THE DYNAM

In this revised and updated second edition of *The Dynamic Constitution*, Richard H. Fallon Jr. provides an engaging, sophisticated introduction to American constitutional law. Suitable for lawyers and nonlawyers alike, this book discusses contemporary constitutional doctrine involving such issues as freedom of speech, freedom of religion, rights to privacy and sexual autonomy, the death penalty, and the powers of Congress. Through examples of Supreme Court cases and portraits of past and present Justices, this book dramatizes the historical and cultural factors that have shaped constitutional law. *The Dynamic Constitution, Second Edition*, combines detailed explication of current doctrine with insightful analysis of the political culture and theoretical debates in which constitutional practice is situated. Professor Fallon uses insights from political science to explain some aspects of constitutional evolution and emphasizes features of the judicial process that distinguish constitutional law from ordinary politics.

Richard H. Fallon Jr. is the Ralph S. Tyler Jr. Professor of Constitutional Law at Harvard University Law School. A former Supreme Court law clerk, he has taught at Harvard Law School since 1982. He has twice been voted the most outstanding teacher at Harvard Law School by graduating students. Professor Fallon has coauthored several constitutional law and federal courts casebooks.

PRAISE FOR *THE DYNAMIC CONSTITUTION*, SECOND EDITION

"If you read just one book on the U.S. Constitution and Supreme Court, Fallon's *Dynamic Constitution* is it. And if you read everything on the subject, this updated edition should be required reading – you will gain fresh and important insights. Why? In two words: breadth and judgment. Across the full range of current Supreme Court decisions, Fallon elucidates doctrine, assesses competing strands of constitutional interpretation, provides historical context enlivened by memorable historical anecdotes, brings into play the background and styles of individual justices, acknowledges the force of practicability in decision making, incorporates recent political science research, and offers a sophisticated judgment of the part politics (only rarely partisan politics) plays in judicial decisions – tracing the Court's interactions with Congress, public opinion, and social movements, and the 'political construction' of its authority. Fallon does it all with clarity and verve and with deep respect for the 'dynamic' constitutional enterprise. We are in the hands of a true master of constitutional law."

– Nancy L. Rosenblum, Senator Joseph Clark Professor of Ethics in Politics and Government, Department of Government, Harvard University

The Dynamic Constitution: An Introduction to American Constitutional Law and Practice

SECOND EDITION

Richard H. Fallon Jr.

Harvard University

CAMBRIDGE
UNIVERSITY PRESS

CAMBRIDGE UNIVERSITY PRESS
Cambridge, New York, Melbourne, Madrid, Cape Town,
Singapore, São Paulo, Delhi, Mexico City

Cambridge University Press
32 Avenue of the Americas, New York, NY 10013-2473, USA

www.cambridge.org
Information on this title: www.cambridge.org/9781107642577

First edition published 2004
Second edition published 2013

Printed in the United States of America

A catalog record for this publication is available from the British Library.

Library of Congress Cataloging in Publication data

Fallon, Richard H., 1952–
The dynamic constitution : an introduction to American constitutional law and practice /
Richard H. Fallon Jr. – Second edition.
    pages cm
Includes bibliographical references and index.
ISBN 978-1-107-02140-2 (hardback) – ISBN 978-1-107-64257-7 (paperback)
1. Constitutional law – United States.   I. Title.
KF4550.F35   2013
342.73–dc23   2012032877

ISBN 978-1-107-02140-2 Hardback
ISBN 978-1-107-64257-7 Paperback

Contents

Preface to the Second Edition   *page* xi
Preface to the First Edition   xv
Prologue: The Affordable Care Act and Other Vignettes   xix

Introduction: The Dynamic Constitution   1
History   2
Original Constitutional Design   5
The Constitution as Higher Law: Foundations of Judicial
    Review   10
Marbury v. Madison: An Enduring Symbol of Judicial
    Power   12
Politics and Judicial Review   17
A Preliminary Perspective on How the Supreme Court
    Interprets the Constitution   19
A Brief History of Judicial Review   24
The Supreme Court Today   33
An Outline of What Is to Come   37

Part I: Individual Rights under the Constitution

1. **Freedom of Speech**   41
    The Foundations of Modern Doctrine   42
    Proximate Origins of Modern Doctrine   44
    Expressive Conduct   54

Shocking and Offensive Speech   58

Remaining Unprotected Categories, Including Obscenity   59

Commercial Speech   63

Campaign Finance and Political Advertising   66

The Broadcast Media   71

Freedom to Associate and Not to Associate   73

Concluding Note   76

2. **Freedom of Religion**   77

Introduction to the Establishment Clause   79

Religion in the Public Schools   82

Governmental Aid to Religious Institutions   85

Symbolic Support for Religion   89

The Free Exercise Clause   92

Voluntary Governmental Accommodations of Religion   97

Tensions between the Free Exercise and Establishment
   Clauses   98

3. **Protection of Economic Liberties**   101

Early History   105

The Fourteenth Amendment   108

Substantive Due Process   111

Modern Contracts Clause Doctrine   118

The Takings Clause   119

Concluding Thoughts   123

4. **Fundamental Rights "Enumerated" in the Bill of Rights** 125

Incorporation of the Bill of Rights against the States   127

Enumerated Rights to Fair Procedures in Criminal Cases   130

Time, Elections, and Change   134

The Law on the Books versus the Law in Practice   135

The Eighth Amendment Prohibition against Cruel and
   Unusual Punishment   138

The Second Amendment and the "Right to Keep and
   Bear Arms"   143

5. **Equal Protection of the Laws**   149
   Equal Protection and the Constitution   152
   Rational Basis Review   156
   Race and the Constitution: Invidious Discrimination   159
   What Did *Brown* Accomplish?   168
   Race and the Constitution: Disparate Impact   169
   Affirmative Action   171
   Gender and the Constitution   179
   Discrimination against Gays and Lesbians   184
   Conclusion   188

6. **"Unenumerated" Fundamental Rights**   191
   The Idea of Fundamental Rights   193
   Voting Rights: A Conceptual Introduction   195
   Voting Rights: The "One-Person, One-Vote" Cases   196
   Beyond One Person, One Vote   198
   Majority-Minority Districting   201
   Equality in the Counting of Votes   203
   Sexual Privacy or Autonomy   207
   Roe v. Wade and Abortion Rights   209
   Gay Rights   214
   Rights Involving Death and Dying   219
   Fundamental Rights Involving the Family   221
   Conclusion   223

Part II: The Constitutional Separation of Powers

7. **The Powers of Congress**   227
   Elements of the "Original Understanding"   230
   Doctrinal and Conceptual History   234
   Crisis and Revision   236

A Course Correction of Uncertain Scope   238
The Necessary and Proper Clause   242
The Spending Power   243
Congressional Regulation of State and Local Governments   245
Coercion through Spending   248
Concluding Thoughts   251

8. **Executive Power**   253
The *Youngstown* Case   256
Foreign Affairs   260
Delegated Power in Domestic Affairs   263
Legislative Vetoes and Line-Item Vetoes   266
Appointments and Removals   270

9. **Judicial Power**   275
The Character of Judicial Power   278
Limits on Judicial Power   283
Anxieties about Judicial Power   289

Part III: Further Issues of Constitutional Structure and Individual Rights

10. **Structural Limits on State Power and Resulting
    Individual Rights**   301
How Federal Power and Federal Law Can Restrict State
    Power   302
The Privileges and Immunities Clause   304
The "Dormant" Commerce Clause   308
The States as "Market Participants"   312
Conclusion   314

11. **The Constitution in War and Emergency**   315
The Power to Initiate War   320
Federal Powers during Wartime   323

War and Individual Rights   324
The Constitution and the "War on Terror"   328
Conclusion   333

12. **The Reach of the Constitution and Congress's
    Enforcement Power**   335
State Action Doctrine   336
The Paucity of "Positive" Fundamental Rights   339
Congressional Power to "Enforce" the Reconstruction
    Amendments   345

13. **Conclusion**   353

Appendix: The Constitution of the United States   363
Index   389

Preface to the Second Edition

On September 25, 2005, John G. Roberts took the oath of office as the seventeenth Chief Justice of the United States. He replaced William H. Rehnquist, for whom he had once served as a law clerk. Roberts's confirmation marked the end of one era in Supreme Court history and the beginning of another. When I wrote the first edition of this book in 2004, Rehnquist had been the Chief Justice since 1986. More significant, in 2004 the composition of the Supreme Court had remained unchanged for ten years, the second-longest period of unaltered membership in the Court's entire history. Because the Supreme Court sits to resolve hard cases that divide the lower courts, change in constitutional law is a constant, even when the Justices stay the same. But in 2004, stable patterns had emerged in many, if not most, areas. It was possible to write with reasonable confidence about the doctrinal equilibria into which the Justices had settled.

The confirmation of John Roberts to replace William Rehnquist, swiftly followed by Samuel Alito's replacement of Sandra Day O'Connor, inevitably brought change. The Chief Justice is almost invariably the most influential of the Justices in the Court's internal workings. Among other things, the Chief Justice gets to decide who writes the majority opinion in any case in which he votes with the majority. The substitution of Justice Alito for Justice O'Connor was especially consequential, too. Through most of the years of the Rehnquist Court, Justice O'Connor was the "swing," or median, Justice – the Justice whose views were most likely to tip the balance between the Court's more conservative Justices and its liberals. When O'Connor retired, to be replaced in 2006 by the more conservative Alito, the Court's center of gravity moved farther to the right. There have been two further membership switches since then, with Sonia Sotomayor replacing David Souter and Elena Kagan succeeding John Paul Stevens.

In this revised second edition, I have updated my discussions of the Supreme Court, of constitutional doctrine, and of the relationship between constitutional law and surrounding political and cultural currents to reflect developments since 2004. As I reflect on them, the intervening changes impress me as both large and interesting, well warranting a new edition.

Another, less important development also deserves mention. Law professors and political scientists have traditionally had quite different perspectives on the Supreme Court. To generalize grossly, law professors have tended to view the Justices as driven by felt obligations of fidelity to distinctively legal ideals, while political scientists have regarded them as ideologically motivated actors with political agendas. In the years since 2004, law professors and political scientists have begun to engage much more with one another's work – to the profit of both, I believe. I remain a law professor, with an abiding conviction that law matters to how the Justices decide cases, but I hope readers will agree that this revised edition is enriched by a number of insights traceable to work by political scientists. Two themes are especially prominent. First, the Supreme Court is a "they," not an "it." To understand what the Court has done in the past and is likely to do in the future, we need to attend closely to the frequently varied thinking of each of the nine individuals who make up the Court. Second, the Supreme Court operates within politically constructed bounds. What the Justices can do successfully at any particular time, and what they can make stick through succeeding rounds of judicial nominations and confirmations, depends on the tolerance of political actors and the American public. There has been enormous change in constitutional doctrine over the sweep of constitutional history, mostly shaped and bounded by the demands and expectations of the American people.

In preparing this revised edition, I have benefited from the help and support of Robert Dreesen of Cambridge University Press and from the comments of two anonymous reviewers of my initial proposal for revising the first edition. Alexander Dryer of the Harvard Law School class of 2012 provided invaluable research and editorial assistance.

Richard H. Fallon Jr.
July 2012

Preface to the First Edition

This book provides an introduction to contemporary constitutional law for intelligent readers who are not, or not yet, lawyers. It is a reasonably short book, which leaves out much detail. I have also done my best to write it in plain language – or at least to explain the jargon used by courts and lawyers before employing it myself. But the book does not talk down to the reader or omit central considerations. It aspires both to inform and to challenge nonlawyers who are interested in constitutional law, as well as law students seeking an introduction to the subject and lawyers who would like a refresher.

I still remember the intellectual thrill of my own first encounter with a book about constitutional law. It came in 1971, when I was a college undergraduate. The book was Robert McCloskey's *The American Supreme Court*, written in 1960. Over the years, when people have asked me to recommend a book introducing constitutional law to nonlawyers, I have usually named McCloskey's. Increasingly, however, I have done so hesitantly. The organization of McCloskey's book is mainly historical. It discusses successive eras in the history of the Supreme Court, often brilliantly, but without attempting to provide the clear portrait of contemporary constitutional law, and of the debates surrounding it, that some readers want. In addition, *The American Supreme Court* has inevitably grown dated with the passage of time, despite able efforts by one of McCloskey's former students to summarize recent developments in additional chapters. McCloskey's book naturally reflects the political and scholarly concerns of the period in which he wrote it, now more than four decades ago. It is time for a new introduction to American constitutional law, written in the twenty-first century for a contemporary audience.

In writing a book for twenty-first-century readers, I have addressed constitutional law from several simultaneous perspectives. First, and perhaps most important, this book sketches the basic outlines of current constitutional doctrine. In chapters with headings such as "The Powers of Congress," "The Freedom of Speech," "The Equal Protection of the Laws," and "The Constitution in War and Emergency," the book discusses leading Supreme Court cases dealing with the powers of Congress and the President and with such issues as hate speech, race and gender discrimination, abortion, gay rights, and affirmative action. It explains why the Court has analyzed these issues as it has, describes debates among the Justices, and anticipates future challenges.

Second, although the book principally focuses on the present, it locates current constitutional doctrines and debates in historical context. Most chapters include a brief account of what the authors and ratifiers of a particular constitutional provision apparently had in mind. I also describe the Supreme Court's historical efforts to interpret the Constitution's language before offering more detailed discussion of contemporary law. In many cases the history is fascinating, often bound up with central currents in the nation's political, economic, and cultural life. In any event, it is often impossible to understand today's law without some awareness of the historical context from which it emerged.

Third, the book refers repeatedly to debates about the Supreme Court's proper role in American government. During the 1930s, when a conservative Supreme Court threatened to thwart President Franklin Roosevelt's New Deal efforts to revive the national economy, critics called passionately for judicial restraint. Many argued that courts should invalidate legislation only when it was clearly unconstitutional, not when there was any room for doubt. Today, another school of so-called originalists argues that the Supreme Court should consistently enforce the "original understanding" of individual constitutional provisions – what those provisions meant to those who wrote and ratified them. Meanwhile, various others have maintained that the Court plays a vital role in adapting vague constitutional language to the needs of changing times. In summarizing current doctrine, I talk about how these and other competing views both do and ought to affect the Court.

Fourth, this book deals openly with the now familiar insight that loosely "political" values and concerns influence Supreme Court decision making. As any reader of newspapers knows, the Court has "liberal" and "conservative" Justices who attract those labels by reaching conclusions that can plausibly be identified as liberal or conservative most of the time. This is a phenomenon that needs to be explained, not ignored, and surely not denied. At the same time, I do not believe that judicial politics are simply a concealed form of partisan electoral politics. In this book I try to explain the ways in which Supreme Court decision making is and is not (or at least should not be) "political."

Before concluding this preface, I should probably say explicitly what is perhaps evident already. Constitutional law is an *argumentative* subject. There are certain facts of the matter – what the Constitution says, what the Supreme Court has held in past cases, and so forth. But lawyers, concerned citizens, and Supreme Court Justices all argue ceaselessly with each other about how the Constitution should be interpreted and applied. At some points, this book tries to stand outside of constitutional arguments and explain them dispassionately. Even then, I am probably too engaged by some issues to adopt a truly neutral perspective. At other points, I join the arguments unabashedly and offer my own opinions, partly because I cannot help myself, because I cannot be indifferent, and partly because constitutional law is ultimately inseparable from constitutional argument. To a large extent, to understand constitutional law is to know how to participate in constitutional debates. There would be no better indication that this book has succeeded in introducing constitutional law successfully than if the reader, at certain points, feels both provoked and empowered to argue with my judgments.

In one sense, this book has been many years in the making. It reflects my reading and writing about constitutional law, and perhaps especially my teaching, over a period of roughly twenty years. In another sense, the book grows directly from a suggestion by Michael Aronson that I write a brief "primer" on constitutional law for nonlawyers. I am very grateful for his encouragement. Ed Parsons gave me enormously helpful editorial advice at a crucial stage in the book's gestation and has continued to provide valuable help through the end. I also owe large debts to a number of friends and colleagues who read earlier drafts. Heartfelt thanks go to David Barron, Erwin Chemerinsky, Jesse Choper, Heather Gerken, Ken Kersch, Sandy Levinson, Daniel Meltzer, Martha Minow, Fred Schauer, Margo Schlanger, and Lloyd Weinreb. Whatever the book's deficiencies, their comments, criticisms, and suggestions made it much better than it would otherwise have been, as did the labors of my extraordinary research assistants, Mark Freeman and Josh Segal.

Prologue: The Affordable Care Act and Other Vignettes

It is emphatically the province and duty of the judicial department to say what the law is. Those who apply the rule to particular cases, must of necessity expound and interpret that rule.

– *Marbury v. Madison* (1803)[1]

[W]hoever hath an absolute authority to interpret any written or spoken laws, it is he who is truly the lawgiver, to all intents and purposes, and not the person who first spoke or wrote them.

– Bishop Hoadly's Sermon, preached before King George I of England, March 31, 1717

On June 28, 2012, the fate of the Patient Protection and Affordable Care Act – or "Obamacare," as many called it – hung in the balance. That statute, which aimed to guarantee health care to virtually all Americans, was the signature achievement of the Obama administration, enacted with great fanfare in 2010. On the night when the bill passed the House in final form, by a vote of 219–212, the President had delivered a short, triumphant speech to the American people, celebrating the accomplishment. Banner headlines appeared in newspapers the following day. Two years later, however, the nation braced for another cliffhanger vote on the Affordable Care Act (ACA), this time by the Supreme Court of the United States.

1 5 U.S. 137, 177 (1803).

The fateful moment came shortly after 10 A.M. As a packed court-room waited and the President watched on television to get the earliest possible report from an observer on the scene (cameras are not allowed in the Supreme Court courtroom), the marshal entered and called out that all in attendance should please rise. The nine Justices – six men and three women – then entered, clad in black robes, and assumed their assigned places behind a large, curved, heavy wooden bench. In the middle Chief Justice John Roberts, a fifty-seven-year-old graduate of Harvard Law School and former Washington lawyer and lower federal court judge, took his seat and called the Court to order. Some observers reported that Roberts looked tired and slightly red-eyed as the Court prepared to "hand down" the results – a term that bespeaks the Court's stature in the constitutional pecking order – in the final three cases of its "Term," which had begun the previous October.

Following brisk announcements about the other two cases, Chief Justice Roberts began to summarize the decision in the Affordable Care Act case, titled *National Federation of Independent Business v. Sebelius*[2] (2012). To the great relief of the Obama administration and to the sore disappointment of others, the Court upheld the most important aspects of the Affordable Care Act by a 5–4 vote. In its most important decision of the year, and possibly its most important decision in many years, the Court did something by essentially doing nothing. It failed to strike down a law enacted by the House and Senate and signed by the President, all following a prolonged national political debate. The Court did not say that the ACA was wise as a matter of policy, as Chief Justice Roberts emphasized in explaining the result, but merely that it did not offend the Constitution. In so holding, Roberts, who is nearly always identified as a judicial "conservative," joined the Court's four "liberals." The other four conservative Justices dissented from the relevant parts of Roberts's opinion.

2 132 S. Ct. 2566 (2012).

What can we learn from *National Federation of Independent Business v. Sebelius*? Quite a lot, I shall argue. But, paradoxically, we should steel ourselves not to try to learn too much. It would be a mistake to treat *National Federation of Independent Business*, or any other single case, as "representative," either of the way that our Constitution works or of the role that the Supreme Court plays in enforcing the Constitution. Anyone searching for a single emblematic case would do well to recall the fable of the blind men and the elephant. Even with our eyes open, we should not mistake a part of the Court's role for the entirety or conclude that what sometimes happens always happens. We will come back very shortly to the Affordable Care Act case. First, to broaden the frame of reference, here are five additional, relatively recent vignettes. Taken in isolation, any one of them might give a quite different picture of constitutional law and the role of the Supreme Court than would *National Federation of Independent Business v. Sebelius* if we were to look at it alone.

First vignette. On September 12, 2005, John Roberts sat at a witness table in the Senate wing of the U.S. Capitol Building, there to testify before the Senate Judiciary Committee. Roberts appeared as a nominee to become the seventeenth Chief Justice of the United States, put up for the post by President George W. Bush. (Like other Justices of the Court, the Chief Justice must be nominated by the President and confirmed by the Senate.) For the decade before Roberts's nomination, the Court had consisted of seven Justices appointed by Republican Presidents and two appointed by Democrats. Although conservatives expressed frustration that the Court was not conservative enough – it continued, for example, to uphold abortion rights under *Roe v. Wade*[3] (1973) – by 2005, liberals worried that the Court had embarked on, and would continue to pursue, what some called an agenda of "conservative judicial activism" that included the invalidation of economic regulatory legislation passed by Congress. Although Roberts was a lifelong conservative who had

3 410 U.S. 113 (1973).

served in the Reagan administration, he sought to allay fears of "judicial activism" by comparing the role of a Supreme Court Justice with that of an umpire:

> Judges and justices are servants of the law, not the other way around. Judges are like umpires. Umpires don't make the rules; they apply them. The role of an umpire and a judge is critical. They make sure everybody plays by the rules. But it is a limited role. Nobody ever went to a ball game to see the umpire.[4]

Following his testimony, Roberts was confirmed as Chief Justice by a Senate vote of 78–22. One of the negative votes came from Barack Obama, then a Senator from Illinois. Obama believed that Roberts's conservative views would make him an unduly conservative Justice.

Second vignette. Two years after his confirmation, Chief Justice Roberts wrote the lead opinion for a bitterly divided Supreme Court in *Parents Involved v. Seattle School District*[5] (2007). By a vote of 5–4, the Court held that local school districts in Seattle, Washington, and Louisville, Kentucky, had violated the Equal Protection Clause when they voluntarily took race into account in assigning students to local public schools for the purpose of promoting racial integration. *Parents Involved* was, in essence, a fight about the legacy of the Supreme Court's iconic decision in *Brown v. Board of Education*[6] (1954), which had condemned racially segregated public education by pronouncing that "[i]n the field of public education," separate, race-based "facilities are inherently unequal."[7] The school districts involved in the *Brown* case all maintained formally designated one-race schools. Regardless of the neighborhood in which they lived, all white children went to a white school and

---

4 Confirmation Hearing on the Nomination of John G. Roberts, Jr. To Be Chief Justice of the United States: Hearing Before the S. Comm. on the Judiciary, 109th Cong. 55 (2005) (statement of John G. Roberts, Jr.).
5 551 U.S. 701 (2007).
6 347 U.S. 483 (1954).
7 Ibid. at 495.

all black children to a black school. Concerned solely with legally mandated segregation, *Brown* did not address the issues that would arise if
residential housing patterns, rather than legal mandates, tended to produce public schools that were nearly all white or all black.

The Court had, however, considered race-based school assignments
in an intervening decision in *Swann v. Charlotte-Mecklenburg Board of
Education*[8] (1971). In *Swann*, a unanimous Supreme Court – in the midst
of upholding a forced busing remedy for past race-based exclusion of
black students from all-white schools – had spoken approvingly of the
possibility that local school districts might want to undertake further,
voluntary efforts (as Seattle and Louisville had done) to promote racial
mixing.

In *Parents Involved*, Chief Justice Roberts dismissed what the Court
had said in *Swann* about race-based assignments for the purpose of
achieving school integration as an ill-considered aside, or "dictum," that
was not necessary to the Court's actual "holding" about the rights and
obligations of the parties before it. What the Court had said in *Swann*
was therefore not binding, he ruled. According to Roberts, *Brown* was
best read as deeply suspicious of, if not flatly condemning, all race-based
school assignments, even those with the purpose of bringing about more
racial integration. "The way to stop discrimination on the basis of race
is to stop discriminating on the basis of race," he wrote.[9] In his view, the
Constitution thus forbade Seattle and Louisville from taking individual
students' race into account in making school assignments.

Four dissenting Justices protested vehemently. According to them,
Brown forbade race-based classifications for the purpose of keeping the
races apart and promoting notions of racial superiority and inferiority, and it should not stop school systems from making modest, voluntary, race-based efforts to achieve racial diversity in their public schools.
Indeed, in the view of the dissenting Justices, *Brown* supplied grounds

8 402 U.S. 1 (1971).
9 Ibid. at 748.

for upholding racially diverse public schools as vital for teaching Americans of all races to live, learn, and work together.

Among the dissenting Justices in *Parents Involved* was John Paul Stevens, who by 2007 had served on the Court for more than thirty years, far longer than any of his colleagues. In a short, unusually personal opinion, he wrote that no member of the Supreme Court that he had joined in 1975 would have agreed with the Court's ruling in *Parents Involved*.[10] Neither Chief Justice Roberts nor any other Justice in the majority contradicted Stevens's claim about how a different Supreme Court with different members would have ruled on the Seattle and Louisville cases in 1975. If one thinks of Justices in terms of an analogy to umpires, one might wonder whether the strike zone had moved.

Third vignette. As I have intimated already, commentators and political scientists invariably classify each of the nine Justices of the Supreme Court as either "liberal" or "conservative." For nearly two decades, the conventional tally has listed five conservatives and four liberals. Given a Court that is so divided, commentators refer to the Justice who is closest to the middle – in this case, the conservative Justice who is most likely to align with the four liberals from time to time – as the "swing Justice." In recent years, the "swing Justice" has been Justice Anthony Kennedy (who, for example, has joined the liberals in upholding gay rights in some cases).

A relatively recent example comes from *Kennedy v. Louisiana*[11] (2008), in which Justice Kennedy held that the Eighth Amendment prohibition against "cruel and unusual punishment" barred the death penalty for a crime (child rape) that did not involve a murder or intended murder. Echoing language from prior cases, Justice Kennedy found executing a child rapist who was not a murderer to be incompatible with "the evolving standards of decency that mark the progress of a maturing society."[12] The four dissenting Justices (the conservatives)

10 See ibid. at 803 (Stevens, J., dissenting).
11 554 U.S. 207 (2008).
12 Ibid. at 419, 435.

argued that the ruling was inconsistent with the original understanding of the Eighth Amendment and was not dictated by any prior precedent. In these respects, they seem correct. The central issues were whether the Constitution's prohibitions should reflect evolving standards of decency and whether the majority had gauged those evolving standards accurately.

Taking note of Justice Kennedy's capacity to push the Court either to the left or to the right, some constitutional lawyers joke sardonically, "This is Anthony Kennedy's country. The rest of us only live here." (If Kennedy were to leave the Court or if its ideological balance shifted, the same Court-focused lawyers would simply substitute the name of the Justice who would then stand closest to the Court's center for Kennedy's.)

Fourth vignette. On May 2, 2011, Navy Seals, acting at the direction of President Barack Obama, mounted a secret raid on a compound in Pakistan where they found and killed Osama bin Laden. Obama was able to direct the raid because the Constitution makes him Commander in Chief of the armed forces.[13] Despite the raid's success, it stirred a fair amount of controversy, including over whether there should have been greater efforts to capture bin Laden, rather than kill him. Yet almost no one seems to have thought that how the President used his power as Commander in Chief in pursuing bin Laden was any concern of the Supreme Court. If bin Laden's heirs had brought suit, they would have had no case.

At roughly the same time as the attack on bin Laden occurred, Congress and the President were locked in highly contentious, ongoing debates about how to stimulate a flagging economy. Should the country cut taxes? Expand stimulus spending? And what should it do about a disturbingly large federal deficit? Once again the Supreme Court stood on the sidelines. It is easy for Court watchers to forget (as when they joke about the importance of Justice Anthony Kennedy), but many of

13 Article II, Section 2, Clause 1.

the most consequential decisions that are made under our Constitution occur with no judicial involvement whatsoever.[14]

Fifth vignette. A number of national civil rights laws prohibit discrimination on the basis of such factors as race, gender, national origin, and religion. Some of the antidiscrimination statutes make exceptions for churches. Others do not. The dispute in *Hosanna-Tabor Evangelical Lutheran Church and School v. Equal Employment Opportunity Commission*[15] (2012) arose when a church fired a church school teacher who had the title of "minister of religion" and she sued to get her job back, claiming employment discrimination in violation of the Americans with Disabilities Act. The Supreme Court did not bother with the details of why the church had fired the woman who brought the suit. Instead, by 9–0, it concluded that a large issue of constitutional principle was at stake and determined the outcome. With John Roberts writing the opinion, the Court held that the Religion Clauses of the First Amendment, which provide that "Congress shall make no law respecting an establishment of religion, or prohibiting the free exercise thereof," forbid Congress from regulating a church's choice of religious "ministers."

The Supreme Court's unanimity in *Hosanna-Tabor* was striking but not particularly unusual. In the "Term" (or year) that it decided *Hosanna-Tabor*, the Court ruled unanimously in 44 percent of its cases. Although it is accurate for many purposes to describe the Supreme Court as ideologically divided between liberals and conservatives, the Justices are not ideologically divided about everything. And if one puts aside the selected sample of cases that come before the Supreme Court, there are far more "easy" constitutional cases than there are "hard" ones. (Going in, not everyone regarded *Hosanna-Tabor* as an easy case.)

Sixth vignette. The Affordable Care Act with which we began was, and is, a nightmare of legal complexity. Before deciding a case, the

---

14 For discussion of the relative significance of judicial and nonjudicial decisions, see Frederick Schauer, "The Court's Agenda – and the Nation's," 120 *Harvard Law Review* 4 (2006).

15 132 S. Ct. 694 (2012).

Supreme Court usually allows the lawyers on the contending sides a total of one hour to present their arguments – thirty minutes per side. In the ACA case, with the constitutionality of a hugely important statute at stake, the Court scheduled six hours of argument, spread over three days. No short summary could do justice to the case. In resuming the discussion, I focus only on the most central and controversial provision – the so-called individual mandate to uninsured individuals (who have incomes too high to qualify for Medicaid) either to purchase health insurance or to pay a penalty. Crucial to the ACA's strategy of ensuring nearly universal coverage was making some Americans buy health insurance that they do not want to buy (typically because they think that they cannot afford it, even with the subsidies that the ACA provides).

Unlike most other national and state governments, the Congress of the United States cannot pass a law such as the ACA unless some provision of the Constitution authorizes it to do so. In other words, it needs to be able to point to a power-conferring provision authorizing it to enact the kind of legislation in question, even if the law that it wants to pass would not otherwise violate anyone's individual rights. To illustrate the distinction, before Congress enacted the ACA, Massachusetts required its citizens to purchase health insurance without attracting a significant constitutional challenge. No provision of the Bill of Rights gives citizens a "right" not to be made to purchase health insurance if a state requires them to buy it. But it is a separate question whether Congress has any enumerated "power" that would permit it to order people to buy health insurance.

In defending the individual mandate, government lawyers relied principally on a provision of the Constitution that authorizes Congress "[t]o regulate Commerce...among the several States."[16] There is a large interstate market in health care and health insurance, they argued, and nearly everyone participates in that interstate market at one time or another, like it or not. Given nearly everyone's participation in the

16 U.S. Constitution, Article I, Section 8, Clause 3.

interstate commercial health-care market, Congress, it was argued, engages in a permissible regulation of interstate commerce when it requires purchases of health insurance, also in an interstate commercial market.

In *National Association of Independent Business v. Sebelius*, Chief Justice Roberts sent one chill into the hearts of the government lawyers who had defended the ACA when he announced, from the bench, that he had written the Court's lead opinion and would summarize its holding. For supporters of the ACA, it would have been a better, more hopeful sign if one of the liberals, or even Justice Kennedy, had written the Court opinion. The Chief Justice delivered another chill as he explained to those in the courtroom why he thought Congress could not mandate the purchase of health insurance under the Commerce Clause: although Congress has broad power to regulate people and businesses who are engaged in interstate commerce, the ACA went too unprecedentedly far by ordering people who were not already engaged in a commercial activity to enter the economic marketplace to buy unwanted health insurance. The power to regulate commerce is a power to regulate commercial activity, not inactivity, he reasoned. On this point, the four conservative Justices essentially agreed with Roberts (even though they did not formally join his opinion). In a significant setback for judicial liberals, *National Federation of Independent Business* thus held that Congress lacks authority under the Commerce Clause to require individuals to buy health insurance.

But Chief Justice Roberts was not done. Having held that Congress could not enact the individual mandate under the Commerce Clause, he turned next to an argument on which the government had placed little reliance: what the ACA termed a "penalty" for failing to buy health insurance could instead be characterized as a "tax" on those who chose not to purchase coverage; and such a tax lay within Congress's power to enact under the Constitution's Taxing and Spending Clause.[17] Although

---

17 U.S. Constitution, Article 1, Section 8, Clause 1.

Congress did not call the ACA penalty a tax, Roberts reasoned, it was collected by the Internal Revenue Service and had many of the hallmarks of a tax. And in the case of reasonable constitutional doubt about whether Congress had the power to enact legislation, he wrote, it was the job of the Supreme Court to get out of the way and let the politically accountable institutions of government – Congress and the President – decide. The four other conservative Justices angrily objected that the individual mandate, which Congress had chosen not to label as a tax, could not be upheld based on bait-and-switch techniques. But the four liberal Justices, who thought that the individual mandate was permissible under the Commerce Clause anyway, also agreed with Roberts about Congress's power to enact the ACA under the Taxing and Spending Clause – the provision under which the Court has long upheld the validity of the Social Security system.

Thus was the individual mandate upheld – as a constitutionally permissible tax, even though Congress had not labeled it a tax! And the "swing" Justice was the Chief Justice, John Roberts, who had almost never before been the sole conservative Justice to join the four liberals and thereby produce a 5–4 ruling that liberals welcomed. Placed on the foundation of the Taxing and Spending Clause, Chief Justice Roberts's opinion was one of the greatest examples of judicial "deference" to Congress and the President – the antithesis of what many people have in mind when they use the loose phrase "judicial activism" – in many decades.

Within days after the decision in *National Association of Independent Business v. Sebelius*, the press, purportedly on the basis of reliable leaks from within the Supreme Court, reported that Chief Justice Roberts had initially planned to vote to invalidate the individual mandate and, more broadly, to join the other four conservative Justices in an opinion striking down the ACA in its entirety. Only at the last minute, the reports said, did he decide to vote to uphold the individual mandate under the Taxing and Spending Power. Roberts switched, the press speculated, to avoid the specter of a Supreme Court dividing along what might have appeared to be partisan lines to invalidate the most important federal statute enacted in many years – and this after the Court had similarly split 5–4, with only Republican-appointed Justices on one side and all Democratic-appointed Justices on the other, in a number of other politically charged cases during Roberts's tenure as Chief Justice. Roberts, the reports said, was moved to his decision by a concern about the Court's long-term stature or "legitimacy." It was vital, he was said to believe, that the public not come to regard the Court as a partisan, political institution that predictably divided along what looked like partisan, political lines in its most important cases. I hasten to emphasize that I do not endorse this account but merely report it. I have no independent basis on which to judge it either true or false. I repeat it, however, not as mere gossip but as an indication of the way that some close-range observers believe that some of the Justices sometimes think and act.

With six vignettes now laid out, I will say candidly, at the outset of this book, that I do not find much illumination in the comparison of Supreme Court Justices to umpires – even if that metaphor captures enough of the myth surrounding the Court, and possibly enough of our hopes for it, to provide some comfort to otherwise skeptical Senators in a judicial confirmation hearing. But the complexity of the landscape that we have traversed already, including unanimous decisions and important constitutional questions that the Court does not address at all, makes me skeptical that any other simple metaphor would serve much better. If we are to understand constitutional law, and the role of the Supreme Court within our constitutional scheme, then we should be prepared to try to understand them on their own terms – as complex, multifaceted, tension ridden, and occasionally inspiring. We should expect the future to reflect the past but occasionally (as we have seen already) to bring dramatic surprises.

Introduction

The Dynamic Constitution

[O]ur Constitution ... is an experiment, as all life is an experiment.
                                    – Justice Oliver Wendell Holmes Jr.[1]

ALTHOUGH THE CONSTITUTION OF THE UNITED STATES IS a single written document, American constitutional law – the subject of this book – is a complex social, cultural, and political practice that includes much more than the written Constitution. Courts, especially the Supreme Court, interpret the Constitution. So do legislators and other government officials as they consider their responsibilities. Very commonly, however, "interpretation" of the Constitution depends on a variety of considerations external to the text. These include the historical practices of Congress and the President, previous judicial decisions or "precedents," public expectations, practical considerations, and moral and political values. By talking about constitutional law as a "practice," I mean to signal that factors such as these are elements of the process from which constitutional law emerges.[2]

Strikingly, arguments about how to interpret the Constitution occur frequently in constitutional practice – not least among Justices of the

---

1 *Abrams v. United States,* 250 U.S. 616, 630 (1919) (Holmes, J., dissenting).
2 For an especially rich practice-based account of law in general and applied to constitutional law in particular, see Ronald Dworkin, *Law's Empire* (Cambridge, MA: Belknap Press of Harvard University Press, 1986).

Supreme Court. (Among the difficulties in studying constitutional law is that the rules of constitutional interpretation are nowhere written down in authoritative form, and any one person's attempt to formulate them would trigger dispute.) Nonetheless, a few fixed points command nearly universal agreement. First, at the center of the frequently argumentative practice of constitutional law stands the written Constitution of the United States. Second, when the Supreme Court decides a case, its ruling binds public officials as well as citizens, despite their possibly contrary views. Supreme Court rulings occasionally encounter resistance. In a few instances they have provoked actual or threatened defiance – matters that I discuss later in this book. Normally, however, the Court gets to say authoritatively what the Constitution means.

In subsequent chapters, I plunge directly into discussions of how particular provisions of the Constitution have been interpreted, especially but not exclusively by the Supreme Court. This introduction explores the textual and historical foundations of our constitutional practice. It first sketches the history that led to the Constitution's adoption, then briefly describes the central provisions of the Constitution itself. Today, we tend to take it for granted that the Supreme Court will interpret and enforce the Constitution. But it was once contested whether the Court should play this role at all, and how the Court should play it is a subject of continuing controversy. As background to current debates, the final sections of this introduction therefore outline a bit more relevant history. I discuss the case in which the Supreme Court first claimed the power of judicial review, *Marbury v. Madison*[3] (1803), and then conclude with a brief survey of the Court's use of its power.

History

At the time of the American Revolution, the fledgling nation seeking independence consisted of thirteen separate colonies. Brought together

3 5 U.S. 137 (1803).

by their common opposition to the taxing policies of the British Parliament, the colonies began sending delegates to a Continental Congress in 1774. This arrangement was initially quite informal. Delegates were elected by the assemblies of their respective colonies. Meeting in Congress, they could vote requests that the various colonies raise troops or furnish funds, but the Congress itself possessed no direct authority to enforce its demands.

In 1777, before the Revolutionary War concluded, the Continental Congress moved to formalize the relationship among the colonies by proposing Articles of Confederation, which were ratified by the assemblies of all thirteen states or colonies and took effect in 1781 as the developing nation's governing legal framework. Like the more informal scheme that had preceded them, the Articles of Confederation established a confederation of equal states, each with one vote in Congress. The national government, such as it was, still had to look to the states to enforce its directives. If it wished to lay a tax, for example, it had to ask the states to assess and collect it. The Articles carefully enumerated the purposes for which the states were united; any power not specifically given to the national Congress was denied to it. The Articles of Confederation did not create an independent executive branch, and there was almost no judicial system. For the Congress to make ordinary decisions, nine states needed to agree. More fundamental actions required unanimity.

As swiftly became clear, the government created by the Articles of Confederation was too weak. Although fighting with Britain stopped in 1781, and a formal peace followed in 1783, the European powers continued to pose threats that could be met only by decisive, coordinated action. At home, an economic downturn revealed the need for a national economic policy including a uniform currency and safeguards against inflation and nonpayment of debts.

To deal with these and related problems, the Continental Congress asked the colonies (or states) to send delegates to a convention in the summer of 1787 to draft proposed amendments to the Articles of

Confederation. When the Constitutional Convention met in Philadelphia, however, the delegates decided almost immediately to ignore their mandate and to draft an entirely new Constitution. The Convention also determined to ignore the Articles of Confederation insofar as they forbade major changes in the scheme of national government without the unanimous approval of the thirteen states voting in Congress. Article VII of the new, draft Constitution provided that it would take effect on ratification by nine states and further directed that the ratifications should be by "conventions" of the people of the states, not by the state legislatures.

The decision of the Constitutional Convention to ignore or defy the Articles of Confederation – which were, after all, the then-prevailing "law" – is at least interesting in its own right and probably possesses enduring significance for American constitutional law.[4] Were the Constitution's authors (or "framers" as they are more commonly called) and ratifiers (those who voted to approve it in separate state conventions) "outlaws" in their own time? Why were they not obliged to follow the Articles of Confederation in all of their written detail? How could valid law, in the form of a Constitution, emerge from actions not authorized by prior written law? It is not enough to say that the framers decided to start over; surely not every group is entitled to "start over" whenever it feels like doing so – for example, by staging a coup or pronouncing itself not bound by current constitutional law. In concluding that they were entitled to ignore the written law of their time, whereas others living under the new Constitution would be bound by it, the framers and ratifiers – followed by subsequent generations who have lionized them – appear to have assumed that unwritten principles of moral and political right pre-exist, and in some sense are more fundamental than, any written law.

---

4 See Bruce Ackerman, *We The People: Foundations* (Cambridge, MA: Belknap Press of Harvard University Press, 1991), vol. 1 (considering the relationship between legality and illegality and the theory of political legitimacy reflected in the framing and ratification of the Constitution). Compare Akhil Reed Amar, "Philadelphia Revisited: Amending the Constitution Outside Article V," 55 *University of Chicago Law Review* 1043 (1988) (asserting the availability of legal justifications for the course of action followed at the Constitutional Convention and thereafter).

In light of the Constitution's origins, it should come as no surprise that debates about whether the Constitution presupposes background principles of moral and political right, even if it does not list them expressly, have echoed throughout American constitutional history.[5]

Original Constitutional Design

By any reasonable measure, the delegates to the Constitutional Convention were an extraordinarily able group. They pursued their work with a mixture of idealism, imagination, practicality, and self-interest. As in the Continental Congress, each state had one vote in the Convention's deliberations. Predictably, the delegations disputed whether each state should retain one vote in the new government's Legislative Branch or whether representation should instead reflect population. The delegates ultimately agreed to a compromise: representation in the House of Representatives depends on population, but each state, regardless of size, gets two Senators.[6]

From a modern perspective, the deliberations at the Convention were striking in several respects. Perhaps most notably, the delegates took it for granted that slavery must continue to exist under the new Constitution. Otherwise the slave states would not have participated. In at least three places the Constitution makes veiled reference to slavery but avoids the shameful term.[7] No women attended the Constitutional

---

5 See Thomas C. Grey, "The Origins of the Unwritten Constitution," 30 *Stanford Law Review* 843 (1978); Suzanna Sherry, "The Founders' Unwritten Constitution: Fundamental Law in American Revolutionary Thought," 54 *University of Chicago Law Review* 1127 (1987).

6 The best relatively recent work on the Convention is Jack N. Rakove, *Original Meanings: Politics and Ideas in the Making of the Constitution* (New York: Knopf, 1997). For an older but still valuable account, see Max Farrand, *The Framing of the Constitution of the United States* (New Haven, CT: Yale University Press, 1913).

7 See Article I, Section 2 (basing a state's representation in the House of Representatives on its free population and three-fifths of "all other Persons" within its territory); Article I, Section 9 (barring Congress from abolishing the slave trade before 1808); and Article 4, Section 2 (providing for the return of runaway slaves).

Convention. Although the Constitution sought to preserve and promote individual liberty, not until after the Civil War could it even plausibly be viewed as a charter of *equal* human freedom.

It also bears note that there were no political parties at the Constitutional Convention. On the contrary, the framers disliked the very idea of parties, which they associated with "factions" hostile to the general or public interest. Nevertheless, a party system quickly developed. For the most part, the parties have worked within a constitutional structure not designed for them.[8]

Although much of the framers' specific thinking now seems embedded in a worldview that is difficult to retrieve, on other issues their aspirations were timeless. At the highest level of abstraction, they wanted to create a national government that was strong enough to deal effectively with genuinely national problems but would not threaten the liberties of a free people – as awkwardly defined to exclude slaves and Native Americans. In pursuing these aims, the basic structure created by the Constitution has impressed most Americans as adequate, and even admirable, for more than two hundred years.

Apart from its brief Preamble, the Constitution – which is reprinted as an appendix to this book for readers who may want to consult it – is not a rhetorical document. Working from the ground up, it literally constitutes the government of the United States. The main structural work occurs in the first three articles.

Article I provides that "[a]ll legislative powers...shall be vested in a Congress of the United States, which shall consist of a Senate and House of Representatives." Following sections that deal with qualifications, apportionment, and election, Article I, Section 8, lists the powers of Congress in a series of seventeen clauses that include the "Power to lay and collect Taxes" and to "regulate Commerce." The list concludes with the so-called Necessary and Proper Clause, authorizing Congress

---

8 One element that was designed with political parties in mind is the Twelfth Amendment, which was ratified in 1804 to accommodate party-based presidential voting.

"to make all Laws which shall be necessary and proper for carrying into Execution the foregoing Powers, and all other Powers vested by this Constitution in the Government of the United States." The Supreme Court has construed the Necessary and Proper Clause as mandating a broad interpretation of Congress's other powers.

Article II confers the executive power on the President of the United States. It provides for the election of the President and Vice President, then specifies the President's powers and duties in a reasonably detailed list. Among other things, the President is made the Commander in Chief of the armed forces and is empowered to make treaties and to appoint ambassadors, judges, and other officers of the United States "by and with the Advice and Consent of the Senate." The President also possesses a power to veto or reject legislation enacted by Congress, subject to override by two-thirds majorities of both Houses.

Article III vests "the judicial Power of the United States" in "one Supreme Court, and in such inferior Courts as the Congress may from time to time ordain and establish." Both in the Constitutional Convention and in the ratification debates, it appears to have been taken for granted that the courts, and especially the Supreme Court, would determine whether legislation enacted by Congress and the states comports with the Constitution.[9] But the text of Article III leaves the power of "judicial review," as it is called, implicit rather than explicit.

Article IV contains miscellaneous provisions. One, the "Privileges and Immunities Clause," imposes an antidiscrimination rule: it limits the freedom of states to discriminate against citizens of other states who might travel or pursue business opportunities within their borders. Another clause of Article IV provides for the admission of new states. A third empowers Congress to legislate for the territories.

Article V establishes the process for amending the Constitution. Unlike ordinary laws, constitutional amendments require the affirmative

9 See Richard H. Fallon Jr., John F. Manning, Daniel J. Meltzer, and David L. Shapiro, *Hart & Wechsler's The Federal Courts and the Federal System*, 6th ed. (New York: Foundation Press, 2009), 11–13.

vote of two-thirds of both Houses of Congress and of three-fourths of the states. The requirement that three-quarters of the states must approve constitutional amendments makes the Constitution extraordinarily difficult to amend.

Article VI states explicitly that "[t]his Constitution, and the Laws of the United States which shall be made in Pursuance thereof...shall be the supreme Law of the Land." This "Supremacy Clause" establishes that whenever state law conflicts with either the Constitution or with federal laws passed by Congress, state law must yield. Article VI also forbids the use of any religious test "as a Qualification to any Office or public Trust under the United States." Article VII provides for the Constitution to be ratified by conventions in the several states, not by state legislatures.

As originally written, the Constitution included only a few express guarantees of rights. To safeguard liberty, it relied on two strategies. First, it divided the powers of government among three separate branches. Second, the Constitution made the federal government one of limited or "enumerated" powers only. The framers saw no need to create an express right to freedom of speech, for example, because they thought that the delegated powers of Congress, properly construed, included no authority to enact legislation encroaching on speech rights. What is more, they trusted the various state constitutions to stop state governments from encroaching on the liberties of their citizens.

During the debates about whether the Constitution should be ratified, the absence of a bill of rights was widely criticized, and the Constitution's main champions – the so-called Federalists – promised to remedy the defect.[10] After the Constitution's ratification, the first Congress proposed twelve amendments, ten of which were quickly approved and took effect in 1791. Known collectively as the Bill of Rights, these ten amendments are today regarded as mainstays of constitutional freedom.

---

10 For a comprehensive and illuminating examination of the ratification debates, see Pauline Mayer, *Ratification: The People Debate the Constitution, 1787–1788* (2010).

The First Amendment guarantees freedoms of speech and religion. The Second provides that "[a] well regulated Militia, being necessary to the security of a free State, the right of the people to keep and bear Arms, shall not be infringed." The Third Amendment forbids the quartering of troops in private homes without the owners' consent, except in time of war. The Fourth creates rights against "unreasonable" searches and seizures. The Fifth forbids deprivations of "life, liberty, or property, without due process of law." Along with the Sixth Amendment, it also provides a variety of rights to people accused of crimes. The Seventh Amendment protects rights to trial by jury. The Eighth bars "cruel and unusual punishments." The Ninth says that "[t]he enumeration in the Constitution, of certain rights, shall not be construed to deny or disparage others retained by the people." Finally, the Tenth Amendment emphasizes the continuingly important role of the states (the powers of which come from their own constitutions and not, interestingly and importantly, from the Constitution of the United States): "The powers not delegated to the United States by the Constitution, nor prohibited by it to the States, are reserved to the States respectively, or to the people."

Surprisingly from a modern perspective, the Bill of Rights originally applied only to the federal government and imposed no restrictions on the states.[11] In other words, it left the states free to regulate speech and religion, for example. In the context of the times, national governmental power obviously aroused more distrust than state power. But trust of the states soon eroded, especially in the long struggle over slavery that increasingly dominated American politics in the first part of the nineteenth century.

That struggle ultimately produced the Civil War, which in turn led to adoption of the Thirteenth Amendment abolishing slavery, the Fourteenth Amendment requiring the states to accord to every person "the equal protection of the laws," and the Fifteenth Amendment forbidding race-based discrimination in voting. Beginning in the twentieth century,

11 See *Barron v. City of Baltimore*, 32 U.S. 243, 247–50 (1832).

the Supreme Court has also construed the Fourteenth Amendment as making nearly all guarantees of the Bill of Rights applicable against the states – a development specifically discussed in Chapter 4. This is a phenomenon of enormous importance, which marks a sharp divide in constitutional history. Since the "Civil War Amendments," twelve further amendments have been ratified, for a total of twenty-seven. Among the most important, the Sixteenth Amendment authorizes Congress to impose an income tax, the Nineteenth guarantees voting rights to women, and the Twenty-Second bars a President from serving more than two terms in office.

One further feature of the Constitution's design deserves emphasis. As is discussed in greater detail in Chapter 12, virtually without exception the Constitution applies only to the government, not to private citizens or companies. Accordingly, if a private company fires an employee for criticizing the boss, it does not violate the constitutional right to freedom of speech – which is only a right against the government. So it also is with other constitutional provisions, including the Equal Protection Clause of the Fourteenth Amendment, which generally prohibits race-based and certain other kinds of discrimination by the government. If private citizens discriminate on the basis of race, their actions be may wrong as a moral matter and may also violate laws enacted by Congress or state or local governments, but they do not violate the Constitution.

The Constitution as Higher Law: Foundations of Judicial Review

Although many changes have occurred subsequently, the Constitution drafted in 1787, as supplemented by the Bill of Rights, created the basic framework of federal law that persists today. On one level there is ordinary law, enacted by ordinary majorities in Congress, state legislatures, and local governments. On another level stands the Constitution, as higher law, which not only establishes and empowers the national government but also imposes limits on what ordinary law can do.

The status of the Constitution as higher law is crucial to the role played by courts, especially the Supreme Court, in the American scheme of government. In nonconstitutional cases, such as those involving questions about whether people have committed crimes or broken contracts, courts routinely interpret and enforce the law. Given the status of the Constitution as higher law, most Americans today probably take it for granted that courts should interpret and enforce the Constitution as well. In fact, allowing the Supreme Court to interpret the Constitution, and treating other branches of government as bound by the Court's decisions, was a choice. It was certainly not an inevitable choice in 1787, when the Constitution was written. Indeed, critics have sometimes questioned whether the Constitution authorizes courts to rule on the constitutionality of legislation at all.

Nowhere does the Constitution say expressly that the courts should have the power to review the constitutionality of legislation. Nor is "judicial review" by any means a logical necessity. In Britain, the source of many American legal principles, the courts traditionally had no role in testing the validity of legislation. The rule was "parliamentary sovereignty": any legislation enacted by Parliament and approved by the monarch was law. To be sure, Britain did not have a written constitution. Even under a written constitution, however, it would be possible to take the same approach. It could have been left to Congress to judge the constitutionality of legislation, and the courts would simply have enforced the law as passed by Congress.

Despite the possibility of constitutionalism without judicial review, and despite the absence of any express reference in the constitutional text, the power of the courts to determine the constitutionality of legislation can fairly be viewed as implicit in Article III, which deals with the judicial power. Article III calls for the federal courts to decide cases "arising under this Constitution" – language best understood as referring to cases in which questions of constitutional law are presented for decision. In addition, Article VI says that state judges are bound by the Constitution, "any Thing in the Constitution or Laws of any State to the Contrary notwithstanding." Again, this language implies that state judges must assess the constitutional validity of state laws. If the power of judicial review is given to state judges, then surely it must exist in the Supreme Court, which the Constitution empowers to hear appeals from state court judgments.

Historical evidence supports this conclusion. Several discussions at the Constitutional Convention anticipated that the courts would exercise judicial review.[12] During the ratification debates, Alexander Hamilton plainly stated in one of the *Federalist Papers* that the Constitution assigned this role to the judiciary.[13] Indeed, several early decisions of the Supreme Court assumed the power of judicial review without anyone paying much attention.[14]

Marbury v. Madison: An Enduring Symbol of Judicial Power

In the early years, however, much was in flux. Government under a written constitution, enforced by an independent judiciary, was a novelty in the history of nations. Many elements of the experiment were precarious, as became plain when a crisis developed in the aftermath of the 1800 presidential election. Although the framers of the Constitution did not envision a role for political parties, partisan divisions emerged almost immediately, and the election of 1800 was bitterly fought between the Federalists supporting John Adams and the Republicans backing Thomas Jefferson. The Federalists, who had dominated the national government during the presidential administrations of George Washington and his successor Adams, generally supported broad national authority, a sound currency, and domestic and foreign policies promoting commercial interests. By contrast, the Republicans were the party of states' rights and political and economic democracy. Many Federalists regarded them as little more competent than a mob to govern the country wisely.

---

12 See Fallon et al., *Hart & Wechsler's The Federal Courts and the Federal System*, 11–13.
13 *The Federalist* No. 78, at 491–94.
14 See *Cooper v. Telfair*, 4 U.S. 14 (1800); *Ware v. Hylton*, 3 U.S. 199 (1796).

After the Republicans won a stunning triumph at the polls, the outgoing Federalists remained in office for a brief period before the inauguration of the new administration. In that interlude, they sought means to safeguard their party and the nation against the anticipated reckless adventures of Jefferson's Republicans. Lacking other plausible options, they decided to rely on the courts. In the time between the election and Jefferson's inauguration, the outgoing Federalists hatched and swiftly implemented a plan to preserve Federalist values through the federal judiciary.[15] First, President Adams named his Secretary of State, John Marshall, as the new Chief Justice of the United States. The Senate then swiftly confirmed him. Second, Congress created sixteen new federal judgeships, to which Adams nominated and the Senate quickly confirmed sixteen new "midnight judges," all Federalists. Finally, in a much less significant move, the outgoing Federalist Congress authorized the President to appoint forty-two minor officeholders, called justices of the peace, for the District of Columbia.

Understandably under the circumstances, Jefferson's Republicans took office in a state of fury about the lame-duck Federalists' efforts to commandeer the federal judiciary. Without compunction, the Republicans set out to stop the Federalists from retaining through the courts the influence that they had lost at the polls. On one front, the Republican Congress abolished the new federal judgeships that its predecessor had created, even though Article III of the Constitution says expressly that federal judges shall "hold their offices during good behavior" – a guarantee ordinarily understood as endowing them with life tenure unless they are impeached for "high crimes and misdemeanors." On another front, Congress enacted legislation that effectively barred the Court from meeting for more than a year, until February 1803. On a third, the

---

15 On the Federalists' maneuvers during the lame-duck period following the 1800 election, see Bruce Ackerman, *The Failure of the Founding Fathers: Jefferson, Marshall, and the Rise of Presidential Democracy* (Cambridge, MA: Harvard University Press, 2005); James F. Simon, *What Kind of Nation: Thomas Jefferson, John Marshall, and the Epic Struggle to Create a United States* (New York: Simon & Schuster, 2002), 104–90.

Jeffersonians set out to "impeach" and remove from office Federalist judges who they believed had abused their powers.[16]

When the Supreme Court finally convened in 1803, it had two cases on its docket arising from the actions of the lame-duck Federalists and the reactions of the newly inaugurated Republicans. One, *Stuart v. Laird*,[17] presented a challenge to the constitutionality of the repeal of the 1801 Judiciary Act that had briefly created the sixteen new federal judgeships. If the Court had held that repeal to be unconstitutional, defiance would likely have ensued, for the Republicans then viewed the Court as a partisan, Federalist institution. Officials of the Jefferson administration would likely have refused to pay the ousted "judges" their salaries. Justices of the Supreme Court who stood against the administration probably would have been impeached. In *Stuart v. Laird*, in what the Justices almost surely regarded as a prudent act of self-preservation, the Court chose simply to ignore the constitutional issue that the unseating of sixteen federal judges presented.[18] Judicial authority had to be won, not assumed, and there was no prospect of winning it in *Stuart v. Laird*.

Although people living at the time might have seen matters differently, history has marked the other case growing out of the aftermath of the 1800 election as the foundation for the practice of judicial review that we know today. *Marbury v. Madison*[19] was a suit brought by one of the forty-two men who had been nominated to serve as a justice of the peace for the District of Columbia. Unfortunately for Marbury, officials of the Adams administration had failed to deliver the "commission" that he needed to assume the office, and the Jefferson administration refused to give it to him. In a suit filed in the Supreme Court, Marbury sought a

16 See Simon, *What Kind of Nation*, 191–219. The Republicans impeached and removed a lower federal court judge and commenced impeachment proceedings against a Supreme Court Justice, although the case against the latter ultimately failed when the Senate, which "tries" impeachment cases, failed to vote a conviction.
17 5 U.S. 299 (1803).
18 For vivid discussion of *Stuart* and the events surrounding it, see Ackerman, *Failure of the Founding Fathers*.
19 5 U.S. 137 (1803).

legal order called a "writ of mandamus" that would have directed Jefferson's Secretary of State, James Madison, to give him his commission.

The political climate surrounding *Marbury v. Madison* was as fraught as that surrounding *Stuart v. Laird*. If the Court ruled for Marbury and ordered Madison to deliver his commission, it was widely expected that Madison – acting at the direction of President Jefferson – would defy the Court's order. As the Court appears to have calculated in *Stuart v. Laird*, Jefferson and Madison could surely have gotten away with defiance in the prevailing partisan climate, and it is even likely that Marshall might have been impeached if he had ruled against the popular new administration. Had events developed in this way, the Supreme Court would have been diminished. If, however, the Court simply ruled against Marbury and in favor of Madison, the precedent of its bowing or appearing to bow before political threats – as it felt forced to do in *Stuart v. Laird* – might have boded equally badly for the constitutional ideal of an independent judiciary.

With remarkable ingenuity, Chief Justice John Marshall found a way to decide *Marbury v. Madison* that has permitted it to serve as an enduring symbol of judicial power, not impotence. On the one hand, Marshall ultimately held that Marbury lost his case. By doing so, he deprived Madison and Jefferson of a judicial order that they could defy. They won, not lost. On the other hand, Marshall managed to decide the case on a basis that required him to claim the power of judicial review and thereby set a precedent for its exercise.

Marshall did so by focusing on a technicality, involving what lawyers call "jurisdiction" or the authority of a particular court to decide a particular case. In plain terms, Marbury had sued in the wrong court. By constitutional design, the Supreme Court functions almost exclusively as an "appellate" court, reviewing decisions already made by lower courts to correct errors on points of law. In only a few categories of cases will the Constitution allow someone to sue directly in the Supreme Court without going to a lower court first. Marbury's suit against Madison did not fall within any of those exceptional categories. As a result, the Supreme

Court had no "jurisdiction" to rule on Marbury's suit against Madison. Although Marshall's opinion ultimately so decided, he arrived at his conclusion by a very circuitous route, which required – or enabled – him to make broad rulings on the Supreme Court's power.

Marshall began his opinion by holding that William Marbury had a right to his commission. He held next that for every right the laws of the United States must furnish a remedy – including, if necessary, the remedy of a judicial order commanding action by high governmental officials such as the Secretary of State. This was an enormous claim of judicial power, which Jefferson and Madison would have denied and indeed defied if the occasion had arisen. But that occasion had not yet arrived, and within the structure of Marshall's opinion it never would, because the Chief Justice had still not reached the jurisdictional question of the Supreme Court's authority to rule on the case at all.

When Marshall finally addressed that question, he might have treated the answer as obvious: under the Constitution, the Supreme Court is mostly supposed to hear appeals, not to act as a trial court in cases such as Marbury's. Instead, Marshall pointed to a statute authorizing the Supreme Court to issue the kind of remedy that Marbury sought, a "writ of mandamus" ordering government officials to perform their legal duties. By enacting that statute, Marshall's opinion reasoned, Congress had attempted to give the Supreme Court jurisdiction to act as a trial court in every case in which one party sought a writ of mandamus. In the view of most commentators, this was a clear misreading of the statute. Read in context, it authorized the Court to grant the remedy of mandamus only in cases that it otherwise had jurisdiction to decide.[20] By twisting the statutory language, however, Marshall managed to create a

---

20 See, for example, Akhil Reed Amar, "Marbury, Section 13, and the Original Jurisdiction of the Supreme Court," 56 *University of Chicago Law Review* 443, 456 (1989). For a rare dissenting argument that Congress actually intended to invest the Supreme Court with a "freestanding" jurisdiction to issue writs of mandamus, see James E. Pfander, "Marbury, Original Jurisdiction, and the Supreme Court's Supervisory Powers," 101 *Columbia Law Review* 1515, 1535 (2001).

constitutional question about the power of the Supreme Court to engage in judicial review: a congressionally enacted statute directed the Court to act as a trial court in all cases involving claims to writs of mandamus, but the Constitution permits the Court to exercise original or trial jurisdiction in only a narrower category of cases. So when a statute conflicts with the Constitution, by ordering what the Constitution forbids, which should a court follow, the statute or the Constitution?

With the question framed in this way, Marshall answered it easily, by giving the ruling for which *Marbury* is famous: it would defeat the purposes of a written Constitution if the courts had to enforce unconstitutional statutes. The courts must exercise judicial review because the Constitution is law, and it is the essence of the judicial function "to say what the law is."

With this conclusion, Marbury lost his case. The Supreme Court could not order Madison to give Marbury his commission as a justice of the peace because it had no jurisdiction to do so. But the chain of reasoning that led to the case's outcome involved assertions of enormous judicial power. Madison won, and Marbury lost, only as a result of a precedent-setting ruling that the Supreme Court must review the constitutionality of acts of Congress.

Politics and Judicial Review

Today, many lawyers regard *Marbury* as perhaps the most important case ever decided by the Supreme Court because it was the first clearly to establish the power of judicial review. If *Marbury* is the foundation of judicial review, however, its status as such is partly ironic. The irony emerges from Marshall's reasoning about the purposes of a written Constitution and about the necessity of judicial review to promote them. As Marshall recognized, the Constitution aims to remove some questions from the domain of political decision making. Without the guarantees of a written constitution, it would be open to Congress and ultimately to political majorities to decide whether to permit or deny freedom of religion, for example, and to determine whether the Supreme Court could exercise original jurisdiction in cases such as William Marbury's.

But it is one thing to say that the Constitution aims to remove certain questions from politics, another to determine which branch of government should interpret the Constitution. In suggesting that a written Constitution would be a nullity without judicial review, Marshall manifested a plain distrust of Congress and other political actors: he assumed that they could not be trusted to interpret the Constitution and the limits that it places on their power. This view is compelling, so far as it goes. Significantly, however, Marshall stopped short of asking any searching questions about the possibility that politics might influence the exercise of judicial power. Although Congress, if left unchecked, might twist and torture the written Constitution in the service of its political goals, is there not also a risk that the Supreme Court might do the same?

In *Marbury* itself, for example, it appears that Marshall may well have concluded that Marbury had to lose in order to avoid the political consequences for the judiciary, potentially including the impeachment of Federalist judges, if a ruling went in Marbury's favor. It also seems likely that Marshall deliberately misconstrued a federal statute in order to frame the question of whether the Constitution authorizes judicial review. He presumably did so partly because, in his view, the governmental framework would be a better one if it included a central judicial role, but he may also have acted as he did partly because he wanted to save his own job and to establish its significance.

In describing *Marbury* as itself possibly influenced by political considerations, I should not put the point too strongly. The term "political" admits of varied usages. If Marshall thought that a strong judiciary would enhance the fairness or stability of government under the Constitution, that would be a political view in one sense of the term, but it would not be objectionably political in the same way, for example, as a decision motivated by a desire to promote the fortunes of a favored political party in the next election. Courts probably cannot help relying on views that are political in the first sense. The Constitution is, among other things, a practical plan of government. In interpreting it, courts necessarily take practical considerations into account. By contrast, it would be scandalous if courts behaved politically in the sense of trying to tip elections to a preferred political party. (A belief that the Supreme Court had crossed this line explains some critics' singular outrage at the ruling in *Bush v. Gore*[21] (2000), a case discussed in Chapter 5, which halted a recount in the state of Florida and thereby resolved all lingering doubt that the Republican George W. Bush had won a disputed presidential election.) Sometimes, however, the line between acceptable and unacceptable judicial politics may grow blurry. *Marbury* itself may be a case in point if the Court predetermined that it must find a way for William Marbury to lose in order to reduce political pressures on the Court and its members, or if it deliberately misread a statute in order to create an opportunity to enhance the power of the Judicial Branch by claiming and exercising the function of judicial review.

A Preliminary Perspective on How the Supreme Court Interprets the Constitution

As this short discussion of politics and judicial review probably suggests, *Marbury v. Madison* presented at least two important questions about judicial power under the Constitution. The first was whether courts have the power of judicial review. On that question, the Court spoke relatively conclusively. Since *Marbury*, the power of courts to "say what the law is" in constitutional cases has largely been seen as settled, though I should probably offer a caution at this preliminary point that this is a somewhat weaker claim than it might appear to be on the surface. As was suggested in the prologue and will become clearer in subsequent chapters, although the Supreme Court has a central, often dominant role in our constitutional practice, the Court is by no means the only relevant actor.

21 531 U.S. 98 (2000).

The second question presented in *Marbury* was how courts ought to interpret the Constitution – what considerations they should take into account in giving constitutional rulings. On that question, *Marbury* said little and settled nothing. In supporting the necessity of judicial review, Chief Justice Marshall cited the possibility of statutes that plainly violated constitutional commands. For example, the Constitution says that no one may be convicted of treason except on the testimony of two witnesses in open court.[22] Surely, he argued, a court could not be required to give effect to a statute authorizing convictions of treason based on the testimony of a single witness.[23] In many cases, however, how the Constitution ought to be interpreted, and whether it permits or condemns a governmental act or policy, will not be obvious.

The question of how the Constitution ought to be interpreted cannot be defined, much less answered, along a single dimension, and it would be a mistake to become bogged down in a lengthy discussion before the reader has encountered a broader sample of cases. Nonetheless, a bit of historical perspective may be helpful. Admittedly treading on contested ground, I would say that if any short statement of the Supreme Court's characteristic approach to constitutional adjudication will stand up, it might be this: the Court typically decides cases in light of what the Justices take to be the Constitution's largest purposes and the values that it presupposes as well as those that it more expressly embodies. If any single sentence encapsulates the Court's outlook, it is probably one written by John Marshall sixteen years after *Marbury* in *McCulloch v. Maryland*[24] (1819): "[W]e must never forget that it is a *constitution* we are expounding." A constitution, Marshall explained, does not "partake of the prolixity of a legal code" and must be construed as "adapt[able] to the various *crises* of human affairs."

A brief review of *McCulloch* may make Marshall's assertion more concrete. The case presented two questions. The first was whether

22 See U.S. Constitution, Article III, Section 3, Clause 1.
23 See *Marbury*, 5 U.S. at 179.
24 17 U.S. 316, 407 (1819).

the Constitution authorized Congress to create a "Bank of the United States" (with branches throughout the country) as a depository for federal funds and as a means of creating networks of commercial credit. Although all agreed that Congress possesses no powers not conferred by the Constitution, and although Article I nowhere refers expressly to a congressional power to create a national bank, Marshall had no difficulty in upholding the Bank of the United States. He reasoned that the Constitution grants Congress a number of "great powers," including those "to lay and collect taxes...; to borrow money...; to regulate commerce...; to declare and carry on a war; [and] to raise and support armies."[25] All of those great powers being given, it would make no sense, he wrote, to read the Constitution as precluding the use of a means – in this case, a national bank – that Congress reasonably thought necessary or appropriate in executing those powers: "[A] government, intrusted with such ample powers, on the due execution of which the happiness and prosperity of the nation so vitally depends, must also be intrusted with ample means for their execution."[26]

With Congress's power to create the bank having been established, the next question was whether it was constitutionally permissible for Maryland to tax the bank. Marshall briskly ruled that it was not. No bit of constitutional language spoke to this issue, but Marshall again appealed to the Constitution's broadest purposes and its underlying assumptions. The power to tax the bank was the power "to destroy" it, he wrote. A Constitution that empowered Congress to create a bank thus could not sensibly be read to leave the states with a power to tax it.

To most commentators on the Constitution, the main methodological assumptions of Marshall's opinion in *McCulloch* have appeared sound. He was right that the Constitution, which does not "partake of the prolixity of a legal code," must be adaptable to "crises of human affairs." What is more, if there are two linguistically plausible interpretations of

25 Ibid.
26 Ibid. at 408.

the Constitution, one of which would make it fairer or more workable than the other, or more capable of realizing its overriding purposes, he was right that courts should take this consideration into account. Good judging requires practical and occasionally moral judgment, not just beady-eyed attention to linguistic detail. This, among other reasons, is why Marshall is generally regarded as perhaps the greatest Justice in Supreme Court history.

The difficulty with Marshall's argument in *McCulloch*, which he never really confronted, is that different people will predictably, sometimes systematically, differ in their views of what would make the Constitution fairer or better or truer to its dominant purposes. Looking at the national bank at issue in *McCulloch*, Marshall emphasized the character of the Constitution in vesting Congress with "great powers," the full effectuation of which should not be frustrated. But an opponent of the bank might as easily have emphasized the plain constitutional design to give Congress only carefully limited powers, as subsequently emphasized by the Tenth Amendment: "The powers not delegated to the United States by the Constitution, nor prohibited by it to the States, are reserved to the States respectively, or to the people."

When Marshall's analysis in *McCulloch* is contrasted with that of a readily imaginable critic, the issue of politics in constitutional adjudication – to which I have alluded already – comes starkly to the fore. If Marshall's methodological assumptions are granted, it seems unavoidable that constitutional decision making should sometimes rest on political considerations of a kind. In determining how the spare language of the Constitution is best interpreted, a judge's views about what is fair and sensible will often come inescapably into play.[27] And if loosely political judgments about what is fair and sensible and most in accord with the Constitution's fundamental purposes often underlie judgments of how best to interpret the Constitution, then loosely political disagreements will often drive disagreements about constitutional law. In *McCulloch*,

27 See Dworkin, *Law's Empire*, 255–56.

Marshall thought it more sensible to read the Constitution as investing Congress with broad powers; those who feared federal authority would have reached the opposite conclusion. (Similar disagreements underlie the division among the Justices in *National Federation of Independent Business v. Sebelius*[28] (2012), which I discussed in the prologue and further discuss in Chapter 7, about whether Congress has authority under the Commerce Clause to require individuals to buy health insurance – a question that the Court answered in the negative by a vote of 5–4.)

In more modern times, those troubled by the prospect of judges' values influencing their rulings have sometimes maintained that judicial decision makers should put their ideological views aside and decide cases strictly in accordance with the "original understanding" of constitutional language. Although I shall say more about "originalism" in Chapter 9, suffice it to say for now that the idea of a determinate original understanding is often a fiction. When the Bank of the United States was first proposed, President George Washington, who had served as presiding officer at the Constitutional Convention, thought the question of whether Congress had the power to create such a bank a doubtful one, and he therefore sought written opinions from his most senior and able Cabinet officials. Secretary of State Jefferson, who opposed the creation of a bank on ideological grounds, also concluded that it would be unconstitutional. Secretary of the Treasury Alexander Hamilton, who favored a bank for economic reasons, concluded that the Constitution indubitably empowered Congress to create one. It is worth pausing over how the positions of Washington, Jefferson, and Hamilton bear on the question of whether it is always possible to identify a historically determinate "original understanding" or "public meaning" of constitutional language adequate to resolve constitutional disputes. Washington, who was surely as well situated to know the original understanding as anyone, was uncertain whether Congress could create a bank. And Jefferson and Hamilton, who should also count as "original understanders" or experts

28 132 S. Ct. 2566 (2012).

on the Constitution's original "public meaning," disagreed along lines reflecting their ideological differences.

From one perspective, it seems troubling that political judgments could influence constitutional law and that political disagreements could underlie constitutional debates, even among those who had participated in the Constitution's framing. Again, however, it is also worth recalling the precise way in which practical and political considerations often enter the picture. In a dispute over whether *McCulloch v. Maryland* was correctly decided, it would not be accurate to say that those on either side had allowed their political views to contaminate a judgment that should have been based on the Constitution alone – whatever that form of words might mean. A good judge or Justice will never ignore the Constitution. It is, indeed, the Constitution that he or she is "expounding." But the meaning of words often depends on their context, and in the context of constitutional adjudication, considerations of fairness, practicality, and good government are almost always relevant to interpretive meaning, even when they are not decisive. The disagreement between Jefferson and Hamilton was a reasoned, reasonable, and conscientious one about the best way to interpret a Constitution that could reasonably have been read to reach either of their preferred conclusions.

A Brief History of Judicial Review

A judicial power to determine how the Constitution is best interpreted can obviously be understood either relatively narrowly – for example, only as a tie breaker when two interpretations of the Constitution are otherwise exactly equally plausible – or more broadly, so that judicial judgments exert a substantially greater influence. That power can also be used either for good or for ill.

History has generally smiled on the exercise of judicial review by the Supreme Court under John Marshall. In broadest terms, Marshall's Court was committed to nation building, including the establishment of federal judicial power as a tool for binding the states into a single, unified country. The Marshall Court upheld the exercise of expansive power by the federal government, but it did not hesitate to invalidate state legislation based on purposive, value-based interpretations of constitutional provisions (few in number, before the Civil War Amendments) conferring rights against the states. Seen in retrospect, Marshall's thirty-four-year tenure as Chief Justice – from 1801 to 1835 – was extraordinary in nearly every way. Marshall forged a remarkable unity among the Justices of his Court, including those appointed by his former political opponents. Dissenting opinions were rare as Marshall presided with casual, unpretentious charm over dinnertime conferences sometimes eased by the consumption of wine. Initially, the wine was reportedly reserved for rainy days. Later the Justices relied on the theory that it was always likely to be raining somewhere in the great territorial mass of the United States.

After Marshall had departed and as the country slid toward Civil War, the Court proceeded less steadily. It took large interpretive liberties in the infamous case of *Dred Scott v. Sandford*[29] (1857), which held that Congress lacked authority to ban the spread of slavery in the federal territories that were not yet states. At the time, questions involving slavery and its spread were literally tearing the country apart. The Court apparently thought it could help to heal the divide by taking one big part of the slavery issue – involving the permissibility of slavery in the territories – "out of politics" and making it pointless for national politicians to fight about it.

In rendering a broad decision predicated on legally dubious reasoning, but one aimed at the goal of stopping the country from splintering over slavery, the Justices may have thought that they acted in the great tradition of *Marbury v. Madison*. They apparently hoped that they could save the country, and, where the end is urgent enough, constitutional reasoning that would be unacceptable under other circumstances may sometimes be what the situation demands. This, after all, is apparently how the esteemed John Marshall had thought about *Marbury*. But

29 60 U.S. 393 (1857).

the *Dred Scott* decision was a fiasco. Besides taking the wrong side of a constitutional issue with profound moral implications, the Justices foolishly, quixotically overestimated the practical reach of judicial power.[30] A Supreme Court ruling had no chance of defusing an issue about which the country would soon descend into war. When it renders otherwise legally dubious decisions in the hope that doing so will be justified by the results that it achieves, the Court more than ever "labors under the obligation to succeed."[31]

After *Dred Scott*, as the bonds of constitutional government frayed, judicial power went into eclipse. During the Civil War, the Supreme Court generally acquiesced in actions by Congress, the President, and the Union Army that quite arguably overstepped constitutional bounds. In a relatively isolated case of judicial resistance to intrusions on civil liberties during wartime, Abraham Lincoln actually defied a ruling by the Chief Justice Roger Taney denying the authority of military officials to hold suspected Confederate sympathizers without bringing them into court and proving them guilty of crimes.[32] The Court thereafter shrank from the limelight. In the immediate aftermath of the Civil War, it declined to exercise powers rather plainly conferred on it by the Civil War Amendments – a matter discussed more fully in Chapter 3.

The Court emerged from its retreat by the end of the nineteenth century and began some of the protection of civil liberties for which it would later earn acclaim. At roughly the same time, however, the Court began to adopt constitutional positions that frustrated "progressive" legislative efforts to prohibit child labor, give workers the right to unionize, and establish minimum wages and maximum hours

---

30 A justice of the current Supreme Court, Stephen Breyer, criticizes the *Dred Scott* decision in "A Look Back at the *Dred Scott* Decision," 35 *Journal of Supreme Court History* 110 (2010).

31 Alexander M. Bickel, *The Least Dangerous Branch: The Supreme Court at the Bar of Politics* (New York: Bobbs-Merrill, 1962), 239.

32 The ruling came in *Ex parte Merryman*, 17 F. Cas. 144 (C.C.D.Md. 1861), a case discussed in Chapter 12.

for laborers. The Court fought its constitutional battle on two fronts. First, in cases challenging federal legislation, the Court frequently held that Congress had exceeded the bounds of its power under Article I of the Constitution when, for example, it sought to regulate child labor. Second, when it was the states that enacted "progressive" legislation, the Court's conservative majority often ruled that restrictions on "the freedom of contract" infringed on individual liberty in violation of the Due Process Clause, which says that no one may be deprived of "life, liberty, or property, without due process of law."

The so-called *Lochner* era, which took its name from a notorious case[33] in which the Supreme Court struck down a state law limiting the hours that could be worked by bakery employees, and was marked by what many observers would characterize as repeated incidences of conservative "judicial activism," stretched into the 1930s. Controversial from the outset, the Court's antiregulatory stance increasingly triggered outrage during the Great Depression, especially as the Supreme Court invalidated central elements of President Franklin Roosevelt's New Deal and threatened to scuttle others. Following a massive triumph in the 1936 elections, and with the programs on which he had won reelection very much at risk, Roosevelt went to Congress and asked for its help in checking the Court: he proposed legislation that would have expanded the Court's size and permitted him to "pack" it by appointing a number of new, pro–New Deal Justices. (Although the Supreme Court has had nine Justices since 1869, the Constitution permits Congress to fix the number by statute. At earlier points in American history, the Court had as few as six and as many as ten Justices.) Roosevelt's Court-packing proposal failed in Congress, but only after it had become unnecessary. In several cases decided during 1937, Justice Owen Roberts, who had cast the crucial fifth vote to invalidate New Deal legislation in some of the earlier cases, switched sides.

33 *Lochner v. New York*, 198 U.S. 45 (1905).

Historians continue to debate whether Roberts was affected by
political currents in general or the Court-packing plan in particular.[34]
Whatever the cause for his changed position, the effect proved dramatic.
In the short term, the New Deal was safe. The Court also gave up closely
scrutinizing state legislation under the Due Process Clause, with the
result that states, too, became free to enact progressive regulatory and
redistributive legislation without judicial obstruction.

The constitutional showdown that occurred in 1937 between Franklin
Roosevelt and the Supreme Court vividly illustrates a number of points
that will be of recurring importance throughout this book. First, the
Supreme Court is a "they," not an "it."[35] Before 1937, the Justices had
been deeply divided about the constitutionality of New Deal legislation.
Even in 1937, at least seven of the nine Justices remained wedded to their
former positions. The decisions of one or two "swing" Justices determined the outcome and brought about what has been described ever
since as "the switch in time that saved nine." It can thus matter a great
deal who sits on the Supreme Court at any particular time. With one or
two different Justices, the Court might have upheld New Deal legislation from the beginning – or it might have continued to invalidate such
programs as Social Security through 1937 and possibly beyond.

Second, as also illustrated by the events surrounding *Marbury v.
Madison* and *Stuart v. Laird*, the Supreme Court operates within what
political scientists call "politically constructed bounds."[36] Although the
Justices exercise enormous power, their decisions can enjoy long-term

---

34 Revisionist works that attribute the "switch in time" less to immediate political pressure than to gradually unfolding changes in constitutional doctrine and prevailing
jurisprudential assumptions include Barry Cushman, *Rethinking the New Deal* (New
York: Oxford University Press, 1998), and G. Edward White, *The Constitution and the
New Deal* (Cambridge, MA: Harvard University Press, 2000).

35 See Adrian Vermeule, "The Judiciary Is a They, Not an It: Interpretive Theory and
the Fallacy of Division," 14 *Journal of Contemporary Legal Issues* 549 (2005).

36 See Keith Whittington, *Political Foundations of Judicial Supremacy: The Presidency,
the Supreme Court, and Constitutional Leadership in U.S. History* (Princeton, NJ:
Princeton University Press, 2007), 4; Mark A. Graber, "Constructing Judicial Review,"
8 *Annual Review of Political Science* 425, 425 (2005).

and sometimes even short-term efficacy only insofar as those decisions remain politically tolerable to Congress and the President, as presumed representatives of the American people. In *Marbury* and *Stuart*, the President could have defied the Supreme Court and got away with it if the Court had ruled differently. In 1937, if Justice Roberts's "switch in time" had not occurred, Roosevelt well might have succeeded in packing the Court. Today, the Court is vastly stronger and less vulnerable, but its remaining so depends on its staying within politically constructed bounds. Normally, there is little risk of its failing to do so. The circumstances of the New Deal were unusually dramatic, but the ordinary processes of judicial retirements, nominations, and confirmations typically suffice to ensure that the Supreme Court will not stray too far out of touch with the aroused sentiments of the American people for too long.[37] When a majority of the Justices take positions that the public finds deeply objectionable, presidential candidates can run against the Court, promising to appoint Justices with different philosophies and thereby bring the Court back into line.

Third, presidential leadership can have a powerful role in shaping the constitutional views of the American people and in reshaping the positions of the Supreme Court, typically through the nominations of new Justices. Franklin Roosevelt had a constitutional vision of expansive governmental power adequate to tame the business cycle, ensure all who were willing to work a living wage, and provide a social safety net for the elderly and disabled. He successfully sold that vision to large majorities of the American people. The contrary view, he argued, reflected an outdated, "horse and buggy" conception of the Constitution.[38] Over the course of more than three presidential terms, Roosevelt was able to appoint eight Justices to the Supreme Court, even without the aid

37 See, for example, Barry Friedman, *The Will of the People: How Public Opinion Has Influenced the Supreme Court and Shaped the Meaning of the Constitution* (New York: Farrar, Straus, and Giroux, 2009).

38 William E. Leuchtenburg, *The Supreme Court Reborn: The Constitutional Revolution in the Age of Roosevelt* (Oxford: Oxford University Press, 1996), 90.

of Court packing. By the time of his death in 1945, the Supreme Court fairly could have been called "the Roosevelt Court." The old regime – defined by a commitment to enforce limits on government's regulatory power – was out. A new regime – defined by a set of constitutional assumptions that accepted sweeping economic regulation and redistributive programs such as Social Security – had taken its place and would reign largely unchallenged for roughly the following fifty years. Policies and programs that once would have been constitutionally unacceptable were then, by nearly consensus understanding, constitutionally permissible.

In remaking the Supreme Court, Franklin Roosevelt self-consciously set out to appoint "liberal" Justices by the standards of his era. In the context of the time, in which "conservatives" had frustrated the enactment of progressive legislation, judicial liberals were generally those who believed that the Supreme Court should give Congress and the state legislatures a relatively free hand. In other words, New Deal liberals preached judicial deference or restraint. As the *Lochner* era gradually faded, however, further reflection on its lessons occurred. Virtually no one advocated a return to the kind of judicial activism that the Court had practiced in the early twentieth century. But while some Justices and commentators took the position that the Court should show "judicial restraint" (and uphold challenged legislation) in nearly all settings, others began to argue that the Court's prior error lay in its effort to protect the wrong substantive rights (such as broad rights of "freedom of contract") under the wrong provisions of the Constitution. In their view, the Court should almost never invalidate economic regulatory legislation enacted by Congress and the state legislatures, but it should not hesitate to protect other rights, including freedom of speech; and, in particular, it should give vigilant protection to the rights of racial and religious minorities.

The latter position, reflecting an evolving, more activist vision of liberal constitutionalism, ultimately rose to ascendancy under the Warren Court, so-called after Chief Justice Earl Warren, who was named to the bench in 1953. One of the early landmarks of his tenure came in 1954, when the Court held in *Brown v. Board of Education*[39] that the Equal Protection Clause of the Fourteenth Amendment forbade race-based discrimination in the public schools. As is discussed further in Chapter 5, this conclusion was probably contrary to the "original understanding" of the Equal Protection Clause, yet nearly everyone regards *Brown* as among the triumphant moments of Supreme Court history. It served as a prelude to other Warren Court decisions that expanded the scope of the constitutional guarantee of equal protection of the laws, First Amendment freedoms of speech and religion, and a variety of rights of criminal suspects.

Warren was a warm, conspicuously decent man. A former governor of California, he had an easy charm and a savvy understanding of politics. During his tenure, the Court assumed something of his personality. From the bench, Warren would sometimes ask counsel who had made technical legal points whether they thought that the results that they urged were fair – not whether they were supportable by legal argument, but whether they were just or decent in a deeper sense. Some thrilled to the approach of the Warren Court. Many law professors were perplexed, often sympathetic to the Court's results but skeptical of the soundness of its constitutional reasoning. And some, of course, were horrified. By any fair account, the Supreme Court was once again at the center of national political controversy through most of the Warren years.

The 1968 presidential election marked the end of the Warren era. During the latter half of the 1960s, as crime rates spiked and court-ordered busing to enforce the desegregation mandate of *Brown v. Board of Education* became deeply unpopular, a shift occurred in the politically constructed bounds within which the Supreme Court operates. In the 1968 presidential campaign, the Republican nominee, Richard Nixon, took clear aim at the Warren Court's decisions, especially those that had expanded the rights of criminal suspects. According to critics, the

39 347 U.S. 483 (1954).

Warren Court's decisions repeatedly loosed dangerous criminals onto the streets on the basis of newly minted legal technicalities (such as the rule requiring *Miranda* warnings, which is discussed in Chapter 4). If elected, Nixon promised, he would appoint "law and order" Justices with a "strict constructionist" philosophy. Nixon's appeal struck a resonant chord. He won. By 1972 he had appointed four new Justices, and the Warren Court was no more.

In the years since Nixon began the process of transformation, the Supreme Court has grown substantially more conservative. It is not always easy to say exactly what it means for the Court to be "conservative" any more than to say what it means for the Court to be "liberal." But a simple measure commonly used by political scientists will suffice for current purposes: judicial decisions count as conservative when they reach substantive outcomes that those with conservative political views could be expected to applaud.[40] As gauged by this standard, the conservative turn began under the Chief Justice that Nixon appointed, Warren Burger, who served from 1969 to 1986. Among its initiatives, the Burger Court inaugurated a pattern of cutbacks in the rights of criminal defendants, as is discussed in Chapter 4. But the turn to the right was not as sharp as some had anticipated. Conservative jurists of the 1960s and 1970s not only felt obliged to adhere to many Warren Court precedents but also retained a kind of elite, secular sensibility. The latter may help explain how the Burger Court could recognize a constitutional right to abortion, by the remarkable vote of 7–2, in its 1973 decision in *Roe v. Wade*.[41]

During the Burger years, the Court's most unyieldingly conservative Justice was William H. Rehnquist, a dissenter in *Roe v. Wade* who was less prepared than any of his colleagues to accept Warren-era precedents. With national politics having taken a further turn to the right with the election of Ronald Reagan in 1980 and the rise of a

---

40 See, for example, Jeffrey A. Segal and Harold J. Spaeth, *The Supreme Court and the Attitudinal Model* (New York: Cambridge University Press, 1993).
41 410 U.S. 113 (1973).

Christian conservative movement, Reagan rewarded Rehnquist's meritorious service as an Associate Justice by nominating him to be Chief Justice upon Burger's retirement. For most of Rehnquist's tenure as Chief Justice from 1986 through 2005, seven of the Court's nine Justices had been appointed by Republican presidents. As was the case with the Burger Court, the Rehnquist Court disappointed political conservatives who had hoped for a complete rollback of all constitutional decisions that they regarded as objectionably liberal – including, for example, *Roe v. Wade* and Warren Court decisions barring prayer in the public schools. Although constitutional law is much influenced by politics, it is also partly autonomous from politics, in ways that I discuss throughout this book. Nevertheless, the Rehnquist Court not only continued to pare away the constitutional rights of criminal defendants but also began to chip at the foundations of the once unquestioned post–New Deal understanding that Congress has nearly boundless powers to regulate any activities that significantly affect the national economy.

The Supreme Court Today

When William Rehnquist died in office in 2005, President George W. Bush nominated John Roberts to be his successor. A former law clerk to Rehnquist, Roberts had worked as a lawyer in the Reagan administration before going on to a career as a Washington lawyer in which he earned renown as a brilliant advocate in cases before the Supreme Court. As Chief Justice, Roberts's votes have marked him as a member of what is invariably described as a five-Justice conservative block. For the most part, he has adhered to a pledge made during his confirmation hearings to be cautious about overruling prior Supreme Court decisions, but one of his most important decisions – which invalidated a federal law that barred spending by corporations to influence the outcome of election campaigns – overruled two cases. Overall, the substitution of Roberts for Rehnquist has made relatively little difference to the Court's voting patterns.

Less cautious than Chief Justice Roberts about overruling precedent are two other members of the conservative block, Antonin Scalia
and Clarence Thomas, both of whom profess to be "originalists," or
adherents to the theory that the Court should decide modern cases
based on the originally understood meaning of constitutional language.
Thomas, the Court's only African American member, is the more strident originalist of the two. Mostly in dissenting or concurring opinions that he writes for himself alone, Thomas professes openness to
the idea that long-settled constitutional precedents – including those
that give Congress broad powers to regulate the national economy and
that bar the states as well as the federal government from supporting
religions – are erroneous as measured against the original understanding of the Constitution and therefore ought to be reversed. In distinguishing himself from Thomas, Justice Scalia, the Court's other self-
proclaimed originalist, was once quoted as saying, "I am an originalist,
but I am not a nut."[42] If quoted accurately, Scalia apparently meant,
in part, that he believes it necessary to accept some, though not all,
prior Supreme Court decisions that he thinks mistaken as an original
matter. (For example, there is a substantial argument that Congress's
creation of Social Security overreaches the original understanding of
congressional power, but the Court has held otherwise, and today millions of Americans depend on Social Security for their livelihood.) Scalia
is an incisive and often humorous questioner of lawyers in oral arguments before the Court. (By comparison, Thomas – who by all accounts
is outgoing and gregarious in his personal life – has not posed even a
single question in any of the Court's public sessions in more than five
years.[43]) Scalia is also one of the most brilliant stylists in the Court's
entire history, although it has been reported that the caustic, mock-
ing tone that he sometimes adopts in dissenting opinions has offended

42 Jeffrey Toobin, *The Nine: Inside the Secret World of the Supreme Court* (New York:
    Doubleday, 2007), 103.
43 Adam Liptak, "No Argument: Thomas Keeps 5-Year Silence," *N.Y. Times*,
    February 13, 2011, A1.

some of his colleagues and thus diminished his capacity to influence them.

More allied with Chief Justice Roberts as a matter of judicial style is Samuel Alito, a graduate of Yale Law School and a veteran of the Reagan administration's legal team, whom President Bush named to the Court in 2006. Alito does not intervene often during arguments before the Court, but it is said that his colleagues listen especially carefully when he does.

Rounding out the conservative block is Justice Anthony Kennedy, who has served on the Court since 1988. Kennedy is routinely referred to as the "swing" Justice, or the conservative most likely to abandon his conservative colleagues to vote for "liberal" outcomes. Although conventional references to the Supreme Court mark periods in its history by reference to the name of Chief Justice, some say it would be more accurate to refer to the current Court as "the Kennedy Court" than as the Roberts Court. Although Kennedy sometimes joins originalist opinions, he is more ready than most of his conservative colleagues to interpret the Constitution in light of what he views as a general aspiration to protect "liberty" and individual "dignity," even when he understands the requirements of liberty and dignity more capaciously than prior generations would have.

Among the four Justices who are commonly denoted as liberals (all nominated to the Court by Democratic presidents), three are women. (There had never been a woman Justice at all until 1981, when President Reagan appointed Sandra Day O'Connor, and the number climbed to three for the first time in 2010.) The most senior liberal as well as the most senior woman is Ruth Bader Ginsburg, named to the Court by Bill Clinton in 1993. During the 1970s, Ginsburg was a pioneering advocate for women's rights in several of the Court's most important cases involving sex discrimination. As a Justice, she has proved cautious and careful, with a preference for deciding cases on narrow bases when possible. She has also continued as a champion of women's rights, sometimes in majority and sometimes in dissenting opinions.

Because the other two women Justices are those with the briefest tenures, their judicial styles are less easy to categorize. Sonia Sotomayor, who joined the Court in 2009 after eleven years as a lower-court judge, is the first Hispanic Justice. The daughter of Puerto Rican immigrants, Sotomayor grew up in the Bronx and worked as a New York district attorney and private lawyer before becoming a judge. Elena Kagan was appointed a year later than Sotomayor after highly successful stints as a law professor, dean of Harvard Law School, and the chief Supreme Court lawyer for the Obama administration. She also previously worked as a top adviser to President Clinton.

The fourth liberal is Stephen Breyer, another former law professor and lower court judge, who has served since 1994. Among the liberal Justices, perhaps none is more attentive than Breyer to questions of how, methodologically, the Court should go about interpreting both the Constitution and federal statutes. He has argued in well-regarded books, in addition to his judicial opinions, that the Justices should attend carefully to the practical implications of their rulings and that they should strive, in particular, to facilitate the fair operation of political democracy (by, for example, invalidating partisan gerrymanders of voting districts and upholding campaign-finance regulations).[44]

It is often remarked that eight of the nine current Justices (Kagan being the sole exception) had served as lower-court judges before their appointments to the Supreme Court. In the past, the Court frequently had more members with national political experience and fewer who had previously been judges. All the sitting Justices attended either Harvard or Yale Law School. Six are Catholics and three are Jews. For the first time in the nation's history, none is a Protestant. Four of the Justices were raised in New York City.

---

44 Stephen Breyer, *Making Our Democracy Work: A Judge's View* (New York: Knopf, 2010); Stephen Breyer, *Active Liberty: Interpreting Our Democratic Constitution* (New York: Knopf, 2005).

An Outline of What Is to Come

Constitutional law is a sprawling subject that does not respect neat divisions. In rough terms, however, the Constitution performs two main functions. First, it creates and structures the government of the United States. Second, it guarantees individual rights against the government.

For the most part, the organization of this book reflects this crude distinction, although it deals with the Constitution's two functions, as I just described them, in reverse order. Part I considers constitutional doctrines involving individual rights. Chapters 1–6 discuss central topics concerning freedom of speech, freedom of religion, economic liberties, a sample of fundamental rights besides speech and religion that are "enumerated" in the Bill of Rights, the equal protection of the laws, and so-called unenumerated rights. (It would be impossible to deal with all of the rights created by the Constitution and to keep the book even reasonably short, and I have therefore had to accept some painful omissions of other important topics.)

Part II of the book discusses constitutional doctrines involving the structure of government under the Constitution. Chapters 7, 8, and 9 deal, respectively, with the powers of Congress under Article I, of the President under Article II, and of the judiciary under Article III. Besides summarizing relevant constitutional doctrine, the chapter on judicial power contains the book's principal discussion of debates about interpretive methodology and about how the power of judicial review ought to be exercised. I postpone detailed consideration of these important issues until Chapter 9 so that readers will be able to assess the various positions against the background of substantive discussions contained in earlier chapters.

The chapters in Part III address topics in which issues of individual rights are not easily separated from issues of constitutional structure and governmental power. Chapter 10 discusses limits on state power resulting from the Constitution's structure and the individual rights to which those limits give rise. Chapter 11 is about the Constitution in war and emergency. Chapter 12 deals with the reach of the Constitution, which generally applies only to the government and not to private conduct, and with Congress's power to "enforce" the Constitution by enacting laws designed to protect constitutional rights. Finally, Chapter 13 summarizes the themes developed in earlier chapters.

Part I   INDIVIDUAL RIGHTS UNDER THE CONSTITUTION

1 Freedom of Speech

Congress shall make no law ... abridging the freedom of speech.
                    – The Free Speech Clause of the First Amendment

The most stringent protection of free speech would not protect a man
in falsely shouting fire in a theatre and causing a panic.
                    – Justice Oliver Wendell Holmes Jr.[1]

MAGINE THAT AMID A SPATE OF TERRORIST ATTACKS ON
American and European cities, an Al Qaeda sympathizer
stands before a sympathetic crowd, exults in the carnage
that has occurred already, and urges jihad against the United States.
He denounces Westerners, Zionists, and Americans as devils reviled
by God. He says that the tide in the battle between the godly and the
ungodly has begun to turn and calls for more suicide bombings and other
terrorist attacks against infidels, throughout the world but especially in
the United States. He urges all lovers of God to launch attacks against
nuclear power plants, water supplies, bridges, and synagogues.

If this imagined Al Qaeda supporter did his speech making elsewhere
in the world, the United States would likely convey a protest to the
appropriate government and demand that it stop him. Speech, we know,
often triggers action. We would dislike having a foreign government
sit by until an attack actually occurred. Most Western governments,

1 *Schenck v. United States*, 249 U.S. 47, 52 (1919).

including those with strong commitments to freedom of speech, would
make an arrest. But if the speaker were an American citizen, living
in the United States, our government would need to adopt a different
posture. The imagined speech would be protected by the First Amendment to the Constitution, as interpreted by the Supreme Court of the
United States – at least unless the Court could be persuaded to change its
mind.

The Foundations of Modern Doctrine

Broad protection for freedom of speech has emerged as one of the
defining features of American constitutional law. Interestingly, however,
modern doctrine does not reflect the original understanding of the First
Amendment. Historians have often emphasized the narrowness of the
framers' vision. According to most accounts, the one clear purpose of the
Free Speech Clause was to prohibit systems of so-called prior restraint,
under which authors had to get the approval of administrative cen-
sors before they could publish their works.[2] Somewhat curiously from a
modern perspective, a constitutional prohibition against prior restraints
would not, by itself, immunize speakers or writers from being punished
for their speech after it was spoken or published. Although such a prohibition bars preclearance requirements, it does not stop the government
from outlawing speech that is lewd or profane, for example, provided
that the punishment does not come until after a speaker has had his or
her say.

Beyond systems of prior restraint, some historians believe that the
First Amendment was originally understood to forbid after-the-fact
punishments for "seditious libel" or criticism of the government.[3] Other
historians regard the evidence as doubtful or believe that the founding

2 See *Near v. Minnesota*, 283 U.S. 697, 713 (1931).
3 See, for example, David A. Anderson, "The Origins of the Press Clause," 30 *UCLA
   Law Review* 455 (1983); William T. Mayton, "Seditious Libel and the Lost Guarantee
   of a Freedom of Expression," 84 *Columbia Law Review* 91 (1984).

generation meant to outlaw prior restraints and nothing more.[4] Almost no one, however, contends that the framers and ratifiers widely understood the Free Speech Clause as doing more than outlawing licensing schemes and, possibly, as protecting critics of the government from punishment for seditious libel. Some among the founding generation may have had broader views, possibly linked to a belief in the existence of "natural rights," but there is little or no evidence of any concrete consensus.[5]

Today, much has changed. As interpreted by the Supreme Court, the First Amendment protects nearly every form of expression, from profanity to commercial advertising to flag burning. What is more, virtually no participant in contemporary constitutional debates seems to object to the departure from the Constitution's originally understood meaning with respect to freedom of speech.

With modern free-speech doctrine lacking firm foundations in the original understanding of the Constitution, it might be thought that the Supreme Court's approach must reflect consensus about the content of a universal human right to free speech. But this suggestion would be mistaken. The United States recognizes speech rights that are substantially broader than those protected by most liberal democracies. To take the most vivid example, most liberal democracies have ratified an international human rights convention that commits signatory nations to banning speech that incites racial hatred.[6] Although the United States participated in the drafting of that convention, this country has never ratified

---

4 See, for example, Leonard W. Levy, *The Emergence of a Free Press* (New York: Oxford University Press, 1985); David Lowenthal, *No Liberty for License: The Forgotten Logic of the First Amendment* (Dallas, TX: Spence Publishing, 1997), 10.

5 See Steven J. Heyman, "Righting the Balance: An Inquiry into the Foundations and Limits of Freedom of Expression," 78 *Boston University Law Review* 1275 (1998).

6 See International Convention on the Elimination of All Forms of Racial Discrimination, Article 4, pledging signatory nations to "declare as an offence punishable by law all dissemination of ideas based on racial superiority or hatred [and] incitement to racial discrimination." See generally Mari J. Matsuda, "Public Response to Racist Speech: Considering the Victim's Story," 87 *Michigan Law Review* 2320 (1989) (discussing practices of other liberal democracies in prohibiting racist speech).

it, largely because of concerns that the convention would violate the First Amendment. Far from suppressing speech that attempts to incite racial hatred, American free-speech doctrine holds racist utterances to enjoy First Amendment protection in most circumstances.

A number of forces have contributed to the development of modern First Amendment law. The Supreme Court has played the principal role in shaping and reshaping a complex body of rules, often in response to the lessons it has gleaned from experiences both happy and unhappy. Cultural forces have also exerted an enormous influence. Supreme Court decisions have proved durable when they resonate with broadly shared values and attitudes, less so when they sound dissonant themes. For the most part, the doctrine reflects a robust optimism about "the marketplace of ideas." People get to decide for themselves what to believe and what not to believe. Some expressions of ideas can be deeply hurtful – racist utterances being a prime example – but neither the surrounding culture nor the judicial doctrine tends to offer much sympathy: American schoolchildren are taught, and many believe, that "sticks and stones can break my bones, but words can never hurt me." Ours is a highly commercialized society, and our First Amendment now protects commercial advertising nearly as fully as it protects political oratory. But this is also a pragmatic nation, skeptical of absolutes, and when the Court believes a particular type of speech to be severely harmful, speech-protective principles will often yield. As Justice Oliver Wendell Holmes wrote in the Supreme Court's first major case interpreting the First Amendment, "The most stringent protection of free speech would not protect a man in falsely shouting fire in a theatre and causing a panic."[7]

Proximate Origins of Modern Doctrine

The origins of modern free-speech doctrine lie in a series of cases decided by the Supreme Court under the 1917 Espionage Act. Before the outbreak of World War I, Congress had enacted little legislation restricting

7 *Schenck v. United States*, 249 U.S. 47, 52 (1919).

speech, and the Court's discussions of freedom of expression had consisted largely of sweeping, mostly unsympathetic generalities. Nor had the Supreme Court applied the First Amendment to strike down state laws. (As discussed in the Introduction, the Bill of Rights, including the First Amendment, did not initially apply to the states. Only during the 1920s did the Court begin to enforce the First Amendment against the states, on the theory that it had been made applicable to them by the Fourteenth Amendment, which was enacted in the aftermath of the Civil War.) In assessing whether the Espionage Act violated the First Amendment, the Court thus found itself relatively free to craft free-speech doctrine as it saw fit.[8]

Passed during World War I, the Espionage Act made it a crime to cause, attempt to cause, or conspire to cause insubordination in the American armed forces or obstruction of military recruiting. The Supreme Court first encountered the statute in *Schenck v. United States*[9] (1919). Schenck and some companions had distributed leaflets to roughly fifteen thousand men drafted for military service. On one side, the leaflets compared the draft with slavery; on the other side, they implored recipients to "Assert Your Rights." Justice Holmes, who would later emerge as a crusading champion of speech rights, wrote the unanimous opinion upholding the defendants' conviction for attempting to cause and conspiring to cause interferences with the American war effort. He first established Schenck's intent: "Of course the document would not have been sent unless it had been intended to have some effect, and we do not see what effect it could be expected to have upon persons subject to the draft except to influence them to obstruct the carrying of it out."[10]

Turning then to the First Amendment issue, Holmes brusquely dismissed any suggestion that all speech might enjoy constitutional protection, even though the First Amendment says literally that "Congress

---

8 On the earlier history of First Amendment litigation, see David M. Rabban, "The First Amendment in Its Forgotten Years," 90 *Yale Law Journal* 514 (1981).
9 249 U.S. 47 (1919).
10 Ibid. at 51.

shall make *no* law...abridging the freedom of speech." As shown by the imagined case of a false cry of fire in a crowded theater, an absolutist interpretation was simply out of the question. Nor, it might be added, does the amendment's language necessarily call for such an approach. As John Marshall had pointed out in an out-of-court debate in the 1790s, the First Amendment does not protect all speech but only "the freedom of speech." The courts must define "the freedom of speech" and thus distinguish speech that is protected from speech that is not.

There are many possible grounds on which the Court might have sought to distinguish protected from unprotected speech. It might, for example, have looked to the original understanding of the First Amendment. But the Court conducted no historical inquiries in *Schenck*. Instead, Justice Holmes – who had been wounded three times in the Civil War and was very much a hard-eyed realist – seized on the criterion of actual or likely harmfulness as the key to identifying speech that lies outside "the freedom of speech" that the First Amendment protects. Speech can be used to deceive, to threaten, and to provoke lawless violence, as well as to inform, amuse, and debate. Focusing on speech's capacity to cause harm, Holmes wrote that "[t]he question in every case is whether the words are used in such circumstances and are of such a nature as to create a clear and present danger that they will bring about the substantive evils that Congress has a right to prevent."[11]

With these words, Holmes articulated the famous "clear and present danger" test for identifying speech that is not protected by the First Amendment. In applying that test, however, Holmes did not initially demand much evidence of the clarity or even the presence of danger. In *Schenck*, the government had not proved that the leaflets distributed by the defendants had caused insubordination or resistance to the draft or that they were likely to do so. Nonetheless, the Court upheld the convictions. The possibility of serious harm to the American war effort, coupled with intent to produce it, was enough.

11 Ibid. at 52.

Holmes applied the "clear and present danger" test with similar lax-
ity in another case decided in 1919, *Debs v. United States*.[12] Eugene V.
Debs was a leading political figure of his day, a four-time Socialist Party
candidate for President who got 6 percent of the total votes cast in 1912.
Despite, or possibly because of, his stature, Debs was indicted and prosecuted under the Espionage Act based on a speech that he delivered
to an Ohio state Socialist Party convention on a Sunday afternoon. In
that speech, he criticized the war; expressed sympathy for those who had
opposed and resisted the draft; and said to his audience that "you need
to know that you are fit for something better than slavery and cannon
fodder."[13] On no more evidence than this, Holmes found the "clear and
present danger" test to be satisfied. Debs had used words with a tendency
to obstruct war recruiting, even if that result never actually occurred.

Schenck and *Debs* got free-speech doctrine off to a bad start. Holmes
was surely right that likely harmfulness is a relevant consideration in
defining "the freedom of speech." But there cannot be any very robust
free-speech doctrine without some focus on why free speech might
deserve constitutional protection – or, if not all speech deserves special protection, why some of it does – even if it is hurtful or poses some
dangers. In *Schenck* and *Debs*, Holmes ignored the value of speech or,
perhaps more precisely, the values in light of which speech might merit
protection even when it poses a risk of producing bad consequences.

The facts of *Schenck* and especially *Debs* illustrate one of the reasons free speech is important: vivid, passionate, occasionally hyperbolic
speech about moral and political matters is vital to public debate in a
political democracy. As Holmes himself would write in a later case, it
would be intolerable for the government first to declare war and then
to imprison those who criticize its policies.[14] Democracy requires the
freedom to dissent. Admittedly, speech criticizing the government's policies might mislead voters, demoralize soldiers, or otherwise lead to bad

12 249 U.S. 211 (1919).
13 Ibid. at 214.
14 See *Abrams v. United States*, 250 U.S. 616, 627–28 (1919) (Holmes, J., dissenting).

results. But protection of political speech is part and parcel of the Constitution's commitment to democracy. In a democracy, the voters need to be trusted to hear all sides of a debate. In the light of history, the Supreme Court's affirmance of Eugene Debs's conviction for making a speech to a political convention was a travesty of the First Amendment.

Within less than a year, Justice Holmes had shifted his perspective and begun to emphasize the values served by freedom of speech. He accepted the mantle of "the great dissenter" beginning in *Abrams v. United States*[15] (1919), involving another prosecution under the Espionage Act, in which he advanced his celebrated marketplace-of-ideas rationale for broad protections of freedom of speech:

> If you have no doubt of your premises or your power and want a certain result with all your heart you naturally express your wishes in law and sweep away all opposition.... But when men have realized that time has upset many fighting faiths, they may come to believe even more than they believe the very foundations of their own conduct that the ultimate good desired is better reached by free trade of ideas – that the best test of truth is the power of the thought to get itself accepted in the competition of the market, and that truth is the only ground on which their wishes safely can be carried out.

Holmes's marketplace-of-ideas rationale for broadly protecting free speech stood in some tension with the "clear and present danger" test to which he still said he adhered: if the Constitution aspires to create an open marketplace in ideas, why would it permit speech – including political criticism of the government – to be censored when it began to prove persuasive enough to pose a clear and present danger? For example, if we want the marketplace of ideas to judge whether obstruction of the draft is a desirable course of action, why should it be permissible to prohibit advocacy of obstructing the draft just at the point that people begin to act on the view that it is? Although Holmes never gave a wholly satisfactory answer to that question, he surely seems right that

15 Ibid. at 630 (1919) (Holmes, J., dissenting).

speech should be deemed presumptively valuable and thus protected by the First Amendment, based on the theory that ideas and debate promote the kind of society in which people will be well situated to decide for themselves which ideas deserve acceptance and which do not. He also seems persuasive in his reinterpretation of the "clear and present" danger test to require an evidentiary showing that harm is in fact likely to occur in the relatively immediate future. Those who wish to censor speech about political matters should not be able to rely on speculations about possible consequences in the remote future but should be required to advance evidence of specific, possibly imminent, harms. (In the classic example, disclosure of secret battle plans or the location of a troopship could cause an immediate, calamitous loss of life in wartime.)

A few years later, Justice Louis Brandeis made a further, enduring contribution to the free-speech tradition in an eloquent concurring opinion in *Whitney v. California*[16] (1927). Brandeis argued that "freedom to think as you will and to speak as you think are means indispensable to the discovery and spread of political truth." The First Amendment, he continued, reflected assumptions "that order cannot be secured merely through fear of punishment for its infraction; that it is hazardous to discourage thought, hope and imagination; that fear breeds repression; that repression breeds hate; that hate menaces stable government; that the path of safety lies in the opportunity to discuss freely supposed grievances and proposed remedies; and that the fitting remedy for evil counsels is good ones."[17] Like Holmes, Brandeis accepted the clear and present danger test, but he, too, proposed to construe it narrowly: "Only an emergency can justify repression"; the "imminent danger" must be clearly apprehended, likely to occur, and "relatively serious."[18]

For more than a decade, Holmes and Brandeis wrote mostly in dissent as Supreme Court majority opinions continued to uphold convictions of those who advocated unlawful action to promote political

16 274 U.S. 357 (1927).
17 Ibid. at 375 (Brandeis, J., concurring).
18 Ibid. at 376–77.

goals – resistance to the draft, or mass strikes that would cripple wartime production, or the overthrow of industrial capitalism. Nonetheless, the power of their arguments rallied opinion gradually to their side, as they personally became heroes of American constitutional culture. Among the shades of conservative gray that defined most Supreme Court Justices of the era, Holmes stood out as a handsome patrician with a rare gift for judicial eloquence and an infectious desire to meet and know the young as well as the famous. Possessing perhaps the sharpest legal mind of any Justice ever to sit on the Court, Holmes drew admiring attention as "the Yankee from Olympus." Brandeis possessed an equal capacity to inspire. The first Jew ever to serve as a Supreme Court Justice, he had championed causes of the poor and disadvantaged before his appointment. He too wrote with unusual flair. By the 1930s and 1940s, the Supreme Court frequently applied the "clear and present danger" test in the searching way that Holmes and Brandeis had said that it should be applied, to protect radical dissenters from mainstream opinion.

A major test for the emerging tradition of speech protectiveness came in *Dennis v. United States*[19] (1951). *Dennis* arose at the height of Cold War anxiety about militant, subversive communism. It involved prosecutions of American Communist Party leaders for advocating the overthrow of the government of the United States by force, not immediately, but at some remote future time. A divided Supreme Court upheld the convictions entered by a lower court. Although the evil of a communist insurrection seemed remote, the Court determined that "imminent" threats were not needed to justify conviction under the "clear and present danger" test. Rather, courts "must ask whether the gravity of the 'evil,' discounted by its improbability, justifies such invasion of free speech as is necessary to avoid the danger."[20]

Like *Schenck* and *Debs*, which were decided in the flush of fear and patriotism accompanying American entry into World War I, *Dennis* was

19 341 U.S. 494 (1951).
20 Ibid. at 510.

very much the product of its fearful time in the McCarthy era, so-called after the bullying Senator Joseph McCarthy who briefly mesmerized the nation with chilling and often baseless allegations of communist infiltration into the highest levels of American government. Seen in that context, the Court's decision in *Dennis* was "quite understandable," as legal scholar John Ely has written, but also very disturbing because the suppression of speech even loosely about politics "mocks our commitment to an open political process."[21] If any lesson can be drawn, it would seem to be this: First Amendment protections of political speech cannot depend on case-by-case judicial judgments of whether particular utterances by particular speakers pose a clear and present danger. In frightened times, judges are as prone as legislators to overestimate the risk that speech criticizing the government's policies or structure may occasion calamity. Some types of speech deserve nearly categorical protection.

Before little more than another decade had passed – and after vigorously protected rights of speech and assembly had proved vital to the success of the civil rights movement of the 1950s and 1960s – the Supreme Court reached this very conclusion. The Court inscribed its lesson into law in *Brandenburg v. Ohio*[22] (1969). Brandenburg, a Ku Klux Klan (KKK) leader, was prosecuted and convicted under a state statute that made it a crime to advocate criminal activity as a means of accomplishing political reform. By a unanimous vote, the Court reversed his conviction. The Court's opinion made no reference to the "clear and present danger" test, which it effectively swept away. Instead, the Court purported to extract from prior decisions "the principle" that a state may never punish the mere advancement of ideas, as opposed to express calls for violation of the law. Earlier cases, the Justices explained, had recognized that the government may not "forbid or proscribe advocacy of the use of force or of law violation except where such advocacy is directed to

21 John Hart Ely, *Democracy and Distrust: A Theory of Judicial Review* (Cambridge, MA: Harvard University Press, 1980), 109.
22 395 U.S. 444 (1969) (*per curiam*).

inciting or producing imminent lawless action and is likely to incite or produce such action."[23]

Despite the Court's suggestion to the contrary, a majority of the Justices had never previously endorsed any "principle" affording so much protection to free speech. Although earlier cases had suggested that only advocacy of violence can be punished, and not the advocacy of abstract political ideas, the Court had never before held that even the express advocacy of violence was protected by the First Amendment, unless it was likely to produce "imminent lawless action." Had the *Brandenburg* test been applied in previous cases, the speakers in *Schenck*, *Debs*, and *Dennis* would all have gone free. In *Schenck* and *Debs*, it is at least arguable that the defendants did not expressly advocate violation of the law, and neither in those cases nor in *Dennis* had the government proved that the speech at issue was likely to incite "imminent," or nearly immediate,[24] violence. Far from merely making explicit a principle already reflected in prior decisions, *Brandenburg* gave broader protection to speech advocating violation of the law than either Holmes or Brandeis had ever defended. To fall outside the protective reach of *Brandenburg*, speech must expressly advocate law violation, not merely create a clear and present danger that such violation may occur, and it must be likely to produce its effects imminently.

Although the *Brandenburg* rule protects more speech than did any previous formulation handed down by the Supreme Court, it does not protect all speech aimed at producing less-than-imminent violence. A court would not construe the First Amendment as protecting a mob boss who directs a "hit" at some relatively distant future time. Nor would *Brandenburg* necessarily protect terrorist cells or those carrying the instructions to activate terrorist plans. In reading Supreme Court cases, good lawyers within our constitutional practice do not always take every word at face value. Instead, they sometimes ask whether a

23 Ibid. at 447.
24 See *Hess v. Indiana*, 414 U.S. 105 (1973) (*per curiam*).

prior case, in which seemingly categorical language appeared, can be "distinguished" from a new case with very different facts. *Brandenburg* involved a speaker who sought to persuade a public audience to accept and act on his political views. Properly interpreted, a rule of constitutional law framed to protect speakers who try to persuade public audiences to adopt their political views need not extend to private speakers promoting nonpolitical crimes (such as mob "hits") or to the coordinated planning (rather than abstract advocacy) of illegal action. Speech used to form or advance the ends of a "conspiracy" – a private agreement to pursue unlawful ends – is almost certainly not protected by the First Amendment, *Brandenburg* notwithstanding. Moreover, just as the Supreme Court devised the *Brandenburg* rule in 1969, it could reject or modify that rule at any time. For now, however, *Brandenburg* furnishes the First Amendment rule applicable to speech publicly advocating violence or other violation of the law, at least when the end to be promoted is even loosely political.

It may or may not be ironic that the first beneficiary of the *Brandenburg* rule was a member of the KKK preaching hatred of racial and religious minorities. As noted in the introduction to this chapter, most other liberal democracies have put speech inciting racial and religious hatred into a category of its own and have prohibited it. The Supreme Court might have followed a parallel course, treating racially and religiously bigoted speech as unprotected by the First Amendment because it is incompatible with an underlying constitutional assumption of human equality. *Brandenburg*, however, drew no such lines. Possibly, the Court considered Brandenburg's speech to be loosely political and deserving of protection on that ground. Possibly, the Justices believed that, contrary to fact, "words will never hurt." Or possibly, the Court recalled, though it did not advert to, a thought uttered by Justice Brandeis in *Whitney v. California*: "that fear breeds repression; that repression breeds hate; [and] that hate menaces stable government."[25] Better to let the hate

25 274 U.S. at 375.

mongers talk openly, the Court may have thought, than to drive them out of the public square and into unseen caldrons. If so, the Court was making an empirical and predictive judgment, quite possibly correct but also contestable. It is important to remember – as Justice Holmes recognized in articulating the "clear and present danger" test – that the Justices do not simply read the Constitution and mechanically determine how its words apply to the facts at hand. As with "clear and present danger," and now with the *Brandenburg* test that succeeded it, they need to devise rules to implement vaguely defined values with real-world consequences in mind. The office of Supreme Court Justices is an eminently practical one.

Whatever *Brandenburg*'s motivating concerns may have been, the case vividly symbolizes the extent to which the First Amendment currently protects freedom to express what Holmes termed "the thought that we hate."[26] For more than forty years now, it has stuck as the law because it reflects a broadly shared cultural commitment to protect the expression even of the most remotely political ideas, even when doing so entails palpable costs – for example, to the targets of hate speech such as Brandenburg's – and larger risks to the society as a whole.

Expressive Conduct

Although the First Amendment refers to freedom of speech, not conduct, the distinction between speech and conduct often proves elusive. Among other things, some conduct is expressive – not just rolling one's eyes or making gestures but also burning flags and draft cards as forms of political protest. It might thus be tempting to say that all expressive conduct enjoys the protection, or at least the presumptive protection, of the First Amendment. But throwing rocks, destroying property, and even committing terrorist murder can sometimes convey messages too. Plainly, therefore, some way must be found to determine which kinds

26 *United States v. Schwimmer*, 279 U.S. 644, 654–55 (1929) (Holmes, J., dissenting).

of expressive conduct deserve First Amendment protection and which do not.

For much of the twentieth century, the Supreme Court struggled to distinguish expressive activities that were principally speechlike from those that principally involved conduct. In *United States v. O'Brien*[27] (1968), the Court embarked on a new course. O'Brien, who had publicly burned his draft card to protest the Vietnam War, was convicted under a federal statute making it a crime to mutilate or destroy a draft certificate. In assessing his First Amendment defense, the Court began by denying "that an apparently limitless variety of conduct can be labeled 'speech' whenever the person engaging in the conduct intends thereby to express an idea."[28] Almost immediately, however, the Court picked up a different theme, by focusing on whether the government's reason for prohibiting the destruction of draft cards was "unrelated to the suppression of free expression."[29] If the statute's only purpose was to stifle critics of the Vietnam War, the Court suggested that it would be invalid. To permit governmental censorship of ideas merely because many people find them offensive or because the government does not trust the public to evaluate them would threaten the central First Amendment principle that people should be able to decide for themselves which ideas to believe (at least in matters of politics and opinion). By contrast, the Court sensibly suggested, if the government were trying to stop harms unrelated to the messages being conveyed by political protestors – such as the destruction of items necessary to the efficient operation of the draft – the protective policies of the First Amendment would be less centrally engaged. To put the point only slightly differently, the Court concluded that the First Amendment condemns deliberate governmental censorship of ideas, but that it does not disable the government from banning conduct, such as the destruction of governmental property, that

27 391 U.S. 367 (1968).
28 Ibid. at 376.
29 Ibid. at 377.

is harmful for reasons independent of any message that it may express. Similarly, the government can bar the inscription of graffiti on public buildings, even though graffiti can be speech, because there are good reasons to prohibit defacing public property, regardless of the message that any particular graffiti artist might wish to communicate.

The approach adopted in *United States v. O'Brien* continues to govern First Amendment cases involving a mixture of speech and conduct. If the government bars a form of conduct as a means of stifling messages that it finds offensive, the courts will almost invariably find a constitutional violation. To cite one vivid example, the Supreme Court invalidated prohibitions against flag burning in *Texas v. Johnson*[30] (1989) and *United States v. Eichman*[31] (1990). The Justices ruled that the government's interest in prohibiting this conduct related to the message that flag burning conveyed and to the offense that it generated. The Court found no sufficient justification for governmental suppression of an attempt to convey ideas.

By contrast, governmental regulation of expressive conduct will be upheld, *O'Brien* established, "if it furthers an important or substantial governmental interest... unrelated to the suppression of free expression; and if the incidental restriction on alleged First Amendment freedoms is no greater than is essential to the furtherance of that interest."[32] Finding the government's purposes to be unrelated to suppression of ideas, the Court has upheld a ban against sleeping on the National Mall in Washington, even as it applied to protestors who wished to dramatize the plight of the homeless.[33] The Court concluded that interests in maintaining the beauty of the Mall justified an across-the-board ban on sleeping and camping there, even when the effect thwarted expressive conduct.

Over time, *O'Brien* has proved among the Supreme Court's most influential free-speech decisions of the modern era. Its significance

30 491 U.S. 397 (1989).
31 496 U.S. 310 (1990).
32 *O'Brien*, 391 U.S. at 377.
33 See *Clark v. Community for Creative Non-Violence*, 468 U.S. 288 (1984).

reaches beyond the special problems posed by expressive conduct. As commentators quickly noticed, even when the government regulates "pure" speech, it may sometimes act for reasons unrelated to the suppression of ideas.[34] For example, a rule that forbids talking in the reading room of a public library applies to speech, not expressive conduct, but the purpose is to facilitate reading and study, not to stifle any particular message. Subsequent cases make clear that rules of this kind – justified by reasons unrelated to the suppression of ideas – will receive deferential treatment from the courts under a test similar to that laid down in *O'Brien*. At the same time, by emphasizing that not all regulations of speech necessarily embody censorial purposes, *O'Brien* helped to crystallize the presumptive offensiveness of those that do. What makes the result in the World War I *Debs* case so offensive is that the government sought to silence Debs because it feared that Debs might persuade people to adopt views of which the government disapproved. In a free country, the people should be able to decide for themselves what to believe, and it is a ground for outrage when the government determines that there are some ideas people cannot be trusted to hear. *O'Brien* is among the leading cases reflecting this now-settled understanding. As the Court routinely recites in a variety of contexts, when the government regulates speech on the basis of its content, a censorial motive most likely explains why some speech is banned but other speech is not, and a strong presumption of constitutional invalidity applies.[35] In nearly all contexts, "content-based" regulations of speech – which try to stop the public from hearing some messages but not others – can be justified only by an exceedingly weighty governmental interest, if at all.

34 Among the most influential early commentaries was John Hart Ely, "Flag Desecration: A Case Study in the Roles of Categorization and Balancing in First Amendment Analysis," 88 *Harvard Law Review* 1482 (1975). See also Laurence H. Tribe, *American Constitutional Law*, 2nd ed. (Mineola, NY: Foundation Press, 1988), 789–94.

35 See generally Elena Kagan, "Private Speech, Public Purpose: The Role of Governmental Motive in First Amendment Doctrine," 63 *University of Chicago Law Review* 413 (1996).

Shocking and Offensive Speech

Another signal step in the development of modern First Amendment law came in *Cohen v. California*[36] (1971). During the era of protests against the Vietnam War, Cohen walked into a courthouse wearing a jacket emblazoned with the legend "Fuck the Draft." The State of California prosecuted and convicted him under a statute that forbade disturbing the peace. The Supreme Court reversed the conviction. In defending Cohen's conviction, the state argued that it had no intent to censor his antiwar message: he was free to express that message however he liked, as long as he did not disturb the peace of his fellow citizens by employing shocking and offensive words. The Court rejected this argument. It deemed Cohen's message inseparable from the words that he chose to express it. Linguistic expression, the Court wrote, has "emotive" as well as "cognitive force,"[37] and Cohen's chosen words conveyed a depth of emotion that other formulations might not have communicated. "[W]e cannot indulge the facile assumption that one can forbid particular words without also running a substantial risk of suppressing ideas in the process," the Court said.[38]

Cohen's reasoning is compelling, even if its conclusion is jarring: the First Amendment protects a right to shock and offend as inseparable from the right to express opinions. Like the partial protection of racist speech in *Brandenburg*, the doctrine established by *Cohen* is not cost-free. Apart from its possible coarsening effect on common sensibilities, shocking speech often confronts unwilling listeners, not just those who thrill to see conventional standards flouted. What is more, the right to shock and offend can be, and sometimes is, exercised maliciously against the most vulnerable groups in American society, including racial minorities. Lines can be drawn in some cases, and prohibitions upheld when

36 403 U.S. 15 (1971).
37 Ibid. at 26.
38 Ibid.

language not only shocks but also conveys a physical threat,[39] but the line drawing grows difficult once *Cohen*'s compelling reasoning is accepted: there is often no distinction between a constitutionally protected substantive message and the form, however shocking or hateful, in which the message is expressed.

Remaining Unprotected Categories, Including Obscenity

In *Chaplinsky v. New Hampshire*[40] (1942), the Supreme Court offered the much-quoted observation that "[t]here are certain well-defined and narrowly limited classes of speech, the prevention and punishment of which has never been thought to raise any Constitutional problem." The Court continued: "These include the lewd and obscene, the profane, the libelous, and the insulting or 'fighting' words – those which by their very utterance inflict injury or tend to incite an immediate breach of the peace."[41]

As illustrated by the subsequent protection of profanity in cases such as *Cohen v. California*, the list of categories of speech that are excluded from First Amendment protection has proved historically variable. ("Libelous" or defamatory speech, another category listed in *Chaplinsky* as outside the protective reach of the First Amendment, has also received an important measure of protection in more recent decisions.) Yet virtually no one has ever suggested that the First Amendment should protect threats, solicitations of bribes, or verbal agreements to fix prices, any more than it protects false cries of fire in a crowded theater. The question is not whether there should be any categories of speech

---

39 See, for example, *Virginia v. Black*, 538 U.S. 343 (2003) (holding that the Constitution would permit the prohibition of cross burning with the intent to intimidate but invalidating a Virginia statute that treated all cross burnings as presumptively intended to intimidate).

40 315 U.S. 568, 571–72 (1942).

41 Ibid.

excluded from the First Amendment but which categories lie beyond the constitutional pale. Among the most interesting disputes has involved "obscenity" – a term that the Court has viewed as somehow linking the sexually explicit with the disgusting, but that has proved astonishingly difficult to define precisely. (Refusing to be stymied by the problem of definition, Justice Potter Stewart once remarked of the category of hard-core sexually explicit material that he thought should be subject to prohibition, "I know it when I see it."[42])

Although obscenity had long been assumed to lie outside the First Amendment, the Supreme Court did not face a case squarely presenting the question until the middle of the twentieth century. In *Roth v. United States*[43] (1957), the Court held that obscenity lacked First Amendment protection, partly because of evidence concerning the original constitutional understanding, partly because obscenity contributed little or nothing to the search for truth, and partly because it threatened the social interest in order and morality.

Notably, however, the Court's surprisingly careless opinion did not define "obscenity" with any precision. The absence of a clear definition proved troublesome when, as the 1950s spilled into the 1960s, magazines and motion pictures pressed the boundaries of constitutional protection. Two Justices, Hugo Black and William Douglas, who sometimes styled themselves as First Amendment literalists or "absolutists," could see no basis for holding sexually explicit speech and pictures to be less protected than other kinds and consistently voted to reverse all obscenity convictions. (Black liked to carry a copy of the Constitution in his pocket, to be available whenever he wanted to make the point with all possible dramatic force that the Constitution says "Congress shall make ... *no law* ... abridging the freedom of speech.") The other Justices continued to wrestle with the definitional issue, with three Justices ultimately concluding that for material to be obscene and thus subject

42 *Jacobellis v. Ohio*, 378 U.S. 184, 197 (1964) (Stewart, J., concurring).
43 354 U.S. 476 (1957).

to legal prohibition, prosecutors must prove it to be "utterly without redeeming social value."[44] Few prosecutions could meet this standard.

In 1973, the Supreme Court – which had grown more conservative since Chief Justice Earl Warren left the bench and since Richard Nixon had made four appointments following his "law and order" election campaign in 1968 – reexamined the issue. In *Miller v. California*,[45] the Court laid down a test for constitutionally unprotected obscenity that has endured through the current day. It defines obscenity as material that (1) "taken as a whole, appeals to the prurient interest," that (2) "depicts or describes, in a patently offensive way, sexual conduct specifically defined by ... applicable state law," and that (3) "taken as a whole, lacks serious literary, artistic, political, or scientific value." In defining obscenity that Congress and the states are entitled to regulate (if they choose to do so), the current doctrine makes no exception for sales or displays of obscene materials only to consenting adults. Adult theaters that admit only people older than twenty-one years old are vulnerable to prosecution.[46]

The Court's toleration of governmental attempts to stifle sexually explicit messages is exceptional in modern First Amendment doctrine. It probably reflects a continuing prudishness, both among the Justices and among significant segments of the population, about the rawest forms of sexual explicitness. In other contexts, the Court permits the content-based regulation of speech only to prevent palpable and serious harms, such as damage to reputation arising from libelous speech and incitements to imminent lawless violence. In contrast, the Court has demanded no proof that obscenity causes any harm apart from its allegedly debasing effects on the character of those who view it. Social scientists have produced some evidence, which is admittedly disputed, suggesting that materials that are not only sexually explicit but also violent may tend to promote increased violence toward women, at least among some

44 *Memoirs v. Massachusetts*, 383 U.S. 413 (1966).
45 413 U.S. 15, 24 (1973).
46 See *Paris Adult Theater v. Slaton*, 413 U.S. 49, 57–58 (1973).

populations.[47] Significantly, however, the Supreme Court has not shaped its definition of prohibitable obscenity to materials plausibly likely to promote sexual violence. Not all obscene films and photographs include violence, and many materials that do eroticize violence are not obscene under the Supreme Court's definition, either because they are not predominantly "prurient" in their appeal – there may be more violence than sex, for example – or because they possess some "serious" value.

The Supreme Court's obscenity doctrine is peculiar in another way as well. Although it permits the prohibition of obscenity, the definition of obscenity is relatively narrow. As a result, *Miller* has done little to stem a mounting flood of sexually explicit materials into American popular culture. The Court's conservative stand against sexually licentious material thus appears to have little practical significance.

The one exception, if that is the proper term, involves child pornography. In *New York v. Ferber*[48] (1982), the Supreme Court upheld a state law prohibiting the production, distribution, and sale of so-called child pornography, defined to include the presentation or depiction of live "sexual conduct" by a child under sixteen years old. A state court had held the statute unconstitutional because it applied to all materials showing children engaged in sexual conduct, without regard to whether the material satisfied the obscenity test of *Miller v. California*. The Supreme Court disagreed. Emphasizing the severe harm to children forced to engage in sexual performances, the Court unanimously upheld the challenged statute. The Court obviously views child pornography, as defined, as not only smutty but also dangerous to children in the highest degree.[49]

47 See Michael B. Salwen et al., *An Integrated Approach to Communication Theory and Research*, 2nd ed. (Oxford: Routledge, 2008); Frederick Schauer, "Causation Theory and the Causes of Sexual Violence," *American Bar Foundation Research Journal* 737 (1987).

48 458 U.S. 747 (1982).

49 Compare *Ashcroft v. Free Speech Coalition*, 122 S. Ct. 1389 (2002) (holding an anti-child-pornography statute unconstitutional insofar as it applied to images that appear to be, but in fact are not, actual minors engaged in actual sexual conduct).

Commercial Speech

Before the 1970s, the Supreme Court accorded no First Amendment protection to commercial advertising.[50] It began to change course in *Virginia State Board of Pharmacy v. Virginia Citizens Consumer Council Inc.*[51] (1976). The Virginia Pharmacy Board forbade pharmacists to advertise the prices that they charged for prescription drugs. The board had adopted its policy to preserve the competitive position of small drug stores, which often needed to charge higher prices than large chains because their costs were higher. According to the board, small neighborhood pharmacies were likely to be more knowledgeable about their individual customers, and thus to give better service and advice, than chain stores. In striking down the Virginia regulation, the Supreme Court majority emphasized the interest of consumers in having access to price information so that they could decide for themselves what to buy and where to buy it. The Court declined to articulate a clear test governing when the regulation of advertising might be permissible. It doubted, however, that the government could ever be justified in barring the dissemination of truthful information simply for the purpose of keeping consumers in the dark.

At the time of the *Virginia Pharmacy* case, the Supreme Court's most "liberal" Justices were those most eager to extend First Amendment protection to commercial advertising, just as they were generally the Justices most protective of First Amendment rights in other contexts (including, for example, the censorship of sexually explicit speech and the suppression of political protestors). Justice William Rehnquist, then the Court's most conservative member, dissented. As a policy matter, he worried that "[u]nder the Court's opinion the way will be open not only for dissemination of price information but for active promotion of prescription drugs, liquor, cigarettes, and other products the use of

---

50 See, for example, *Valentine v. Chrestensen*, 316 U.S. 52 (1942).
51 425 U.S. 748 (1976).

which it has previously been thought desirable to discourage."[52] Rehnquist dissented again from the Court's ruling in *Central Hudson Gas &
Electric Corp. v. Public Service Commission*[53] (1981), which established
a test for the permissibility of restrictions on commercial advertising
that the Supreme Court has never abandoned. Under that test, for
commercial speech to be entitled to First Amendment protection at all,
it "must concern lawful activity and not be misleading." If that threshold
is crossed, government may regulate commercial advertising only if the
regulation directly promotes a "substantial" governmental interest and
"is not more extensive than is necessary to serve that interest."[54]

From a loosely political perspective, the Justices in *Virginia Pharmacy* and *Central Hudson* might easily have seemed misaligned but in a
way not much noticed at the time. In both cases, the challenged restrictions on speech were parts of a broad framework of economic regulation.
The state of Virginia licensed pharmacies such as that involved in the *Virginia Pharmacy* case and closely regulated their business practices. Similarly, the party claiming free speech rights in *Central Hudson* was a highly
regulated electric power company – indeed, a licensed monopolist –
challenging a restriction on the promotional aspect of its business. As the
Nobel Prize–winning economist Ronald Coase has pointed out, in the
decades following the New Deal, liberals generally championed broad
regulation of economic markets but maintained that the government
had no business regulating speech under the First Amendment.[55] During the same period, conservatives protested governmental intervention
in economic markets but tended to support the regulation of speech in a
variety of contexts (including the prohibition of obscenity and the suppression of speech by subversive organizations such as the Communist
Party). According to Coase, both positions were inconsistent. On the one

52 Ibid. at 781 (Rehnquist, J., dissenting).
53 447 U.S. 557 (1980).
54 Ibid. at 566.
55 See generally Ronald H. Coase, "Advertising and Free Speech," 6 *Journal of Legal
   Studies* 1 (1977).

hand, if the government was good at regulating economic markets (as liberals thought), it was unlikely to be much less good at regulating speech markets or, at least, at regulating the advertising of economic transactions. On the other hand, if government intervention into economic markets tended to bring bad consequences (as conservatives maintained), the government was unlikely to perform better when it regulated speech.

Since Coase offered his comment, the position of judicial liberals has not changed a great deal but that of judicial conservatives has. In recent years they have emerged as enthusiastic champions of commercial speech rights. Indeed, in *Lorillard Tobacco Co. v. Reilly*[56] (2001), the Court's five most conservative Justices outvoted four typically more liberal dissenters to invalidate a Massachusetts statute barring billboard advertising of tobacco products within one thousand feet of a school or playground.[57] Without disputing the state's claims that tobacco advertising helps attract children to addictive and deadly products, the Court's majority ruled that the burdens on speech imposed by the state law were too "onerous" to survive constitutional scrutiny.

The decision in *Lorillard* demonstrates the tendency of legal doctrine to deal in abstraction. In the eyes of the law, companies engaged in the business of selling cigarettes became "speakers" protected under the First Amendment, even though the sole aim of their "speech" – consisting mostly of misleading images of healthy and sexy-looking people on billboards – was to promote the sale of a deadly product. But *Lorillard* also represents a weighing of competing values. No more today than in Justice Holmes's time is all speech absolutely protected under the First Amendment. False cries of fire in crowded theaters of course remain subject to prohibition. And the same Justices who joined the *Lorillard* majority continued to hold that the states can regulate obscenity, simply to preserve state interests in morality. In *Lorillard*, the Justices might have held that the state's interest in protecting its children outweighed

56 533 U.S. 525 (2001).
57 Justice Sandra Day O'Connor wrote the Court's opinion, relevant parts of which were joined by Chief Justice Rehnquist and by Justices Scalia, Kennedy, and Thomas.

the speech interests of tobacco companies eager to market their products. Instead, the majority concluded that the balance of considerations tipped the other way.

Campaign Finance and Political Advertising

If commercial speech cases involve a fusion of economic markets with what Justice Holmes called the First Amendment "marketplace of ideas," the same might be said of cases arising from congressional efforts to regulate the expenditure of money in political campaigns. To a large extent, political campaigns are exercises in speech, as candidates and their supporters try to persuade others to embrace their positions. And for campaign speech to be effective in the modern world takes money. Campaign organizations need staff, phone and mailing lists, brochures, websites, bumper stickers, signs, and the like. In addition, advertising in the media – and particularly on television, which can be enormously expensive in some markets – is hugely important. Although campaign advertising is surely subject to the solicitude of the First Amendment, donations and expenditures of money to generate political speech can also threaten the integrity of American political democracy. In the crudest example of corruption, moneyed interests can trade cash with dishonest politicians for specific, expressly requested political favors. Even in the absence of formal bargains, big donors effectively buy access to politicians, and access – possibly coupled with implicit promises of more donations to future campaigns or tacit threats to support other candidates – often translates into influence. Some find it antithetical to democratic ideals that economic power should translate so readily into political power.

Beginning with the Tillman Act in 1907 and the Federal Corrupt Practices Act in 1910, Congress has enacted a variety of measures aimed at protecting American politics from the corrupting influence of money. Because these measures and the judicial decisions evaluating them have included innumerable complexities, any short summary must oversimplify some points. Roughly speaking, however, attempted regulations fall into two main categories. One deals with *contributions*, or gifts of money by individuals or corporations to candidates or candidates' political committees, for the candidates – not the donors – to use to generate political speech. Other regulations have attempted to limit direct *expenditures* of money by individuals or organizations to create and disseminate political advertising. By way of illustration, if the Acme Corporation gives a check for $10,000 to a candidate for public office, it has made a contribution. If Acme itself spends $10,000 to place an Acme-produced advertisement supporting that candidate on a local television station, it has made a direct expenditure.

The Supreme Court's first major encounter with the constitutional issues raised by campaign finance regulation came in *Buckley v. Valeo*[58] (1976). The Court in *Buckley* reviewed the amendments to the Federal Election Campaign Act that Congress had passed in response to the shakedown fund-raising tactics employed by President Richard Nixon's reelection campaign committee in the 1972 elections. *Buckley* drew a sharp First Amendment line between regulations of campaign contributions and regulations of direct expenditures. *Buckley* upheld the contribution limitations that Congress had imposed. According to the Court's majority, direct gifts to candidates posed a risk of corruption, by which the Court appeared to mean something very close to bribery (which no one thinks is protected by the First Amendment), or the appearance of corruption. By contrast, *Buckley* invalidated restrictions on expenditures by candidates and, of equal importance, on "independent" expenditures by a candidate's supporters on campaign advertising. In the Court's view, independent expenditures – which, by definition, could not be coordinated with a candidate or a candidate's committee – pose a much lesser risk of corruption than do gifts of money directly to a candidate's campaign. In response to the argument that the government has an interest in stopping wealthy individuals from achieving undue political

58 424 U.S. 1 (1976).

influence as a result of their expenditures, the Court took the position that restriction of some speakers on the ground that their speech might prove too influential was antithetical to the First Amendment. According to the Court, it was a basic premise of First Amendment doctrine that more speech is better than less and that citizens, and voters, should be able to decide whom or what to believe in an unregulated marketplace of ideas.

In the years following *Buckley*, money continued to pour ever more voluminously into political campaigns, with more spent in each election cycle than in the one that preceded it. Much of the influx came through purportedly "independent" expenditures by corporations and labor unions, often to broadcast "attack" ads targeting candidates whom they wished to defeat. Spurred by the crusading efforts of Senators John McCain and Russell Feingold, Congress responded in 2002 by enacting the Bipartisan Campaign Reform Act of 2002[59] (BCRA). The act plugged a loophole in the previous law by limiting the contributions that individuals and organizations could make to political parties. Even more important, it barred corporations and labor unions from running advertisements that refer by name to any candidate for federal office within thirty days of a primary or sixty days of a general election.

In 2003, in *McConnell v. Federal Election Commission*,[60] the Supreme Court, by a 5–4 vote, upheld all of BCRA's main elements. To do so, it essentially put corporations and labor unions in a class by themselves. Although Congress could not stop individuals from running political advertisements because of a concern that their speech would give them undue influence, it was permissible, the Court said, for Congress to enact legislation "aimed at 'the corrosive and distorting effects of immense aggregations of wealth that are accumulated with the help of the corporate form and that have little or no correlation to the public's

59 Pub. L. No. 107–155, 116 Stat. 81 (codified primarily in scattered sections of 2 and 47 U.S.C.).
60 540 U.S. 93 (2003).

support for the corporation's political ideas.' "[61] The four dissenting Justices registered their disagreement in especially caustic opinions. In their view, the Court's decision violated the fundamental First Amendment principle – sometimes called "the persuasion principle"[62] – that the government may not silence speakers, at least about political matters, based on a concern that the speakers might persuade their audiences.

The 5–4 decision in *McConnell* came at a time when observers regularly described the Supreme Court as comprising five conservative and four liberal Justices. As in the *Lorillard* case, which involved tobacco advertising, the liberal Justices voted to uphold regulations of speech that they thought necessary to serve important governmental interests, and the conservatives generally adhered to the principle that the government should not be able to restrict speech, including speech by corporations, on the basis of a fear that it may prove persuasive. *McConnell* came out differently from *Lorillard* because one of the conservative Justices, Sandra Day O'Connor – the only Justice who had ever run for public office herself (the Arizona Legislature) – thought that corporate spending on political advertisements was sufficiently harmful to justify governmental regulation. In *McConnell*, Justice O'Connor coauthored the most important sections of the majority opinion.

I said in the Introduction that the Supreme Court is a "they," not an "it." After Justice O'Connor retired from the Court in 2006 and Samuel Alito took her place, the Justices voted to reconsider *McConnell*. In *Citizens United v. Federal Election Commission*[63] (2010), the Court overruled *McConnell* and held that the provision of BCRA that limits campaign advertising by corporations and labor unions violates the First Amendment. It is as objectionable for the government to stifle political speech by corporations as political speech by individuals, the majority held, because corporations are ultimately just collections of individuals

61 Ibid. at 205.
62 David A. Strauss, "Persuasion, Autonomy, and Freedom of Expression," 91 *Columbia Law Review* 334 (1991).
63 130 S. Ct. 876 (2010).

and because the voters should be able to decide for themselves whether or not to be persuaded by corporate speech. No one believes that the government should be able to regulate the political speech of media corporations on the editorial pages of their newspapers, regardless of how much influence a media corporation might achieve. In the view of the *Citizens United* majority, there is no principled ground for treating other kinds of corporations differently. Under *Citizens United*, the government can require corporations to disclose that they have funded campaign advertising, so that voters can assess its truthfulness in light of the source, but it cannot forbid corporations from engaging in political speech.

Four outraged dissenters lambasted the majority's decision as conservative judicial activism at its worst. The majority had invalidated an act of Congress rather than deferring to Congress's judgment about the urgent practical need for regulation. In overruling a recent decision, the Court showed no respect for precedent. And with corporations historically having been subject to a host of regulations not applicable to individuals, the majority could find no firm anchor for its ruling in the original understanding of the First Amendment, the dissenters argued.[64]

In the aftermath of *Citizens United*, more money, including corporate money, has flooded into politics than ever before. There is no neutral ground from which to appraise the Court's decision. In the view of some, *McConnell* was a First Amendment travesty on a par with *United States v. Debs*: to allow the silencing of political speech by corporations on the ground that it is likely to prove too persuasive with the voters was wholly incompatible with the First Amendment's commitment to a marketplace of ideas. In the view of others, *Citizens United* is among the most ruinous decisions in the history of American democracy: it turns the political marketplace of ideas into an economic market, dominated not by those who have the best ideas but by those with the most money.

---

64 Justice Scalia responded in a concurring opinion that the founding generation would have viewed speech by collections of individuals – which corporations are, in his view – as protected. See ibid. at 929.

The Broadcast Media

Perhaps surprisingly, different First Amendment rules sometimes apply to different media of communication. As long as newspapers and magazines do not print material that is altogether outside the protection of the First Amendment, such as obscenity or false advertising, the First Amendment gives them nearly complete immunity from governmental regulation. By contrast, the broadcast media (radio and television) have historically enjoyed less protection. The original justification for differential treatment of the print and broadcast media lay in public ownership of the airwaves, a scarce resource owned by the government. To prevent a chaos of competing voices attempting to broadcast over the same frequencies, the Federal Communications Commission (FCC) licenses use of the broadcast spectrum, and the Supreme Court has held that the FCC may use its licensing power to demand programming in the public interest.[65] For example, the FCC can require that the broadcast media provide news coverage. In *Red Lion Broadcasting Co. v. FCC*[66] (1969), the Court also upheld the constitutionality of the commission's now-abandoned "fairness doctrine," which required balanced coverage of public issues.

In *FCC v. Pacifica Foundation*[67] (1978), the Supreme Court went further in holding that the FCC may enforce regulations prohibiting broadcast over the public airwaves of speech that the Commission deems "indecent," even if it is not "obscene" under the test of *Miller v. California*, at least during times when children may be listening. The *Pacifica* case arose when a San Francisco radio station played a recorded monologue by the comedian George Carlin titled "Filthy Words," featuring seven words that Carlin himself described as barred from the public airwaves – "the ones that will curve your spine, grow hair on your hands and maybe, even bring...peace without honor...and a bourbon."[68] The

65 On the history of broadcast regulation, see Lucas A. Powe Jr., *American Broadcasting and the First Amendment* (Berkeley: University of California Press, 1987).
66 395 U.S. 367 (1969).
67 438 U.S. 726 (1978).
68 Quoted in ibid. at 751.

monologue repeatedly used the seven "filthy" words to comic effect but not to the amusement of the FCC. When the FCC threatened to enforce a regulation barring the broadcast of "indecent" material, Pacifica claimed a violation of its rights under the First Amendment. The Supreme Court disagreed. Although Carlin could not have been punished for delivering his monologue in a theater or a nightclub (because it was not "obscene" under the test of *Miller v. California*), a majority of the Justices concluded that Pacifica could be penalized for broadcasting it over the public airwaves. Relying on different arguments from those they had advanced in *Red Lion*, the Justices emphasized two considerations in holding that the First Amendment gives less protection to the broadcast media than to other kinds of speakers: radio and television broadcasts come directly into the home, and they are uniquely accessible to children. A more recent decision holds that the FCC cannot penalize broadcasters for transmitting indecent programming unless it makes clear in advance what is prohibited and what is permitted,[69] but the Court has not retreated from the view that special First Amendment rules apply to the broadcast media.

Having held that the radio and television stations broadcasting over the public airwaves are subject to different First Amendment rules than the print media, the Supreme Court has naturally been pressed to clarify the rules applicable to cable television. Like the over-the-airwaves media, cable television comes directly into the home and is widely accessible to children. But unlike the traditional broadcast media, cable operators deliver their signals through privately owned wires, not publicly owned and licensed airwaves. Most, if not all, of the current Supreme Court Justices therefore agree that the special First Amendment rules permitting federal regulation of the broadcast media do not apply to regulation of cable companies.[70]

69 See *Federal Communications Commission v. Fox Television Stations, Inc.*, 132 S. Ct. 2307 (2012).

70 See, for example, *Denver Area Educational Telecommunications Consortium, Inc. v. FCC*, 518 U.S. 727 (1996). The Court has suggested, however, that cable broadcasters can be required to ensure the effective blocking of channels that feature sexually explicit programming when a subscriber specifically so requests.

In the long run, as cable television spreads to more and more homes, it seems doubtful that a sharp distinction between the First Amendment status of broadcast television and cable television will continue to make any practical sense (if it does now). And although predictions are hazardous, in a variety of contexts, the Court seems increasingly insistent that all content-based regulations are invalid unless "necessary" to promote "compelling" governmental interests. It may be only a matter of time until the regulation of over-the-air broadcasting must also meet this standard.

This already appears to be the case with regulation of speech on the Internet. In *Reno v. American Civil Liberties Union*[71] (1997), the Court struck down a federal statutory provision barring the sending or display of "patently offensive" (but not necessarily "obscene") material in a manner available to anyone younger than eighteen years of age. As the Court noted, this prohibition effectively restricted the messages that could be sent to chat rooms or newsgroups, and it would have imposed prohibitively expensive burdens on speakers with websites to verify that all of their users are adults. The Court thus ruled that the prohibition swept too broadly and thereby violated the First Amendment, despite serious concerns about children's access to inappropriate materials.[72]

Freedom to Associate and Not to Associate

The First Amendment contains no explicit reference to freedom to associate for expressive purposes. Nonetheless, the Supreme Court has held that such a right exists, largely because of the role of association in helping to promote speech: people often join groups to be able to advocate their causes more effectively. An important case in the development of the doctrine was *NAACP v. Alabama*[73] (1958), in which the

---

71 521 U.S. 844 (1997).
72 The Court also invalidated a statutory provision that barred the knowing transmission of indecent messages to any recipient under eighteen years of age on the ground that the term "indecent" was excessively vague and potentially overbroad.
73 357 U.S. 449 (1958).

state had demanded that the local chapter of the National Association for the Advancement of Colored People (NAACP), a civil rights organization, disclose its membership lists. In Alabama in 1958, public identification of NAACP members almost certainly would have subjected them to widespread hostility, if not violence. In addition, the threat of future identification would have discouraged membership in civil rights organizations. Confronted with these facts, the Court held that the Constitution protects a right to associate for expressive purposes. It then ruled that for Alabama to force public disclosure of the NAACP's membership rolls would impose a burden on that right and that the Constitution forbade the imposition of such a burden in the absence of a powerful reason, which the state had not demonstrated.

Once recognized, the right to freedom of association for expressive purposes implies a right not to associate. Like-minded people who join expressive groups have at least a presumptive right to exclude people who hold different views. To cite an obvious example, the NAACP should not have to admit white racists, nor should the KKK have to admit African Americans. At the same time, the right not to associate should not be defined too broadly. Otherwise it would threaten the government's power to bar discrimination on the basis of race, religion, and gender whenever an affected group or business claims an expressive purpose. A bigoted employer who prefers not to hire blacks or Jews should not be able to claim a constitutional right of freedom of association strong enough to override obligations imposed by the nation's civil rights laws. To date, the precise scope of the constitutional right not to associate remains uncertain.

Roberts v. U.S. Jaycees[74] (1984) presented a question about the right of expressive organizations to discriminate on the basis of gender. The Jaycees are a nonprofit national corporation, organized to promote educational, charitable, and civic purposes. By rule, the Jaycees restricted regular membership to men between the ages of eighteen and

74 468 U.S. 609 (1984).

thirty-five. When Minnesota enacted an antidiscrimination statute that forbade the Jaycees from excluding women, the Jaycees claimed a violation of their right to freedom of association. The Supreme Court disagreed. It rested its conclusion on two considerations, without making clear whether either alone would have sufficed. First, the government had a "compelling" interest in preventing discrimination on the basis of gender.[75] Second, the Jaycees had failed to establish that the challenged statute impeded their ability to communicate their "preferred views" because they had presented no evidence that "women might have a different attitude" from men concerning the political, economic, and charitable issues on which the group sometimes spoke.[76]

To be contrasted with *Roberts* is *Boy Scouts of America v. Dale*[77] (2000), in which the Court found that a state antidiscrimination statute did violate rights to freedom of association. The Scouts removed Dale as an assistant scoutmaster upon learning that he was gay, was the co-president of the Rutgers University Lesbian/Gay Alliance, and had been quoted in the press on the need for gay role models. After a New Jersey court ordered Dale's reinstatement under a state antidiscrimination statute, the Scouts pressed a freedom of association claim in the Supreme Court. By a 5–4 vote, the Court ruled for the Scouts. The majority opinion found that the Scouts were an expressive organization, seeking to instill moral values. It also accepted the Scouts' claim, vigorously contested by the dissenting opinion, that the Scouts had a longstanding position that homosexual behavior was morally inappropriate. With these findings in place, the Court held in essence that Dale's continued presence in the Scouts would have sent a pro-gay message at odds with the message that the Scouts wished to send. In the view of the majority, it was as if Dale were a walking pro-gay billboard, and the Scouts, as an expressive association, could not be forced into an association that

75 Ibid. at 623.
76 Ibid. at 627–28.
77 530 U.S. 640 (2000).

would dilute their message by commingling it with his. The Court distinguished *Roberts* on the ground that forcing the Jaycees to admit women did not "materially interfere with the ideas" that the Jaycees wished to express.[78]

Concluding Note

For better or for worse, *Boy Scouts of America v. Dale* illustrates the "firstness" of the First Amendment within contemporary constitutional doctrine. In a collision with core principles of free speech and freedom of association, competing values – including those associated with ideals of human equality – typically give way. But a concluding note of caution is also in order. If my carefully framed conclusion about the firstness of the First Amendment is correct, it is because it captures the First Amendment's frequently absolute pretensions ("Congress shall make *no* law...abridging the freedom of speech"), while also acknowledging its capacity for occasional compromise and equivocation through recognition that only "core principles" are unyielding. ("The most stringent protection of free speech would not protect a man falsely shouting fire in a theatre.") In determining the outer boundaries of First Amendment protections, judges and Justices must make difficult, often contestable, judgments.

78 Ibid. at 657–58.

2 Freedom of Religion

Congress shall make no law respecting an establishment of religion, or prohibiting the free exercise thereof...

– Religion Clause of the First Amendment to the Constitution

[Freedom of religion] embraces two concepts, – freedom to believe and freedom to act. The first is absolute but, in the nature of things, the second cannot be.

– Cantwell v. Connecticut[1]

N 1967, THE HEAVYWEIGHT BOXING CHAMPION OF THE world, Muhammad Ali, was stripped of his title and sentenced to five years in jail for refusing to report for induction into the army. The country was then at war in Vietnam. The nation had a draft. But when called, Ali refused to take what the Supreme Court described as "the traditional step forward,"[2] and he was prosecuted as a result. His defense was straightforward: the draft law then in force provided exemptions for those who, because of sincere religious belief, were conscientiously opposed to war in any form. As a newly converted member of the Nation of Islam, Ali claimed entitlement to "conscientious objector" status.

1 310 U.S. 296, 303 (1940).
2 See *Clay*, aka *Ali v. United States*, 403 U.S. 698, 700 (1971).

Although the appeals process took five years, in *Clay*, also known as
Ali v. United States[3] (1971), the Supreme Court overturned Ali's conviction. The Court based its decision entirely on the draft laws then in effect.
It held that draft officials had erred in their consideration of whether Ali
was entitled to a draft exemption as a religiously motivated conscientious
objector. Nevertheless, difficult, controversial, and tangled constitutional
issues were not far in the background. To grasp why is to understand
what is perhaps the central issue in constitutional doctrines involving
freedom of religion.

The First Amendment includes two clauses dealing with religion. The
first, the Establishment Clause, provides that "Congress shall make no
law respecting an establishment of religion." The second, the Free Exercise Clause, immediately adds that neither may Congress "prohibit[] the
free exercise thereof." Taken together, the two Religion Clauses reflect a
commitment to religious voluntarism or freedom of religious conscience.
The Establishment Clause forbids governmental efforts to impose religious beliefs or practices. The Free Exercise Clause stops the government from barring or discouraging religious observance.

The difficulty is that general propositions do not resolve hard cases,
as the statute at the center of *Clay v. United States* nicely illustrates.
From one side, a serious argument could be mounted that Ali had a
constitutional right to be excused from the draft, even if Congress had
not provided an exemption. If the government had required him to fight
despite his religious beliefs, or sent him to jail for refusing to do so, it
would arguably have violated his right to the free exercise of his religion.
According to this view, the Free Exercise Clause establishes that people
cannot be punished for doing what their religion dictates, at least in the
absence of a compelling governmental interest supporting the imposition
of punishment.

From another side, however, an equally serious argument holds that
the government's provision of a draft exemption only for religiously

3 Ibid. at 698 (1971).

motivated objectors (and not, for example, for those opposed to war on philosophical but not religious grounds) creates a preference for religious believers over nonbelievers in violation of the Establishment Clause. According to this view, a law that takes note of religious belief for purposes of affording favored treatment (as in the form of draft exemptions) "respect[s] an establishment of religion," in contravention of the Constitution.[4]

When the debate is framed in these terms, there is something to be said for both of these nearly polar arguments – and perhaps, thus, a natural disposition for the Supreme Court to adopt a mediating position. But a mediating position clearly could not satisfy everyone, and any particular mediating position risks pleasing no one. Perhaps as a result, there is widespread disagreement about how the Religion Clauses ought to be interpreted, even though some points of doctrine are reasonably clear.

Although issues under the Religion Clauses are often interconnected, the Supreme Court typically resolves Establishment Clause issues within one doctrinal framework and Free Exercise Clause issues within another. In tracing the outlines of contemporary doctrine, I begin by following the same approach, treating first the Establishment Clause and then the Free Exercise Clause, before reconnecting the discussions at the end.

Introduction to the Establishment Clause

Disputes about the Establishment Clause, like disputes about the meaning of most constitutional provisions, begin (although they do not necessarily end) with efforts to identify the clause's originally understood meaning. It is easy to discover statements by members of the founding

---

4 Obviously troubled by this objection, the Supreme Court, in *Welsh v. United States*, 398 U.S. 333, 344 (1970), interpreted the statutory provision providing exemptions for those opposed to war on religious grounds to encompass "all those whose consciences, spurred by deeply held moral, ethical, or religious beliefs, would give them no rest or peace if they allowed themselves to become a part of an instrument of war." See also *United States v. Seeger*, 380 U.S. 163, 165–66 (1965).

generation demanding rigid separation of church and state. Yet the federal government had scarcely begun operation before both Houses of Congress hired chaplains, to be paid from public funds, and before President George Washington proclaimed a national day of prayer and thanksgiving.[5] In modern disputes, those who favor strict separation of church and state, and who believe that the government should not become entangled with religious institutions or accord preference to those with religious motivations, point to expressions of separationist ideals as the best evidence of the original understanding. On the other side, those who believe that religion ought to play a greater role in American public life and that the government should be able to make laws accommodating religious beliefs (such as by furnishing draft exemptions) cite historical practice involving such matters as congressional chaplains and national days of prayer as evidence that the Establishment Clause originally was understood relatively narrowly – perhaps barring only official designation of a state church, explicit coercion of religious practice, and taxes specifically to fund a single established religion.[6]

There are no early Supreme Court decisions interpreting the Religion Clauses. Indeed, only two Establishment Clause cases received any significant consideration by the Supreme Court before 1947,[7] which commentators typically treat as the beginning of the "modern" era of Establishment Clause jurisprudence.[8] Challenges to federal action under the Religion Clauses were rare, if not nonexistent, during the early years,

---

5 See, for example, *Wallace v. Jaffree*, 472 U.S. 38, 98–103 (1985) (Rehnquist, J., dissenting).

6 See, for example, *County of Allegheny v. ACLU*, 492 U.S. 573, 659 (1989) (Kennedy, J., joined by Rehnquist, C. J., and White and Scalia, J. J., concurring in the judgment in part and dissenting in part).

7 See *Bradfield v. Roberts*, 175 U.S. 291 (1899) (upholding federal appropriations to a Catholic hospital in the District of Columbia); *Quick Bear v. Leupp*, 210 U.S. 50 (1908) (upholding disbursement of federal funds held in trust for the Sioux Indians to Catholic schools designated by the Sioux).

8 The watershed case was *Everson v. Board of Education*, 330 U.S. 1 (1947).

and those clauses – like other provisions of the Bill of Rights – were originally understood not to apply to the states.[9]

Two slightly overdrawn positions will help illuminate current controversies about the Establishment Clause. "Strict separationists" believe that the government has no business supporting religious beliefs or institutions in any way – for example, by providing tax breaks to churches, assisting parochial schools, including prayers or benedictions in public ceremonies, or inscribing "In God We Trust" on the currency. But strict separationists struggle with the significance of long-standing practice. If the first Congress hired and paid chaplains without either the founding generation or most of their successors seeing a constitutional problem in doing so, and if "In God We Trust" has been on the currency since 1864, when Abraham Lincoln approved the addition, then how can these and similar practices be deemed unconstitutional today?

Opposed to the strict separationists are a loose coalition of what might be called "religious accommodationists."[10] Emphasizing historical practice, they maintain that the Establishment Clause forbids governmental efforts to coerce the citizenry to practice or support any single religion, but they deny that it mandates hostility or even indifference to religion in general. As long as the government does not favor one sect above others but instead shows equal respect for a plurality of faiths, religious accommodationists believe that the Constitution tolerates noncoercive acknowledgments and accommodations of religious

9 Indeed, at the time of the Constitution's ratification, a number of states maintained "established" churches, supported by public tax revenues. Against this background, one of the apparent purposes of the federal Establishment Clause was to bar Congress from interfering with state establishments of religion. Nonetheless, the Supreme Court has assumed that the Establishment Clause, like most of the rest of the Bill of Rights, was made applicable against the states by the Fourteenth Amendment, adopted in the aftermath of the Civil War. See *Everson, supra* note 8. Today, the Establishment Clause bars state governments, fully as much as the federal government, from making laws "respecting an establishment of religion."

10 See, for example, Michael W. McConnell, "Religious Freedom at a Crossroads," 59 *University of Chicago Law Review* 115 (1992).

beliefs. Religious accommodationists can well explain why certain entrenched social practices (such as the inscription of "In God We Trust" on the currency) were not historically perceived as presenting constitutional difficulties: the relevant practices are not coercive and do not prefer one narrow sect over another. But accommodationists have a harder time explaining and, indeed, may have to reject Supreme Court rulings that now seem well accepted, including the decision that prayer in the public schools violates the Establishment Clause.[11]

To date, neither the strict separationists nor the religious accommodationists have achieved their fullest aspirations. Supreme Court doctrine reflects a contested mix of competing views. In recent years, however, the Court has tilted increasingly away from strict separationism and toward a religious accommodationist approach.

Religion in the Public Schools

In pathbreaking decisions in the 1960s, the Supreme Court held that officially organized prayer and Bible readings in the public schools violate the Establishment Clause.[12] The decisions sparked immediate controversy. Their historical foundations were doubtful. Nevertheless, the decisions manifested an alluring ideal of religious voluntarism that can reasonably be ascribed to the Religion Clauses: just as the government should not directly coerce its citizens into practicing a religion that they do not believe, neither should it intentionally subject them to social pressures to adapt their beliefs to a prescribed religious norm. Children in the public schools are particularly impressionable. School-sponsored prayer sends a signal to children that prayer not only is normal but also is viewed as normatively desirable within our society.

From the 1960s through the mid-1980s, the Supreme Court exhibited considerable sensitivity to the social effects of governmental policies in

11 See *Engel v. Vitale*, 370 U.S. 421 (1962).
12 See ibid. (prayer); *Abington School Dist. v. Schempp*, 374 U.S. 203 (1963) (Bible reading).

promoting religion, especially in the public schools, and found Establishment Clause violations rather readily. During this period the Court developed a stringent test for Establishment Clause violations – often referred to as "the *Lemon* test" – under which a statute would be deemed invalid if either its "purpose" or its "principal or primary effect" was to promote religion, or if it promoted excessive "entanglement" between church and state.[13] In *Epperson v. Arkansas*[14] (1968), the Court struck down a statute forbidding public schoolteachers to teach the theory of evolution. A majority found it "clear that fundamentalist sectarian conviction was and is the law's reason for existence."[15] In *Stone v. Graham*[16] (1980), the Court similarly invalidated a Kentucky statute that mandated posting the Ten Commandments on the wall of public school classrooms. Once again, the Court determined that the statute's likely purpose and effect were to advance religion.

Near the high-water mark of strict separationism, in 1985 the Court held unconstitutional a state law authorizing a moment of silence in the public schools "for meditation or voluntary prayer." The opinion in *Wallace v. Jaffree*[17] (1985) emphasized that a previous statute had called for the school day to begin with a one-minute period of silence "for meditation." By taking the further step of authorizing "voluntary prayer," the Court reasoned, the legislature manifested a "purpose" of promoting religion. The Court suggested, but did not expressly hold, that a statute simply prescribing a moment of silence, without reference to prayer, would pass constitutional muster.

The Court's opinion in *Wallace v. Jaffree* provoked strong dissenting opinions arguing that the Court should drastically revise its interpretation of the Establishment Clause.[18] These opinions protested, accurately,

---

13 The test took its name from *Lemon v. Kurtzman*, 403 U.S. 602 (1971).

14 393 U.S. 97 (1968).

15 Ibid. at 107–08.

16 449 U.S. 39 (1980).

17 472 U.S. 38, 40–41 (1985).

18 The dissenting opinions were written by Chief Justice Warren Burger, Justice Byron White, and then Justice William Rehnquist.

that if the Court were serious about invalidating every statute with either the purpose or the primary effect of promoting religion, as it purported to do under the *Lemon* test, a variety of historically entrenched practices would need to fall. There could be no more national days of prayer, "In God We Trust" would need to be banished from the currency, and so forth.

In the years since *Wallace v. Jaffree*, the Supreme Court has grown less quick to find Establishment Clause violations, even in the context of public education, where schoolchildren remain notoriously impressionable. For example, the Court has held that when public schools open their classrooms and gymnasiums to use by nonreligious groups (such as chess and drama clubs), they not only may but must permit religious organizations to use the same facilities on a nondiscriminatory basis, notwithstanding any possible effects in promoting religion.[19]

Nevertheless, a majority of the Justices have continued to treat public schools and schoolchildren as triggering elevated concerns under the Establishment Clause. In *Lee v. Weisman*[20] (1992), for example, the Court held that it was constitutionally impermissible for a public school graduation ceremony to include a religious invocation or benediction. Because the graduation ceremony was a public event, including adults as well as children, the cases that had forbidden school prayer on ordinary school days did not obviously dictate the outcome. As lawyers say, they were "distinguishable." Even so, a narrow majority of the Justices concluded that the context placed impermissible "public pressure, as well as peer pressure, on attending students" to participate in the school-sponsored prayer.[21] The majority reached this conclusion even though an earlier, accommodationist decision had found that a state legislature

---

19 See *Good News Club v. Milford Central School*, 533 U.S. 98 (2001).

20 505 U.S. 577 (1992).

21 Ibid. at 593. See also *Santa Fe Independent School Dist. v. Doe*, 530 U.S. 290 (2000) (invalidating a school district policy of electing students to deliver a brief invocation or message at high school football games).

did not violate the Establishment Clause by hiring a chaplain to lead prayers at the beginning of legislative sessions attended predominantly, if not exclusively, by adults.[22]

Governmental Aid to Religious Institutions

Throughout American history, religious institutions have received governmental benefits. Some of these benefits, such as police and fire protection, have flowed to churches on the same basis as to other groups and individuals. But other traditional benefits have gone to churches on more selective terms. For example, from the beginning of constitutional history, churches have been widely exempted from state and local property taxes. Charitable institutions other than churches may also qualify for tax relief, but in comparison with noncharitable organizations, churches stand on a preferred footing. Noting the traditional status of tax benefits for churches, the Court found in *Walz v. Tax Commission*[23] (1970) that a state law exempting churches from property taxes (along with other educational and charitable institutions) did not violate the Establishment Clause. The *Walz* decision is notable in part because it comes from the same era in which the Court formulated the *Lemon* test and in which it adopted strongly separationist views in other settings. Even for Justices otherwise committed to strict separation, the combination of history and entrenched expectations gave pause. But the Court's opinion in *Walz* was narrow. It suggested that although the government could permissibly exempt churches from taxes, it would be problematic under the Establishment Clause for the government to give money directly to a religious institution. Even though the cash value of a tax exemption and a government check might be precisely the same, the Court, in *Walz*, thought that there was a symbolic difference between them: transferring money

22 See *Marsh v. Chambers*, 463 U.S. 783 (1983).
23 397 U.S. 664 (1970).

directly to a religious institution somehow seemed like a stronger form of endorsement than did excusing churches from tax obligations imposed on most but not all others.

Through most of constitutional history, it was uncommon for the government to give money or other items of value (other than broadly shared public services and tax breaks) directly to religious institutions. But the permissibility of direct governmental aid emerged as an important political issue beginning in the 1960s. Parochial schools, nearly all operated by the Roman Catholic Church, initially lay at the center of the controversy.[24] Citing a desire to promote the public interest in effective education, local and national governments began to furnish aid to parochial schools or to parents who wished to send their children to such schools. But public support for parochial schooling also attracted strong opposition. Some regarded the public initiatives as special-interest legislation, enacted for the benefit of Catholics. Others feared that churches' bids for public support would provoke an entanglement with the state that was likely to prove unhealthy for church and state alike.

The Supreme Court initially reacted with a mix of skepticism and confusion. During its relatively strict separationist period from the 1960s through the mid-1980s, the Justices invalidated numerous governmental programs aiding parochial schools. But the Court did not strike down every aid program that came before it. Even constitutional specialists had a hard time making sense of the pattern of decisions.

Then, in the 1980s and 1990s, the social and political climate changed.[25] First, beginning with the so-called Reagan revolution, American national politics veered to the right, with religious conservatives playing a prominent role in the emerging governing coalition. Second, conservative Protestant denominations began to operate church schools

24 For an insightful social, political, and legal analysis of the unfolding history of the debate about the constitutionality of public funding for parochial schools, see John C. Jeffries Jr. and James E. Ryan, "A Political History of the Establishment Clause," 100 *Michigan Law Review* 279 (2001).

25 See Jeffries and Ryan, "A Political History of the Establishment Clause."

in larger numbers. As they did so, the issue of aid to parochial schools increasingly affected Protestants as well as Catholics. Third, central elements of the conservative coalition that formed during the 1980s and 1990s believed that private institutions, including churches, could provide a variety of services more effectively than could the bureaucratic public sector, which seemed to some to have done a particularly poor job with public education, especially in urban school districts. From this perspective, it made good sense for the government to subsidize private service organizations, including churches, as an alternative to direct public provision of education and other traditional public services (such as treatment for drug and alcohol abuse).

Against the background of these trends, a Supreme Court that grew increasingly conservative as a result of appointments by Presidents Ronald Reagan and George H. W. Bush gradually relaxed the Establishment Clause restrictions on governmental aid to parochial schools and other religious organizations. The doctrine that emerged is difficult to describe with both brevity and precision, partly because divisions existed within the conservative majority that decided the most important cases and partly because it is impossible to be sure how a majority of the current Court – which has been nudged even further in a conservative direction by appointments made by President George W. Bush – would resolve those divisions. But a central theme involves neutrality: when the government offers benefits to secular schools or drug-abuse programs, it ought not be required to discriminate against religious ones, and it may extend benefits on a neutral basis to secular and religious institutions alike. The relevant cases divide into two general categories.

One involves the direct provision of governmental aid to religious schools and other organizations. Overturning several decisions from earlier decades, the Supreme Court held in *Mitchell v. Helms*[26] (2000) that it was constitutionally permissible for the government to provide educational materials directly to parochial schools on the same basis that

26 530 U.S. 793 (2000).

it provided those materials to other private schools. None of the opinions in the case garnered five votes. The plurality opinion joined by the Court's four most conservative Justices (at the time) found no Establishment Clause violation when two conditions were met: the materials distributed by the government were "secular," not inherently religious, and they went to parochial and nonparochial schools on a "neutral" basis.[27] Justice O'Connor's concurring opinion, which was necessary to make the majority, added the further requirement that the secular materials provided by the government not be "diverted" for use in specifically religious indoctrination.[28] (For example, an overhead projector could be used in math or history classes, but not in a class on religious dogma – even though there would be no way to stop a religious school from using the money saved by the government's donation of an overhead projector to buy specifically religious instructional materials out of its own, rather than the government's, budget.) A dissenting opinion protested that the Court set a dangerous precedent by allowing the government to provide direct aid to religious institutions, supported by the taxes of those who objected to such aid.

A second category of cases involves the government's provision of financial aid to parents who prefer to send their children to religious rather than to public schools. The most important case is *Zelman v. Simmons-Harris*[29] (2002), which upheld the constitutionality of a school-voucher program. Under the program, parents of school-age children receive governmental vouchers, worth a certain number of dollars toward school tuition, which they can use at either a parochial school or a secular private school (if they choose not simply to send their children to public school). Challengers argued that the scheme involved in *Zelman* would promote religion by encouraging increased attendance at parochial schools and, what is more, that it would effectively coerce

27 See ibid. at 812–21 (opinion of Thomas, J., joined by Rehnquist, C. J., Kennedy, J., and Scalia, J. J.).
28 See ibid. at 839 (O'Connor, J., joined by Breyer, J., concurring).
29 536 U.S. 639 (2002).

taxpayers into paying for explicitly religious instruction. By a 5–4 vote, the Supreme Court disagreed. According to Chief Justice William Rehnquist's majority opinion, the crucial point involved the "neutrality" of the voucher program: parents could qualify for vouchers regardless of their religious beliefs, and the vouchers could be redeemed at secular as well as at religious schools. The voucher program thus did not promote religion or coerce tax payments for the purpose of promoting religion but merely facilitated "the genuine and independent choices of private individuals,"[30] regardless of whether those choices were religious or nonreligious. A dissenting opinion joined by four Justices argued, to no avail, that the majority's talk of neutrality blinked the reality that most vouchers were redeemed at religious schools and that vouchers would therefore tend to promote religious belief.[31]

Symbolic Support for Religion

The neutrality rationale of *Mitchell v. Helms* and *Zelman v. Simmons-Harris* does not lack appeal, at least on the surface. If the government provides aid to private secular schools (and also operates secular public schools), a mandatory exclusion of religious schools smacks of discrimination. It would be a mistake, however, to believe that an ideal of neutrality has emerged as the centerpiece of the current Court's overall approach to Establishment Clause issues. A tolerance for nonneutrality is most evident in cases involving what might be thought of as "symbolic" support for religion through such practices as inscription of "In God We Trust" on the currency, presidential proclamations of national days of prayer, and the designation of Christmas as a national holiday. Indeed, the Supreme Court begins its own sessions with a

---

30 Ibid. at 649.

31 Justice Souter wrote the principal dissenting opinion, joined by Justices Stevens, Ginsburg, and Breyer. Justice Breyer wrote an additional dissenting opinion, which Justices Stevens and Souter joined.

ringing summons by the marshal that includes the words "God save the United States and this honorable Court."

Even the Justices who otherwise are strict separationists have never questioned the constitutional permissibility of practices such as these, although they have felt some discomfiture in explaining why official tributes and appeals to God do not offend separationist ideals. A favorite explanatory trope has involved the notion of "ceremonial deism" – the idea, roughly speaking, that some references and appeals to God have been part of the nation's heritage for so long that their continuing, rote recitation has lost its religious significance in most people's minds.[32] Nearly everyone agrees that historical practice is relevant to constitutional interpretation. It is difficult to say that the founding fathers misunderstood the Constitution when they proclaimed days of prayer and thanksgiving and began sessions of Congress with prayers led by chaplains, or that Abraham Lincoln behaved culpably when he approved the inscription of "In God We Trust" on the currency. Yet sometimes the Court has held that historically accepted practice violates the Constitution in light of modern understandings of traditional ideals. For example, as will be discussed in Chapter 5, the Court has ruled that forms of race- and gender-based discrimination that were accepted by the framers and ratifiers of the Equal Protection Clause nevertheless violate that clause as appropriately interpreted today. Another factor that may influence even otherwise strict separationist Justices is a sense of what I described in the Introduction as the "politically constructed bounds" within which judicial review operates. A judicial ruling that required the root-and-branch removal of all references to God from American public life would provoke widespread outrage that the Justices were misusing their

---

32 The former dean of Yale Law School Walter Rostow coined the phrase "ceremonial deism" in 1962. For a detailed account of the concept, see Steven B. Epstein, "Rethinking the Constitutionality of Ceremonial Deism," 96 *Columbia Law Review* 2083 (1996). The Supreme Court discussed ceremonial deism explicitly in *Lynch v. Donnelly*, 465 U.S. 668, 716 (1984) (Brennan, J., dissenting), *County of Allegheny v. ACLU*, 492 U.S. 573 (1989), and *Elk Grove Unified School District v. Newdow*, 542 U.S. 1, 37 (2004) (O'Connor, J., concurring).

positions to impose their own elitist, secular preferences on the American people. With the process of nominating and confirming Justices to the Supreme Court being a political one, one might well question whether a Supreme Court ruling that purported to forbid any symbolic governmental support for religion could long endure.

Although no Justice has ever demanded an end to all symbolic support for religion, the Justices have divided deeply and sometimes angrily over where to draw the line. Public displays of crèches at Christmastime and of the Ten Commandments in various settings have served as flash points.[33] Three principal positions have emerged. The Court's strictest separationists have most often applied the *Lemon* test, which would bar all governmental references to religion that have either the purpose or the primary effect of promoting religion. During her years on the Court, Justice Sandra Day O'Connor applied a test – in which some other Justices sometimes joined her – asking whether a well-informed "reasonable observer" would view particular crèches and Ten Commandments displays as constituting endorsements of religion.[34] In one crèche case, four Justices took the extremely accommodationist stand that governmental action should not be deemed to violate the Establishment Clause unless it rises to the level of coercion or sustained, one-sect proselytization.[35] Among the currently sitting Justices, at least three appear to subscribe to this last position (Justices Scalia, Thomas, and Kennedy) and two more (Chief Justice Roberts and Justice Alito) may. Overall, the Court appears more accommodationist than at any previous time since the 1950s.

33 See, for example, *County of Allegheny v. ACLU*, 492 U.S. 573 (1989) (invalidating display of crèche but upholding display of eighteen-foot Chanukah menorah); *Lynch v. Donnelly*, 465 U.S. 668 (1984) (upholding display of crèche); *McCreary County v. ACLU*, 545 U.S. 844 (2005) (invalidating display of the Ten Commandments); *Van Orden v. Perry*, 545 U.S. 677 (2005) (upholding display of the Ten Commandments on the same day as the *McCreary County* decision).

34 *McCreary County*, 545 U.S. at 883 (O'Connor, J., concurring); *County of Allegheny*, 492 U.S. at 630–32 (O'Connor, J., concurring in part and concurring in the judgment)

35 *County of Allegheny*, 492 U.S. at 659–60 (Kennedy, J., concurring in the judgment in part and dissenting in part).

The Free Exercise Clause

The Supreme Court's first major decision interpreting the Free Exercise Clause came in *Reynolds v. United States*[36] (1878). At issue was whether the Free Exercise Clause precluded the enforcement of a federal antipolygamy statute against a religious Mormon at a time when the Mormon Church considered polygamy a religious duty. The Court rejected Reynolds's claim of right under the Free Exercise Clause and upheld the prosecution.

Reynolds exemplifies the central issue in interpreting and applying the Free Exercise Clause: when, if ever, must the government make exceptions to generally applicable laws (such as a law against polygamy) for people who have religiously motivated reasons to engage in conduct that those laws prohibit or burden? To answer that question, the *Reynolds* Court invoked a distinction between religious belief, which was immune from regulation, and religiously motivated conduct, which was not: "Congress was deprived of all legislative power over mere opinion, but was left free to reach actions which were in violation of social duties or subversive of good order."[37] This is a plausible position but also a harsh one. The government confronts its citizens with what the late Justice Potter Stewart – one of the Court's most lucid writers and clever phrase makers – once termed "a cruel choice" when it demands that they either breach their religious duties or violate the secular law.[38] It is not implausible to read the Free Exercise Clause as requiring the government to make reasonable accommodations to spare its citizens choices of this kind.

During the 1930s and 1940s, the Supreme Court gradually softened the harsh stance it had adopted in *Reynolds* and began to hold that the Free Exercise Clause sometimes protects conduct, at least when religiously motivated conduct is coupled with speech. The Court required an

36 98 U.S. 145 (1878).
37 Ibid. at 164.
38 *Braunfeld v. Brown*, 366 U.S. 599, 616 (1961) (Stewart, J., dissenting).

especially striking exemption for religiously motivated conduct in *Wisconsin v. Yoder*[39] (1972), which held that a state must except the Old Order Amish from a requirement that parents send their children to school through the age of sixteen. An Amish parent, whose fifteen-year-old daughter had already completed the eighth grade, argued that for him to subject her to further public schooling would violate his religious obligation to maintain his family apart from the world and worldly influences. Although acknowledging the importance of education, the Court concluded that the state's interest in compelling an additional year or two of high school attendance was insufficient to outweigh the interests of the Amish community under the Free Exercise Clause.

The decision in *Yoder* followed a similar ruling in *Sherbert v. Verner*[40] (1963). *Sherbert* involved a claim to unemployment benefits by a Sabbatarian who had lost her job because she refused to work on Saturday. (When she was hired, the work week was five days, but her employer subsequently added mandatory Saturday shifts.) The government concluded that Sherbert's unemployment was voluntary and denied her claim pursuant to a rule that barred benefits for those who willingly left their jobs. But the Supreme Court held, in essence, that Sherbert was entitled to an exemption from the otherwise applicable rule unless the government could demonstrate that enforcement of the rule against her (and others who acted on the basis of perceived religious duties) was necessary to promote a "compelling state interest."[41]

If *Reynolds* represented a narrow interpretation of the Free Exercise Clause, *Yoder* and *Sherbert* articulated a far-reaching one. Under the "strict scrutiny" test laid out in *Sherbert*, people claiming to act on the basis of religious duties were entitled to exemptions from otherwise applicable laws unless the government could demonstrate a "compelling interest" that necessitated denying such exemptions. Although this test is easy enough to state, its application gave rise to impressive difficulties.

39 406 U.S. 205 (1972).
40 374 U.S. 398 (1963).
41 Ibid. at 403, 406.

As a succession of cases demonstrated, conflicts between legal duties and religious duties abound in our religiously diverse nation. In some contexts, *Sherbert*'s compelling state interest test seemed to the Supreme Court to ask the government to bend too much. In one case, for example, the Old Order Amish asserted a religious objection to paying Social Security taxes.[42] To have to allow religious exemptions from ordinary tax obligations would be an administrative nightmare for the government. The Court therefore rejected the claim. But if the result was sensible, the reasoning was more troublesome. If "administrative convenience" counts as a compelling governmental interest, then that strict-looking standard has been diluted quite considerably.

What is more, an interpretation of the Free Exercise Clause that mandates preferential treatment for those claiming religious motivations may lead to tension with other constitutional values, notably including those embodied in the Establishment Clause.[43] If the government grants exemptions to otherwise applicable legal duties for religious believers but not for nonbelievers, it arguably promotes religion.

In light of concerns such as these, the Supreme Court reversed course once again and held that the Free Exercise Clause generally does not mandate exemptions for religiously motivated conduct, in *Employment Division v. Smith*[44] (1990). At issue was whether a state that criminalized possession of the mildly hallucinogenic drug peyote must make an exception for those who wished to use the drug as part of Native American religious rituals. In holding that no exemption was required, the Court refused to apply *Sherbert*'s compelling interest test. According to Justice Antonin Scalia's majority opinion, the Free Exercise Clause does not create a right to exemptions from "neutral, generally applicable laws," such as a bar against peyote use.[45] Instead, much more narrowly, the

42 See *United States v. Lee*, 455 U.S. 252 (1982).
43 See, for example, Christopher L. Eisgruber and Lawrence G. Sager, "The Vulnerability of Conscience: The Constitutional Basis for Protecting Religious Conduct," 61 *University of Chicago Law Review* 1245 (1994).
44 494 U.S. 872 (1990).
45 Ibid. at 881.

Free Exercise Clause forbids the government only from singling out religiously motivated practices and prohibiting them simply because "they are engaged in for religious reasons, or only because of the religious belief that they display."[46] Within this framework, neutral and generally applicable laws, such as laws prohibiting peyote use by everyone, simply raise no issue under the Establishment Clause; their enforcement against religiously motivated conduct does not trigger a "compelling state interest" test or otherwise require special justification.

Employment Division v. Smith drew and, indeed, has continued to draw angry objections from constitutional scholars,[47] among others. (The critics included large majorities in both Houses of Congress, who enacted a statute called the Religious Freedom Restoration Act that directed the courts to assess claims to religious exemptions from general statutes under a compelling interest test. As discussed in Chapter 12, however, the Supreme Court held that statute to be unconstitutional.) One criticism holds that *Smith* misinterprets the original understanding of the Free Exercise Clause – a claim disputed by both the Supreme Court majority and by other scholars. Another protests that the Court's approach treads callously on religious minorities, whose interests are less likely to be accommodated by legislatures than are those of mainstream religions. For example, during the Prohibition era, when the possession of alcohol was otherwise illegal, the government made an exception for communion wine. By contrast, the Oregon statute barring peyote use that was at issue in *Employment Division v. Smith* provided no comparable accommodation for the religious rites of the Native American Church. (Interestingly, however, in the aftermath of the *Smith* decision, the Oregon legislature amended the state's drug laws to permit possession and use of peyote for religious purposes only.)

Decisions subsequent to *Smith* have made clear that its rule of decision is subject to a few exceptions, several of which the Court carefully

46 Ibid. at 877.
47 See, for example, Michael W. McConnell, "Free Exercise Revisionism and the Smith Decision," 57 *University of Chicago Law Review* 1109 (1990); Douglas Laycock, "The Remnants of Free Exercise," 1990 *Supreme Court Review* 1 (1990).

drew in *Smith* itself, mostly to permit the Court to reconcile its newly prescribed approach with the outcomes reached in, though not the reasoning of, prior cases. (Under the doctrine requiring courts to respect "precedent," the Supreme Court is generally believed to have a greater obligation to accept that prior cases reached the right outcome than that they reasoned soundly in arriving at that outcome.) One of those subsequent decisions is highly consequential. At issue in *Hosanna-Tabor Evangelical Lutheran Church and School v. Equal Employment Opportunity Commission*[48] (2012), to which I referred in the prologue, was whether Congress can subject church decisions involving the hiring and firing of clergy to neutral laws that bar various forms of employment discrimination. By unanimous vote, the Justices held that the Free Exercise Clause mandates an exception to employment discrimination laws for religious organizations' choice of clergy. The *Smith* rule applies only to statutes that prohibit "outward physical acts" by individuals, Chief Justice Roberts wrote, and has no applicability to cases involving governmental interference with an "internal church decision that affects the faith and mission of the church itself."[49] "By imposing an unwanted minister, the state infringes the Free Exercise Clause, which protects a religious group's right to shape its own faith and mission through its appointments," the Chief Justice explained.[50]

Time will tell whether the *Hosanna-Tabor* case augurs further changes in Free Exercise Clause doctrine. For now, subject only to relatively narrow exceptions, *Smith* states the law: although the Free Exercise Clause bars the government from prohibiting religious conduct "only because of the religious belief" that prompts it, the clause does nothing to ameliorate the "cruel choice" that arises when a neutral, generally applicable statute forbids conduct (such as the sacramental use of peyote) that some citizens think is their religious duty to perform.

48 *Hosanna-Tabor Evangelical Lutheran Church & School v. Equal Employment Opportunity Commission*, 132 S. Ct. 694 (2012).
49 Ibid. at 707.
50 Ibid. at 706.

Voluntary Governmental Accommodations of Religion

A final set of difficult issues arises under the Religion Clauses when the government voluntarily exempts persons engaged in religiously motivated conduct from otherwise applicable duties. As I noted in the introduction to this chapter, an issue of this kind lay in the background in *Clay v. United States*. A comparable issue would be raised by Oregon's amended drug laws, which still include a general prohibition against peyote use but now make an exception for persons using peyote for religiously motivated purposes. Do exemptions specifically and solely applicable to religiously motivated conduct violate the Establishment Clause?

Only a few Supreme Court cases directly address issues of this kind. Although some are difficult to reconcile with others,[51] their general tenor suggests that when the government imposes a burden – for example, by forbidding conduct – it may selectively lift that burden to accommodate religious beliefs, at least as long as its doing so does not impose substantial burdens on others and could not reasonably be understood as endorsing the underlying beliefs.[52] It perhaps bears emphasis, however, that the cases are few and their teachings less than wholly clear. In cases decided during the Vietnam War era, the Court construed the statute granting draft exemptions to those who opposed war on religious grounds to make the same exemptions available to people who were not religious in the traditional sense but who nevertheless opposed all wars

---

51 Compare *Corporation of Presiding Bishop of Church of Jesus Christ of Latter-Day Saints v. Amos*, 483 U.S. 327 (1987) (upholding a statutory exemption that benefited religious groups only) with *Texas Monthly, Inc. v. Bullock*, 489 U.S. 1 (1989) (invalidating a state sales-tax exemption for religious periodicals).

52 See, for example, *Corporation of Presiding Bishop v. Amos*, *supra* note 51; *Texas Monthly, Inc. v. Bullock*, *supra* note 51, 489 U.S. at 18, n.8 (plurality opinion). See also *Cutter v. Wilkinson*, 544 U.S. 709 (2005), which upheld a federal statute that requires state and local governments to relax rules that otherwise would stop institutionalized persons from practicing their religions unless a burden on religious practice furthers "a compelling governmental interest" and does so by "the least restrictive means." The Court emphasized that the statute in question "alleviates exceptional government-created burdens" and does not impose excessive burdens "on nonbeneficiaries." Ibid. at 720.

for reasons of conscience.[53] The Court may have believed that granting an exemption only to believers in a traditional God would have created difficulties under the Establishment Clause.

Tensions between the Free Exercise and Establishment Clauses

For anyone who believes both (1) that the Establishment Clause forbids the government to prefer or promote religion and (2) that the Free Exercise Clause requires the government to spare its citizens the "cruel choice" between obeying the law and obeying their religion whenever it can reasonably do so, the two clauses will often be in conflict. The Free Exercise Clause will require exemptions from otherwise applicable legal duties that the Establishment Clause will forbid (because exemptions for the religiously observant may tend to promote religion). To put the same point another way, it is impossible to maintain what might be regarded as "strong" interpretations of both clauses – a strict separationist view of the Establishment Clause and a demand that the government accommodate religious beliefs under the Free Exercise Clause.

Although there are various ways in which a conflict between the two clauses might be avoided, the current Supreme Court has dealt with the situation by adopting relatively "weak" interpretations of both. Notwithstanding the exception carved out in the recent *Hosanna-Tabor* case, *Employment Division v. Smith* gives a weak reading of the Free Exercise Clause, under which the government virtually never needs to accommodate individual religious believers by exempting religiously motivated conduct from generally applicable laws. The Court's interpretation of the Establishment Clause, which allows the government to inscribe "In God We Trust" on the currency and to supply valuable goods and services to religious institutions as long as it does so on a "neutral" basis, is similarly weak. Indeed, the Court's interpretation of the Establishment Clause appears to allow the government voluntarily to lift the burden

---

53 See *Welsh v. United States* and *United States v. Seeger, supra* note 4.

that governmental regulations impose on religiously motivated conduct on a nonneutral basis, without providing comparable exceptions for others, at least some of the time.

The conjunction of weak Free Exercise Clause doctrine with weak Establishment Clause doctrine gives elected governmental officials a great deal of discretion in dealing with matters involving religion: the government is seldom required to accommodate religious beliefs, but it has relatively broad freedom to do so if it chooses.

This doctrinal structure well serves the interests of those with mainstream religious beliefs. The political process will seldom impose significant burdens on mainstream views, and mainstream believers are unlikely to be affronted by such practices as putting "In God We Trust" on the currency and making Christmas Day a national holiday. If the doctrinal structure should be faulted, it is for failing to provide adequate protection of religious minorities.

It should be remembered, however, that the category of "religious minorities" includes two subgroups. One consists of the religiously devout who wish greater governmental accommodation of their beliefs – more exemptions from generally applicable laws, expanded voucher or other programs to facilitate the religious education of their children, and so forth. The other subgroup comprises religious or irreligious outsiders who feel demeaned and marginalized by governmental programs supporting and accommodating religious beliefs that they do not share. Religion Clause doctrine could give fuller protection to the interests of either of these minority subgroups, but it could not give fuller protection to both.

3 Protection of Economic Liberties

The Constitution was essentially an economic document based upon the concept that the fundamental private rights of property are anterior to government and morally beyond the reach of popular majorities.

– Charles A. Beard[1]

[A] constitution is not intended to embody a particular economic theory.... It is made for people of fundamentally differing views.

– Justice Oliver Wendell Holmes Jr.[2]

WHEN THE HISTORIAN CHARLES BEARD WROTE IN 1913 that "[t]he Constitution was essentially an economic document," he claimed too much. The founders intended the Constitution to protect many values, not just property. Nevertheless, property and contract rights ranked high among those that the Constitution was initially designed to safeguard. Prominent framers and ratifiers worried particularly about legislation excusing debtors from obligations to their creditors.[3] They viewed such legislation as immoral because it violated the sanctity of promises and as

---

1 Charles A. Beard, *An Economic Interpretation of the Constitution of the United States* (New York: Macmillan, 1913), 324.

2 *Lochner v. New York*, 198 U.S. 45, 75 (1905) (Holmes, J., dissenting).

3 See *The Federalist*, No. 10 (Madison) (characterizing "[a] rage for paper money, for an abolition of debts," as among the phenomena demonstrating a need for a new constitution).

imprudent because it discouraged commercial lending. (If the legislature could excuse promises to repay money, banks would be less willing to loan money in the first place.) In one of the rare provisions of the original Constitution that creates rights enforceable against the states (rather than the federal government), Article I, Section 10, provides that "[n]o State shall...pass any...Law impairing the Obligation of Contracts." The Fifth Amendment forbids the federal government from taking "private property...for public use, without just compensation." The Fourteenth Amendment, which was added to the Constitution in 1868, forbids state and local governments, as much as the national government, to deprive anyone of property without due process of law.

Regardless of the framers' intent, the original understanding of the Constitution, or the situation that prevailed in Charles Beard's time, the modern Supreme Court affords very little constitutional protection to property rights. A 2005 case, *Kelo v. City of New London*,[4] illustrates both the present state of the law and some of the ferment that may surround current doctrine. For much of the twentieth century, New London, Connecticut, was home to several Navy and Coast Guard facilities, which attracted major defense contractors and created thousands of jobs. As the Cold War drew to a close, however, the work began to disappear. Soon, the city's unemployment rate was twice the national average, its population was at the lowest level since 1920, and its crime rate was climbing. City officials responded with an ambitious plan to attract new businesses and residents. That plan depended heavily on the promised efforts of the private, nonprofit New London Development Corporation (NLDC) to transform the working-class Fort Trumbull neighborhood into a modern "urban village," with shops, restaurants, and condominiums surrounding a new $300 million research center for the pharmaceutical giant Pfizer.

When NLDC set about acquiring the necessary land, however, it found that some Fort Trumbull residents refused to leave. Wilhelmina

4 545 U.S. 469 (2005).

Dery, whose grandmother settled in the neighborhood in the 1890s after arriving from Italy, declined to sell the home her family had owned since 1905. Dery herself had been born there in 1918 and had lived there her entire life. Another resident, Susette Kelo, had moved to Fort Trumbull only the year before the redevelopment efforts began, but she was equally determined not to sell her small pink cottage. She had restored the home herself and treasured its sweeping water views. Unwilling to allow a handful of resistant home owners to derail the redevelopment plan, the city and the NLDC wheeled out their trump card: the so-called power of eminent domain, or the authority of governments to take property for "public use," as long as they pay the "just compensation" that the Constitution's Takings Clause requires.[5]

Still refusing to yield, Kelo and Dery, joined by several others who had declined to sell, sued the city in federal court. They acknowledged that they had been offered payment for their land. They further acknowledged that the government would have been entitled to take it (upon payment of just compensation) to build a road, or a fort, or a fire station. Kelo's and Dery's complaint was that by taking their homes to transfer them to another private party, New London had run afoul of the Takings Clause's implicit guarantee that private property may not be taken at all except for public use.

By a vote of 5–4, the Supreme Court ruled that Kelo and Dery had no case. In the majority opinion, Justice John Paul Stevens explained that New London had "carefully formulated an economic development plan that it believes will provide appreciable benefits to the community."[6] Citing earlier decisions that had construed the Fifth Amendment's "public purpose" requirement broadly, particularly in the context of urban renewal, he reasoned that the city's interest in promoting redevelopment justified it in forcing private property owners to cede their family homes to a private development corporation. (Justice Kennedy concurred to

5 For a rich account of New London's plan and those who resisted it, see Jeff Benedict, *Little Pink House* (New York: Grand Central, 2009).
6 Ibid. at 483.

explain that "a more demanding standard" might apply in some cases involving private transfers.[7])

Justice Sandra Day O'Connor – a former Arizona state legislator widely noted for being attuned to public sensibilities in addressing hot-button legal issues – wrote for the dissenters. She criticized the majority for giving the government "license to transfer property from those with fewer resources to those with more."[8] When "[a]ny property may...be taken for the benefit of another private party," she warned, the "beneficiaries are likely to be those citizens with disproportionate influence and power in the political process, including large corporations and development firms."[9]

Public response to the *Kelo* decision was almost wholly negative. Americans, who care about property rights, empathized with the evicted home owners, whom they thought had been treated unfairly. In the years following *Kelo*, forty-three states rewrote the state laws conferring government authority to "take" private property for ostensibly public use. When constitutional amendments to limit use of the eminent domain power appeared on state election ballots, more than 60 percent of California voters registered their support, as did nearly 70 percent of Florida voters and 80 percent of Michigan voters.

Kelo may, or may not, signal that modern Supreme Court doctrine regarding the protection of property and other economic rights is sufficiently out of touch with prevailing public views to be due for a major rethinking. Only time will tell. But to understand the body of constitutional doctrine that currently exists, it is important to grasp how we got to where we are.

The story of how we got here includes at least two strands. One involves past misadventures by Courts that tried to give strong protection to property and other economic rights – misadventures that attracted even more vehement criticisms and stronger rebukes of the Court than

7 Ibid. at 493.
8 Ibid. at 505.
9 Ibid.

that which followed *Kelo*. During the late nineteenth and early twentieth centuries, the Court's protection of economic rights under the Due Process Clause (during the so-called *Lochner* era, which took its name from the case of *Lochner v. New York*[10]) occasioned enormous controversy and ultimately helped bring the Court, if not the country, to the edge of catastrophe in the 1930s. The other strand of the story involves the astonishing difficulty, as a purely analytical matter, in determining when it can fairly be said that the obligations of contract have been "interfere[d]" with or when a "taking" of property has occurred. This difficulty also plays a large role in explaining the Court's relatively hands-off approach since the 1930s, even though the Court has never wholly renounced the protection of economic rights, as the *Kelo* dissenters made clear.

Early History

As noted already, the Takings Clause of the Fifth Amendment – which prohibits the taking of private property for public use without just compensation – did not originally apply to the states. Nor, before the Civil War, did the federal government engage in many uncompensated expropriations. As a result, few early cases arose under the Takings Clause.

By contrast, decisions under the Contract Clause loomed relatively large in the early history of the Supreme Court. *Sturges v. Crowninshield*[11] (1819) invalidated a state bankruptcy law that excused debtors from contractual obligations created before the law's adoption. Under the statute, debtors who declared bankruptcy and surrendered all of their property for division among their creditors could be discharged from further obligation to pay their old debts. The Court ruled that the law impaired the obligation of contracts.

In another famous case, *Fletcher v. Peck*[12] (1810), Chief Justice John Marshall rejected a state's effort to withdraw rights to land that it had

10 198 U.S. 45 (1905).
11 17 U.S. 122 (1819).
12 10 U.S. 87 (1810).

previously granted to private parties in exchange for the payment of money. He found the state's nullifying effort to be condemned by the Contract Clause and by "general principles which are common to our free institutions."[13] The latter phrase is telling. Many of the Justices of the early Supreme Court viewed the Constitution as embodying "natural rights," including rights to property and economic liberty, which they regarded as given by God or nature or as otherwise morally self-evident.[14] These Justices naturally read provisions such as the Contract Clause in light of their moral and constitutional theories. For them, the more difficult question was whether the Court should invalidate legislation that violated moral rights even if it did not transgress any specific constitutional limitation (such as the Contract Clause) at all. Justice Samuel Chase offered a celebrated statement that the courts should decline to enforce morally wrongful legislation in *Calder v. Bull*[15] (1798), in which he cited as an example "a law that takes property from A and gives it to B: It is against all reason and justice, for a people to entrust a Legislature with SUCH powers; and, therefore, it cannot be presumed that they have done it."

A rare Contract Clause case to divide the Marshall Court – and to reveal a potential gap in the natural rights philosophy – was *Ogden v. Saunders*[16] (1827). As did *Sturges v. Crowninshield*, *Ogden* involved a state law providing for the discharge of debts in cases of bankruptcy. The contracts at issue in *Ogden*, however, had all come into existence after the enactment of the bankruptcy statute. Over the sharp dissent of Chief Justice Marshall, the Court reasoned that state laws existing at the time of a contract's formation in effect became part of the contract. Under this reasoning, the debtor in *Ogden* had not promised categorically

---

13 Ibid. at 139.

14 See generally Suzanna Sherry, "The Founders' Unwritten Constitution," cited in note 5 of the Introduction to this book.

15 3 U.S. 386, 388 (1798) (Chase, J.) (*seriatim* opinion).

16 25 U.S. 213 (1827).

to pay the money that he owed but only to pay *unless* he became insolvent and was discharged in a bankruptcy proceeding. The law thus did not impair the obligations created by preexisting contracts; instead, it conditioned or regulated the obligations that subsequent contracts could create.

It is easy to understand the allure of *Ogden*'s reasoning. Surely, private parties should not be able to escape the reach of state regulatory legislation simply by making a contract. Suppose, for example, that state law prohibits the use of a pesticide that is damaging to the environment. Suppose, further, that I enter a contract to pay Jones $500 to treat my lawn with that forbidden chemical. Under these circumstances, surely neither Jones nor I should be able to claim successfully that the state's regulatory legislation "impairs" the obligation created by our contract and thereby violates the Constitution. Rather, the state law must be allowed either to operate as a condition of the contract, forcing the substitution of some other pesticide, or to bar the contract from ever taking effect.

It is equally plain, however, that the reasoning of *Ogden v. Saunders* threatens to drain nearly all substance from the Contract Clause. If state regulatory legislation always forms a part of all subsequently enacted contracts, and if there are no constitutional limits on the legislation that states may enact, then the states can effectively limit contract rights in any way that they choose – as long as they do so prospectively, before a contract has been formed. Chief Justice Marshall dissented for this reason.

Viewed together, the majority and dissenting opinions in *Ogden v. Saunders* frame a central issue in defining constitutionally protected economic liberties: how can the courts distinguish permissible regulation of the terms on which parties may contract from forbidden impairments of the right to make contracts and have them enforced? As *Ogden* demonstrates, that issue arises under the Contract Clause. But it can also be framed as arising under other provisions of the Constitution, as subsequent constitutional developments have demonstrated.

The Fourteenth Amendment

In the aftermath of the Civil War, Congress proposed and the states ratified the Fourteenth Amendment to the Constitution. Although principally intended to guarantee the civil rights of former slaves and their descendants, the Fourteenth Amendment deliberately speaks in more general terms: "No State shall make or enforce any law which shall abridge the privileges or immunities of citizens of the United States; nor shall any State deprive any person of life, liberty, or property, without due process of law; nor deny to any person within its jurisdiction the equal protection of the laws."

At the very least, there is a serious historical argument that the Fourteenth Amendment's framers and ratifiers intended the first quoted clause, prohibiting state abridgement of the "privileges or immunities" of citizenship, to protect certain basic economic liberties. The language of the Privileges or Immunities Clause of the Fourteenth Amendment closely parallels the Privileges and Immunities Clause of Article IV. As is discussed in Chapter 10, the Privileges and Immunities Clause is essentially an antidiscrimination provision: it contemplates the existence of a set of privileges and immunities of state citizenship; leaves it to the states to define their content; and says that a state may not withhold those privileges and immunities, however it chooses to define them, from citizens of other states who happen to be within its borders. During congressional debates leading to adoption of the Fourteenth Amendment, prominent members of Congress cited a judicial decision listing the privileges and immunities of state citizenship under Article IV as identifying the privileges or immunities that would henceforth be recognized as rights of national citizenship, and thus defined by the Supreme Court of the United States, under the proposed new Privileges or Immunities Clause.[17] In that decision in *Corfield v. Coryell*[18] (1823), Justice Bushrod

17 For discussion of the legislative history, see Alexander M. Bickel, "The Original Understanding and the Segregation Decision," 69 *Harvard Law Review* 1 (1955).
18 6 F. Cas. 546 (No. 3230) (C.C.E.D. Pa. 1823).

Washington – nephew of George Washington – said that Article IV protected all privileges "which are, in their nature, fundamental; which belong, of right, to the citizens of all free governments."[19] Under traditional understandings, economic rights to own property and to practice a lawful trade occupied the category of fundamental rights and constituted privileges and immunities of state citizenship.

The crucial judicial test of the meaning of the Fourteenth Amendment's Privileges or Immunities Clause came in *The Slaughter-House Cases*[20] (1872). The state of Louisiana licensed a slaughterhouse monopoly for the city of New Orleans and barred all others from the profession. In the Supreme Court, challengers maintained that the right of butchers "to exercise their trade" was a traditional right of economic liberty protected against unreasonable state regulation by the newly ratified Privileges or Immunities Clause of the Fourteenth Amendment and that the Court must therefore judge the reasonableness of the state legislation creating a slaughtering monopoly. By a 5–4 vote, the Court disagreed. In a tortured opinion, the Court simply refused to believe that the Fourteenth Amendment had elevated the traditional privileges or immunities of state citizenship under Article IV, such as the right to pursue a lawful trade, to the status of privileges or immunities of national citizenship, which would need to be defined and enforced by the federal courts. Instead, it held, the Privileges or Immunities Clause of the Fourteenth Amendment had merely ratified the existence of a few rights of national citizenship already implicit in the original Constitution, such as the right to travel from one state to another.

The Court's reluctance to recognize a set of newly conferred privileges or immunities of national citizenship that included property, contract, and other economic rights is easy to understand in its historical context. In the aftermath of the disastrous *Dred Scott* decision and the ensuing Civil War – both briefly discussed in the Introduction – the Court

19 Ibid. at 551.
20 83 U.S. 36 (1872).

understandably felt vulnerable and uncertain. It was reluctant to claim large new responsibilities likely to enmesh it in further controversy, such as those that the Privileges or Immunities Clause appeared to thrust upon it. If the Fourteenth Amendment created judicially enforceable privileges or immunities of national citizenship, it would have fallen to the Court to define those privileges or immunities and to give them substantive content. Historical understandings might have provided some guidance. Nonetheless, the Court's new responsibilities would have been large and the implications for the states – which would have been subjected to a potentially sweeping array of constitutional limitations whenever they restricted long-standing privileges or immunities involving business and trade – nearly revolutionary. As the majority put it, "such a construction...would constitute this court a perpetual censor upon all legislation of the States."[21] Again, it bears emphasis that before the Civil War, the Constitution created very few judicially enforceable rights against the states.

Even so, the Court's reasoning in *The Slaughter-House Cases* is difficult to defend. As the Court had to acknowledge, the Privileges or Immunities Clause plainly says that no state may abridge the privileges or immunities of citizenship; and when it says so, it unmistakably refers to privileges or immunities of national citizenship. By holding that the Privileges or Immunities Clause ratified only the existence of privileges or immunities of national citizenship that were already implicit in the Constitution, the *Slaughter-House* majority ruled that a principal provision of the Fourteenth Amendment, adopted specifically to alter the relationship between state and national governments in the wake of a bloody Civil War, essentially changed nothing. It was, as a dissenting opinion protested, "a vain and idle enactment."[22] This interpretation of the Privileges or Immunities Clause was and remains intellectually untenable. It also remains unaltered. Since *The Slaughter-House Cases*, the Court has

21 Ibid. at 78.
22 Ibid. at 96 (Field, J., dissenting).

treated the Privileges or Immunities Clause of the Fourteenth Amendment as a virtual constitutional nullity.[23]

Ironically, however, within a few years of *The Slaughter-House Cases*, the Court began to do under the Due Process Clause what it had refused to do under the Privileges of Immunities Clause: the Court began to scrutinize state legislation to determine whether it unreasonably interfered with liberty or deprived people of property without due process of law (rather than depriving citizens of "the privileges or immunities" of national citizenship).

Substantive Due Process

The era of "substantive due process" review of economic legislation under the Due Process Clause began around 1890. The assumptions that underlay the Court's decision making are hard to recapture. The Court took for granted that the states are entitled to enact regulatory legislation to promote the public health, safety, and morals. But the Court also assumed that regulation lacking in fundamental fairness should be deemed to deprive its targets of liberty or property "without due process of law." Critics have challenged the very idea of "substantive due process" as a contradiction in terms – "sort of like 'green pastel redness,'" as one critic put it.[24] According to those who take this line, the Due Process Clause is obviously a guarantee of fair procedures, and it was a flat-out mistake to use this clause to invalidate legislation on grounds of substantive, rather than procedural, unfairness. Perhaps so, perhaps not – there may be some outcomes that are so substantively unfair that no process

---

23 *Saenz v. Roe*, 526 U.S. 489 (1999), was unusual in relying on the Privileges or Immunities Clause as the constitutional home of a traditionally recognized right to travel, but the Court gave no indication that it intended any broader revitalization of the clause. See Laurence H. Tribe, "*Saenz* Sans Prophecy: Does the Privileges or Immunities Revival Portend the Future – Or Reveal the Structure of the Present?," 113 *Harvard Law Review* 110, 197–98 (1999).

24 John Hart Ely, *Democracy and Distrust: A Theory of Judicial Review* (Cambridge, MA: Belknap Press of Harvard University Press, 1980), 19–20.

that produced them could count as "due." In any event, in hundreds of substantive due process cases from the late 1800s through the 1930s, the Court asked either or both of two questions: First, does state regulatory legislation have a valid public purpose? Second, if so, does the challenged regulation represent a fair and sensible means of pursuing that purpose?

If the notion of substantive due process makes sense at all, the Court's approach sounds reasonable. Certainly it would have sounded reasonable if the Court had conducted precisely the same inquiries to determine whether legislation violated the "privileges or immunities" of national citizenship – as, but for *The Slaughter-House Cases*, it might well have done. In practice, however, acute difficulties arose because the Court's administration of substantive due process review reflected narrow, grudging views of what counted as valid public purposes and as reasonable means of promoting them. The Court thus became what the *Slaughter-House* majority had feared, "a perpetual censor upon all legislation of the States."

The Court began implementing substantive due process review near the dawn of the so-called Progressive Era in American history. During that period, legislatures recurrently enacted regulatory legislation aimed particularly to protect miners and factory workers, including children, from brutally long hours, low wages, and oppressive conditions of employment. With considerable frequency, the Court found such legislative efforts invalid on the ground that they interfered unreasonably with rights to freedom of contract protected by the Due Process Clause.

Lochner v. New York[25] (1905), the decision from which this era of judicial history takes its name, exemplified the Court's approach. *Lochner* struck down a New York statute imposing a sixty-hour limit on bakery employees' work weeks. In finding the statute invalid, the Court first imagined that it might have been passed for the special benefit of bakery workers, to give them an advantage in bargaining with bakery owners. But for the state simply to try to benefit one class of citizens

25 198 U.S. 45 (1905).

(bakery workers) at the expense of another (their employers) was not, in the Court's view, a valid public purpose. To the Court, legislation designed to benefit only one otherwise competent group of citizens, especially by improving their situation relative to others, aimed to promote class interests, not the general public interest. It was the equivalent of the plainly unjust statute that Justice Chase had imagined in *Calder v. Bull*, taking from A and giving to B simply because the state preferred B to A.[26]

Alternatively, the *Lochner* Court imagined that the statute limiting bakery workers to sixty-hour weeks might have been enacted for the purpose of protecting bakers' health (rather than promoting their economic well-being at the expense of others). For the state to promote the health of its citizens was a permissible public purpose, the Court acknowledged, but it then scrutinized the state's chosen means and found them wanting. There was insufficient evidence, the Court ruled, that working more than sixty hours a week as a baker posed a significant threat to health. Absent such evidence, the state's regulation was unreasonable and potentially tyrannical. Under the state's theory, the Court wrote, "[n]ot only the hours of employees, but the hours of employers, could be regulated, and doctors, lawyers, scientists, all professional men, as well as athletes and artisans, could be forbidden to fatigue their brains and bodies by prolonged hours of exercise."[27] Three Justices dissented on this point. They believed the evidence sufficient to uphold the statute as a health measure.

Justice Oliver Wendell Holmes, later to emerge as a champion of free speech rights, dissented on more fundamental grounds. The Court, he objected, was reading the Constitution through the lens of a particular, controversial economic philosophy that looked skeptically on all governmental regulation of economic markets. It assumed that if a factory

---

26 On the concern of the *Lochner*-era Court concerning class legislation, see Howard Gillman, *The Constitution Besieged* (Durham, NC: Duke University Press, 1993), 10, 127.

27 *Lochner*, 198 U.S. at 60.

owner and factory laborers wished to contract for seventy-hour work weeks at pennies an hour, they had a natural right to do so, and any governmental interference was a suspect deprivation of liberty. The difficulty, Holmes wrote, was that this was "an economic theory which a large part of the country does not entertain."[28] Where the Court saw voluntary transactions among willing contractors, others saw self-sustaining social structures conspiring to keep the poor, poor and the rich, rich. Where the Court saw natural liberty, others saw socially constructed inequality in which some had too much bargaining power and others had too little. Given the division of views, Holmes thought that elected officials and ultimately the voters, not the Justices of the Supreme Court, should chart the nation's economic and regulatory policy.

From the 1905 decision in *Lochner* through 1937, the Supreme Court applied substantive due process review to roughly four hundred economic regulatory statutes. The Justices invalidated about half. The decisions do not form a pattern of perfect consistency. The Court had difficulty distinguishing legislation promoting genuine "public" interests in protecting those not competent to protect themselves (such as children and sometimes, in the Court's view, women) from legislation that impermissibly attempted to promote some citizens' interests at the expense of others. The Court also varied in its willingness to credit evidence showing that legislation reasonably promoted worker health and safety. But the Court maintained its basic analytic framework with remarkable consistency in the face of unrelenting public and legislative opposition.

That opposition grew angrier as time passed. *Lochner* was a due process case invalidating economic regulatory legislation enacted by a state. But the *Lochner*-era Supreme Court invalidated regulatory legislation under other provisions of the Constitution as well. Most notably, the Court frequently struck down federal legislation regulating economic activity as lying beyond Congress's power to enact under Article I (the provision from which Congress derives most of its powers). From

28 Ibid. at 75 (Holmes, J., dissenting).

the perspective of a majority of the Justices, Congress and the states were trying to eliminate vital freedoms of contract that the framers of the Constitution had regarded as God given. From the perspective of those on the other side, the Justices were unreasonably trying to impose antiquated economic notions on an unwilling nation. In this view, the Justices' antiregulatory stance had become untenable in a modern industrial economy, especially when rampant unemployment made it impossible for employees – who could easily be fired and replaced – to bargain effectively with their employers for decent working conditions or a living wage.

When anger and frustration with the Court reached an apex in the mid-1930s, with President Roosevelt credibly proposing to "pack" the Supreme Court to save the New Deal (as discussed in the Introduction), the Court sharply altered course. With respect to substantive due process, the signal decision came in *West Coast Hotel Co. v. Parrish*[29] (1937), which upheld a state law mandating a minimum wage for women. Reflecting its dramatic rejection of the *Lochner*-era assumption that an unregulated market economy provided fair opportunities for the exercise of natural liberty, the Court wrote, "The exploitation of a class of workers who are in an unequal position with respect to bargaining power and are thus relatively defenseless against the denial of a living wage is not only detrimental to their health and well-being, but casts a direct burden for their support upon the community."[30] In this formulation, an unregulated "free market" is neither sacrosanct nor even presumptively just. The government violates no protected liberty when it identifies economic "exploitation" and enacts regulatory legislation to correct it.

In the wake of *West Coast Hotel* and parallel decisions sustaining Congress's regulatory power under the Commerce Clause, the principal monuments of the *Lochner* era all tumbled within a few short years. As noted in the Introduction, the process of change included a number

29 300 U.S. 379 (1937).
30 Ibid. at 399.

of elements, all illustrative of the ways in which constitutional law evolves. To begin with, the Supreme Court is a "they," not an "it," and the Justices had long been divided about when, if ever, economic regulatory legislation should be deemed so "unreasonable" as to violate the Due Process Clause. One or two of the Justices seemed subtly to shift their positions in 1937, possibly in response to political pressure. Not all of the changes occurred overnight, however, and not all were due to a couple of Justices' altered stances. President Franklin Roosevelt had a constitutional as well as a political vision, and he successfully sold that vision to large majorities of the American people. As viewed by FDR, the Constitution does not merely tolerate but actually invites broad governmental intervention in the national economy and the creation of a social safety net – including programs, such as Social Security, that the founding generation could never have imagined but that the Constitution's large generalities nevertheless authorize. Within a few years, the conservative stalwarts of the *Lochner* era had departed the bench. President Roosevelt got to remake the Supreme Court with Justices who shared his constitutional vision, which thus became and remained ascendant in the courts for several generations of constitutional politics. In the history of American constitutional law generally, but perhaps especially in the parts involving property rights and the government's regulatory authority, FDR is a towering figure.

In the jurisprudential regime that Roosevelt more than anyone else brought into being, it became an unquestionable premise of constitutional reasoning that all economic regulatory legislation enjoys a presumption of constitutionality and should be upheld as long as it is supported by any conceivable rational basis. What is more, it became the conventional wisdom, taught to generations of law students, that *Lochner*'s underlying theory was not only erroneous but also disgracefully so. Summarizing the lessons that the Court had drawn from the *Lochner* experience, Justice Hugo Black – the first man named to the Supreme Court by Franklin Roosevelt and a constitutional literalist who believed that the Due Process Clause conferred no substantive guarantees of property rights – wrote in 1963 that "[u]nder the system of government created by our Constitution, it is up to legislatures, not courts, to decide on the wisdom and utility of [economic regulatory] legislation."[31] He continued: "There was a time when the Due Process Clause was used by this Court to strike down laws which were thought unreasonable, that is, unwise or incompatible with some particular economic or social philosophy.... [That approach] has long since been discarded.... It is now settled that States have power to legislate against what are found to be injurious practices..., so long as their laws do not run afoul of some specific federal constitutional prohibition, or of some valid federal law."[32]

Perhaps significantly, the Supreme Court has never wholly renounced the scrutiny of economic legislation under the Due Process Clause. It continues to ask whether such legislation is rationally related to a legitimate public purpose. Yet not since 1937 has the Court invalidated economic regulatory legislation on "substantive due process" grounds.[33] More than seventy years later, the taint of the *Lochner* era remains strong. Modern liberals continue to share the main elements of Franklin Roosevelt's constitutional vision. Conservatives today may question some elements of that vision, but when they think of substantive due process, they tend to see *Lochner* as the direct ancestor of their own constitutional bête noire, the protection of abortion rights under *Roe v. Wade*[34] (1973), which is discussed in Chapter 6. *Lochner* thus remains prominent in what is sometimes described as the "anti-canon" of constitutional law, the catalog of cases that nearly everyone reviles and regards as dreadful constitutional mistakes.

---

31 *Ferguson v. Skrupa*, 372 U.S. 726, 729 (1963).

32 Ibid. at 729–31 (internal quotation marks omitted).

33 In *Eastern Enterprises v. Apfel*, 524 U.S. 498 (1998), however, Justice Kennedy's conclusion that an economic regulatory statute violated substantive due process was necessary to the Court's decision that the statute was unconstitutional – a conclusion that four other Justices reached under the Takings Clause.

34 410 U.S. 113 (1973).

Modern Contracts Clause Doctrine

Since the demise of *Lochner*, the Supreme Court has not shown much more enthusiasm for invalidating economic regulatory legislation under the Contract Clause than under the Due Process Clause. Indeed, the Court's retreat from strong enforcement of the Contract Clause actually began before the end of the *Lochner* era, in *Home Building Loan Association v. Blaisdell*[35] (1934). At the height of the Great Depression, the State of Minnesota enacted a statute barring mortgage foreclosures for a two-year period. On the surface, this might have appeared to be precisely the kind of debtor-relief legislation that the Contracts Clause was meant to forbid: it effectively stopped banks and other creditors from enforcing their contractual rights to foreclose on the property of nonpaying debtors. Nonetheless, the Court upheld the statute.

The Court's *Blaisdell* opinion emphasized two themes. The first involved the statute's emergency nature. The Court quoted Chief Justice John Marshall's opinion in *McCulloch v. Maryland*[36] (1819) for the proposition that the Constitution was "intended to endure for ages to come, and consequently, to be adapted to the various crises of human affairs."[37] The second crucial strand in the Court's reasoning expanded the doctrine, traceable to *Ogden v. Saunders*, that private contracts must be read to incorporate preexisting legal rules and regulations. According to *Blaisdell*, "the reservation of essential attributes of sovereign power" – that is, the right of the state to enact subsequent legislation adjusting contract rights – "is also read into contracts as a postulate of the legal order."[38]

This formulation bears close attention. Under it, the Contracts Clause no longer establishes an absolute barrier to state laws that retroactively impair the obligation of contracts; even after contracts have been formed, the state may exercise its "sovereign power" to enact

35 290 U.S. 398 (1934).
36 17 U.S. 316 (1819).
37 *Blaisdell*, 290 U.S. at 443 (quoting *McCulloch*, 17 U.S. at 415).
38 Ibid. at 435.

regulatory legislation with the effect of nullifying or adjusting contract rights, as long as that legislation is itself reasonable. The duty to distinguish reasonable from unreasonable adjustments of contract rights falls, of course, to the Supreme Court, which – in the post–New Deal and post-*Lochner* era – has tended to judge reasonableness with a tolerant disposition. In only one subsequent case have the Justices invalidated state legislation adjusting rights under contracts solely involving private parties.[39]

The Takings Clause

The Takings Clause of the Fifth Amendment says that "private property [shall not] be taken for public use, without just compensation." As the language makes plain, the Takings Clause does not absolutely bar the taking of private property for public use; on the contrary, it presupposes that governments must possess the power to take such property as they need for public purposes. The Takings Clause only requires that if the government takes private property for public use, it must pay just compensation. Takings Clause cases can thus present either or both of two questions. First, has a "taking" of property occurred? Second, if so, was the taking for "public use"? (This was the question in the *Kelo* case, discussed at the beginning of this chapter.) A third, typically less interesting question is whether the "compensation" offered by the government is "just."

The first of these questions, involving whether a "taking" has occurred at all, frequently turns out to be one of extraordinary complexity. The answer is obvious when the government occupies and uses private property to build a fort or a road, for example. But matters can be much more complex when the government engages in activities that interfere with the enjoyment of private property but does not physically occupy it. In *United States v. Causby*[40] (1946), the government's

---

39 See *Allied Structural Steel Co. v. Spannaus*, 438 U.S. 234 (1978).
40 328 U.S. 256 (1946).

recurrent use of airspace for military flights made it impossible for
Causby to continue to use his land as a chicken farm. The Supreme Court
found a taking. According to the Court, the taking was "as complete as
if the United States had entered upon the surface of the land and taken
exclusive possession of it."[41]

To be distinguished from cases involving the government's occupa-
tion and use of property are cases involving the regulation of property uses. The leading case is *Pennsylvania Coal Co. v. Mahon*[42] (1922).
In Pennsylvania coal country, coal companies commonly purchased or
retained underground mining rights, separate from the ownership rights
in surface property held by others. Against this background, the Pennsylvania Legislature enacted a statute prohibiting the mining of coal in any
manner that would cause the "subsidence," or downward collapse, of surface property. The statute effectively barred coal companies from exercising some of their mining rights, even though they technically retained
ownership of all the subsurface coal that they had previously purchased.

In legal doctrinal terms, the question posed by cases such as *Mahon*
is this: when, if ever, should governmental regulatory legislation that
diminishes the value of property rights (in this case, by forbidding any
use of those rights that would cause subsidence) be deemed to constitute a "regulatory taking" that requires just compensation? The question
arises in innumerable contexts. For example, it comes up whenever the
government enacts land-use or zoning regulations. Has a taking occurred
whenever a zoning ordinance prohibits operating gasoline stations in residential neighborhoods, and a property owner who would like to open
a gasoline station is forbidden from doing so? Whenever environmental protection statutes prohibit filling wetlands to make them suitable
for housing lots? According to legal historians, the Takings Clause was
not originally understood to create a barrier to or to require the payment of just compensation for regulatory legislation that affects land

41 Ibid. at 261.
42 260 U.S. 393 (1922).

use (and thereby diminishes the value of particular properties).[43] To the founders, the Takings Clause protected only against governmental occupations and use of property (as in the cases of roads and forts). But members of the founding generation almost surely did not anticipate either the scope of modern land-use regulation or the problems that have spurred its enactment. Perhaps for this reason, almost no one seems to think that Takings Clause cases – in interesting contrast with some other ones – should always be decided based on the original constitutional understanding.[44]

Confronting the takings issue in *Mahon*, the Supreme Court found that the Pennsylvania antisubsidence legislation constituted a taking. In an opinion by Justice Holmes, the Court did not question that the government enjoyed broad regulatory powers. (Holmes had dissented in *Lochner.*) Nor did Holmes suggest that landowners were entitled to just compensation whenever governmental regulation of permissible property uses diminished the value of their property. But there must be a limit, he wrote. If governmental regulation goes "too far," it becomes effectively indistinguishable from appropriation or destruction of property, and just compensation must be paid.[45]

Since *Mahon*, the Supreme Court has developed a complex body of doctrine guiding the judicial inquiry into when governmental regulation of property uses goes "too far" and thus triggers a just compensation requirement under the Takings Clause. The Court's inquiries are largely "ad hoc," it has said, but in recent decades it has noted that "three

---

43 See, for example, William Michael Treanor, "The Original Understanding of the Takings Clause and the Political Process," 95 *Columbia Law Review* 782 (1995).

44 See *Lucas v. South Carolina Coastal Council*, 505 U.S. 1003, 1028 n.15 (1992). As Justice Scalia, who often champions originalism, explained, because practice in the states before the Court applied the Takings Clause to them was "out of accord with *any* plausible interpretation of [its] provisions," and because "the text of the Clause" – unlike "the text originally proposed by Madison" – "can be read to encompass regulatory as well as physical deprivations," the Court should not interpret the Clause in light of the "early American experience."

45 *Mahon*, 260 U.S. at 415.

factors... have 'particular significance': (1) the economic impact of the regulation on the claimant; (2) the extent to which the regulation has interfered with distinct investment-backed expectations; and (3) the character of the governmental action."[46] For the most part, the Court has applied this test in a deferential manner and has allowed the enforcement of land-use regulations even when they dramatically reduce the economic value of land. In doing so, it has followed an approach that closely parallels its post-*Lochner* jurisprudence under the Due Process and Contracts Clauses: just as the Court does not absolutely prohibit regulatory legislation adjusting contractual and property rights, neither will it make regulation economically infeasible by too readily requiring payments of "just compensation" to regulated parties.

It should perhaps be no surprise, however, that in recent years, an increasingly conservative Supreme Court has shown a renewed interest in the Takings Clause.[47] (In ordinary political parlance, those who generally disfavor economic regulatory legislation, including environmental legislation, are almost invariably described as "conservative.") So far, the Court has not altered the main elements of a doctrinal framework that gives the government broad regulatory flexibility before it can be said to have gone "too far." Neither, so far, has the Court retreated from post-*Lochner* precedents that grant the government broad discretion in determining which takings of property are fairly described as being for "public use." Nevertheless, the Justices undoubtedly took note of the outrage that the *Kelo* decision provoked. It remains to be seen whether a political climate that appears increasingly supportive of claims that governmental policies interfere with property rights will influence future decisions under the Takings Clause.

---

46 *Connolly v. Pension Benefit Guaranty Corp.*, 475 U.S. 211, 225 (1986) (internal quotation marks omitted).

47 For a provocative sketch of the conservative path that the Court has so far declined to travel, see Richard A. Epstein, *Takings: Private Property and the Power of Eminent Domain* (Cambridge, MA: Harvard University Press, 1985).

Concluding Thoughts

The central difficulty confronting the Supreme Court under the Takings Clause is in many ways the same as the central difficulty that the Justices face under the Due Process and Contracts Clauses. From the perspective of fairness, it might appear disturbing when a landowner loses millions of dollars as a result of being denied the "right" to build on wetlands, for example. But a logically prior question is whether the landowner should be seen as having that claimed "right" in the first place. If it is assumed that there is a natural or constitutional "right" to be absolutely free from governmental regulation, then land-use regulation, of course, violates that right and constitutes a "taking" of property – just as other economic regulatory legislation interferes with the "right" to do whatever one wants or to enter whatever contracts on whatever terms one chooses. As the Supreme Court recognized in renouncing *Lochner*, however, to assume that the economy should operate on laissez-faire principles or that there is a general right to freedom from regulation is to assume a controversial economic philosophy that many people do not share and that the Constitution does not necessarily impose.

In the context of the Takings Clause, the philosophy that views all regulation as a deprivation of natural or constitutional rights is particularly untenable. A wetlands owner undoubtedly possesses a property right, but the answer to whether that right includes a privilege to haul in landfill and disrupt drainage and environmental ecosystems cannot be extracted from the necessary meaning of the concept of property. Property and contract rights need to be defined before they can be protected. Almost no one thinks that just because property is mine, I am entitled to use it to emit noises that keep my neighbors awake all night or to spew out fumes, the smell of which would sicken my neighbors and ruin their use of their land. With property rights needing to be defined, Congress, the state legislatures, and city councils all have a role.

Under the Constitution, the courts must oversee the political process to ensure that legislative judgments are reasonable and do not intrude on prerogatives that constitutional guarantees minimally and necessarily entail. But the enduring lesson of the *Lochner* debacle is that economic rights invite specification and adjustment by the political branches of government, exercising their regulatory powers, and not merely interpretation by the courts. As Holmes wrote in his famous *Lochner* dissent, the Court should hesitate to read into the Constitution a single, restrictive economic philosophy that reasonable political majorities need not share.

4 Fundamental Rights "Enumerated" in the Bill of Rights

I N UNITED STATES V. CAROLENE PRODUCTS (1938),[1] THE
Supreme Court considered the constitutionality of a federal
statute that prohibited interstate shipments of "filled milk" –
skimmed milk compounded with nonmilk fats, such as vegetable oil.
Although government lawyers maintained that filled milk might con-
tain threats to human health, the supporting evidence was flimsy. The
real purpose of the statute was almost certainly to protect the dairy
industry, which possessed considerable political clout at the time, against
unwanted competition from a cheaper substitute. Yet the Supreme Court
resoundingly upheld the statute. Less than a year after the demise of the
Lochner regime, judicial deference to legislative judgments was the order
of the day. The bitter lessons taught by *Lochner*'s collapse had sunk in.

But what exactly were those lessons? Was aggressive judicial review
to protect individual liberties to be rejected across the board? Earlier
chapters in this book have shown that the answer was no. In the years
following its *Carolene Products* decision, the Court quickly developed
a new agenda, foreshadowed by a remarkable footnote in that case
that Supreme Court Justice Lewis F. Powell once called "the most celebrated footnote in constitutional law."[2] In that footnote, the Court
explained that although it had largely abandoned review of economic

1 304 U.S. 144 (1938).
2 Lewis F. Powell Jr., "*Carolene Products* Revisited," 82 *Columbia Law Review* 1087
(1982).

legislation for fairness or reasonableness under the Due Process Clause, it would not defer to Congress and the state legislatures with respect to all matters. Most famously, the Court said that statutes "directed at particular religious, or national, or racial minorities" might continue to warrant exacting judicial review[3] – a development later reflected in some of the Court's most lauded decisions under the Equal Protection Clause, including *Brown v. Board of Education*[4] (1954), which forbade race discrimination in the public schools.

Perhaps less famous, but just as important, the *Carolene Products* footnote also insisted that "[t]here may be a narrower scope for operation of the presumption of constitutionality when legislation appears on its face to be within a specific prohibition of the Constitution, such as those of the first ten Amendments, which are deemed to be equally specific when held to be embraced within the Fourteenth [Amendment]." Today, the Court is zealous in protecting many of the guarantees listed in the Bill of Rights, as the first ten amendments are collectively called, including the freedoms of speech and religion discussed in Chapters 1 and 2. Lawyers and judges typically refer to the rights listed in the Bill of Rights as "enumerated," or specifically identified. This terminology aims to mark a contrast with the "unenumerated" or unlisted rights that the Court has sometimes protected in a line of substantive due process cases that once featured the now-rejected *Lochner v. New York*[5] (1905), which recognized a right to freedom of contract, and currently includes *Roe v. Wade*[6] (1973), which recognizes a right to abortion. According to widely prevalent understandings, substantive due process adjudication is suspect, whereas the enforcement of enumerated rights is not.

Having devoted entire chapters to the freedoms of speech and religion, this book cannot discuss all of the rights in the Bill of Rights. To avoid turning a brief introduction to constitutional law into a sprawling

3 304 U.S. at 152 n.4 (citations omitted).
4 347 U.S. 483 (1954).
5 198 U.S. 45 (1905).
6 410 U.S. 113 (1973).

treatise, this chapter deals with just three topics concerning enumerated rights. The first involves the Supreme Court's efforts to enforce provisions of the Bill of Rights that confer procedural guarantees on people who are suspected of criminal behavior or prosecuted for crimes. The right to an attorney is a well-known example. The second topic is the application of the Eighth Amendment's prohibition against cruel and unusual punishments to the death penalty. The third is the Second Amendment right to bear arms. I have chosen to discuss these three topics in part because they are especially politically salient and in part because they provide good vehicles for advancing some of this book's general themes about doctrinal evolution within the dynamic, argumentative practice of constitutional law.

Before addressing these substantive matters, however, I shall say a few words about how the Bill of Rights has come to apply to the states as well as to the federal government. Insofar as the *Carolene Products* agenda requires a distinction between enumerated rights protected by the Bill of Rights and other rights protected by substantive due process, the explanation of this evolution in the Bill of Rights' application abounds in ironies.

Incorporation of the Bill of Rights against the States

As noted in the Introduction, those who wrote and ratified the Bill of Rights saw no need to make its protections applicable against the states, most of which already included bills of rights in their state constitutions. The language of some of the first ten amendments leaves little doubt on this score. For example, the First Amendment begins by mandating that "*Congress* shall make no law," wholly without reference to the states. The Supreme Court resolved any question about the rest of the Bill of Rights when it held in *Barron v. Baltimore*[7] (1833) that other provisions did not apply against the states either.

7 32 U.S. 243 (1833).

In the aftermath of the Civil War, when Congress deliberated whether to propose constitutional amendments to "reconstruct" the Union and especially the South, the states appeared less trustworthy than they had at the founding of the republic. Unlike the Bill of Rights, the Thirteenth, Fourteenth, and Fifteenth Amendments all are written to create rights against the states. Moreover, although the matter has long been freighted with controversy, a number of historians believe that the Privileges or Immunities Clause of the Fourteenth Amendment was originally understood by most observers as encompassing some or all of the guarantees of the Bill of Rights among the "privileges or immunities" that it aimed to protect against the states.[8] As we have seen already, however, the Supreme Court held otherwise in *The Slaughter-House Cases*[9] (1872), discussed in Chapter 3. After *The Slaughter-House Cases*, the Privileges or Immunities Clause was a constitutional dead letter.

The judicial nullification of the Privileges or Immunities Clause left a functional void that the Supreme Court, again as discussed in Chapter 3, turned to the Due Process Clause to fill. During the *Lochner* era, the Court notoriously held that the Due Process Clause gave substantive protection to economic liberties. In an equally significant development that began in the late nineteenth century, the Court started to hold that some of the rights enforceable against the federal government

---

8 Justice Black first argued that the Privileges or Immunities Clause of the Fourteenth Amendment was understood as encompassing some of the guarantees of the Bill of Rights in *Adamson v. California*, 332 U.S. 46, 70–92 (1947) (Black, J., dissenting). Black's *Adamson* dissent included a substantial appendix reviewing the legislative history of the amendment. Ibid. at 92. Soon afterward, Stanford law professor Charles Fairman responded with a lengthy article that most observers thought effectively refuted Black's argument. See Charles Fairman, "Does the Fourteenth Amendment Incorporate the Bill of Rights?," 2 *Stanford Law Review* 5 (1949). More recent research, however, reveals a more complicated picture. See, for example, Akhil Reed Amar, *The Bill of Rights: Creation and Reconstruction* (New Haven, CT: Yale University Press, 1998); William E. Nelson, *The Fourteenth Amendment: From Political Principle to Judicial Doctrine* (Cambridge, MA: Harvard University Press, 1988); Michael K. Curtis, *No State Shall Abridge: The Fourteenth Amendment and the Bill of Rights* (Durham, NC: Duke University Press, 1986).

9 83 U.S. 36 (1872).

under the Bill of Rights – including the First Amendment right to freedom of speech – were part of the "liberty" protected against state interference by the Due Process Clause. In other words, the Supreme Court began enforcing some but not all of the rights included in the Bill of Rights against the states as a matter of substantive due process. The *Carolene Products* footnote left this bizarre, evolving situation in place when it contemplated aggressive judicial review of legislation "within a specific prohibition of the Constitution, such as those of the first ten Amendments, *which are deemed to be equally specific when held to be embraced within the Fourteenth [Amendment]*."

Questions involving which provisions of the Bill of Rights were "incorporated" in the Fourteenth Amendment represented a subject of sometimes fierce controversy from the 1940s through the 1960s. The debates among the Justices were as complex as they were heated, and I shall not attempt to summarize them. Suffice it to say that by the late 1960s and early 1970s, "incorporation doctrine" – which specifies which provisions of the Bill of Rights are "incorporated" within the Due Process Clause of the Fourteenth Amendment and thus apply against the states – had reached a rough equilibrium that has remained relatively stable ever since. That equilibrium has three main components. First, the Due Process Clause incorporates those guarantees of the Bill of Rights that the Supreme Court deems "fundamental." Second, in determining whether a particular right is fundamental, the Court will inquire whether it is "fundamental to the American scheme of justice" as it has existed historically. Under this test, the Court has held that nearly all of the provisions of the Bill of Rights are fundamental but that a few – such as the Seventh Amendment right to trial by a jury (rather than a judge) in civil suits for money damages – are not. Third, when a right is incorporated by the Fourteenth Amendment, it ordinarily applies to states in exactly the same way as it applies to the federal government, but it does not always do so. For example, the Court has held that the Sixth Amendment right to trial by jury in criminal cases forbids the federal government to authorize convictions by less-than-unanimous juries, but that states, if they wish, can provide for less-than-unanimous convictions.[10]

Among the resulting ironies is this: the Supreme Court's enforcement of "enumerated" rights is often contrasted with its identification of "fundamental" rights as a matter of substantive due process (as, for example, in *Roe v. Wade*). Yet, under the incorporation doctrine, the Court must engage in a comparable inquiry to determine which of the rights of the Bill of Rights are sufficiently "fundamental" to be incorporated against the states under the Due Process Clause.

Enumerated Rights to Fair Procedures in Criminal Cases

Many of the rights enumerated in the Bill of Rights are rights to fair procedures in criminal cases. Though ancient in origin, a number of these rights began to assume their modern form during the 1950s and 1960s, when the liberal Warren Court engaged in a controversial reshaping effort. That effort continues to attract criticism, even though it has substantially endured to the current day.

The Warren Court's liberal activism – for so it is almost invariably described – represented a novel development in constitutional history. In appointing the Justices who buried *Lochner*, President Franklin Roosevelt had wanted a Court that would stand out of the way of progressive social legislation, not embark on crusades of its own. The Warren Court, which began to take shape after the appointment of Earl Warren as Chief

---

10 The Court adopted the formula that the Fourteenth Amendment incorporated the procedural rights included in the Bill of Rights that were "fundamental to the American scheme of justice" in *Duncan v. Louisiana*, 391 U.S. 145, 149 (1968). Before the 1960s, the Court had held some of the guarantees of the Bill of Rights to be applicable against the states but only insofar as they were "implicit in the concept of ordered liberty." *Palko v. Connecticut*, 302 U.S. 319, 325 (1937). Under this formula, the demands of due process were "less rigid and more fluid" than the more specific guarantees of the Bill of Rights, and "[t]hat which may, in one setting, constitute a denial of fundamental fairness... may, in other circumstances, and in the light of other considerations, fall short of such denial." *Betts v. Brady*, 316 U.S. 455, 462 (1942).

Justice in 1953, broke with the pattern that the Roosevelt-appointed Justices had established, though not so dramatically as is sometimes imagined. Whether consciously or unconsciously, the Warren Court substantially adopted the philosophy of the *Carolene Products* footnote.[11] Under the Court's "incorporation" rulings, its criminal procedure decisions enforced the "specific" prohibitions of the Bill of Rights governing such matters as freedom from "unreasonable searches and seizures" and the right of criminal defendants to the "assistance of counsel." By no means coincidentally, the Warren Court also construed and extended those rights with the aim of making them meaningful to the disadvantaged, mostly poor Americans who disproportionately found themselves in the maw of the criminal justice system.

In doing so, the Warren Court imposed many new obligations and burdens on state and local governments, with great optimism about the effects that its rulings would achieve. One of the Justices, William Brennan, liked to tell his law clerks that in the Supreme Court, the most important number was five, because with five votes, anything was possible.[12] As we will see, it turned out not to be so. The story of the Warren Court's efforts includes a number of important lessons involving the possibility of doctrinal innovation by the Supreme Court, the importance of public and political responses to the Court's decisions, and the apparently limited capacity of decisions involving criminal procedure to produce fundamental changes in out-of-court behavior by the police.

A brief survey of three lines of cases gives a flavor of the Supreme Court's evolving interpretations of the Bill of Rights provisions that confer rights on suspects in criminal investigations and on criminal defendants. The Sixth Amendment guarantees the right to be represented by counsel. Historically, the right was meaningful, as a practical matter, only to those who could afford lawyers or were lucky enough to be served by

11 See John Hart Ely, *Democracy and Distrust: A Theory of Judicial Review* (Cambridge, MA: Harvard University Press, 1980), 73–77.
12 See H. Jefferson Powell, *Constitutional Conscience: The Moral Dimension of Judicial Decision* (Chicago: University of Chicago Press, 2008), 16.

volunteers. The Justices of the Warren Court considered the resulting situation unfair to poor defendants. In *Gideon v. Wainwright*[13] (1963), the Court expanded the right to the "assistance of counsel" from a right of those who could afford lawyers to be assisted by them into a right to court-appointed lawyers for those accused of serious crimes who could not afford to pay attorneys' fees.[14] Reflective of the Warren Court's concern with the rights of disadvantaged minorities, *Gideon*'s transparently driving concern was equal justice for the poor.

Another line of cases enforces the Fifth Amendment guarantee that no person "shall be compelled in any criminal case to be a witness against himself" by requiring that police provide specific warnings before questioning criminal suspects held in custody. The central decision came in *Miranda v. Arizona*[15] (1966), which prescribes that for a confession uttered during a custodial interrogation to be admissible into evidence, a suspect must be advised "that he has the right to remain silent, that anything he says can be used against him in a court of law, that he has the right to the presence of an attorney, and that if he cannot afford an attorney one will be appointed for him prior to any questioning if he so desires."[16]

Miranda again manifested the Warren Court's characteristic approach, in at least two ways. First, the Court undoubtedly saw *Miranda*, like *Gideon* before it, as ensuring that those who were too poor or unsophisticated to ask for lawyers would benefit from constitutional guarantees on a more nearly equal basis with those who were better off or more sophisticated. Second, without worrying too much about the niceties of constitutional "interpretation," the Court set out to devise a rule that would work effectively in practice to vindicate underlying constitutional

---

13 372 U.S. 335 (1963).

14 *Gideon* itself involved a conviction for a felony, an especially serious crime. Subsequent cases extended the reach of the principle enunciated in *Gideon* to any case in which the defendant receives a jail or prison sentence.

15 384 U.S. 436 (1966).

16 Ibid. at 479.

values. Not every confession obtained in the absence of a *Miranda* warning would constitute compelled self-incrimination in the literal sense. As the Court saw it, however, modern techniques of "custodial police interrogation"[17] brought risks of both psychological and physical coercion that it could not detect effectively on a case-by-case basis. To forestall the risk, the Court laid down the rule, which has as little foundation in the constitutional text as it does in constitutional history, that suspects must receive *Miranda* warnings or their equivalents.

A third line of decisions, beginning with the Warren Court's ruling in *Mapp v. Ohio*[18] (1961), applies the so-called exclusionary rule to state criminal prosecutions. The exclusionary rule is a judge-made rule holding that if the police obtain evidence by violating a person's constitutional rights, the illegally acquired evidence cannot be used against that person in a criminal case. In cases governed by the exclusionary rule, a constitutional violation has already occurred – commonly a police search for evidence in violation of the Fourth Amendment right to be free from "unreasonable searches and seizures." The Fourth Amendment does not say that evidence obtained through unreasonable searches or seizures cannot be admitted in court. Other remedies might exist. For example, the police officer who conducted the unreasonable search might be subjected to discipline or sued for damages. Nevertheless, the Supreme Court has introduced the exclusionary rule as a rule of criminal procedure, barring the use of illegally obtained evidence to prove the commission of a crime. In making the exclusionary rule applicable to prosecutions in state court, the Warren Court again adopted an approach designed to work effectively in practice to protect underlying constitutional values – in this case, by deterring police from violating constitutional rights in the first place. Police officers, the Court reasoned, are less likely to engage in "unreasonable" searches if they know that the fruits of such searches cannot be used to convict a criminal defendant. Again,

17 Ibid. at 439.
18 367 U.S. 643 (1961).

the Court's decision came at an obvious cost to other values. When a court applies the exclusionary rule, a person whose guilt could have been established by the excluded evidence often goes free.

Time, Elections, and Change

Although some observers applauded the Warren Court's commitment to equal justice and even were inspired by it, others were disturbed by the Court's willingness to be pathbreaking. Indeed, in the turbulent 1960s, when many Americans saw traditional values and institutions as under siege, the Warren Court actually frightened some, who perceived its decisions as undermining law enforcement and releasing known criminals on legal "technicalities" (involving, for example, police failures to give *Miranda* warnings or to observe Fourth Amendment prohibitions against "unreasonable" searches and seizures).[19] As I noted in the Introduction, Richard Nixon made an issue of the Warren Court in the 1968 presidential election campaign, in which he pledged to appoint "strict constructionist" Justices to the Supreme Court. Within a year of his inauguration as President, Nixon had nominated the conservative Warren Burger to replace Earl Warren, who retired, as Chief Justice. In fewer than four years, three more Nixon appointments had substantially reshaped the Court.

In the era of the Burger Court (1969–86), and then of the Rehnquist and Roberts Courts that succeeded it, the Warren Court's expansion of criminal defendants' procedural rights has mostly come to a halt. Indeed, over the past three decades, the Court has engaged in notable cutbacks in many areas. Unlike the substantive due process decisions of the *Lochner* era, however, the Warren Court's leading criminal procedural decisions remain on the books. The right to counsel established by *Gideon v. Wainright* endures unchallenged. Perhaps more surprising,

19 See generally John Morton Blum, *Years of Discord: American Politics and Society, 1961–74* (New York: W. W. Norton, 1991), 207–17, 313–14.

Miranda, too, seems securely entrenched, at least in the shrinking category of cases to which it applies. For some time, conservatives held up *Miranda* as a textbook example of judicial "activism" that was threatening to public safety, and they called for the Supreme Court to overrule it. But when the Court finally did expressly reconsider *Miranda* in *Dickerson v. United States*[20] (2000), some of the most conservative Justices joined a 7–2 majority sustaining *Miranda*'s authority. Over time, *Miranda* has woven itself into the fabric of constitutional law. What is more, police practice has adjusted to it, and it has emerged as among the best-known symbols of American constitutional law in film and on television. For a Court that relies on the doctrine of precedent, or respect for prior rulings, to sustain its own decisions in the future, the costs of overruling *Miranda* plainly seemed larger than the benefits.

The Law on the Books versus the Law in Practice

Although the Burger, Rehnquist, and Roberts Courts have left standing the principal landmark decisions of the Warren Court involving constitutional criminal procedure, it would be a mistake to assume that those decisions have effectively achieved all of their aims. Although poor defendants continue to have a right to court-appointed lawyers, such lawyers typically are underpaid and overworked. They have more clients than they can handle. And they respond, in a huge proportion of cases, by steering their clients into a "plea bargain," under which the defendant pleads guilty to a crime but typically receives a shorter sentence than the prosecutor had initially sought. In the absence of a more serious commitment by state governments to fund criminal defenses, poor defendants may thus get little more than an agent to help with plea negotiations, not a committed defender.[21] (Within our criminal justice

20 530 U.S. 428 (2000).

21 The Supreme Court has held that the right to assistance of counsel requires at least minimally competent representation in the plea bargaining process. See, for example, *Lafler v. Cooper*, 132 S. Ct. 1376 (2012), and *Missouri v. Frye*, 131 S. Ct. 1399 (2012).

system as it operates today, well more than 90 percent of convictions for felonies, or serious crimes, come from guilty pleas.[22]) As a result, the gap between criminal justice for the poor and criminal justice for the rich remains huge.

The subsequent histories of *Miranda* and the "exclusionary rule" are harder to chart, in part because the Supreme Court has introduced a number of complex, important exceptions, the details of which are too intricate to consider here.[23] An equally important element of the story is easier to identify in broad terms, though harder to document with full precision. In both *Miranda* and in its exclusionary rule cases, the Warren Court attempted to use constitutional rules involving the evidence that can be introduced in court (confessions and the fruits of illegal searches) to alter what it believed to be wrongful and abusive police practices outside of court (coercive interrogation techniques and unreasonable searches and seizures).[24] There is abundant reason to question how far the Court's rules have achieved their intended out-of-court results. Of perhaps most critical importance, criminal suspects are free to waive their *Miranda* rights and to confess to a crime without speaking to a lawyer, or to consent to searches that would otherwise be unreasonable, thereby taking them out of the constitutionally forbidden "unreasonable" category. Americans, it turns out, waive their *Miranda* rights and consent to police searches with remarkable frequency. Although most Americans have probably heard the *Miranda* warning often enough on

22 In the most recent years for which statistics are available, guilty pleas accounted for more than 96 percent of federal felony convictions and 94 percent of state felony convictions. See *Administrative Office of the U.S. Courts – AOUSC Criminal Master Data File* (Washington, DC: Department of Justice, Bureau of Justice Statistics, 2009); Sean Rosenmerkel, Matthew Durose, and Donald Farole Jr., *Felony Sentences in State Courts, 2006 – Statistical Tables* (Washington, DC: Department of Justice, Bureau of Justice Statistics, 2009), table 4.1.

23 Among the most significant, *Berghuis v. Thompkins*, 130 S. Ct. 2250 (2010), requires a detainee to make an affirmative invocation of *Miranda* rights to benefit from them.

24 See William J. Stuntz, "The Substantive Origins of Criminal Procedure," 105 *Yale Law Journal* 393, 436–39 (1995).

television to be able to recite it verbatim, in one study nearly 80 percent of suspects waived their right to an attorney and agreed to answer police questions without having an attorney present.[25] Nor was it only the innocent who talked: nearly two-thirds of the suspects who waived their *Miranda* rights gave incriminating statements, partial admissions of guilt, or full confessions to their interrogators.[26]

Waiver is an even larger issue with respect to Fourth Amendment rights. If a police officer approaches a random person on the street and asks to search her purse or backpack, for example, the officer has no obligation to advise her that in the absence of her consent the search would be unreasonable and that any fruits of an unreasonable search could not be admitted in court to prove her guilty of a crime. Nor need the officer ask nicely or explain to the target of his requests (or demands) that she has a right to say no. Under these circumstances, many people may well think that they have no choice but to "consent" to searches and seizures. For example, a study of warrantless highway stops in Maryland found that 96 percent of drivers consented to have their cars searched, including many who were transporting large quantities of illegal drugs.[27] In these and other contexts, "consent" comes even to the kind of unreasonable and invasive searches that the Fourth Amendment was designed to prevent, and it comes especially often from the poor and the legally uninformed. In the rare cases in which consent is not forthcoming, some observers claim that the police frequently lie and say that it was.[28]

In the eyes of some legal scholars, experience with *Miranda* and the exclusionary rule illustrates the difficulty, if not the impossibility, of using in-court rules of procedure (involving the admissibility of evidence) to

25 See Richard A. Leo, "Inside the Interrogation Room," 86 *Journal of Criminal Law & Criminology* 266, 276 (1996).
26 See ibid. at 280.
27 See Samuel R. Gross and Katherine Y. Barnes, "Road Work: Racial Profiling and Drug Interdiction on the Highway," 101 *Michigan Law Review* 651, 672, 699–700 (2002).
28 See, for example, Yale Kamisar, "In Defense of the Search and Seizure Exclusionary Rule," 26 *Harvard Journal of Law & Public Policy* 119, 130–31 (2003).

reform the out-of-court practices of institutions such as the police. The same experience highlights a point too often overlooked in legal scholarship: frequently, a large gap exists between constitutional law as it appears on the books and constitutional law as it operates in practice.

The Eighth Amendment Prohibition against Cruel and Unusual Punishment

After a criminal suspect has been convicted of a crime, the Eighth Amendment prohibits the infliction of "cruel and unusual punishments." In determining which punishments are cruel and unusual, the Supreme Court, since the Warren era, has said that it will look to "the evolving standards of decency that mark the progress of a maturing society."[29] This formulation contemplates that some punishments that might have seemed acceptable in the eighteenth century, when the Bill of Rights was initially adopted, would not pass constitutional muster today.

The most controversial cases applying the Eighth Amendment have involved the death penalty. When the Constitution was written, every one of the thirteen states authorized capital punishment for some crimes. The Bill of Rights, adopted soon afterward, refers to "capital" cases.[30] By the middle of the twentieth century, however, serious arguments had emerged that the Supreme Court should hold the death penalty unconstitutional. Those arguments had two main components. First, as measured by evolving standards of decency, capital punishment has become morally objectionable. (In the view of some, its objectionability, if any, would depend on the question – to which investigation still appears to have yielded no clear answer[31] – about whether it is an effective

---

29 *Trop v. Dulles*, 356 U.S. 86, 101 (1958).

30 U.S. Const., Amend. V.

31 See, for example, John J. Donohue and Justin Wolfers, "Uses and Abuses of Empirical Evidence in the Death Penalty Debate," 58 *Stanford Law Review* 791, 804–21 (2005); Jeffrey Fagan, "Death and Deterrence Redux: Science, Law, and Causal Reasoning on Capital Punishment," 4 *Ohio State Journal of Criminal Law* 255, 269–89 (2006).

deterrent to homicides.) Second, the processes that lead prosecutors to request and juries to impose death sentences are too prone to caprice and mistake to be acceptable in practice, even if there are some cases in which capital punishment would be permissible in principle.[32] Among other things, death sentences exhibit troubling racial disparities. Blacks are more likely to receive the death penalty than are whites, and people who kill whites are more likely to be sentenced to death than are people who kill blacks.[33] Worse yet, there can be no certain guarantee that a state will not sometimes execute the innocent.

In 1972, in *Furman v. Georgia*,[34] the Supreme Court shocked nearly all observers by announcing the stunning conclusion that the death penalty as then administered in the United States was cruel and unusual and thus violated the Eighth Amendment. The Court that decided *Furman*, and thereby invalidated the death penalty statutes of thirty-nine states, was badly fractured. Four Justices dissented, each in a separate opinion, with Justice Lewis Powell protesting that the Constitution's text and history made the ruling wholly unsupportable.[35] What is more, the five Justices who composed the majority did not agree in their reasoning, with each writing a separate opinion to explain his thinking. (One observer described *Furman* as "not so much a case as a badly orchestrated opera, with nine characters taking turns to offer their own

32 See, for example, Charles L. Black Jr., *Capital Punishment: The Inevitability of Caprice and Mistake* (New York: W. W. Norton, 1974); Samuel R. Gross, "The Risks of Death: Why Erroneous Convictions Are Common in Capital Cases," 44 *Buffalo Law Review* 469 (1996); Michael Burkhead and James Luginbuhl, "Sources of Bias and Arbitrariness in the Capital Trial," 50 *Journal of Social Issues* 103 (1994).

33 See, for example, David C. Baldus, Charles Pulaski, and George Woodworth, "Comparative Review of Death Sentences: An Empirical Study of the Georgia Experience," 74 *Journal of Criminal Law and Criminology* 661 (1983). The Supreme Court considered this study at length in *McCleskey v. Kemp*, 481 U.S. 279 (1987). See also U.S. General Accounting Office, *Death Penalty Sentencing: Research Indicates Pattern of Racial Disparities* (Washington, DC: Report to the House and Senate Judiciary Committees, 1990), which reviews twenty-eight different studies on the racially disparate application of the death penalty.

34 408 U.S. 238 (1972).

35 Ibid. at 417–19 (Powell, J., dissenting).

arias"[36] in the form of more than 230 pages worth of opinions.) Among the Justices in the *Furman* majority, two appeared to believe that the death penalty had ceased to comport with contemporary standards of fairness. Three other Justices lodged versions of a related but different objection. Although thirty-nine states and the federal government maintained death penalty statutes on their books, by 1965, the total number of executions in the United States had fallen to seven. By 1972, no executions had occurred for five years (in part because of aggressive legal challenges mounted by the National Association for the Advancement of Colored People's Legal Defense Fund). With executions occurring so rarely, and with there being so little apparent consistency in prosecutors' decisions whether to seek the death penalty and juries' decisions whether to inflict it, three Justices thought that the death penalty was cruel and unusual "in the same way," as Justice Potter Stewart put it, that "being struck by lightning is cruel and unusual."[37]

Just as *Furman* stunned the country, the country's response to *Furman* must have stunned the Court. Within a few years, thirty-five states had reenacted death penalty legislation, crafted to attempt to avoid the caprice in administration that some of the Justices had found objectionable. The new statutes took one or the other of two tacks. Some attempted to create greater consistency in application by directing judges and juries to look at particular factors in determining whether to impose capital punishment on particular defendants. Other statutes abolished sentencing discretion altogether by making the death penalty mandatory for specified crimes.

In *Gregg v. Georgia*[38] (1976), the Supreme Court gave its blessing to the first of these two strategies. Like other schemes that the Court has subsequently approved, the Georgia statute at issue in *Gregg* prescribed a two-stage sequence in capital cases. First, a jury determines

---

36 Robert Weisberg, "Deregulating Death," *1983 Supreme Court Review* 305, 315.
37 *Furman*, 408 U.S. at 309 (Potter, J., concurring).
38 428 U.S. 153 (1976).

guilt or innocence. Then, if the defendant is found guilty, a decision about whether to impose death or a lesser penalty is made separately. In the second, penalty phase, the sentencing body (whether a jury or a judge[39]) must be given statutory guidance about "aggravating" factors (beyond those involved in less heinous murders, typically punished by imprisonment) that might tend to make execution an appropriate punishment. At the same time, the sentencer must also be permitted to consider "mitigating" factors, such as aspects of the defendant's character or upbringing, that might make execution unduly harsh. In another pair of decisions, handed down on the same day, the Court invalidated statutes that wholly eliminated sentencing discretion by making the death penalty mandatory for some crimes.[40] The conjunction of these rulings establishes that a statute authorizing the death penalty must structure and limit a judge's or jury's deliberation about the appropriateness of execution as punishment for a particular offender but cannot categorically mandate capital sentences. The first of these requirements reflects a demand for consistency; the second demands individualized judgments of desert, with opportunity for the exercise of leniency. There is an obvious tension between these mandates, though perhaps not one that rises to the level of a logical contradiction.[41]

---

39 Although *Gregg* and the companion case *Jurek v. Texas*, 428 U.S. 262 (1976), involved statutory schemes that assigned the sentencing decision to the jury, in *Proffitt v. Florida*, 428 U.S. 242 (1976), also decided the same day, the Court upheld a scheme that assigned the decision to the trial judge.

40 See *Woodson v. North Carolina*, 428 U.S. 280 (1976), and *Roberts v. Louisiana*, 428 U.S. 325 (1976).

41 See *Callins v. Collins*, 510 U.S. 1141, 1144 (1994) (Blackmun, J., dissenting from the denial of certiorari) ("Experience has taught us that the constitutional goal of eliminating arbitrariness and discrimination from the administration of death can never be achieved without compromising an equally essential component of fundamental fairness – individualized sentencing."). See also ibid. at 1141–43 (Scalia, J., concurring in the denial of certiorari) (agreeing that the commands are "incompatible" and criticizing "the creation of false, untextual, and unhistorical contradictions within 'the Court's Eighth Amendment jurisprudence.'").

Roughly a decade after *Gregg*, in *McCleskey v. Kemp*[42] (1987), the Justices confronted arguments that race-based disparities in capital sentencing rendered the death penalty unconstitutional under either the Eighth Amendment or the Equal Protection Clause. By a 5–4 vote, a bitterly divided Court answered in the negative. General statistics about sentencing outcomes could not prove that racism caused particular charging and sentencing decisions, the Court held, and it was unwilling to authorize postconviction inquiries into the thought processes of prosecutors and jurors in particular cases. Given unrefuted statistical evidence of racial disparities in the imposition of capital sentences – including a study showing that defendants charged with killing white victims were 4.3 times more likely to be sentenced to death than defendants charged with killing blacks – the majority concluded that a different ruling would have made the death penalty nearly impossible to enforce. The majority refused to countenance that result.

Although the Supreme Court has held consistently since 1976 that the death penalty is not categorically impermissible, it has ruled in an expanding sequence of cases that capital punishment is morally excessive, or "grossly disproportionate," as a punishment for offenses other than murder (including rape, even when the victim is a child).[43] The Court has also held that the death penalty is cruel and unusual as applied to particular categories of offenders, including juveniles,[44] the insane,[45] and people with mental retardation.[46] In all of these cases, the Court's

---

42 481 U.S. 279 (1987).

43 In *Enmund v. Florida*, 458 U.S. 782 (1982), for example, the Court held the death penalty unconstitutional as applied to a getaway car driver for a robbery in which two murders occurred, because the driver did not intend that a killing would take place and did not himself kill or attempt to kill the victims. In *Coker v. Georgia*, 433 U.S. 584 (1977), the Court held that capital punishment was an unconstitutional penalty for the rape of an adult, and in *Kennedy v. Louisiana*, 554 U.S. 407 (2008), it extended this holding to the rape of a child.

44 *Roper v. Simmons*, 543 U.S. 551 (2005).

45 *Ford v. Wainwright*, 477 U.S. 399 (1986).

46 *Atkins v. Virginia*, 536 U.S. 304 (2002).

decisions have provoked bitter dissents that the results lacked support in the Constitution's text and history and constituted judicial overreaching.

The Second Amendment and the "Right to Keep and Bear Arms"

Uniquely among the provisions of the Bill of Rights, the Second Amendment has its own preamble: "A well regulated Militia, being necessary to the security of a free State, the right of the people to keep and bear Arms, shall not be infringed." When the Second Amendment was drafted and ratified in the eighteenth century, "the militia" consisted of the free males within a state who were capable of bearing arms.[47] So defined, the militia was widely believed "necessary to the security of a free state" for two reasons. First, it stood ready to repel foreign invaders. Second, the militia provided the people with an ultimate safeguard in case the government itself – like the government of King George III – should ever became tyrannical.

The Supreme Court first confronted a question about the meaning of the right "to keep and bear Arms" in *United States v. Miller*[48] (1939), a case involving a federal statute that prohibited transporting unregistered sawed-off shotguns (among other firearms) across state lines. The Justices concluded unanimously that the statute did not violate the Second Amendment. Noting the textual linkage of the right to bear arms to the needs of "a well regulated Militia," the Court pointed out that sawed-off shotguns had no plausible military usage. (As the historian Garry Wills once put it, "To bear arms is, in itself, a military term. One does not bear arms against a rabbit."[49])

With *Miller* on the books, several generations of constitutional lawyers largely took it for granted that both the federal government and

47 Mark V. Tushnet, *Out of Range: Why the Constitution Can't End the Battle over Guns* (Oxford: Oxford University Press, 2007), 10.

48 307 U.S. 174 (1939).

49 Gary Wills, "To Keep and Bear Arms," *New York Review of Books*, September 21, 1995, at 62, 64.

the states could ban the possession and use of firearms except insofar as the states deemed their possession necessary to service in a well-regulated militia. Over this period, "gun control" legislation became progressively more stringent in some parts of the country, partly in response to an alarming rise in violent crime in the 1960s and 1970s. During these decades, restrictions on gun possession and use fit with an anticrime agenda that political conservatives favored as much as liberals.

The politics of gun control changed substantially during the latter decades of the twentieth century, however, as many conservatives began to perceive prohibitions on gun ownership as threats to the lifestyles of hunters, sportsmen, and those who cherished traditional rights of self-defense. Over this period, the National Rifle Association became a zealous defender of rights to handguns as well as rifles. As gun control became a partisan political issue, opponents of regulation increasingly presented themselves as champions of Second Amendment rights.[50]

For only the second time in its history, the Supreme Court considered the constitutionality of gun-control legislation in the 2008 case of *District of Columbia v. Heller.*[51] *Heller* presented a challenge to one of the most stringent regulatory statutes in the country. The District of Columbia banned virtually all handguns, and it required that other firearms – including rifles – be kept under conditions that would render them useless for defense against sudden threats, including home invasions. By a 5–4 vote, the Court found in *Heller* that the Second Amendment protects a personal right to possess guns for self-defense.

Writing for the Court, Justice Antonin Scalia – a self-described "originalist" – canvassed a broad range of historical sources. Although he acknowledged that the perceived need for a militia may have motivated the drafting and ratification of the Second Amendment, he concluded

---

50 See Reva B. Siegel, "Dead or Alive: Originalism as Popular Constitutionalism in *Heller*," 122 *Harvard Law Review* 191 (2008).
51 554 U.S. 570 (2008).

that the right protected by what he called the Amendment's "operative clause," as opposed to its preamble, was originally understood as encompassing a broader, personal entitlement to possess weapons for hunting and self-defense, especially in the home. Having recognized that the Second Amendment creates personal rights to keep and use guns for self-defense, Justice Scalia then noted ways in which that right might be limited. He explained that "nothing in our opinion should be taken to cast doubt on longstanding prohibitions on the possession of firearms by felons and the mentally ill, or laws forbidding the carrying of firearms in sensitive places such as schools and government buildings, or laws imposing conditions and qualifications on the commercial sale of arms."[52] Justice Scalia also wrote that the Second Amendment protects only the right to possess weapons "in common use." As Justice Scalia recognized, limiting gun rights to weapons in common use means that "the Militia" could not today perform the functions that the Second Amendment's preamble contemplated. Without highly sophisticated weapons, a modern militia could neither defend a state against foreign invasion nor fight off a tyrannical national government. "But the fact that modern developments have limited the degree of fit between the prefatory clause and the protected right cannot change our interpretation of the right," Scalia wrote.[53] The upshot is that, under *Heller*, Second Amendment rights are wholly disjoined from the founders' purpose of preserving a well-regulated militia. On the one hand, the right to "bear arms" extends to the use of nonmilitary weapons for sport and self-defense. On the other hand, it bestows no right to the kind of weapons that a militia would need to discharge "a well regulated Militia['s]" historical functions.

There were two dissenting opinions in *Heller*, each representing the views of four Justices. One, by Justice Breyer, argued that even if the Second Amendment protected a right to possess weapons for self-defense, that right should be subject to reasonable regulation to

52 Ibid. at 626–27.
53 Ibid. at 627–28.

protect the public interest. So reasoning, he thought that the District of Columbia's regulation, "which focuses upon the presence of handguns in high-crime urban areas, represents a permissible legislative response to a serious, indeed life-threatening, problem."[54] The other dissenting opinion, by Justice Stevens, was as ostensibly originalist as the majority opinion, but it came to the opposite conclusion. Examining largely the same historical materials as Justice Scalia, Stevens thought it clear that those who wrote and ratified the Second Amendment had sought to create a constitutional right to the kinds of guns necessary for a well-regulated militia, not a right to keep handguns for personal use.

With all nine Justices in *Heller* having either written or joined opinions that purported rest on the Second Amendment's original understanding, it is striking that the Court nevertheless divided 5–4 concerning the outcome – and that the Justices did so along what commentators routinely identify as ideological lines. The Court's five most conservative Justices reached a result that most political conservatives undoubtedly welcomed. Correspondingly, the Court's four more liberal Justices arrived at a conclusion that most liberals would applaud for policy reasons, whatever the history might have been. Even when taking guidance from history, the Justices may be engaged in the search for a "usable" past that supports practically sensible results in the modern world. Even if they are not consciously motivated to do so, modern psychological research shows that most people – presumably including most Justices – have strong predispositions to view evidence as supporting conclusions that they find congenial.[55] It could perhaps go without saying that liberals and conservatives characteristically tend to differ in their views about which regulations of gun possession would be practically sensible.

---

54 Ibid. at 681–82 (Breyer, J., dissenting).

55 For a fascinating discussion of the modern psychological research and its pertinence to constitutional adjudication, see Dan M. Kahan, "The Supreme Court, 2010 Term – Foreword: Neutral Principles, Motivated Cognition, and Some Problems for Constitutional Law," 125 *Harvard Law Review* 1 (2011).

Two years after *Heller*, in *McDonald v. City of Chicago*[56] (2010), the Court again divided along a conservative/liberal fault line in holding, 5–4, that the Second Amendment right to bear arms is a "fundamental" one that the Fourteenth Amendment incorporates, and thus makes applicable against the states, via the Due Process Clause.

---

56 130 S. Ct. 3020 (2010). Justice Thomas, in a concurring opinion that no other Justice joined, would have held that incorporation occurred via the Privileges or Immunities Clause. See ibid. at 3059 (Thomas, J., concurring).

5   Equal Protection of the Laws

No State shall...deny to any person within its jurisdiction the equal
protection of the laws.
> – Equal Protection Clause of the Fourteenth Amendment

I N 1994, JENNIFER GRATZ APPLIED FOR ADMISSION TO THE
University of Michigan. Gratz was a good student. Her
adjusted high school grade-point average was 3.8 on a 4-point
scale, and she had achieved a solid but not top-notch score on a standardized college admissions test. At many colleges, this record would
have ensured admission. At the University of Michigan, it did not. After
applying in the fall, Gratz received a letter in January notifying her that
she would need to wait until April for a final decision: although she was
"well qualified," she was "less competitive than the students who have
been admitted on first review." In April a second letter arrived, this one
with the news that Gratz had been rejected.

Unwilling to accept this result, Gratz filed suit in federal court, alleging that the University of Michigan had violated her Fourteenth Amendment right not to be deprived of "the equal protection of the laws." In
particular, Gratz, who is white, argued that Michigan unconstitutionally
discriminated against her by granting race-based admissions preferences
to members of historically underrepresented minority groups.

The facts of *Gratz v. Bollinger*[1] (2003) were complicated, in part because the University of Michigan's undergraduate admissions policy – like those at many elite colleges – took a number of factors into account. Under the system that Gratz challenged in the Supreme Court, the university ranked applicants on a scale that included 150 possible points. Of those, 110 were based on high school grades, standardized test scores, and the rigor of an applicant's high school program. Beyond these relatively objective indicia of academic achievement, it was possible to earn points for leadership, the quality of an application essay, or residence in the state of Michigan. "Legacy" applicants – those whose parents had attended the University of Michigan – received four points. One category grouped together, and provided twenty points for, being a member of an underrepresented racial minority group, coming from a socioeconomically challenged background, being a recruited athlete, or being designated by the provost for special treatment.

Under this system, Gratz would have been admitted if she had come from a socioeconomically challenged background, was a recruited athlete, or had been assigned a preference by the provost (perhaps because of family ties or wealth, some of which might have been dangled as available for donation to the university). Gratz would also have earned admission if she had recorded sufficiently better grades or test scores and possibly if she had demonstrated more leadership or had a parent who was a Michigan graduate. But Gratz did not complain about being "discriminated against" on any of these bases. She argued solely that the University of Michigan denied her the equal protection of the laws by giving a twenty-point preference to members of racial minority groups.

The Supreme Court agreed and held Michigan's undergraduate admissions scheme to be unconstitutional – although, as I subsequently explain, in a separate case decided on the same day, the Justices upheld the different affirmative action program used by the University of Michigan Law School, in which race was taken into account but made

1 539 U.S. 244 (2003).

a smaller and less rigid difference. Many complications thus lie ahead. Even without those complications, however, *Gratz v. Bollinger* illustrates the central features of modern equal protection doctrine and raises many of the questions that surround it. A few bear noting at the outset.

The Equal Protection Clause does not prohibit all forms of governmental classification or discrimination, nor do all bases for governmental discrimination trigger searching judicial scrutiny. The University of Michigan gives preferences to applicants with high grades over applicants with low grades and to Michigan residents over residents of other states. It prefers athletes to nonathletes and the children of alumni to applicants who are not the children of alumni. Had Gratz argued that the University of Michigan could not discriminate on any of these grounds, her argument under the Equal Protection Clause almost surely would have failed. (This, presumably, is why Gratz raised no such challenges.) But why does the Equal Protection Clause permit so much governmental discrimination? Why would the Court have upheld governmental policies that discriminate against applicants who have relatively weak grades or test scores, come from states other than Michigan, or are not star athletes or the children of alumni?

In contrast with nearly all other bases for governmental decision making, race-based classifications draw heightened judicial scrutiny. When Gratz claimed that she was discriminated against on the basis of race, she had a winning argument. The Court treats race-based classifications as "suspect," unlike classifications based on test scores or, in some contexts, family background (as in the case of alumni children). But what is so different and special about race? Or if it is obvious what is "special" about race, what other grounds for governmental classification, if any, should be viewed as similarly "suspect" and thus as presumptively unconstitutional? Should classifications based on gender be treated as suspect? Classifications based on homosexuality?

In treating some bases for discrimination as "suspect" and others as not, modern equal protection doctrine appears not to reflect the original understanding of the Equal Protection Clause. There is little or no evidence that the Equal Protection Clause, adopted in the aftermath of the Civil War, was originally understood to bar race-based preferences for racial minorities – the kind of "race discrimination" challenged by Jennifer Gratz. Indeed, although many Americans might be surprised to learn it, the evidence suggests that the framers and ratifiers of the Equal Protection Clause did not even view it as banning all laws discriminating against racial minorities. This is one reason, though by no means the only one, that it took until 1954 – nearly a hundred years after the ratification of the Equal Protection Clause – for the Supreme Court to invalidate legally segregated education in *Brown v. Board of Education*.[2] How, then, did the Court arrive at its celebrated decision in *Brown*? Do the arguments supporting the result in *Brown* point clearly to the conclusion that the affirmative action program at issue in *Gratz* violated the Equal Protection Clause?

Whether or not the Supreme Court admits it, it inevitably makes lots of moral judgments in applying the Equal Protection Clause. But are those pure judgments of personal morality, or do other considerations come into play? If the latter, what considerations tend to influence the Court's decisions?

In the course of surveying modern equal protection doctrine, this chapter elaborates on the points that I have highlighted and attempts to answer the questions that I have just raised.

Equal Protection and the Constitution

Although the Declaration of Independence proclaimed that "all men are created equal," the original Constitution included no general guarantee of equal protection of the laws. Indeed, as noted in the Introduction, the original Constitution contemplated the continued existence of slavery. Following the Civil War, Reconstruction Congresses proposed and the states ratified the Thirteenth Amendment, which abolished

2 347 U.S. 483 (1954).

slavery, and then the Fourteenth Amendment, which provides that "[n]o State shall...deny to any person within its jurisdiction the equal protection of the laws." Today, the equal protection guarantee ranks among the centerpieces of the Constitution. No provision more profoundly reflects the nation's ideals. As with some other constitutional guarantees, however, current doctrine under the Equal Protection Clause owes far more to historically unfolding cultural forces than to original understandings.

As perhaps the most obvious measure of cultural influence, the Supreme Court today applies the equal protection guarantee to federal as well as to state legislation, even though the Equal Protection Clause refers only to what "no State" may deny. This practice traces to a 1954 decision in which the Court pronounced it simply "unthinkable" that the Constitution could tolerate race-based discrimination by the federal government while condemning identical discrimination by the states.[3] To justify its conclusion, the Court held that the Due Process Clause of the Fifth Amendment includes a guarantee of basic governmental fairness that condemns race discrimination. This ruling drew no support from history or original constitutional understanding, and the Court did not pretend otherwise. The Fifth Amendment was adopted at a time when the Constitution provided for slavery; then, no one thought it barred race discrimination.

Cultural forces have played nearly as large a role in shaping judicial doctrine under the Equal Protection Clause itself. By all accounts, the principal purpose of the Fourteenth Amendment (in which the Equal Protection Clause appears) was to protect former slaves and their descendants against the most invidious forms of state discrimination. But the framers and ratifiers of the Fourteenth Amendment inhabited a pervasively racist world, much of which they apparently did not intend to challenge, at least immediately. Congress itself maintained segregated viewing galleries throughout its debates about the Fourteenth

3 *Bolling v. Sharpe*, 347 U.S. 497, 500 (1954).

Amendment. In addition, almost no one appears to have thought that the Fourteenth Amendment barred state and local governments from operating racially segregated public schools or from prohibiting interracial marriages.[4] Among the states then operating segregated schools, none changed its practices upon the amendment's ratification.

In attempting to explain the original meaning of the Fourteenth Amendment, historians have emphasized that the principal drafters intended the centrally operative provision to be the Privilege or Immunities Clause (which was briefly discussed in Chapter 3): "No State shall make or enforce any law which shall abridge the privileges or immunities of citizens of the United States." According to the most widely accepted account, the framers recognized at least two categories of rights – "fundamental" or "civil" rights, on the one hand, and lesser rights, including "social" rights, on the other hand.[5] The framers apparently expected the Privileges or Immunities Clause to guarantee fundamental rights to everyone, including African Americans, but not necessarily to mandate equality in all spheres of governmental conduct. According to this same account, the framers regarded the Equal Protection Clause as reinforcing the demand for equality with respect to fundamental rights but not necessarily as guaranteeing that all rights, including rights to sit in public galleries or to attend public schools, must be distributed without regard to race.

Although this is probably the most commonly accepted account of the background history, it should not be pressed too dogmatically. With

---

4 See Michael J. Klarman, "An Interpretive History of Modern Equal Protection," 90 *Michigan Law Review* 213, 252, n.180 (1991) (citing and discussing authorities). For a rare dissenting view, based largely on unsuccessful congressional efforts to forbid school segregation under the 1875 Civil Rights Act, see Michael W. McConnell, "Originalism and the Desegregation Decisions," 81 *Virginia Law Review* 947 (1995). For a critical response, see Michael J. Klarman, "Brown, Originalism, and Constitutional Theory," 81 *Virginia Law Review* 1881 (1995).

5 See Alexander M. Bickel, "The Original Understanding and the Segregation Decision," 69 *Harvard Law Review* 1, 12–17, 56–58 (1955). See also Klarman, "An Interpretive History of Modern Equal Protection," 235, n.95 (reviewing subsequent debate including the view that most of the Fourteenth Amendment's ratifiers viewed it as protecting only fundamental rights).

the Fourteenth Amendment, as with other constitutional provisions, the framers and ratifiers did not reach consensus on their expectations and write those expectations into law. On many points, they undoubtedly disagreed among themselves. They also worked against the background of a moral tradition opposing slavery and celebrating the ideal of natural rights, shared by all human beings. Some historians and constitutional theorists thus maintain that the Equal Protection Clause constitutionalizes a moral ideal and that it is the moral ideal of equality, not the framers' specific expectations, that ultimately ought to matter in constitutional adjudication.[6] Again, however, virtually no one contends that a majority of the framers and ratifiers specifically expected or intended the Fourteenth Amendment to outlaw all forms of race-based discrimination.

As discussed in Chapter 3, the Supreme Court dashed the framers' expectations for the Privileges or Immunities Clause in *The Slaughter-House Cases*[7] (1872), which construed the Privileges or Immunities Clause so narrowly as to render it almost meaningless. Within a few years, however, the Equal Protection Clause took on a life of its own and has since achieved a significance apparently never contemplated by the framing generation. Under current doctrine, most governmental classifications are subject to judicial scrutiny under a "rational basis" test similar to that applied to economic regulatory legislation under the Due Process Clause in the post-*Lochner* era. But the Court deems a few bases for classification, such as race, to be constitutionally "suspect." Suspect classifications attract "strict" judicial scrutiny and will be upheld only if "necessary to promote a compelling governmental interest."

6 See, for example, William E. Nelson, *The Fourteenth Amendment: From Political Principle to Judicial Doctrine* (Cambridge, MA: Harvard University Press, 1988) (arguing that the framers and ratifiers were mostly concerned with general moral ideals and did not attempt to reach clear understandings with respect to many specific applications); Ronald Dworkin, *Freedom's Law* (Cambridge, MA: Harvard University Press, 1996), 8–10 (arguing that whatever the framers' specific expectations, the Equal Protection Clause embodies a moral principle, which must be interpreted in light of its ultimate moral meaning).
7 83 U.S. 36 (1872).

Rational Basis Review

Most if not all laws create classifications and provide different treatment for people in different categories. Tax laws sometimes require those who earn larger incomes to pay higher rates than those who earn smaller incomes. The blind cannot get driver's licenses. Even criminal laws have a classificatory effect. A law against theft sorts people into two categories, thieves and nonthieves. The government punishes the lawbreakers but not the law abiding. As these examples demonstrate, the Equal Protection Clause cannot sensibly command that the government treat everyone "the same." The rich can be treated differently from the poor in setting tax rates and the blind treated differently from the sighted in distributing driver's licenses. Instead of insisting that everyone be treated "the same," the Equal Protection Clause mandates only that "like cases" – those who are the same in relevant ways – should be treated alike. In other words, the clause's guiding principle condemns discriminations only among those who are relevantly similar. Thus comes the central question for equal protection analysis: When are cases "alike," or when are people sufficiently similar in relevant respects, so that they must be treated the same?

In its central range of operation, equal protection doctrine answers this question by applying a test of means-ends rationality to governmental classifications. The government can award drivers' licenses to those with good vision while withholding licenses from the blind because this classificatory scheme rationally advances a legitimate governmental interest in highway safety. Viewed in light of that interest, the blind and the sighted are not similarly situated: the blind are less likely to be safe drivers. By the same token, the government can classify thieves differently from nonthieves and impose restraints on the former but not on the latter because this difference in treatment rationally promotes a legitimate governmental interest in deterring theft.

As already noted, the rational basis test used to test ordinary or nonsuspect classifications under the Equal Protection Clause closely parallels the rational basis test used in the post-*Lochner* era to assess economic regulatory legislation under the Due Process Clause. Perhaps for that reason, the equal protection test is similarly deferential in most applications.[8] The Supreme Court hesitates to say either that the government's ends or purposes are not legitimate or that there is no rational connection between ends and means. In the post-*Lochner* world, if the government chooses to tax the rich at a higher rate than the poor (or a lower one), or to assist dairy farmers but not cranberry growers, the Court will not second-guess its judgments.

This is why, as I have suggested, the Court would almost certainly have upheld most if not all of the nonracial criteria used by the University of Michigan in its undergraduate admissions process. The university wants to admit good students who will make the best use of a college education. This is a legitimate purpose, to which selection based on high school grades and test scores is rationally related. It is also legitimate for the university to want competitive athletic teams. Preferences for recruited athletes rationally promote this goal. Preferences for alumni children may pose slightly greater difficulties, but they too are probably acceptable. Within a highly deferential framework for evaluation, alumni preferences might be thought to advance legitimate interests in maintaining good relations with past graduates (who may be good candidates to make financial contributions to the school). Such preferences might also be defended by reference to an interest in admitting those students who are likely to have the longest-standing desires to attend the University of Michigan. Nor is it a problem that the university's policies promote a variety of purposes, not just one. A single law or policy may aim to advance multiple goals, and a classification will be upheld if it is rationally related to any.

Although the Supreme Court almost always accords great deference to legislative judgments in applying rational basis review, there are

---

8 See, for example, *FCC v. Beach Communications, Inc.,* 508 U.S. 307, 313–14 (1993) (emphasizing that rational basis review "is a paradigm of judicial restraint").

occasional exceptions. A revealing study identified 110 cases in which the Court applied the rational basis test during the twenty-five-year period from 1971 to 1996.[9] In one hundred of those cases, the Court upheld the challenged statute or regulation, but in ten cases, or about 9 percent of the total, the Court found a constitutional violation. More interesting is that the Court, in those ten cases, appeared to apply what the study's author termed a "heightened" form of rationality review. In other words, although the Court purported to apply the same test in all 110 cases, in fact it conducted a far more searching inquiry in a subset of the cases than it did in most of the others.[10]

U.S. Department of Agriculture v. Moreno[11] (1973) illustrates the pattern. *Moreno* held that a federal statute offended equal protection principles by denying food stamps to "any household containing an individual who is unrelated to any other member of the household."[12] The Court might easily have upheld the statute by ruling that Congress could permissibly choose to subsidize only households that resemble traditional families. In determining eligibility for spending programs, Congress generally enjoys great flexibility to protect the public treasury by drawing lines, and lines that give preferences to families and family members are permissible in many contexts. Instead, despite its frequent assertions that legislation will be upheld if there is any imaginable basis on which it might be supported, the Court focused on what it said was the statute's real purpose – to exclude "hippie" communes from achieving eligibility. Pronouncing that "a bare congressional desire to harm a politically unpopular group cannot constitute a *legitimate* governmental interest,"[13] the Court invalidated the challenged statutory exclusion.

9 See Robert C. Farrell, "Successful Rational Basis Claims in the Supreme Court from the 1971 Term through Romer v. Evans," 32 *Indiana Law Review* 357, 370 (1999).
10 See ibid. at 357–58.
11 413 U.S. 528 (1973).
12 Ibid. at 529.
13 Ibid. at 534.

In contrast with the Court's dominant line of highly deferential deci-sions, *Moreno* exhibits what might be termed an occasional or recessive judicial willingness to engage in serious review of the substantive fair-ness of legislative classifications, even in "rational basis" cases. Plainly implicit in this approach is an assumption that fairness is at least not wholly in the eye of the beholder. Although most legislative judgments fall within a permissible range, some do not. It bears emphasis that the Court rarely adopts the morally judgmental disposition that it displayed in *Moreno*, at least in rational basis cases. The Court's dominant ten-dency is to perform review so deferential as to amount to a rubber stamp, including in cases in which some legislatively preferred special interests receive benefits denied to or escape burdens imposed on others. (Think again of a statute giving tax breaks to dairy farmers but not cranberry growers.) But the recessive disposition to assess the substantive fairness of legislative classifications refuses to disappear entirely. It crops up from time to time, sometimes in unexpected cases, such as *Moreno*.

Race and the Constitution: Invidious Discrimination

In contrast with the rational basis review that the Supreme Court applies in most cases, the modern Court treats all race-based classifications as "suspect" or presumptively unconstitutional. As discussed already, this approach appears not to reflect the original understanding of the Equal Protection Clause. Nor did the Supreme Court always take the modern view.

In the notorious case of *Plessy v. Ferguson*[14] (1896), the Court upheld a Louisiana law requiring that passenger railroads provide "equal but separate accommodations for the white, and colored races." After being excluded from the "white" car, Homer Plessy argued first that he was only one-eighth black and thus was white, not black, within the mean-ing of the law. That claim failing, he argued next that the race-based

14 163 U.S. 537, 540 (1896).

classification violated the Equal Protection Clause. The Supreme Court disagreed. Asserting that the Fourteenth Amendment was not "intended to abolish [all] distinctions based upon color, or to enforce social, as distinguished from political, equality,"[15] the Court held that the legislature had the power to enact race-based classifications – at least within the domain of "social" rights – as long as those classifications were "reasonable."

In this aspect of its ruling, *Plessy* appears to have tracked what many believe to be the historically understood meaning of the Equal Protection Clause: it barred governmentally mandated race-based discrimination with respect to a limited class of fundamental rights but not with respect to social rights. Almost immediately, however, the Court encountered a complication. It assumed that all governmentally mandated discrimination – whether based on race, sightedness, age, or educational attainment – must at least be "reasonable" to be legally permissible and must be "enacted in good faith for the promotion of the public good, and not for the annoyance or oppression of a particular class." Applying this requirement, the Court readily accepted that it was reasonable for Louisiana to accommodate prevailing social attitudes by mandating "separate but equal" railroad cars for whites and blacks. The difficulty involved whether the separate accommodations could really be adjudged equal. In reality, the white cars were often more comfortable than the black cars. Increasing the awkwardness was that whites were in fact permitted to sit in the black cars, which often doubled as smoking cars, if they so chose, whereas blacks were wholly excluded from the white cars. The Court dealt curtly with objections such as these: "We consider the underlying fallacy of the plaintiff's argument to consist in the assumption that the enforced separation of the two races stamps the colored race with a badge of inferiority. If this be so, it is not by reason of anything found in the act, but solely because the colored race chooses to put that construction upon it."[16]

15 Ibid. at 544.
16 Ibid. at 551.

From a modern perspective, this assertion is hard to take seriously. Among all of the opinions of the Supreme Court, this may be the point, Charles Black once wrote, at which "[t]he curves of callousness and stupidity intersect at their respective maxima."[17] At the time of its decision, however, *Plessy v. Ferguson* attracted no stir. During the last two decades of the nineteenth century, race relations in the United States sank to a historic low, especially in the South. For most of the country, as for most of the Justices, it may have been almost unimaginable that the Constitution could mandate what the Court described as the enforced "commingling" of the races. Justices of the Supreme Court tend to embody the characteristic outlooks of their time and to see constitutional issues in light of them. For people who perceived racial discrimination as natural, not invidious, it may even have been possible to believe that the accommodation of white preferences for separation carried no necessary message of black inferiority. As I noted in Chapter 4, psychological research now confirms what unscientific observation had long revealed: people have strong tendencies to believe what they find it convenient or comforting to believe.

But it was plainly also possible to perceive the reality of the situation. "The thin disguise of 'equal' accommodations for passengers in railroad coaches will not mislead any one," Justice John Marshall Harlan wrote in a solitary dissenting opinion.[18] Very much a man of his time, Harlan spoke unapologetically of the special virtues and accomplishments of "[t]he white race."[19] "But in view of the constitution," he wrote in the same paragraph, "there is in this country no superior, dominant, ruling class of citizens.... Our constitution is color-blind."[20]

Despite Harlan's protest, *Plessy*'s regime of "separate but equal" endured for more than fifty years. Over time, its morally shameful character – a matter by no means wholly dependent on the original

17 Charles L. Black Jr., "The Lawfulness of the Segregation Decisions," 69 *Yale Law Journal* 421, 422, n.8 (1960).
18 *Plessy*, 163 U.S. 562 (Harlan, J., dissenting).
19 Ibid. at 559.
20 Ibid.

understanding of any constitutional provision – grew ever more apparent to increasing numbers of Americans. Not surprisingly, the Supreme Court manifested acute discomfort with race-based discriminations in its next major consideration of their constitutionality. Nevertheless, the Court expressly upheld a race-based military order excluding all persons of Japanese ancestry from designated areas of the West Coast in *Korematsu v. United States*[21] (1944).

The exclusion order followed the Japanese attack on Pearl Harbor in December 1941. Fearing that people of Japanese descent posed a sabotage risk, military officials ordered all persons of Japanese ancestry to leave the West Coast and submit to detention in "relocation centers." The military orders applied to roughly 112,000 people, of whom more than 65,000 were American citizens. Confronted with a challenge to the exclusion policy, the Court began its *Korematsu* opinion by announcing that "all legal restrictions which curtail the civil rights of a single racial group are immediately suspect" and subject to "the most rigid scrutiny."[22] This assertion was in one way remarkable. The Equal Protection Clause does not apply to the federal government, and the Court was still a decade away from holding expressly that the Due Process Clause establishes identical antidiscrimination norms. Nonetheless, the Court assumed that race-based classifications are inherently suspect under the Constitution and call for "the most rigid scrutiny."

In *Korematsu*, however, the reality of the Court's analysis did not match its language. The majority upheld the government's race-based exclusion order on the basis of scanty evidence contained in what a dissenting Justice described as an "unsworn, self-serving statement, untested by any cross-examination," offered by the general who had ordered all persons of Japanese descent to leave the West Coast.[23] Writing for the Court, Justice Hugo Black insisted that "[t]o cast this case into

21 323 U.S. 214 (1944).
22 Ibid. at 216.
23 *Korematsu*, 323 U.S. at 245 (Jackson, J., dissenting).

outlines of racial prejudice...merely confuses the issue."[24] Critics have charged otherwise. Today, *Korematsu* is frequently grouped with *Dred Scott v. Sandford* (1857) and *Lochner v. New York* (1905) as part of the constitutional "anti-canon" of cases that illustrate egregiously misguided constitutional analysis from which lessons now have been learned and that the Supreme Court should not ever repeat.

In the years after *Korematsu*, social attitudes concerning race and race discrimination continued to evolve at an accelerating pace. Following World War II, President Harry Truman ordered the desegregation of the U.S. Armed Forces, which had remained racially divided throughout the war. Increasing numbers of blacks assumed positions of professional and intellectual prominence. The 1948 platform of the Democratic Party included a strong civil rights plank for the first time. Meanwhile, lawyers for the National Association for the Advancement of Colored People (NAACP) had begun a brilliant legal campaign attacking segregation in public education.[25] Initially, NAACP lawyers accepted the "separate but equal" framework traceable to *Plessy v. Ferguson*. In one setting after another, they demonstrated that the separate educational facilities maintained for racial minorities were not, in actual fact, at all equal to those enjoyed by whites. Having won a number of victories with this strategy, the lawyers prepared to argue that racially discriminatory education was inherently unequal and thus unconstitutional.

The NAACP pressed this argument before the Supreme Court in *Brown v. Board of Education*[26] (1954). In their initial deliberations, the Justices found themselves troubled and divided. However unjust segregation might be, some worried that they lacked an adequate legal basis to upset the rule that had prevailed for more than fifty years under *Plessy v. Ferguson*. They also worried that it might lie beyond the proper reach of judicial power to decree a revolutionary change in racial relations in a

24 Ibid. at 223.
25 See Mark V. Tushnet, *The NAACP's Legal Strategy against Segregated Education, 1925–50* (Chapel Hill, NC: University of North Carolina Press, 1987).
26 347 U.S. 483 (1954).

significant portion of the United States. (The disgrace of the *Lochner* era and the threat of Court packing, brought on by perceived judicial over-reaching, lay fewer than twenty years in the past.) With early discussions "indicat[ing] a vote somewhere between five to four for sustaining school segregation and six to three for striking it down,"[27] the Justices decided to take the unusual step of asking for a second round of arguments in the case. Before the second argument occurred, Chief Justice Fred M. Vinson – a Kentuckian who had seven times won election to the House of Representatives before joining the Court and who was generally unsympathetic to the challengers' case – died. To replace Vinson, President Dwight Eisenhower nominated the far more progressive Earl Warren, a former governor of California. With the *Brown* case in mind, Justice Felix Frankfurter is said to have remarked, "[T]his is the first solid piece of evidence I've ever had that there really is a God."[28]

Under the leadership of the new Chief Justice, the Court decided *Brown* by the astonishing vote of 9–0, ruling that legally mandated segregation in public education violated the Equal Protection Clause. Historical inquiries, conducted by the parties at the Court's request, gave the Justices little help in reaching that conclusion: at best, the history revealed no clear intent to abolish discrimination in public education. At worst, it showed an understanding of education as a less than fundamental right with respect to which race-based separations were permitted. But the Court refused to be deterred. "In approaching this problem, we cannot turn the clock back to 1868 when the [Fourteenth] Amendment was adopted, or even to 1896 when *Plessy v. Ferguson* was written," Warren wrote.[29] Focusing on the present day, he emphasized that education had become "perhaps the most important function of state and local governments"[30] and that segregation, as a matter of social and

27 Michael Klarman, "An Interpretive History of Modern Equal Protection," 241–42.
28 Phillip Elman and Norman Silber, "The Solicitor General's Office, Justice Frankfurter, and Civil Rights Litigation, 1946–1960: An Oral History," 100 *Harvard Law Review* 817, 840 (1987).
29 *Brown*, 347 U.S. at 492.
30 Ibid. at 493.

psychological fact, communicated a message of race-based inferiority.[31] In an opinion lacking further rhetorical flourishes, the Court held that "in the field of public education the doctrine of 'separate but equal' has no place."[32]

Although *Brown* mandated a revolutionary change in the organization of Southern education and signaled that there would be future demands for the abolition of other discriminatory practices, the Supreme Court did not insist that the educational revolution begin immediately. Instead of ordering immediate school desegregation, the Court called for yet a third argument in the case. Nearly a year later, the Justices issued a second decision, devoted solely to the issue of remedies for school segregation.[33] In that decision, the Court pronounced that responsibility for school desegregation rested in the first instance with state and local officials, not the federal courts, and said that such officials must proceed, not necessarily posthaste, but with "all deliberate speed."[34] A long period of foot-dragging ensued. As I shall explain more fully later, the Supreme Court did not begin to insist firmly on effective desegregation of the public schools until the mid-1960s, after Congress had shown its strong commitment to the ideal of racial equality by enacting the 1964 Civil Rights Act, the most sweeping civil rights legislation since Reconstruction. (A few courageous judges on the lower federal courts took firmer stands, sometimes at considerable risk to themselves and their families.)

To some extent, the Supreme Court appears to have been waiting, attempting to create as few waves as possible, hoping for public opinion to rally to its side and, in particular, for white Southerners to become reconciled to the need for change. In a number of decisions throughout the 1950s, the Justices quietly applied the rule of *Brown v. Board of Education* to end publicly mandated segregation in facilities such as parks, golf courses, and playgrounds. Mandating an end to

31 Ibid. at 493–94.
32 Ibid. at 495.
33 See *Brown v. Board of Education* (II), 349 U.S. 294 (1955).
34 Ibid. at 301.

segregation in these areas was thought to tread less on Southern sensibilities than ending segregation in primary education, which involved small children. At the same time, the cases to which the Court applied the desegregation mandate subtly expanded *Brown*'s rationale. As originally written, the Court's decision had emphasized the special character of education and had expressly banished "separate but equal" only from the realm of public schooling.

But even while broadening *Brown*'s sphere of application, the Court went out of its way – some would say shamefully so – to avoid a collision over the issue of interracial marriage. In *Naim v. Naim*[35] (1955), the Court essentially refused to rule on an appeal challenging a Virginia statute that forbade whites to marry nonwhites (except, bizarrely, the descendants of Pocahontas). Justice Frankfurter, a former Harvard Law School professor who had also been a close advisor to Franklin Roosevelt and who had as much confidence in his political as his legal instincts, was the force behind the Court's refusal. Frankfurter apparently persuaded his fellow Justices that interracial marriage aroused such "deep" and hostile feeling that a Court pronouncement would undermine support for *Brown* and school desegregation.[36] On a pretext, the Court dismissed the appeal and permitted the statute to be enforced.

By 1967, the public climate had changed, and the Court finally was prepared to condemn statutes barring interracial marriage. In *Loving v. Virginia*,[37] the Justices ruled unanimously that such statutes violated the Equal Protection Clause. Within a few more years, the Court had formulated the still-applicable "strict scrutiny" test under which it invalidates all statutes that discriminate on the basis of race unless they are "necessary to promote a compelling government interest."

Since then, the Court's position has not waivered. *Palmore v. Sidoti*[38] (1984) reflects its insistence that classifications rooted in attitudes

35 350 U.S. 891 (1955).
36 See Klarman, "An Interpretive History of Modern Equal Protection," 243.
37 See *Loving v. Virginia*, 388 U.S. 1 (1967).
38 466 U.S. 429 (1984).

of racial hostility are deeply suspect and virtually never permissible. *Palmore* arose from the efforts of a divorced white father to have his daughter removed from the custody of his ex-wife after she married a black man. A state court ruled in favor of the father on the ground that the transfer of custody would promote the best interests of the child – the usual legal standard in child custody matters – because if the daughter remained in a biracial household, "social stigmatization...is sure to come." The Supreme Court rejected this reasoning. By a unanimous vote, the Court ruled that even if private prejudices might lead to "social stigmatization," they could not be permitted to influence a child custody decision: "The Constitution cannot control such prejudices but neither can it tolerate them. Private biases may be outside the reach of the law, but the law cannot, directly or indirectly, give them effect."[39]

Although the Court did not use the language of "strict scrutiny" in *Palmore*, its approach also helps illustrate what strict scrutiny means. In some minimal way, it might have been "rational" for a court to consider whether a child is likely to suffer social stigmatization from living in a biracial household as one factor relevant to determining the child's best interests. Under strict scrutiny, however, the mere fact that it would be "rational" (in some minimal sense) to take race into account does not suffice.

When the social and doctrinal developments are viewed in hindsight, it is remarkable how fast a firm national consensus emerged that publicly enforced race discrimination, which had been a familiar feature of American life from the very beginning, was morally and constitutionally intolerable. In the 1950s, the correctness of *Brown v. Board of Education* was a much-debated issue. By the 1970s, *Brown* enjoyed almost unanimous support in the legal community. Today, anyone who maintained that the case was wrongly decided would be disqualified from service on the Supreme Court. The President would not nominate, and the Senate would not confirm, a person who took that view.

39 Ibid. at 433.

If we pause to probe why *Brown* enjoys iconic status, the answer has nothing to do with fidelity to the original understanding of constitutional language. More commonly, *Brown* is said to epitomize the role of the Supreme Court as a guarantor of minority rights: under the theory of the *Carolene Products* footnote, which I briefly discussed in Chapter 4, the Court has a special responsibility to protect "discrete and insular minorities." If that judgment is correct, it bears noting that *Brown* did not come until 1954, nearly a hundred years after the ratification of the Fourteenth Amendment and nearly sixty years after *Plessy v. Ferguson*, at a time when a majority of Americans outside the Deep South had already come to believe that race-based segregation was morally wrongful, even if they were not yet ready to join a crusade for segregation's abolition. If the Court pushed ahead of national public opinion (outside the Deep South) in its condemnation of race discrimination, it did not do so by much.

What Did *Brown* Accomplish?

Although almost no one today doubts that the Supreme Court should have decided *Brown v. Board of Education* as it did, or that *Brown* established a morally compelling principle of constitutional law, recent decades have witnessed a contentious debate about how much the Court's ruling, by itself, actually accomplished. In *Brown*'s immediate wake, political leaders throughout the South embarked on a program of "massive resistance" to its desegregation mandate. Within a relatively few years, the border states had begun to desegregate, but for roughly a decade, the states of the Deep South continued to maintain one-race schools in the overwhelming majority of communities. As late as 1964, only about 1 percent of the black children in the South attended racially mixed schools.[40] Only thereafter, following Congress's enactment of

40 See Michael J. Klarman, *Brown v. Board of Education and the Civil Rights Movement* (New York: Oxford University Press, 2007), 123–24.

the landmark 1964 Civil Rights Act and its commitment of the federal government to enforcing immediate school desegregation, did the number of integrated schools in the South shoot up sharply, reaching roughly 90 percent in 1973.[41]

In the eyes of revisionist historians, this sequence of events invites questions about *Brown*'s causal efficacy in bringing school segregation to its ultimate end.[42] According to some who hold this view, credit for bringing about school desegregation should go less to the Supreme Court than to the largely African American–led civil rights movement that took to the streets to demand racial justice and to the Congress that enacted the 1964 Civil Rights Act.[43] Regardless of how one judges this revisionist claim, events in the decade following *Brown* vividly illustrate the point – also made in Chapter 4 – that there can be profound disparities between the principles decreed by the Supreme Court and the actual practice of public officials, who do not always bend to judicial mandates.

Race and the Constitution: Disparate Impact

Governmental statutes and policies can disadvantage racial minorities in at least two ways. As in *Plessy v. Ferguson* and *Korematsu v. United States*, they can withhold benefits or impose burdens on an expressly

---

41 Ibid.

42 See, for example, Gerald N. Rosenberg, *The Hollow Hope: Can Courts Bring About Social Change* (1991).

43 In a subtle variation on this position, Michael J. Klarman, *From Jim Crow to Civil Rights: The Supreme Court and the Struggle for Racial Equality* (New York: Oxford University Press, 2004), argues that *Brown* helped bring about the civil rights movement and the 1964 Civil Rights Act but did so largely by creating a "backlash" among angry Southern whites that manifested itself in acts of unspeakable violence against African Americans, including children trying to integrate Southern schools, and against civil rights demonstrators. Viewing this violence on television, the national political majority grew convinced that support for civil rights was a moral imperative. On this account, politics and the 1964 Civil Rights Act (rather than *Brown*) were the proximate cause of the end of officially sanctioned school segregation, but *Brown*, and the ugly backlash that it caused, played important roles in the causal chain.

racial basis. Or, even if they do not formally mention race at all, they may have a greater adverse impact on one racial group than another.

Washington v. Davis[44] (1976) exemplifies the phenomenon of racially "disparate impact." Under a rule adopted by the District of Columbia, candidates to become police officers had to score above a certain level on a test designed to measure verbal ability and reading comprehension. Black candidates failed the test at four times the rate of whites. Citing the test's racially skewed impact, challengers argued that it was racially discriminatory in effect, even if not in form, and that it should receive heightened judicial scrutiny under equal protection principles (rather than be subject merely to rational basis review). The Supreme Court disagreed.

According to the Court, racially disparate impact does not by itself constitute forbidden race discrimination. Nor are statutes with a racially disparate impact constitutionally "suspect" and therefore invalid unless necessary to promote a compelling governmental interest. Such statutes do not even trigger a heightened burden of governmental justification. Instead, rational basis review applies unless a challenger can prove that a statute or policy with a racially discriminatory impact was enacted for the discriminatory purpose of harming a racial minority group.

Washington v. Davis was an extremely important case. Racial minorities may suffer two kinds of disadvantage. One arises from hostility. The other is a relative dearth of sympathy, empathy, or concern. If a test systematically disadvantaged whites, rather than blacks, then public officials might well reconsider whether the test was a good one or otherwise readjust governmental policy. Under *Washington v. Davis*, the Equal Protection Clause bars legislation that reflects race-based hostility, but it leaves the problem of racially selective sympathy and indifference wholly unaddressed.

The Court's reasoning in *Washington v. Davis* was relatively explicit. In American society, there are likely to be many rules and policies under

44 426 U.S. 229 (1976).

which blacks on average fare less well than whites. If all rules and policies with racially disparate impacts were invalid absent a compelling justification, the Court reasoned in *Washington v. Davis*, courts could expect to have to apply that test to "a whole range of tax, welfare, public service, regulatory, and licensing statutes that may be more burdensome to the poor and [thus] to the average black [who is more likely to be poor] than to the more affluent white."[45] What is more, governmental bodies (for better or for worse) would feel a subtle pressure to pay attention to race in order to avoid racially disparate impacts that could cause them to be sued. In light of its assessment of the costs and benefits, the Supreme Court refused to license serious constitutional challenges to every statute or policy with a racially skewed effect. It defined the race discrimination forbidden by the Constitution as purposeful race discrimination only and read the Equal Protection Clause as requiring no special judicial scrutiny of statutes with racially disparate effects.

Affirmative Action

When the Supreme Court began to treat race-based discrimination as constitutionally "suspect," it did so in cases in which the government's purpose was to exclude, burden, or stigmatize minorities. Not immediately obvious, at least to everyone, was whether race-based decision making would be deemed comparably suspect when used for other, nonstigmatizing purposes, including promoting racial integration and enhanced opportunities for racial minorities. Indeed, in the aftermath of *Brown* and the passage of the 1964 Civil Rights Act, the Court began to insist that previously segregated school districts must make race-based school assignments in order to dismantle past discriminatory regimes. Because many neighborhoods are predominantly white or predominantly black, a transition from all-white and all-black schools to neighborhood schools – which often came after years of resistance – continued to leave many students in nearly all-white or all-black classes.

45 Ibid. at 248.

When previously segregated school districts then adopted "freedom of choice" plans, whites refused to attend previously all-black schools, and blacks who contemplated moving to previously all-white schools confronted threats and intimidation. In response to these developments, the Justices, in the late 1960s and early 1970s, stiffened their position about what previously segregated school systems had to do to satisfy the Constitution. In *Brown*, the Court had apparently contemplated that it would suffice merely to end expressly race-based assignments of whites to all-white schools and of blacks to all-black schools. By the late 1960s and early 1970s, the Court demanded meaningful integration, with substantial numbers of white and black students actually attending the same schools.[46] Where necessary to achieve this effect, the Court – in a highly controversial development – began to uphold lower-court orders requiring the busing of some students from the schools closest to their homes to schools in other neighborhoods.[47]

In cases involving court-ordered busing, the Supreme Court treated race-based school assignments as a remedial necessity. Its position invited (though did not require) the inference that race-based classifications, including student assignments, were constitutionally acceptable, not suspect, when employed for the purpose of achieving the integration of racial minorities into traditionally white environments. The relevant Court decisions all involved race-based school assignments for the purpose of remedying past unlawful practices, but on at least one occasion – as noted in the prologue – the Court welcomed voluntary actions by school officials (not required as remedies for past unlawful actions) to take account of students' races as a means of creating integrated school environments. In *Swann v. Charlotte-Mecklenburg Board of Education*[48] (1971), the Court wrote: "School authorities ... might well

46 See, for example, *Green v. County School Board*, 391 U.S. 430 (1968).
47 See, for example, *Swann v. Charlotte-Mecklenburg Board of Education*, 402 U.S. 1 (1971).
48 402 U.S. 1, 16 (1971).

conclude...that in order to prepare students to live in a pluralistic society each school should have a prescribed ratio of Negro to white students reflecting the proportion for the district as a whole." I shall say more about voluntary efforts to achieve racial diversity in the public schools later.

Another possible use of race to include rather than to exclude racial minorities involved what came to be called "affirmative action" by traditionally selective state universities, which (unlike the public schools, which educate everyone) admit some students while refusing admission to others, and by government agencies making decisions about whom to hire or promote and to whom to award government contracts. Prior to *Brown*, voluntarily adopted programs of this kind, aimed at benefiting rather than disadvantaging racial minorities, would have been politically unthinkable. Within twenty years after *Brown*, affirmative action programs began to draw challenges by whites, some of whom claimed to be the victims of constitutionally intolerable "reverse discrimination." The question for the Court was whether race-based classifications are as objectionable when they are used for purposes of inclusion or integration as when they are used to separate or demean.

In explaining why strict scrutiny was appropriate in cases involving discriminations against minorities, commentators had often cited the *Carolene Products* theory that heightened judicial scrutiny is needed to protect "discrete and insular" minority groups from the effects of "prejudice" in the political process.[49] Under *Carolene Products*, affirmative action programs should not occasion elevated judicial concern. Such programs benefit members of minority groups rather than harm them, and they are not likely to be motivated by "prejudice" against the white majority.

Affirmative action would also appear to escape strict judicial scrutiny if the Supreme Court were to assess it from a strictly originalist

---

49 See, for example, John Hart Ely, *Democracy and Distrust: A Theory of Judicial Review* (Cambridge, MA: Harvard University Press, 1980), 135–79.

perspective. There is no indication that the framers and ratifiers of the Equal Protection Clause regarded race-based preferences for disadvantaged minorities as unfair or constitutionally impermissible. In the years immediately surrounding the ratification of the Fourteenth Amendment, Congress repeatedly enacted statutes providing benefits for "colored" soldiers and sailors and women and children. A judicial decision to subject affirmative action programs to strict judicial scrutiny therefore cannot rest on the original understanding, any more than it can reflect a commitment to protecting discrete and insular minorities.

In the view of many, however – including some commentators and Justices who profess to be originalists in other contexts – affirmative action is inherently unfair because it classifies people according to what ought to be the biological irrelevancy of their race. According to this view, the sacrosanct precedent of *Brown v. Board of Education* authorizes and indeed requires the Court to treat affirmative action as a species of race discrimination and therefore as constitutionally suspect.

Even when the debate is put on grounds of fairness, affirmative action has ardent champions. Some defenders see a need to remedy historical injustices that have led to a current situation in which whites, on average, are substantially better educated and earn significantly higher incomes than blacks, on average. Others cite continuing discrimination in contemporary society. Others contend that a racially diverse society requires racially diverse leadership to function effectively. (According to one study, "[u]nder race-blind policies, Blacks would make up only 1.6 to 3.4 percent" of the students in accredited law schools, and "[e]liminating affirmative action from medical education would reduce Black enrollment by 90 percent."[50]) Nor do most defenders of affirmative action believe that it requires moral apologies to whites (or Asian Americans who may also be disadvantaged by affirmative action in some contexts). According to proponents of what is often called an "antisubordinationist" view, race-based classifications are objectionable only when used to

---

50 Sylvia A. Law, "White Privilege and Affirmative Action," 32 *Akron Law Review* 603, 620 (1999).

demean, suppress, or stigmatize. Apart from our long history of reliance on race-based laws to enslave and stigmatize racial minorities, it is no more morally objectionable to classify based on race than based on many other traits, including such "immutable" ones as age, blindness, and possibly IQ.

In the law's development to date, considerations of fairness and wise social policy have dominated the Supreme Court's thinking about affirmative action, with originalism and *Carolene Products* playing little if any role. In a lengthening string of cases, the Court has held – often by narrow majorities – that affirmative action programs are as constitutionally suspect as any other form of race-based discrimination and thus trigger strict judicial scrutiny. So far, however, the Court has not ruled out affirmative action altogether.

For many years, the leading case has been *Regents of the University of California v. Bakke*[51] (1978), which involved an affirmative action program by the medical school of the University of California at Davis. Each year the medical school enrolled one hundred students. Some years there were no minority students; without affirmative action, the school never admitted more than a handful. In response to this situation, the medical school decided to set aside sixteen places solely for minorities. Alan Bakke, a white who applied and got rejected, brought a challenge under the Equal Protection Clause. In *Bakke*, four Justices favored rejecting the equal protection challenge and upholding the medical schools' admissions policy as an acceptable remedy for historical and continuing societal discrimination. Four other Justices concluded that any use of race in the admissions process was forbidden by a federal statute. That division left the decisive vote in the hands of Justice Lewis Powell, a moderate conservative from Virginia whose instincts were resolutely pragmatic. He appears to have wanted to save affirmative action, which he recognized to be deeply socially divisive, by limiting the circumstances under which it could be practiced.

---

51 438 U.S. 265 (1978).

In his opinion, much of which was joined by no other Justice (but which nonetheless stated the controlling position because the other Justices were split 4–4), Powell held that race-based affirmative action triggered strict judicial scrutiny: it was permissible under the Equal Protection Clause only if necessary to promote a compelling governmental interest. But Powell, unlike those completely opposed to affirmative action, recognized at least two circumstances under which race-based preferences might pass that test. First, he believed that affirmative action could be permissible as a remedy for specifically identified past discrimination by particular institutions – though not, he emphasized, as a remedy for general, possibly pervasive societal discrimination. Second, he found that educational institutions had a compelling interest in achieving a diverse student body – one that would produce rich classroom discussions and help prepare students for success in a racially diverse world. Powell thus authorized affirmative action but only on a narrow basis. He insisted that the Equal Protection Clause requires that any affirmative action program be no broader than necessary to achieve its purpose. He specifically declared rigid racial "quotas" constitutionally impermissible (and thus invalidated the minority set-aside employed by the University of California at Davis medical school). He wrote that educational institutions seeking diversity could consider race as one relevant factor among many, but that they must give individualized consideration to every applicant. In effect, educational institutions could take race into account as long as they did not do so too openly (for example, by employing quotas) or let it count for too much.

Subsequent decisions have generally followed the path laid out in *Bakke*. In *Gratz v. Bollinger*,[52] the facts of which were presented at the beginning of this chapter, a 6–3 majority struck down a rigid program under which applicants from underrepresented minorities received a large (and fixed) total of 20 points out of a possible 150 on the school's admissions index. Although the Court assumed that the university had

52 539 U.S. 244 (2003).

a "compelling" interest in achieving a diverse student body, it ruled that the uniform twenty-point bonus was too large and mechanical to be narrowly tailored to a legitimate interest in the kind of diversity in student background and outlook that the university could legitimately claim to value under Justice Powell's *Bakke* opinion. At the same time, in the companion case of *Grutter v. Bollinger*,[53] a 5–4 majority upheld the affirmative action program employed by the University of Michigan Law School, under which admissions officers took race into account in seeking to achieve a diverse student body but did so on an individualized basis without quotas or a point system. Justice Sandra Day O'Connor, a moderate conservative who often tried to follow the difference-splitting approach of Justice Powell, wrote the *Grutter* opinion.

In sometimes caustic dissenting opinions, the four Justices in the *Grutter* minority argued that in its search for a "critical mass" of minority students, the University of Michigan Law School made race count for too much. In their view, the numbers proved that the school, in practice, sought to achieve rough racial proportionality rather than merely making race a modest "plus" in achieving the kind of diversity that enhances educational quality. Justices Antonin Scalia and Clarence Thomas registered a more fundamental and passionate complaint that affirmative action is a form of race-based discrimination and that it is therefore unfair.

Whether the Supreme Court will continue to uphold affirmative action programs such as that involved in *Grutter* remains to be seen. As I have emphasized, the Supreme Court is a "they," not an "it," and in 2006 the moderate conservative Justice O'Connor was succeeded by the more conservative Justice Samuel Alito. With Alito's appointment, the "swing" Justice whose vote will control the outcome of future cases – including one pending before the Court as I write these words – will almost certainly be Justice Anthony Kennedy (until more appointments to the Court shift its ideological balance one way or the other). I offer this

53 539 U.S. 306 (2003).

observation with some diffidence due to anxiety that it may sound cynical or world-wearily "realist," as if the Justices' preferences were everything and law did not matter in the Supreme Court. In my view, most and perhaps all of the Justices genuinely want to follow the law, and they regard the obligation to adhere to precedent as a significant constraint in many contexts. But in areas of the law in which concerns about fundamental fairness play a driving role in decisions about how "best" to interpret vague constitutional language, one cannot expect a Justice with strong morally charged views to adopt all of the reasoning of a relatively recent precedent, such as *Grutter*, if he or she believes its analysis to be seriously mistaken.

A prefiguring of the next major affirmative action decision may have come in *Parents Involved in Community Schools v. Seattle School District No. 1*[54] (2007), a case – discussed briefly in the prologue – raising the question of whether a city or county school district that has not engaged in race-based discrimination in the past, or has completed its remedial obligations, can take race into account in assigning children to one school rather than another for the purpose of promoting racial integration. There are some differences between primary and secondary education, on the one hand, and the university admissions process at issue in *Grutter*, on the other hand. But there are obvious similarities, too, and the reasoning of *Parents Involved* thus becomes relevant to more traditional affirmative action issues.

In *Parents Involved*, the Court, by a 5–4 vote, invalidated the race-based elements of the school assignment plans of the Seattle, Washington, and Jefferson County, Kentucky, school districts. In an opinion joined in whole by three other Justices and in part by a fourth, Chief Justice John Roberts expressed deep skepticism about the constitutional permissibility of any form of race-based classification, even when utilized for purposes of achieving racial diversity. "The way to stop discrimination on the basis of race," as he thought *Brown* mandated, "is [for the

54 551 U.S. 701 (2007).

government] to stop discriminating on the basis of race," he wrote. The fifth vote to invalidate the challenged plans came from Justice Kennedy, who joined the Chief Justice's opinion only in part. Kennedy's own concurring opinion pointedly refused to rule out absolutely all uses of race-based classifications for inclusionary rather than exclusionary purposes, but he insisted that it was acceptable to classify people by race only as a last resort, when no other means would let the government achieve truly urgent goals. Four dissenting Justices protested angrily that the majority had betrayed what they viewed as the "integrationist" ideals of *Brown v. Board of Education*. In their view, *Parents Involved* ignored what had been rightly recognized since *Brown* as a compelling "interest in helping our children learn to work and play together with children of different racial backgrounds," as well as "an interest in overcoming the adverse educational effects produced by and associated with highly segregated schools."

As I noted in the prologue, among the *Parents Involved* dissenters was John Paul Stevens, then the Court's longest-serving Justice, who wrote: "It is my firm conviction that no Member of the Court that I joined in 1975 would have agreed with today's decision."[55] He may well have been right. The Justices in 2007 were different from the Justices in 1975. So was the country, however – and so were the outlooks of the presidents who had appointed and the Senators who had confirmed the Justices who had joined the Court after Stevens. The next chapter in the saga involving the use of race to promote inclusion or integration remains to be written. It will be a chapter in the racial and political history of the country, not just in the history of the Supreme Court.

Gender and the Constitution

Through most of constitutional history, discrimination against women was accepted as a matter of course. The Supreme Court reviewed

55 551 U.S. at 803 (Stevens, J., dissenting).

gender-based classifications under the rational basis test but invariably approved them. In an 1873 case upholding a statute that denied women the right to practice law, the Court observed that "[t]he natural and proper timidity and delicacy which belongs to the female sex evidently unfits it for many of the occupations of civil life."[56] The Court's tone had not changed notably by 1948, when it upheld a law barring most women from obtaining bartender's licenses: "The fact that women may now have achieved the virtues that men long claimed as their prerogatives and now indulge in vices that men have long practiced, does not preclude the State from drawing a sharp line between the sexes."[57]

The first decision invalidating a statute that discriminated on the basis of sex came in 1971.[58] The timing reveals much. By 1971, cultural attitudes about women's roles were changing dramatically. Shortly afterward, in a case challenging the military's policy of automatically providing "dependency" or spousal support allowances to married male but not to married female members of the armed forces, Ruth Bader Ginsburg, then a relatively young lawyer, forcefully argued that sex-based classifications should be deemed constitutionally suspect, just like those based on race. Ginsburg, a pioneering advocate for sex equality who would be named a Supreme Court Justice two decades later, maintained that sex, like race, was an immutable trait, crucial to self-identity, "which the dominant culture views as a badge of inferiority justifying disadvantaged treatment." Ginsburg won the case, *Frontiero v. Richardson*[59] (1973), with eight of the nine Justices agreeing that women were disadvantaged unfairly. But she could persuade only four Justices, one short of a majority, that statutes that discriminate on the basis of sex should be analyzed in the same way as statutes that discriminate on the basis of race.

The Court's hesitation was understandable. Ginsburg was right that sex, like race, is a highly salient characteristic: people always notice the

56 *Bradwell v. Illinois*, 83 U.S. (16 Wall.) 130, 141 (1872).
57 *Goesaert v. Cleary*, 335 U.S. 464, 465 (1948).
58 See *Reed v. Reed*, 404 U.S. 71 (1971).
59 411 U.S. 677 (1973).

gender of others. She was also right that women have historically been disadvantaged on the basis of sex and that the disadvantages remained palpable in 1973: women on average earned lower incomes than men, remained subject to various forms of formal and informal employment discrimination, and had achieved few prominent positions of political leadership. But if the struggle for gender equality has obvious parallels to the struggle for racial equality, there are important differences as well. First, the physiological differences between men and women are more than skin deep: only women can get pregnant, men on average are stronger and heavier than women, and so forth. Second, whereas race would likely be irrelevant in an ideal world, gender would not. Sexual attraction would remain, as might sex-linked desires for privacy (for example, in separate restrooms, showers, and similar facilities), and there would continue to be correlations between sex and average height, strength, and weight. A third complicating factor is that women are a (small) majority of the American population, not a "discrete and insular minority." None of these considerations remotely suggests that sex discrimination is not a problem of constitutional dimension. Nevertheless, issues of sex-based discrimination present distinctive complexities.

With respect to the "standard" for judicial review, the Supreme Court ultimately decided to split the difference between the strict scrutiny it applies to race-based classifications and the rational basis review it uses in most other cases. In *Craig v. Boren*[60] (1976), the Court held that gender-based discriminations should be deemed invalid unless they "serve important governmental objectives" and are "substantially related to achievement of those objectives." To this formula it later added the gloss that gender-based discriminations are impermissible unless supported by "an exceedingly persuasive justification."[61]

At issue in *Craig* was an Oklahoma statute that forbade men between the ages of eighteen and twenty-one, but not women of the same age, to

---

60 429 U.S. 190, 197 (1976).
61 See *United States v. Virginia*, 518 U.S. 515, 524 (1996).

buy low-alcohol beer. The state defended the statute as a means of stopping drunk driving, to which it said that young men were more prone
than young women. The Court, however, found the supporting evidence
insufficient to justify the differential treatment. Its decision reveals a
good deal about both the "intermediate" scrutiny to which it subjects
gender-based discrimination and the concerns that motivate the Court's
analysis.

Although many of the arguments for treating gender-based classifications as suspect involve historical discrimination against women, in
Craig, the Court applied elevated scrutiny to invalidate a statute that
discriminated against young men. Nor was *Craig* unusual in this respect:
the Justices regularly scrutinize statutes that disadvantage men under
precisely the same test applicable to statutes that disadvantage women.
In insisting on parallel treatment, the Court may believe statutes that
discriminate against men to be as presumptively unfair as those that discriminate against women. It may also believe that gender stereotypes are
the mirror images of one another. If so, a statute based on a stereotype
of males as prone to engage in risky behavior such as drinking and driving may tend to reinforce a parallel stereotype of women as cautious and
risk averse. In the long run, gender-based stereotypes probably tend to
limit the opportunities open to men and women alike.

It also bears notice that although the statute involved in *Craig* failed
"intermediate" scrutiny, it would almost certainly have passed the
rational basis test. The state had a legitimate interest in reducing drunk
driving. It was not irrational to try to reduce drunk driving by prohibiting
alcohol sales to a group who might reasonably be thought especially
prone to drink and then drive. Indeed, the state actually had some
evidence suggesting that although men between the ages of eighteen and
twenty-one displayed at least a modest tendency to drive while drunk,
women of the same age almost never did. In short, it was probably
"rational," in a narrowly instrumental sense, for the state to forbid
the purchase of low-alcohol beer to eighteen- to twenty-one-year-old
men and equally "rational" to exclude women from the prohibition.
Nevertheless, the Court refused to permit the discrimination between

men and women. Even when gender-based discrimination is otherwise rational, the Court apparently concluded, it can have a moral and perhaps a social cost – possibly, once again, by reinforcing cultural stereotypes. To put the point somewhat more bluntly, *Craig v. Boren* appears to construe the Equal Protection Clause as committed to fighting gender-based stereotypes by forbidding gender-based discrimination, even when such discrimination is otherwise rational, unless it is "substantially related" to an "important" governmental objective.

Although *Craig* both established a test for the constitutionality of statutes that discriminate on the basis of gender and highlighted the Court's concern with gender-based stereotypes, subsequent decisions do not form a simple pattern. The Court has invalidated formulas that designate men for higher pay. Nearly all statutes that expressly exclude women from jobs and opportunities are also invalid, but there are exceptions. The Court has upheld a statute effectively excluding women prison guards from duty in "contact" positions in all-male facilities. In doing so, it credited concerns that women would be less capable of maintaining order and more likely to attract sexual assaults.[62] The Court also upheld a statute providing that men, but not women, must register for the draft.[63] Once again, a majority of the Justices thought that physiological differences between men and women (rather than unconsidered stereotypes) justified differential treatment.

In *United States v. Virginia*[64] (1996), the Court held that a state violated the Equal Protection Clause by excluding women from a prestigious state college offering a distinctive educational program – at least when the state did so without offering a comparably excellent program exclusively for women. The opinion's author was Justice Ruth Bader Ginsburg, the trailblazing attorney for the plaintiff in *Frontiero* who became the second woman ever to serve on the Supreme Court when she was nominated by President Bill Clinton in 1993. In a footnote, the Court said that it did not mean to rule on the question of whether

62 See *Dothard v. Rawlinson*, 433 U.S. 321 (1977).
63 See *Rostker v. Goldberg*, 453 U.S. 57 (1981).
64 518 U.S. 515 (1996).

separate classes for men and women would be permissible as long as equally good opportunities existed for both.[65] But it emphasized that states may not discriminate between men and women on the basis of stereotypes or overbroad generalizations.

The difficulty, of course, is that stereotypes and overbroad generalizations can be difficult to distinguish from the reasoned awareness of "real differences" that can sometimes justify gender-based classifications. On the one hand, real physiological differences between men and women probably justify single-sex athletic teams (although the Court has not had occasion to say so expressly). On the other hand, the Court held in *United States v. Virginia* that the state relied on an impermissible stereotype in concluding that women could not profit from the physically and psychologically arduous educational method employed at Virginia Military Institute.

Against this backdrop, *United States v. Virginia* – decided by a Supreme Court that included two female Justices – may be especially important for its emphatic location of the burden of justification in cases of gender-based discrimination: "Parties who seek to defend gender-based government action must demonstrate an 'exceedingly persuasive justification' for that action.... The burden of justification is demanding and it rests entirely on the State."[66]

Discrimination against Gays and Lesbians

Recent decades have witnessed widespread, often heated debates about the constitutionality of statutes that discriminate against homosexual persons and acts. At one level, these debates have involved a relatively

---

65 See ibid. at 533, n.7.

66 Ibid. at 531, 533. That *United States v. Virginia* did not sound the death for all gender-based classifications became clear in *Nguyen v. Immigration and Naturalization Service*, 533 U.S. 53 (2001), which upheld a statute giving American women a preference over American men in passing on their American citizenship to out-of-wedlock children who are born abroad. Foreign-born, out-of-wedlock children of American mothers automatically become citizens (provided the mother meets certain residency requirements), whereas those of American fathers do not.

straightforward clash of moral and social outlooks. From the perspective of gay rights advocates, gays are a classic discrete and insular minority that is the victim of prejudice: traditional taboos against homosexuality lack reasoned justifications. Gays should be as free to find gratification and fulfillment through gay relationships, including marriage, as heterosexuals are through heterosexual relationships. Discrimination against gays is a form of bigotry that ought to be condemned. By contrast, cultural conservatives believe that open gay sexuality and (especially) gay marriage threaten traditional moral values built around the monogamous two-parent family, defined to include one father and one mother. In their view, gay sex reflects a perversion of the order of nature (and in the eyes of many, the order ordained by God). For those who take this view, discrimination based on homosexuality seems natural and appropriate, whether to show moral disapproval or to protect society from the spread of corruption.

As a matter of culture and politics, the tide of the battle appears to have turned, even if losses continue to be incurred in the short run. In 1961, all fifty states prohibited homosexual sodomy. By the time the Supreme Court invalidated an antisodomy ordinance in 2003 (in *Lawrence v. Texas*[67]), the number had fallen to thirteen. When President Bill Clinton attempted to end the military's ban on service by homosexuals in 1993, he met a firestorm of opposition by Congress and military leaders and had to back down. "Don't ask, don't tell" emerged as a compromise. By 2010, Congress authorized the abolition of "don't ask, don't tell" and the substitution of a nondiscrimination policy. A few decades ago, gay marriage had almost no supporting political constituency. A number of states now permit it, some as the result of legislative initiatives. Perhaps more important, young people tend to be much more accepting of gay lifestyles than are older people. Polling data show that seven out of ten voters younger than age thirty-five favor gay marriage.[68]

67 539 U.S. 558 (2003).
68 Frank Newport, "For First Time, Majority of Americans Favor Legal Gay Marriage," *Gallup* (May 20, 2011), http://www.gallup.com/poll/147662/first-time-majority-americans-favor-legal-gay-marriage.aspx.

Regardless of what happens in the courts, one can thus predict that legal discriminations against gays will continue to wane in the years ahead (although, as Yogi Berra once said, "It's tough to make predictions, especially about the future").

As prevailing attitudes toward homosexuality have evolved in American society as a whole, profound changes have also occurred in constitutional law. Nevertheless, the current state of affairs is not easy to describe, partly because statutes that disadvantage gays present a surprisingly diverse array of constitutional issues. More specifically, the loose category of "gay rights litigation" has involved challenges to at least three different kinds of statutes: (1) those involving explicit discriminations against gays – for example, barring them from certain jobs or opportunities (such as service in the U.S. military); (2) those that apply only to same-sex behavior (such as prohibitions against same-sex sodomy and gay marriage); and (3) those with a discriminatory effect on gays, such as statutes that prohibit all sodomy (heterosexual as well as homosexual). The Supreme Court has dealt with cases in the third category under the Due Process Clause rather than the Equal Protection Clause, and the hardest cases in the second category are ones in which the discrimination involves what the Court has termed "fundamental rights." Although this division is not wholly satisfactory, I therefore postpone consideration of due process and fundamental rights issues until Chapter 6 and deal here only with governmental classifications that expressly designate some people as homosexual and discriminate against them on that basis.

The Supreme Court's first decision marking the advent of a new era – and still its leading statement on the permissibility of discrimination against gays – came in *Romer v. Evans*[69] (1996). *Romer* arose when Colorado voters approved a ballot question amending the state's constitution to bar the enforcement of either state or local legislation affording gays "any minority status, quota preferences, protected

69 517 U.S. 620 (1996).

status or claim of discrimination." That Colorado voters would have been asked to approve such an amendment showed that cultural attitudes were shifting: the proposed amendment reflected cultural conservatives' reaction against an emerging tendency by state and local governments not only to repeal antisodomy statutes but also to pass legislation barring discrimination against gays. By any standard, however, the Colorado amendment was poorly written and unclear. At a minimum, it prohibited the enactment within Colorado of legislation specifically protecting gays against public or private discrimination (in the way that civil rights legislation frequently bars discriminations on the basis or race or gender, for example). It arguably, but only arguably, took the further step of leaving gay people without legal redress under Colorado law if they were discriminatorily denied rights otherwise conferred on *all* Colorado citizens, such as the right to ride on public transportation (after paying the fare) or to receive protection from the police and fire departments.

In a decision that surprised many observers, the Supreme Court held by 6–3 that the Colorado amendment violated the Equal Protection Clause. In so ruling, the Court importantly and revealingly assumed that discriminations against gay people are subject only to rational basis review, not strict judicial scrutiny. Nevertheless, Justice Anthony Kennedy's majority opinion found that the Colorado amendment failed rational basis review because it was "at once too narrow and too broad": "It identifies persons by a single trait and then denies them protection across the board. . . . A law declaring that in general it shall be more difficult for one group of citizens than for all others to seek aid from the government is itself a denial of equal protection of the laws in the most literal sense."[70] The only explanation for such a law, Justice Kennedy wrote, was that it "was born of animosity toward the class of persons affected"[71] and thus lacked the legitimate purpose required by rational

70 Ibid. at 633.
71 Ibid. at 634.

basis review. The three dissenting Justices denounced that conclusion as unprecedented and misguided. In their view, the Colorado amendment reflected a permissible moral judgment, not an expression of prejudice.

Following *Romer, Lawrence v. Texas*[72] (2003), which I discuss in Chapter 6, invalidated a prohibition against homosexual sodomy. Although the majority opinion in that case rested its holding on the Due Process Clause, it hinted that the Equal Protection Clause might have dictated the same result and emphasized that the Constitution mandates recognition of the equal "dignity of [homosexual] persons."[73] As this book goes to press, a very live question – almost certain to come before the Supreme Court soon – is whether prohibitions against gay marriage are "irrational" or otherwise constitutionally impermissible under the Equal Protection Clause. The equal protection doctrine that emerges from *Romer* still appears to contemplate that there can be rational as well as irrational discriminations against gay people, with the courts needing to draw the line between the two. Time will tell where exactly a majority of the Justices will place that line or whether they may abolish it altogether.

Conclusion

It is often suggested that modern equal protection doctrine reflects a theory, traceable to *United States v. Carolene Products Co.*[74] (1938), under which the courts defer to legislative judgments except when classificatory schemes reflect prejudice against discrete and insular minorities. The *Carolene Products* theory explains the correctness of the Court's approach in *Brown v. Board of Education*: African Americans are the paradigmatic "discrete and insular minority," long victimized by prejudice. The *Carolene Products* rationale also helps justify most applications of rational basis review: in cases not involving discrete and insular

72 539 U.S. 558 (2003).
73 Ibid. at 575.
74 304 U.S. 144 (1938).

minorities, the political process can usually be relied on to do at least rough justice, and searching judicial review would risk repeating the mistakes of the *Lochner* era by intruding unnecessarily on legislative prerogatives.

Increasingly, however, the Supreme Court has adopted positions that are incompatible with the *Carolene Products* theory. On the one hand, the Court treats certain classificatory schemes as suspect or semisuspect even when they disadvantage majority rather than minority groups. For example, it strictly scrutinizes race-based affirmative action schemes that disadvantage whites, not blacks. Similarly, it treats all gender-based classifications as semisuspect, even though women are a statistical majority (not a minority) of the population and even though it would be bizarre to think that men, as a class, are the victims of widespread prejudice. On the other hand, the Court refuses to confer suspect status on a number of classifications involving genuine minority groups against whom prejudice seems very real – persons with mental retardation, for example[75] – when it believes that classificatory legislation is likely to be both practically sensible and morally acceptable.

Modern doctrine seems equally divorced from the original understanding of the Equal Protection Clause, which was ratified in 1868. For better or worse, the Supreme Court has treated equal protection as a moral ideal to which the courts must give content, partly in light of Justices' and judges' personal judgments and partly in light of the evolving understandings of the American people. Seldom, if ever, does the Court describe its function in these daunting terms. But that, in essence, is what the Court does – subject, of course, to the now familiar caveat that the Supreme Court is a "they," not an "it." When the American people are sharply divided, their divisions are likely to find reflection in the Supreme Court.

---

75 See, for example, *City of Cleburne v. Cleburne Living Center*, 473 U.S. 432 (1985); *Heller v. Doe*, 509 U.S. 312 (1993).

6 "Unenumerated" Fundamental Rights

"[L]iberty" is not a series of isolated points pricked out in terms of ... freedom of speech, press, and religion ... and so on. It is a rational continuum which, broadly speaking, includes a freedom from all substantial arbitrary impositions and purposeless restraints.

– Justice John Marshall Harlan[1]

The Court is most vulnerable and comes nearest to illegitimacy when it deals with judge-made constitutional law having little or no cognizable roots in the language or design of the Constitution.

– Justice Byron White[2]

AS THE SUPREME COURT NOTED IN THE FIRST SENTENCE of its opinion, the case of *Skinner v. Oklahoma*[3] (1942) "touche[d] a sensitive and important area of human rights." The state of Oklahoma sought to sterilize Jack T. Skinner against his will. In the state's view, Skinner was a "habitual criminal," convicted three times of crimes involving "moral turpitude" – twice for "robbery," once for stealing chickens. Oklahoma's "Habitual Criminal Sterilization Act" called for repeat offenders to be sterilized in order to stop people

---

1 *Poe v. Ullman*, 367 U.S. 497, 543 (1961) (Harlan, J., dissenting).
2 *Bowers v. Hardwick*, 478 U.S. 186, 194 (1986), overruled by *Lawrence v. Texas*, 539 U.S. 558 (2003).
3 316 U.S. 535, 536 (1942).

with manifest criminal tendencies from passing those tendencies to future generations.

In doctrinal terms, *Skinner* was not an easy case. Or, perhaps to state the same point differently, from one perspective it seemed too easy. To Skinner and indeed to the Justices of the Supreme Court, Oklahoma's Habitual Criminal Sterilization Act may have looked cruel and offensive, jarringly similar in some respects (though not, of course, in all) to the "eugenics" policies then being implemented in Nazi Germany. But what provision of the Constitution, if any, did the Oklahoma law violate? So close to the ignominious *Lochner* era, the Court would not have been willing to find a violation of substantive due process. And although the Eighth Amendment forbids "cruel and unusual punishments" for crimes, in 1942 the Court had not yet held that the Eighth Amendment imposes limits on the states, as well as on the federal government (under the "incorporation" doctrine discussed in Chapter 4). So Skinner's lawyer emphasized the Equal Protection Clause: the statute's defect, he argued, was that it singled out some three-time convicts, but not others, for sterilization. More particularly, it rather systematically and unequally excluded white-collar criminals from the sterilization that it imposed on three-time chicken thieves.

To a person not versed in constitutional law, this might seem a sound basis for objection. The problem, for the Supreme Court, lay in the rational basis test it normally applied under the Equal Protection Clause (as explained in Chapter 5). To prevent the inheritance of criminal tendencies was a "legitimate" governmental purpose. And for the state to single out some criminals as more likely than others to pass on dangerous criminal tendencies was probably not wholly irrational either. (Surely, neither chicken thieves nor any other subcategory of criminals, defined by their offenses, constitutes a suspect class, discrimination against which would trigger strict judicial scrutiny.) As Chief Justice Harlan Fiske Stone wrote in a concurring opinion, "[I]f we must presume that the legislature knows...that the criminal tendencies of any class of habitual offenders are transmissible,...I should suppose that we must likewise presume that the legislature, in its wisdom, knows that the criminal tendencies of some classes of offenders are more likely to be transmitted than those of others."[4]

To raise this argument, however, is to presuppose that the rational basis test applies. *Skinner v. Oklahoma* held that it did not. In an opinion by Justice William O. Douglas, the Court began and ended by emphasizing the obvious fact that the challenged legislation intruded on a "basic civil right[]," involving "[m]arriage and procreation," that was "fundamental to the very existence and survival of the race."[5] When legislation draws lines that affect so fundamental a right, the Court ruled, "strict scrutiny" rather than "rational basis" review applies – even in cases such as *Skinner* that involve no "suspect classification." Applying strict scrutiny, the Court invalidated the Oklahoma Habitual Criminal Sterilization Act, substantially on the ground that it was unfair to sterilize Skinner while exempting white-collar criminals. Again, however, the decision to apply strict scrutiny was itself a crucial, doctrinally innovative step in the Court's analysis. It was only because the Supreme Court classified the right to procreate as what the Justices would now call a "fundamental right" that strict scrutiny applied and Skinner won his case.

The Idea of Fundamental Rights

When *Skinner* was decided, the notion of "fundamental" rights that were not specifically listed or "enumerated" in the Bill of Rights was a doctrinal novelty on which the Court did little to expand in the years immediately following. Although the authors of the Fourteenth Amendment contemplated the existence of fundamental rights constituting the privileges or immunities of national citizenship, the Supreme Court rendered the Privileges or Immunities Clause effectively meaningless in *The Slaughter-House Cases*[6] (1872), as discussed in Chapter 3. Nor did the

4 Ibid. at 544 (Stone, C. J., concurring).
5 Ibid. at 541.
6 83 U.S. 36 (1872).

idea of fundamental rights play any role in the *Lochner* era, when the Court purported to inquire equally into the reasonableness of all restrictions on liberties, without ranking them in terms of fundamentality, or in the immediate aftermath of the *Lochner* era. But beginning in the late 1950s, and especially during the 1960s and 1970s, the Court has designated some rights protected by the Due Process and Equal Protection Clauses as more "fundamental" than others. Among the rights assigned to this category are the rights to vote, to marry, to raise one's children, and to have an abortion. Under modern doctrine, statutes that infringe judicially identified fundamental rights trigger "strict" judicial scrutiny and are invalid unless "necessary to promote a compelling governmental interest." To give a snapshot of the resulting doctrine, statutes thus attract the same "strict" scrutiny if they either discriminate on "suspect" bases, as was discussed in Chapter 5, or, alternatively, burden fundamental rights, as will be discussed in this chapter.

The Supreme Court's fundamental rights jurisprudence is deeply controversial, at least in some of its aspects. From the perspective of critics, the Court properly protects "enumerated" rights such as freedom of speech, but "unenumerated" fundamental rights – such as the rights to vote, to marry, and to have an abortion – are illicit judicial creations. Although the distinction between "enumerated" and "unenumerated" rights is so well entrenched in constitutional debates that I have accepted it for purposes of discussion, it is frequently more misleading than illuminating.[7] For example, the Constitution refers specifically to "the freedom of speech" but not to the freedom of association. Should recognized rights to freedom of association be deemed "unenumerated" and therefore suspect or even illegitimate? Virtually no one seems to think so. Are recognized rights to engage in expressive conduct, such as picketing and displaying signs, unenumerated because the First Amendment mentions only "speech"? Again, virtually no one seems to think

---

7 See Ronald Dworkin, "Unenumerated Rights: Whether and How Roe Should Be Overruled," 59 *University of Chicago Law Review* 381 (1992).

so. It might be suggested that certain rights are properly recognized as implicit in the First Amendment and thus should count as enumerated even if not identified specifically but that other provisions of the Constitution cannot similarly generate implicit rights. But this position is arbitrary and untenable. Furthermore, some rights have long been recognized as implicit in the structure of the Constitution as a whole. The right to travel from state to state, which is discussed at greater length in Chapter 10, furnishes one historically recognized example. Although the right to travel is not listed anywhere in the Constitution, it is presupposed by the Constitution's structure, which creates a unified nation. In this example, as in other cases, a categorical distinction between enumerated and unenumerated rights is more likely to confuse than enlighten. What matters is whether a right is implicit in the Constitution in some meaningful sense or is presupposed by it. If so, a second question arises, involving how weighty or important that right is.

Today, judicial conservatives often insist that tradition provides the exclusive touchstone for the identification of fundamental rights. Liberals normally are more open to the possibility that historical understandings, though relevant, are not necessarily controlling. But these are generalizations. In no one's eyes are all of the rights that the Supreme Court has deemed "fundamental" created equal.

Voting Rights: A Conceptual Introduction

Harper v. Virginia Board of Elections[8] (1966) exemplifies the Court's stance in denominating voting rights as fundamental. The case presented a challenge to provisions of the Virginia state constitution that made payment of an annual $1.50 "poll tax" a prerequisite to voting. The tax's aims were to raise revenues and to restrict voting to those who were most likely to vote wisely. Willingness to pay the fee was at least a crude measure of a citizen's interest in public affairs. Furthermore, as

8 383 U.S. 663 (1966).

a dissenting opinion pointed out, "it was probably accepted as sound political theory by a large percentage of Americans through most of our history, that people with some property have a deeper stake in community affairs, and are consequently more responsible, more educated, more knowledgeable."[9] Nevertheless, the Court's majority invalidated the poll tax. Although acknowledging that "the right to vote in state elections is nowhere expressly mentioned" in the Constitution, the majority thought that such a right could fairly be said to be implicit in the Constitution's structure. The right to vote on an equal basis is closely linked in popular understanding to the right to equal citizenship. What is more, the right to vote, within a political democracy, is the right that must normally be relied on by citizens to protect and preserve their other rights in legislative deliberations. Given the Constitution's implicit commitment to political democracy, and the importance of the right to vote as a guarantor of equal citizenship within political democracy, the Court concluded that voting rights deserve recognition as being "fundamental." In determining whether voting rights had been infringed, the Court would therefore not stop upon determining that a rule or classification that precluded some people from voting was minimally "rational." It would unapologetically apply a more rigorous form of scrutiny that has today evolved into a compelling state interest test.

Voting Rights: The "One-Person, One-Vote" Cases

The Supreme Court's most celebrated cases involving voting rights are the so-called one-person, one-vote cases, symbolized by *Reynolds v. Sims*[10] (1964). *Reynolds* involved a challenge to legislative districts in the state of Alabama. When the Court decided the case in 1964, the Alabama legislature had not once "reapportioned" itself since 1901. Over the intervening sixty-three years, shifts in population had made it

---

9 Ibid. at 685 (Harlan, J., dissenting).
10 377 U.S. 533 (1964).

possible for voters in districts that included only about 25 percent of the state's citizens to elect a majority of the members in both the state Senate and state House of Representatives. Cities, which had grown larger, were underrepresented. Rural areas had disproportionate influence. Nor was the Alabama legislature likely to fix the problem. Fair reapportionment would have required many legislators to vote themselves out of jobs. Similar situations existed in other states.

In *Reynolds*, Alabama voters in underrepresented areas claimed that the state's electoral scheme violated the Equal Protection Clause. Their claim was different from that involved in *Harper*, and in some ways more difficult. At stake in *Harper* was the right of citizens who could not afford the poll tax to be able to vote at all. *Reynolds* did not involve total exclusions from voting but rather the right to an equally weighted vote. At the time the case was argued, *Reynolds* appeared to raise extraordinary difficulties. On the one hand, voting arrangements that let minorities dominate state politics seemed inherently unfair. On the other hand, it was far from obvious that the right to an equally weighted vote should be regarded as implicit in the Constitution's overall theory or structure. With each state entitled to two Senators in the U.S. Senate, voters in small states have relatively more voting power in senatorial elections than do voters in large states.

Finally, many observers shared a concern to which Justice Felix Frankfurter had given passionate voice in an earlier decision: that judicial oversight of legislative districting would plunge the Court into a dangerous "political thicket."[11] In Alabama or any other state, there are many ways that lines might be drawn to create voting districts of roughly equal population. That being so, any selection was likely to advantage either Democrats or Republicans. If the courts got involved at all, Frankfurter feared that they would quickly become embroiled in partisan controversies. Beyond a few plain constitutional limits, such as those forbidding discrimination on the basis of race or gender in the distribution

---

11 *Colegrove v. Green*, 328 U.S. 549, 556 (1946).

of voting rights, he also doubted the availability of judicially manageable standards to decide how political power ought to be allocated. For Frankfurter, electoral districting questions were political to the core. He thought that courts should treat them as coming within the "political question" doctrine, discussed in Chapter 9, and thus as committed entirely to the "political branches" of government.

In *Reynolds v. Sims* and a series of other one-person, one-vote cases during the 1960s, the Supreme Court dismissed these concerns. Reasoning that voting rights are "fundamental" rights under the Equal Protection Clause, and that their purpose is to give equal political power to all voters as a measure of their equal citizenship, it held that "seats in both houses of a bicameral state legislature must be apportioned on a population basis"[12] following each decennial census. Although the one-person, one-vote cases provoked fierce controversy at the time, within as little as a decade they – like *Brown v. Board of Education* – had won nearly universal acceptance. A rule demanding equal populations in electoral districts turned out to pose few problems in implementation: legislatures know the standard that they must meet to achieve judicial acceptance of their plans. When tempers had cooled, the idea that everyone's vote should have equal weight also accorded with almost everybody's notion of basic fairness – as, apparently, did the idea that in a political democracy, the right to vote should be regarded as "fundamental."[13]

Beyond One Person, One Vote

The one-person, one-vote cases resolved one problem in ensuring that voting power is fairly distributed – but as it turned out, only the simplest one. A further question involves the proper role of the courts, if any, in ensuring that equally sized legislative districts (which thus satisfy the

12 *Reynolds*, 377 U.S. at 568.

13 There are, to be sure, some important ambiguities in the one person, one vote formulation. For discussion, see Sanford Levinson, "One Person, One Vote: A Mantra in Need of Meaning," 80 *North Carolina Law Review* 1269 (2002).

one-person, one-vote requirement) permit fair representation of all relevant groups. In recent decades, the most vehement squabbles about fair representation have involved political parties' efforts to draw district lines that advantage them over their rivals. *Davis v. Bandemer*[14] (1986) well illustrates the problem. In the aftermath of the 1980 census, when legislatures throughout the nation needed to be reapportioned to comply with the one-person, one-vote requirement, the Republican Party controlled the Indiana legislature. Employing a long-practiced technique known as "gerrymandering," Indiana Republicans set out to do what Democrats tried to do in states in which they had legislative majorities – create voting districts that would help their candidates and disadvantage the other party. Relying on well-known methods, the Indiana Republicans "packed" as many likely Democratic voters as possible into some legislative districts. These districts became "safe" seats for Democrats, but their design also ensured that the Democrats, in winning them by huge margins, would "waste" many votes that might have helped elect Democrats in other districts. Having arranged for lots of Democratic votes to be "wasted," the Indiana Republicans then drew a series of district lines that "split" other geographical concentrations of Democrats by assigning some to one district and some to another, each with a Republican majority. The design worked. In the 1982 elections, Republican candidates captured fifty-seven seats in the Indiana State House of Representatives to the Democrats' forty-three, even though Democratic candidates won 52 percent of the total votes cast statewide.

When Indiana Democrats challenged the constitutionality of the Republicans' gerrymander in *Davis v. Bandemer*, the Supreme Court could not agree on a majority opinion. Three Justices believed that challenges to partisan gerrymandering present "political questions" not fit for judicial decision at all; this would have meant that party-based gerrymanders violate no judicially enforceable constitutional rights.[15] Nearly

14 478 U.S. 109 (1986) (plurality opinion).
15 See ibid. at 164 (O'Connor, J., joined by Burger, C. J., and Rehnquist, J., concurring in judgment).

at the opposite extreme, two Justices believed that gerrymanders are inherently unfair and that courts should hold them unconstitutional whenever they are effective.[16] In the middle, a plurality of four ruled that partisan gerrymanders violate the Constitution only when they "consistently degrade a voter's or a group of voters' influence on the political process as a whole."[17]

In essence, *Davis v. Bandemer* recognized a fundamental constitutional right to be free from partisan gerrymanders but defined that right very narrowly and made violations almost impossible to prove: proof of "consistent degrad[ation]" could apparently emerge only from a series of elections in which one party was grossly underrepresented in the legislature (relative to the total number of votes won by its candidates). That the Indiana gerrymander had worked for one election in 1982 did not suffice. Writing for the plurality, Justice Byron White adopted that position quite self-consciously. On the one hand, he believed that electoral districting was an inherently political exercise and that state legislatures, in performing it, were incorrigibly partisan. He thus thought it would be naive and unworkable to hold that partisan scheming in the design of legislative districts always violated the Equal Protection Clause. On the other hand, he thought that the Court must define some limit, marked by the consistent degradation of the votes of one or the other party. *Davis v. Bandemer* thus reflected an uneasy compromise. Although forbidding the grossest partisan excesses, it did not develop a more affirmative theory concerning the fair distribution of voting power beyond the one-person, one-vote requirement.

In practice, the test prescribed by the *Davis* plurality proved both difficult for lower courts to apply and impossible for those who wished to challenge partisan gerrymanders to satisfy. Troubled by one or both aspects of this state of affairs, the Supreme Court agreed to revisit the

16 See ibid. at 164 (Powell, J., joined by Stevens, J., concurring in part and dissenting in part).
17 Ibid. at 132 (plurality opinion).

issues presented by party-based gerrymanders in *Vieth v. Jubelirer*[18] (2004). Once again, however, the Justices proved unable to agree on a majority opinion. This time around, four Justices believed that there were no "judicially manageable standards" by which courts could judge the permissibility of partisan gerrymanders. In their view, courts should therefore dismiss all challenges to such schemes as presenting "political questions" not fit for judicial resolution. The decisive vote was cast by Justice Anthony Kennedy, who agreed with the plurality that the case should be dismissed, and further agreed that no judicially manageable standards had yet emerged, but refused to rule out the possibility that an extreme partisan gerrymander might violate the Constitution. To date, no Supreme Court opinion has ever held that a partisan gerrymander is unconstitutional, nor has a majority of the Supreme Court ever agreed on a standard for determining when, if ever, it could be said that partisan gerrymandering goes too far. This is an unhappy state of affairs but, among the political thickets about which Justice Frankfurter used to worry, that involving partisan gerrymanders is perhaps the thickest.

Majority-Minority Districting

The Supreme Court has taken a more aggressive stance against deliberate state efforts to create "majority-minority" districts in which statewide racial minorities (such as African Americans) enjoy majority status. States might attempt to create majority-minority districts for a number of reasons, but perhaps the most common involves efforts to comply with a federal statute, the Voting Rights Act (VRA). Congress originally enacted the VRA to stop states, especially in the South, from deliberately drawing district lines that disadvantaged racial minorities. It later amended and toughened the VRA when it thought that the Supreme Court had done too little to ensure that minorities were treated fairly. As interpreted by the Supreme Court, the amended VRA requires states

18 541 U.S. 267 (2004).

to create majority-minority districts when (1) a minority community is large and compact enough to constitute the majority in a properly drawn district, (2) the minority community is politically cohesive, and (3) the majority has itself engaged in racially polarized voting.[19]

In a series of cases, the Supreme Court has ruled that although the VRA requires the states to keep race in mind in order to create majority-minority districts when they can readily do so, the Constitution forbids them from making race the "predominant factor" in districting decisions. The predominant factor test emerged gradually from cases involving oddly shaped districts, the strange contours of which defied explanation on grounds other than race-based decision making. Such districts, the Court wrote in *Shaw v. Reno*[20] (1993), "reinforce[] the perception that members of the same racial group – regardless of their age, education, economic status, or the community in which they live – think alike, share the same political interests, and will prefer the same candidates at the polls."

Dissenting Justices have emphasized that legislatures can and some-times do create oddly shaped districts to benefit groups other than racial minorities. For example, Justice John Paul Stevens, who grew up in the politically tribal Chicago of the 1920s and 1930s, sharply disagreed with the majority's analysis in *Shaw v. Reno*. Writing in dissent, he protested: "If it is permissible to draw boundaries to provide adequate represen-tation for rural voters, for union members, for Hasidic Jews, for Polish Americans, or for Republicans [as it generally is, as long as the districts observe one-person, one-vote principles], it necessarily follows that it is permissible to do the same thing for members of the very minority group whose history in the United States gave birth to the Equal Protection Clause. A contrary conclusion could only be described as perverse."[21]

The Justices in the majority – who are the same Justices who are most skeptical of affirmative action – reject that reasoning. In their eyes, race

19 See *Thornburg v. Gingles*, 478 U.S. 30 (1986).
20 509 U.S. 630, 647 (1993).
21 Ibid. at 679 (Stevens, J., dissenting).

is different because it is peculiarly divisive and unfair as a basis for governmental decision making, especially when it is plainly the predominant factor in producing decisions. (In majority-minority districting cases, as in affirmative action cases, the controlling position seems to be that race can be taken into account but cannot be allowed to count for too much.)

The majority's position in cases such as *Shaw v. Reno* is invariably classed as "conservative." If taken at face value, that characterization is a revealing one, which illustrates an important distinction between judicial politics and electoral politics. Even when Republicans have had congressional majorities, they have made no serious move to repeal provisions of the VRA that pressure states to create majority-minority districts. The reason lies at least partly in partisan concerns. Almost without exception, majority-minority districts are packed with an overwhelming proportion of Democrats and thus "waste" Democratic votes that might help elect more Democratic candidates if some were spread across more districts. On this issue, however, conservative Supreme Court Justices have not allied themselves with the interests of congressional Republicans. In imposing constitutional obstacles to majority-minority districts, conservative Supreme Court Justices read the Constitution in light of views that are "political" in one sense, involving judgments of fairness, but they are not "partisan" in the sense of seeking to promote the fortunes of any political party. By the same token, the Court's more liberal Justices have consistently voted to sustain the constitutionality of majority-minority districts, presumably without regard to the electoral interests of the Democratic Party. In short, both the conservative and the liberal Justices' positions reflect judgments of moral and constitutional principle, not partisan political calculation.

Equality in the Counting of Votes

If the Supreme Court's divisions are reassuringly nonpartisan in cases involving majority-minority districts, *Bush v. Gore*[22] (2000) drew angry

22 531 U.S. 98 (2000).

charges of partisan decision making from more than a few. The case grew
out of the messy aftermath of the 2000 presidential election. Following
a close vote nationwide, the election's outcome depended on which candidate had carried Florida. After a machine count and recount of ballots left the Democrat Al Gore trailing the Republican George Bush by
fewer than one thousand votes, a series of legal battles developed about
whether there could be a manual recount of ballots on which the machine
tabulation had failed to reflect any presidential choice. Many of the ballots were punch cards on which voters using a stylus had apparently left
"hanging chads" or produced "dimples" but had made no full perfora-
tion. In a highly controversial ruling, a narrow majority of the Florida
Supreme Court ordered a recount in which they directed election officials and lower courts to attempt to discern "the intent of the voter" in
determining which ballots to count, but the state supreme court gave no
further specification of precisely how to identify what the intent of the
voter was. The court's ruling kept the hopes of Gore and his supporters
temporarily alive.

Opposing a recount, the Bush legal team rushed to the Supreme
Court of the United States. In an extraordinary motion, they asked the
Justices to "stay" or halt the recount while the parties prepared and filed
their legal briefs and awaited a Supreme Court ruling on whether allowing a recount to go forward would violate the Constitution. By a vote
of 5–4, with the Court's five most conservative Justices constituting the
majority, the Court granted the stay. Proceeding on a fast-paced, emergency basis, the Court then heard argument in the case and announced
its decision within just a few days. On the merits, the Court held that a
recount conducted under the vague "intent of the voter" standard would
have violated the "fundamental" right of Florida voters to have their
votes valued equally: "[T]he standards for accepting or rejecting contested ballots might vary not only from county to county but indeed
within a single county from one recount team to another."[23] Then, in

23 Ibid. at 106.

an even more controversial aspect of its opinion, the Court held that it was too late for the Florida Supreme Court to fix the problem by giving further instruction to the officials conducting the recount to ensure reasonable consistency.

The Supreme Court's opinion in *Bush v. Gore* had no identified author. It was issued "per curiam," or by the Court. But the Court was far from unanimous. Justices Stevens, Ginsburg, and Breyer – all of whom were generally counted as "liberals" – wrote or joined opinions flatly denying that an equal protection violation had occurred.[24] Justice David Souter agreed with them in protesting that even if a constitutional problem existed, the Florida Supreme Court should be given a chance to fix it by issuing clearer vote-counting instructions, rather than having the recount simply halted in its tracks.

When the dissenting votes were tallied and identified, it thus became clear that the Court's five most conservative Justices made up the majority. Yet in other cases under the Equal Protection Clause, the conservatives are those who are usually least likely to find rights violations (except in cases challenging affirmative action). The decision was unusual in other respects as well. The majority paid no heed to historical practices involving the counting and recounting of ballots. Before the advent of voting machines, all ballots had been counted by hand, often with no more direction than the Florida Supreme Court had given. Several Justices who joined the majority opinion frequently insist that the Court has no authority to condemn practices that were historically accepted as constitutional – a principle that they ignored in *Bush v. Gore*. Finally, the Court's opinion paid no heed to the inequalities that its ruling left unredressed, including that resulting from using different types of voting machines with varying degrees of accuracy across different parts of the state. Instead, the Court said this: "Our consideration is limited to the present" facts involving "the special instance of a statewide recount under the authority of a single state judicial officer" who had the

24 See ibid. at 124, 128 (Stevens, J., joined by Ginsburg, J., and Breyer, J., dissenting).

authority to prescribe uniform vote-counting standards but had failed to do so.[25] In the years since *Bush v. Gore*, the Supreme Court has never once relied on it to hold that any other state practice involving the counting or recounting of votes infringes the fundamental right to vote and have one's vote counted fairly.

The majority Justices may have felt that extraordinary features of the situation surrounding *Bush v. Gore* justified extraordinary action. For example, they may have believed that a partisan Florida Supreme Court dominated by Democrats was trying to steal an election that Bush had fairly won, or that a recount under partisan pressures and a national media spotlight would surely prove unfair, or that continued uncertainty about the election's outcome risked a national crisis that the Court needed to resolve decisively.[26] Reflecting on the partisanship that perhaps inevitably surrounded the vote count in Florida, some believed in December 2000 and continue to believe now that the Justices in the majority not only supplied cool and disinterested judgment but also saved the nation from dangerous confusion that could have resulted from continued uncertainty about the election's outcome. Others maintain that the Justices either descended into rank partisanship or at least lost their bearings in resolving what Justice Oliver Wendell Holmes would have called a "great case." As Holmes explained, "great cases are called great not by reason of their real importance in shaping the law of the future, but because of some accident of immediate overwhelming interest which appeals to the feelings and distorts the judgment."[27] Even today, we may still stand too close to *Bush v. Gore* for anyone to judge disinterestedly.

---

25 Ibid. at 109.

26 For a position of this general kind, see Richard A. Posner, *Breaking the Deadlock: The 2000 Election, the Constitution, and the Courts* (Princeton, NJ: Princeton University Press, 2001).

27 *Northern Securities Co. v. United States*, 193 U.S. 197, 400 (1904) (Holmes, J., dissenting).

Sexual Privacy or Autonomy

Most critics of the Supreme Court's fundamental rights jurisprudence tend to put voting rights cases in a class by themselves, perhaps along with some cases involving the right to travel, as involving rights that really are implicit in the Constitution. The most enduringly controversial fundamental rights cases have involved sexual privacy or autonomy. The Court laid the foundation for these cases with its 1942 decision in *Skinner v. Oklahoma*, but no further building occurred for more than two decades. Doctrinal development, and the controversies surrounding it, began with *Griswold v. Connecticut*[28] (1965). *Griswold* presented a challenge to a state statute that barred the distribution or use of "any drug... or instrument for the purpose of [contraception]." As interpreted, the statute allowed doctors to prescribe contraceptives to protect physical and psychological health – a loophole widely exploited by physicians serving middle- and upper-class patients. But the law posed a threat to clinics expressly offering family-planning assistance to the less affluent. In *Griswold*, two doctors challenged their convictions for prescribing contraceptives for use by married couples for no purpose other than contraception. By a vote of 7–2, the Court invalidated the statute, despite obvious anguish about the rationale for the result. (In contrast with *Skinner* and the voting rights cases, in *Griswold* the Court could not rest its decision on the Equal Protection Clause because the challenged statute prohibited everyone, not merely one particular class, from using birth control devices solely for purposes of contraception.)

Justice Douglas wrote the Court's opinion. Also the author of *Skinner*, Douglas had been named to the Court in the aftermath of the discredited *Lochner* era and was pledged not to repeat its mistakes. In *Griswold*, Douglas flatly denied that the decision involved the identification of a fundamental right protected by the Due Process Clause. "Overtones of some arguments suggest that *Lochner*... should be our

28 381 U.S. 479 (1965).

guide...[b]ut we decline that invitation,"[29] he wrote. In a brisk but confusing opinion that approached gibberish at crucial points, Douglas instead reasoned that several provisions of the Bill of Rights give rise to "peripheral" or "penumbral" rights that "create zones of privacy."[30] As an example, he cited the recognized First Amendment right to freedom of association, which is not expressly mentioned in the Constitution, as constituting a "penumbra where privacy is protected from governmental intrusion."[31] Similar "penumbras" of privacy surround other constitutional guarantees, Douglas continued, and the relation of marital intimacy – which Connecticut sought to regulate by denying contraceptives to married couples – fell "within the zone of privacy created by" one or more of those guarantees or penumbras,[32] although Douglas did not say which. Other Justices, who wrote concurring opinions, thought it less necessary to establish that the Connecticut statute violated "some right assured by the letter or penumbra of the Bill of Rights."[33] In the view of one concurring Justice, "the concept of liberty" protected by the Due Process Clause "protects those personal rights that are fundamental, and is not confined to the specific terms of the Bill of Rights."[34]

Although confusing in other respects, *Griswold* clearly suggested that the most disturbing feature of the Connecticut statute was its intrusion into intimate aspects of the marital relationship, some protection for which the Constitution might reasonably be said to presuppose: surely those who wrote and ratified the Constitution took it for granted that people would be able to marry and to enjoy sexual intimacy within marriage. Without explanation, however, the Court simply abandoned that limitation on *Griswold*'s rationale in *Eisenstadt v. Baird*[35] (1972), which

29 Ibid. at 481–82.
30 Ibid. at 483, 485.
31 Ibid. at 483.
32 Ibid. at 485.
33 See ibid. at 499 (Harlan, J., concurring in the judgment). Justice Goldberg also wrote a concurring opinion, in which Chief Justice Warren and Justice Brennan joined.
34 Ibid. at 486 (Goldberg, J., concurring).
35 405 U.S. 438 (1972).

invalidated a Massachusetts law that forbade the distribution of contraceptives to single people. "If the right of privacy means anything," the Court wrote, "it is the right of the individual, married or single, to be free from unwanted governmental intrusion into matters so fundamentally affecting a person as the decision whether to bear or beget a child."

The decision in *Eisenstadt* came near the height of what has been described as a sexual revolution, and it expressed the prevailing spirit of the age. Yet the decision also reflected a more timeless jurisprudential assumption that the Constitution presupposes, and thus authorizes the Supreme Court to identify and protect, certain fundamental liberties that it does not expressly mention. This jurisprudential assumption is very broadly shared, at least when it is not made explicit. To recur to previously discussed examples, the First Amendment refers only to freedom of speech, but it is fairly read to presuppose a right to freedom of expressive association. The Constitution does not state explicitly that there is a fundamental right to vote in state elections, but the idea that it implicitly creates or presupposes such a right now occasions almost no dispute. Most commentators believe that *Griswold v. Connecticut* similarly reached the right result, principally on the ground that a Constitution that protects speech and religion and that creates a right to be free from unreasonable searches and seizures (among other firmly recognized rights) should be read as presupposing a right to marry and to enjoy sexual intimacy in marriage. If one accepts the principle that the Constitution implicitly recognizes or presupposes some unenumerated fundamental rights, the difficult questions all involve application: which rights should the Supreme Court identify as fundamental, and to which criteria should it look in reaching its judgments?

Roe v. Wade and Abortion Rights

If ever concealed, the difficulty of those questions burst into prominence in *Roe v. Wade*[36] (1973). As is well known, *Roe* held that the Due

36 410 U.S. 113 (1973).

Process Clause protects a fundamental right to abortion. The Court's analysis unfolded in two crucial steps. First, the Court found that "the right...to be free from unwanted governmental intrusion into matters so fundamentally affecting a person as the decision whether to bear or beget a child" – which was prefigured in *Skinner v. Oklahoma* and expressly recognized in *Eisenstadt v. Baird* – encompasses a fundamental right to abortion. Second, the Court asked whether restriction of that right could be justified under the strict scrutiny test as necessary to promote a compelling governmental interest. Only when a fetus reached the stage of viability, the Court ruled, does the state's interest in fetal life become "compelling." Before that, a woman has a protected constitutional right to terminate an unwanted pregnancy.

Roe's reasoning is controversial at both steps. At the first, critics maintain that the Court's definition of the right to decide whether "to bear or beget a child" omits the most morally important point: abortion inherently involves the destruction of a human fetus. Abortion opponents claim that there can be no right, fundamental or otherwise, to cause the loss of an innocent life. At the second step, critics assert that the state's interest in preserving fetal life is morally compelling from the moment of conception.

As an enormous literature has abundantly demonstrated, there are many things that can be said in *Roe*'s defense, just as there are many things that can be said in opposition. Amid the continuing debate, it remains remarkable that seven Justices of the generally conservative Burger Court could have joined the *Roe* opinion. The Court's majority obviously failed to anticipate how endlessly divisive the abortion issue would prove to be. In contrast with some of their successors, even the most conservative Justices on the Burger Court were predominantly secular in orientation. From their perspective, *Roe* must have seemed a judicious compromise: it protected a woman's right to control the use of her body before the point of fetal viability, while permitting the state to protect unborn life thereafter.

Additionally, *Roe*, like *Skinner* and *Griswold* before it, had an "equal rights" as well as a "fundamental rights" dimension. Most obviously, only women can be come pregnant, and the law virtually never requires anyone other than a pregnant woman to risk his or her life, or to make bodily sacrifices comparable with those exacted by pregnancy, to protect or preserve the life of another. (The closest analogy may involve compelled military service in wartime – a burden that was imposed on men but not on women in the past.) In addition, because some states regulated abortion only lightly, by 1973, a woman with sufficient funds and education could typically procure a lawful abortion by traveling to a state where abortion was legal. By contrast, women who were poorer and less well educated often lacked access to legal abortion. Many thousands sought illegal abortions instead. According to some estimates, the mortality rate for illegal, unlicensed abortions was more than ten times higher than the mortality rate for legal abortions.[37]

Whatever the Justices may have thought, *Roe v. Wade* sparked a furor that has still not subsided roughly forty years later. Abortion opponents have never accepted *Roe*'s legitimacy. Within a short time after its decision, conservative presidential candidates began to promise to appoint prolife Justices to the Supreme Court. The Republican Party platform called for *Roe* to be reversed. By 1992, after Republican Presidents Ronald Reagan and George H. W. Bush had appointed five new Justices to the Supreme Court (and Democrats none), *Roe* appeared ripe for overruling.

The Court thus surprised most observers when it affirmed "*Roe*'s essential holding" in a bitter 5–4 decision in *Planned Parenthood of Southeastern Pennsylvania v. Casey*[38] (1992). Three themes dominated

---

37 See, for example, Jesse H. Choper, "Consequences of Supreme Court Decisions Upholding Individual Rights," 83 *Michigan Law Review* 1, 185 (1984) (stating that "the risk of death from an illegal abortion is twelve times greater than from a legal one").

38 505 U.S. 833 (1992).

the *Casey* plurality opinion that was jointly authored by Justices Sandra Day O'Connor, Anthony Kennedy, and David Souter – all of whom were nominated to the Court by Presidents who had pledged to seek prolife Justices. First, if *Roe* was a mistake at the time of its decision, it was at least not an obvious one. An unwanted pregnancy subjects women to enormous burdens. Decisions such as *Skinner, Griswold*, and *Eisenstadt* made it plausible to rely on precedent to hold as a matter of law that women had a fundamental right to decide whether to bear an unwanted child.[39] Second, a generation of women had shaped their lives in partial reliance on *Roe*. They had entered relationships and built careers in the expectation that unplanned pregnancies would not force them into unwanted childbearing. Third, the plurality worried openly that the Court's "legitimacy" would be compromised if it were to overrule *Roe* "under fire" and thus foster an impression that political pressure could trigger a change in constitutional law.[40] Precisely because the authors of the *Casey* plurality opinion had been appointed to overrule *Roe*, they felt, when the occasion actually arose, that they ought not do so. *Casey* marked the first time that a Supreme Court opinion ever openly expressed such a thought.

Although preserving *Roe*'s "central holding," *Casey* grants the states more flexibility than before to regulate and discourage abortion. Under *Roe*, nearly all impediments to abortion attracted strict judicial scrutiny. Under *Casey*, the states can impose waiting periods for having an abortion and require those performing abortions to provide information on alternatives, as long as those efforts do not amount to what the Court judges an "undue burden" on the ultimate abortion right.

In the Supreme Court, the most heated divisions about the meaning of the "undue burden" test have come in cases involving statutes that barred so-called partial-birth abortion (or what medical professionals

39 See ibid. at 849–53 (plurality opinion).
40 See ibid. at 864–69.

more typically refer to as intact dilation and extraction). In this procedure, which is sometimes used to terminate second-trimester pregnancies, doctors partially deliver an intact (but not yet viable) fetus before crushing its skull. In the first of two partial-birth abortion cases the Court, by 5–4, struck down a statute prohibiting the practice, partly because the law made no exception for situations in which doctors might choose this method over others on the basis of concerns about the health of the mother.[41] In a dissenting opinion, Justice Kennedy, who had voted with the majority in *Casey*, maintained that it was not an "undue burden" on the abortion right to ban a procedure that was, in his view, so closely analogous to infanticide.[42] In an indication of the moral and legal gulf that divided the Justices, a concurring opinion suggested that it was flatly irrational to ban partial-birth abortion when a mother's health might be at stake and when an alternative abortion procedure would leave the fetus dead anyway.[43]

A few years later, the Court largely replayed the same debate in *Gonzales v. Carhart*[44] (2007), but this time with a different outcome. The principal difference contributing to the change in results was the retirement of Justice O'Connor and her replacement by Samuel Alito. Now writing for the majority instead of being in dissent, Justice Kennedy argued that among the reasons Congress might wish to ban partial-birth abortion was to save women from postabortion regret and depression that might come from knowing "that [they] had allowed a doctor to pierce the skull and vacuum the fast-developing brain of [their] unborn child."[45] Ruth Bader Ginsburg, the only female Justice in 2007, filed a dissenting opinion in which she protested angrily that the Court had adopted a stereotyped, patronizing attitude toward women while, at the

41 *Stenberg v. Carhart*, 530 U.S. 914 (2000).
42 Ibid. at 963 (Kennedy, J., dissenting).
43 Ibid. at 946–47 (Stevens, J., concurring).
44 550 U.S. 124 (2007).
45 Ibid. at 159–60.

same time, "depriv[ing them] of the right to make an autonomous choice, even at the expense of their safety."[46]

Although there have been no major developments in the Supreme Court since *Carhart*, it surely did not represent the Court's last word on abortion, any more than did *Roe* or *Casey* before it. Abortion cases will continue to arise as state legislatures and possibly Congress enact statutes that test the meaning of the undue burden standard and even invite the Court to reconsider *Roe* and *Casey*. Whatever one might think about abortion rights, it is certainly not inappropriate for state legislatures to press the Court to reverse itself in some cases. Legislatures did so throughout the *Lochner* era. In yet an earlier period, Abraham Lincoln argued eloquently that Congress should continue its efforts to ban the spread of slavery in territories not yet admitted into the Union as states, notwithstanding the Supreme Court's ruling in *Dred Scott v. Sandford*[47] (1856) that Congress lacked authority to do so.[48] In the final analysis, the justifiability of legislative refusals to accept that the Supreme Court has settled a matter definitively depends at least in part on the moral and constitutional merits of the underlying position. In the case of *Roe v. Wade*, those merits remain subject to dispute.

Gay Rights

In 1986, while conservative opposition to *Roe v. Wade* mounted, the Supreme Court confronted another case implicating deeply held social, cultural, and moral values: a challenge to a Georgia statute forbidding sodomy. As written, the statute drew no distinction between homosexual and heterosexual sodomy. In practice, however, prosecutions for consensual heterosexual sodomy never occurred. Criminal prosecutions for

---

46 Ibid. at 184 (Ginsburg, J., dissenting).

47 60 U.S. 393 (1857).

48 See, for example, Lincoln's speech at Springfield, Illinois, on July 17, 1858, reproduced in Abraham Lincoln, *Speeches and Writings, 1832–1858* (New York: Library of America, 1989), 460, 472–79.

homosexual sodomy were also rare, but unusual circumstances resulted in the filing of charges against Michael Hardwick: when police arrived at his home to question him about another matter, a roommate led them directly to Hardwick's bedroom, where they observed him engaged in homosexual sodomy. Although the state ultimately dropped the prosecution, Hardwick decided to press the issue. He sought a judicial ruling that the antisodomy statute deprived him of a constitutionally protected fundamental right to sexual autonomy in the privacy of his bedroom.

In *Bowers v. Hardwick*[49] (1986), the Supreme Court rejected that claim. Several threads ran through the Court's opinion and the concurring opinions of the Justices in the 5–4 majority. The first involved anxiety about the judicial role in recognizing fundamental rights amid the fallout from *Roe v. Wade*. Writing for the Court, Justice Byron White, one of the two dissenters in *Roe*, observed that "[t]he Court is most vulnerable and comes nearest to illegitimacy when it deals with judge-made constitutional law having little or no cognizable roots in the language or design of the Constitution."[50] He further maintained that the Court could properly treat as "fundamental" only those rights that were either "implicit in the concept of ordered liberty" or "deeply rooted in this Nation's history and tradition."[51] This formulation would have justified the ruling in *Griswold v. Connecticut* but seemed intentionally ambiguous about if not flatly inconsistent with *Roe v. Wade*.

The second, sometimes latent theme in the Court's opinion was contempt for homosexual conduct. The Court refused to consider whether the Constitution would permit application of the Georgia statute to heterosexual sodomy.[52] In a concurring opinion, Chief Justice Warren Burger quoted an eighteenth-century English jurist who had termed sodomy a crime worse than rape.[53] Citing historical prohibitions against

49 478 U.S. 186 (1986).
50 Ibid. at 194.
51 Ibid. at 191–92.
52 See ibid. at 188, n.2.
53 See ibid. at 197 (Burger, C. J., concurring).

sodomy, the majority opinion caustically concluded that "to claim that a right to engage in [homosexual sodomy] is 'deeply rooted in this Nation's history and tradition' or 'implicit in the concept of ordered liberty' is, at best, facetious."[54]

A third strand in the Court's opinion involved an unwillingness to recognize a fundamental privacy or autonomy right embracing all forms of private, voluntary sexual conduct. The Court said that "it would be difficult, except by fiat, to limit the claimed right to homosexual conduct while leaving exposed to prosecution adultery, incest, and other sexual crimes even though they are committed in the home."[55]

Justice Harry Blackmun wrote a powerful dissenting opinion in *Bowers*. He derided the majority's preoccupation with the anatomical details of private, consensual acts of sexual intimacy. At stake, he wrote, was not an isolated right to engage in homosexual sodomy but "the fundamental interest all individuals have in controlling the nature of their intimate associations with others."[56] In his view, the Constitution presupposed a right of all persons to control "the most intimate aspects of their lives,"[57] at least through voluntary conduct in the privacy of their homes that posed no palpable threats to themselves or others. He thought it cruel and bigoted to deny to homosexuals the lawful opportunity for sexual intimacy that others take for granted.

Seventeen years later, the Court largely adopted Blackmun's position when it squarely overruled *Bowers v. Hardwick* in *Lawrence v. Texas*[58] (2003). The Court's decision in *Lawrence* was bold. The Justices could have ruled in favor of the challengers on narrow equal protection grounds. The Texas statute involved in the case prohibited homosexual, but not heterosexual, sodomy. The Court thus might have held that even if all sodomy could be prohibited, the distinction between homosexual and heterosexual sodomy was simply irrational and thus

54 Ibid. at 194 (majority opinion).
55 Ibid. at 195–96.
56 Ibid. at 206 (Blackmun, J., dissenting).
57 Ibid. at 199–200.
58 539 U.S. 558 (2003).

unconstitutional. (Justice O'Connor took this position in a concurring opinion.) But Justice Kennedy, who wrote the majority opinion joined by four other Justices, insisted on going further, to make clear that a state could not prohibit homosexual sodomy even if it also barred heterosexual sodomy. He also made clear the Court's central concern with the dignity of those threatened with prosecution: "When homosexual conduct is made criminal by the law of the State, that declaration in and of itself is an invitation to subject homosexual persons to discrimination both in the public and in the private spheres. The central holding of *Bowers* has been brought in question by this case, and... [i]ts continuance as precedent demeans the lives of homosexual persons."[59] The three Justices generally viewed as the Court's most conservative – Chief Justice William Rehnquist and Associate Justices Antonin Scalia and Clarence Thomas – filed a strident dissent (written by Justice Scalia).

In accord with my frequent reminders that the Supreme Court is a "they," not an "it," the readiest explanation for the Court's movement from *Bowers* to *Lawrence* involves a shift in membership. The precedents on which the *Lawrence* majority principally relied all dated to before *Bowers*. Justice Kennedy thus pointedly wrote that "*Bowers* was not correct when it was decided, and it is not correct today.... *Bowers v. Hardwick* should be and now is overruled."[60] But Justice Kennedy also noted that whereas in 1961 all states outlawed sodomy and twenty-four continued to do so in 1986 (when *Bowers* was decided), by 2003 the number was down to thirteen, of which four barred only homosexual sodomy. The social trend may have fortified the majority's confidence that it reflected an emerging moral consensus of the American people when it concluded that the "liberty" protected by the Due Process Clause should embrace broad rights of sexual autonomy.

In describing the constitutionally protected "liberty" that *Lawrence* upheld, Justice Kennedy departed from precedent in a small but potentially significant way: he did not use the terminology of fundamental

59 Ibid. at 575.
60 Ibid. at 578.

rights or strict judicial scrutiny. This was surely a deliberate choice. In making it, he may have meant to undermine the sharp distinction between strict scrutiny and rational basis review and to claim a judicial authority to make more nuanced judgments. Justice Kennedy also took pains to describe the protected liberty as one involving the conduct of "*private* lives in matters pertaining to *sex*." This formulation appeared designed to distinguish the right upheld in *Lawrence* from the right to homosexual marriage that the Justices surely knew would soon be claimed. The Court has previously described marriage as a "fundamental right," denials of which would trigger strict judicial scrutiny, but it remains uncertain how the protected right to "marriage" will be defined. It might be defined by reference to tradition as referring exclusively to a relationship between a man and a woman, or it might be viewed as a status of legal union from which homosexual couples cannot be excluded.

Dissenting in *Lawrence*, Justice Scalia argued that the Court had abused its authority by taking a partisan position in a "culture war" between liberals and social and religious conservatives and by "largely sign[ing] on to the so-called homosexual agenda...[of] eliminating the moral opprobrium that has traditionally attached to homosexual conduct."[61] Scalia may have intended his reference to the Court's taking sides in a "culture war" as hyperbole, although possibly he did not. There seems little doubt, and the Court did not deny, that it had made a judgment of fairness: it was wrong to deny to those wishing to engage in homosexual conduct the same opportunities for lawful sexual intimacy that the Court's precedents had previously ensured to heterosexuals. If this issue is the subject of a culture war, neutrality may not be an option. Nor will it be an option when the Court inevitably addresses issues involving claims of a constitutional right to gay marriage.

---

61 Ibid. at 602 (Scalia, J., dissenting).

Rights Involving Death and Dying

In 1997, the Supreme Court decided two important cases rejecting claims of what the press recurrently termed a constitutional "right to die." This was a misnomer. Die we all shall, with or without a constitutional right to do so. To speak technically and precisely, the issues before the Court involved the constitutionality of state laws forbidding people to receive the assistance of a willing physician in committing suicide. In *Washington v. Glucksberg*[62] (1997) and *Vacco v. Quill*[63] (1997), the Court ruled that the Constitution creates no general right to physician-assisted suicide.

Chief Justice William Rehnquist wrote the majority opinions in both cases. In considering whether patients who were terminally ill had a fundamental right to assisted suicide, Rehnquist employed substantially the same narrow test that the Court had used in *Bowers v. Hardwick*. Under it, he found no fundamental right to assisted suicide because no such right was "deeply rooted in this Nation's history and tradition."[64] On the contrary, all states had once prohibited assisted suicide, and all but one continued to do so.

In denying any right to assisted suicide, however, Rehnquist drew an important distinction. Most states traditionally have acknowledged the right of competent persons to refuse unwanted medical treatment – including life support or dialysis or chemotherapy – even when the refusal would predictably lead to death. Because that more limited right to refuse treatment had the support of "tradition[]," Rehnquist and the rest of the Court assumed (although they had no need to hold expressly) that it occupied the status of a fundamental right guaranteed under the Due Process Clause.[65]

Five Justices of the Court, in concurring opinions not joined by the Chief Justice, also appeared to believe that terminal patients have a

62 521 U.S. 702 (1997).
63 521 U.S. 793 (1997).
64 *Glucksberg*, 521 U.S. at 721.
65 See ibid. at 720.

constitutional right to the assistance of a willing physician in obtaining medication adequate to control their pain.[66] For some patients whose suffering is especially acute, a dosage sufficient to bring pain relief may also predictably cause death. Doctors and theologians have developed the so-called doctrine of double effect to deal with this situation. Under it, doctors may permissibly administer medication necessary to alleviate pain, even if a secondary and unintended (even though foreseeable) effect is to occasion death.

With the Court having recognized a fundamental right of competent persons to refuse unwanted medical treatment, and with at least five Justices apparently believing that there is a fundamental right not to be deprived of medication necessary to alleviate terminal suffering, the doctrinal picture that emerges from *Washington v. Glucksberg* is somewhat complex. Within it, seeming anomalies may exist. A terminal patient may direct a doctor to turn off a respirator; that step would constitute the exercise of a fundamental right to refuse treatment, even if death will result immediately. But a terminal patient not on a respirator has no right to the assistance of a physician in obtaining drugs for suicide.

If disparities such as this seem troubling, at least two considerations support the Court's piecemeal approach. First, the likely effects of authorizing physician-assisted suicide are much debated. Some believe that legalized physician-assisted suicide would corrupt the doctor-patient relationship. It might also give rise to cruel pressures on the elderly to choose suicide as an alternative to expending all their assets or consuming scarce medical resources. Under the circumstances, it may be prudent to wait to see what happens in states or countries that voluntarily choose

66 Justice O'Connor's concurring opinion, joined by Justices Ginsburg and Breyer, expressly raised and reserved this question. See ibid. at 736–37 (O'Connor, J., concurring). Although Justice Stevens was less specific, his concurring opinion suggested that individual liberty interests should outweigh competing state interests in at least some cases. See ibid. at 741–42, 745 (Stevens, J., concurring in the judgment). Justice Souter also reserved the question of whether individual interests might prevail over state interests in preserving life under some conditions. See ibid. at 782 (Souter, J., concurring in the judgment).

to authorize physician-assisted suicide. Second, as Justice O'Connor wrote in her concurring opinion in *Washington v. Glucksberg*, "[e]very one of us at some point may be affected by our own or a family member's terminal illness."[67] Issues involving assisted suicide have drawn and will continue to draw public attention. The Court can expect to profit from deliberation in the political arena before reconsidering issues involving "the right to die" at a later date.

Fundamental Rights Involving the Family

Fundamental rights involving the family are among the most firmly rooted in tradition and thus among those that are least controversially recognized as protected by the Due Process and Equal Protection Clauses. In several cases, the Court has characterized the right to marry as "fundamental."[68] The Court has also held that parents have constitutionally protected fundamental interests in the care, custody, and control of their children. But the precise scope of protected parental rights requires careful definition. For example, the state can obviously forbid parents to treat their children abusively. The state can also enforce compulsory education and vaccination laws,[69] parental wishes to the contrary notwithstanding.

Troxel v. Granville[70] (2000), which presented a novel question involving parents' rights to control who could visit with their children, demonstrates the difficulty of line drawing. A Washington statute permitted "any person" to petition a court for visitation rights and authorized the court to grant such rights whenever "visitation may serve the best interest of the child." In *Troxel*, in which grandparents had asked a court to grant them visitation rights and there was no determination of parental

67 Ibid. at 737 (O'Connor, J., concurring).
68 See, for example, *Loving v. Virginia*, 388 U.S. 1 (1967); *Zablocki v. Redhail*, 434 U.S. 374 (1978).
69 See *Jacobson v. Massachusetts*, 197 U.S. 11 (1905).
70 530 U.S. 57 (2000).

unfitness, the Supreme Court held that the statute gave too much discretionary power to judges and retained too little for parents. Interestingly, however, the Justices could not agree on a majority opinion specifying when, if ever, a state might permissibly grant visitation rights to nonparents, including grandparents, despite a parent's objection. Nor did the plurality opinion in the case, joined by four Justices, invoke the strict scrutiny formula often applied in other fundamental rights cases. Instead, the plurality inquired more loosely into the reasonableness of the particular infringement on parents' traditional rights that was at issue.

This approach made practical sense under the circumstances. Like the property rights discussed in Chapter 3, fundamental liberty rights need to be defined before they can be enforced. Again, as with property rights, state law has at least some role to play in the process of definition. If a state requires that schoolchildren observe a dress code, and if parents object that the code interferes with their fundamental right of control over their children, the issue should not be whether the infringement on parental rights is "necessary to promote a compelling governmental interest." The logically prior question is whether this modest limitation on parental powers actually intrudes on a parent's fundamental right – as that right has historically been understood or would sensibly be defined – at all. A similar analysis helps to explain many familiar and widely accepted restrictions on the fundamental right to marry. As Justice Potter Stewart once wrote, "[s]urely…a State may legitimately say that no one can marry his or her sibling, that no one can marry who is not at least 14 years old, that no one can marry without first passing an examination for venereal disease, or that no one can marry who has a living husband or wife."[71] Rules such as these do not infringe the right to marry so much as define it – even though, as Justice Stewart continued, surely "there is a limit beyond which a State may not constitutionally go"[72] in confining the definition of fundamental rights.

---

71 *Zablocki v. Redhail*, 434 U.S. at 392 (Stewart, J., concurring in the judgment).
72 Ibid.

Conclusion

Especially since *Roe v. Wade*, controversy abounds about which rights should be regarded as implicit in the Constitution or as presupposed by it. There are similar debates, equally heated, about whether "fundamental rights" must be grounded in history or can be identified by direct appeal to moral fairness or changing social norms. On the most basic point, however, more agreement exists than is often acknowledged, even if that agreement is sometimes obscured in debates about whether particular rights ought to be recognized: in creating individual rights against the government, the Constitution implies or presupposes more than it says expressly.

Part II   THE CONSTITUTIONAL SEPARATION OF POWERS

7 The Powers of Congress

> The powers delegated by the proposed Constitution to the federal government are few and defined.
>
> – The Federalist No. 45

N 1994, IN SEPTEMBER OF HER FRESHMAN YEAR AT Virginia Polytechnic Institute (better known as Virginia Tech), Christy Brzonkala reported that she had been raped by two members of the school's varsity football team, one of whom allegedly told her, "You'd better not have any diseases." When Brzonkala pressed a complaint through the college's disciplinary system, officials dismissed the charges against one of her alleged assailants. They found the other student guilty and initially suspended him for two semesters, but the school's provost overturned that punishment as "excessive" in light of the penalties in similar cases.

Rape is, of course, a crime under Virginia law, and Brzonkala might have sought action by the state's criminal justice system. In general, however, private citizens cannot force prosecutors to bring criminal charges. For a variety of reasons, prosecutors sometimes hesitate to file rape cases, perhaps especially against members of a public university's popular football team. So Brzonkala filed a civil (rather than criminal) lawsuit of her own in which she sought not to have her alleged assailants sent to jail but to have them pay money damages directly to her. She did so under the Violence against Women Act, a federal statute Congress enacted in 1994.

In *United States v. Morrison*[1] (2000), the Supreme Court ordered the dismissal of Brzonkala's lawsuit. The Court made no finding that Brzonkala had not been raped or that the defendants were not her rapists. By a 5–4 vote, the Court ruled instead that the federal statute that authorized her to sue was unconstitutional – not because the defendants would have had a right to rape Brzonkala (they would not) but because Congress had no power under the Constitution to enact a statute generally forbidding or penalizing violence against women.

From several perspectives, *United States v. Morrison* reveals a good deal about congressional power under the Constitution of the United States. As emphasized in the prologue, in a preliminary discussion of the Affordable Care Act (ACA) and *National Federation of Independent Business v. Sebelius*,[2] the government of the United States continues to be what the Supreme Court, echoing the Constitution's framers, calls one of "limited powers." Unlike state governments, which generally can pass any law that they wish unless the Constitution forbids them to do so, Congress can enact legislation only if it can point to some specific provision of the Constitution that authorizes it. Article I lists Congress's powers in a long string of clauses. (A few other grants of congressional authority are scattered in other parts of the Constitution, including the Thirteenth, Fourteenth, and Fifteenth Amendments.) The length and specificity of Article I's list support the inference that powers not named are withheld. The Tenth Amendment makes that conclusion unmistakable. It provides that "[t]he powers not delegated to the United States by the Constitution, nor prohibited by it to the States, are reserved to the States respectively, or to the people."

In *United States v. Morrison*, all involved conceded that no clause in the Constitution said expressly that Congress could prohibit or punish violence against women. In their eighteenth-century world, the framers

1 529 U.S. 598 (2000).
2 132 S. Ct. 2566 (2012).

and ratifiers of the Constitution apparently assumed that the states, rather than the federal government, would have responsibility for punishing most acts of violence. Defenders of the Violence against Women Act therefore had to stretch a bit in arguing that the statute was constitutionally valid. They claimed that Congress had authority to enact the Violence against Women Act under the Commerce Clause, which says that "[t]he Congress shall have Power...to regulate Commerce... among the several States."[3]

Although it might initially seem far-fetched to argue that the Commerce Clause empowers Congress to prohibit violence against women, that argument was actually wholly plausible under previous cases decided by the Supreme Court. (Indeed, four Justices of the Supreme Court accepted it in *Morrison*.) When no other provision of the Constitution clearly empowers congressional action, yet Congress believes regulatory legislation to be desirable or even urgently necessary, both Congress and the courts have recurrently looked for some connection, however tenuous, between a regulated activity and interstate commerce. For example, Congress has relied on the Commerce Clause to enact minimum wage legislation, environmental protection statutes, and civil rights laws prohibiting discrimination by private employers (which, unlike the government, are not directly covered by the Equal Protection Clause). In the case of violence against women, Congress relied in part on data indicating that such violence costs the national economy billions of dollars a year in health care and in lost economic activity and thus results in fewer sales of goods and services in interstate commerce.

Like the Justices of the Supreme Court, constitutional law scholars disagree about whether *United States v. Morrison* was consistent with the Court's prior cases. Either way, the case frames questions of great constitutional importance. How did we get to the current situation, in which many of the most important statutes enacted by Congress need to be justified by reference to the Commerce Clause, even when they do not straightforwardly regulate the sale or movement of goods in commerce

3 U.S. Constitution, Article I, Section 8, Clause 3.

from one state to another? Does a great deal of modern law rest on an outright evasion of the Constitution's language and intent? Does the Court's invalidation of the Violence against Women Act – when coupled with its subsequent ruling in *National Federation of Independent Business* that Congress could not invoke the Commerce Clause to justify requiring individuals to purchase health insurance – mean that a number of other federal statutes, including those that prohibit race discrimination by restaurants and private businesses, are at risk of being struck down as well?

These questions regarding the Commerce Clause have parallels in some other constitutional provisions conferring powers on Congress, especially the taxing and spending power conferred by Article I, Section 8, Clause 1, which authorizes Congress to lay taxes and spend money to "provide for the ... general Welfare of the United States." It is under the Taxing and Spending Clause that Congress has created many of the features of the modern welfare state, including Social Security, that would have been unimaginable to the Constitution's framers – even if their language permits what they could not have foreseen. It is also under the Taxing and Spending Clause that a closely divided Supreme Court ultimately upheld the Affordable Care Act's individual mandate to purchase health insurance in *National Federation of Independent Business v. Sebelius*. In this chapter, I focus mostly on the commerce power, both because it is centrally important and because debates about congressional authority under other provisions have often tracked Commerce Clause debates. But I also discuss the Taxing and Spending Clause. Because *National Federation of Independent Business v. Sebelius* appears prominently in a number of places in the discussion that follows, readers who only dimly recall the account of that case that appeared in the prologue may want to look back to refresh their recollections before reading on.

Elements of the "Original Understanding"

In thinking about the reach of congressional power, as about most constitutional questions, the starting point lies in the constitutional text and its historical purposes. But the historical purposes of the Commerce Clause are hard to reconstruct in a neutral way because the framers and ratifiers inhabited a political, economic, and intellectual world so different from ours. On the one hand, the framers clearly anticipated that the states, not Congress, would be the principal lawmakers. They also appeared to contemplate that the states would retain what they called the "police power" – probably to the exclusion of Congress – to enact legislation to protect the public health, safety, and morals. On the other hand, the framers viewed the Constitution as empowering Congress to deal with all matters of genuinely national dimension.[4]

Formidable intellectual puzzles arise in attempts to integrate the various elements of the framers' views and to discern their relevance to modern problems. To be slightly more concrete, today there are many problems that appear genuinely national in scope that the framers could never have anticipated. For example, interstate trafficking in child pornography may involve threats to public safety and morals, and the framers thus

---

4 See Jack N. Rakove, *Original Meanings: Politics and Ideas in the Making of the Constitution* (New York: Knopf, 1996), 177–80 (describing the Constitutional Convention's efforts to give determinate meaning to a proposal to confer national legislative power "in all cases to which the separate States are incompetent, or in which the harmony of the United States may be interrupted by the exercise of individual Legislation"); Robert L. Stern, "That Commerce Which Concerns More States Than One," 47 *Harvard Law Review* 1335, 1341 (1934); Donald H. Regan, "How to Think about the Federal Commerce Power and Incidentally Rewrite *United States v. Lopez*," 94 *Michigan Law Review* 554, 556 (1995). By noting that the framers apparently intended to empower Congress to deal with all genuinely national problems, I do not intend to imply that they viewed the Commerce Clause as reaching all such problems. For a range of views, see, for example, William Winslow Crosskey, *Politics and the Constitution in the History of the United States* (Chicago: University of Chicago Press, 1953), 1:50–292 (arguing that the Commerce Clause authorized regulation of all gainful activities); Randy E. Barnett, "The Original Meaning of the Commerce Clause," 68 *University of Chicago Law Review* 101 (2001) (arguing that the Commerce Clause authorized only the regulation of the trade of goods and the shipment of goods for trade); Grant S. Nelson and Robert J. Pushaw Jr., "Rethinking the Commerce Clause: Applying First Principles to Uphold Federal Commercial Regulations but Preserve State Control over Social Issues," 85 *Iowa Law Review* 1 (1999) (adopting an intermediate view).

might have considered the problem the exclusive concern of the states. But suppose that Congress attempts to address the problem, which centrally involves the abuse of children, by forbidding shipment of child pornography across state lines. Legislation of this form arguably regulates "commerce" (or trade "among the several States") in the most literal sense, even if its purpose involves considerations of safety and morality that the framers might have expected to be the province of state rather than federal regulation.

An additional element of the framers' worldview further complicates the picture insofar as their expectations remain paramount (although it is not obvious that they should). The founding generation regarded each of the states as a "sovereign," which had retained its sovereignty even after the ratification of the Constitution. To the eighteenth-century mind, "sovereignty" implied supremacy. Reconciliation of state sovereignty with national sovereignty thus would appear to have required that there be no overlap of state and national powers: if the federal government could regulate the same conduct as a state, and thereby displace state legislation, this would have implied that the state was not really sovereign or supreme. Operating with this categorical scheme, many members of the founding generation appear to have assumed that there was a distinction between the manufacture of products, which should be subject only to state and not to congressional regulation, and the shipment and sale of goods in interstate commerce, which would come within Congress's commerce power. But suppose that a manufacturing plant spews pollution into the atmosphere, that the pollution flows across state lines, and that it damages agriculture, health, and thus economic productivity in other states. Should Congress today be deemed powerless to enact regulatory legislation because of an anachronistic eighteenth-century understanding that the regulation of manufacturing is a power reserved to the states? Isn't pollution a genuinely national problem today, even if it was not in 1787? And didn't the framers and ratifiers intend to empower Congress to deal with all genuinely national problems?

As modern lawyers and judges struggle with questions such as these, more is at stake than abstract issues of fidelity to the Constitution's "original understanding,"[5] as the debate surrounding the Affordable Care Act case makes vivid. On the whole, political liberals tend to favor a broad interpretation of Congress's commerce power as necessary to promote liberal goals such as the enactment of environmental, economic, and workplace safety regulation. To be effective, such regulation often must occur at the national level. For example, it may be impossible for one state acting alone to protect its environment effectively if air pollution from other states sweeps across its borders. It may be almost equally impossible for one state on its own to require employers to provide pensions or medical benefits to their employees if surrounding states do not do likewise. If a single state, or only a few, were to impose such obligations, many businesses likely would flee to other states, where their costs would be lower.

Whereas liberals tend to favor broad congressional power, conservatives characteristically regard such power with more skepticism – and not simply because they have different views about the nature or significance of the Constitution's original understanding. Part of their opposition reflects resistance to one-size-fits-all national regulation. In at least some cases, state and local governments may enjoy distinctive advantages in tailoring legislation to local problems and values. Conservatives also tend to believe that "that government is best which governs least," at least in the area of business regulation. Recognition of sweeping federal regulatory power increases the likelihood that regulation will be enacted at some level of government. According to conservatives, regulation not only diminishes liberty but also threatens to create costly economic inefficiency.[6]

5 For a lucid and balanced discussion of constitutional debates about federalism and their underlying stakes, see David L. Shapiro, *Federalism: A Dialogue* (Evanston, IL: Northwestern University Press, 1995).

6 For a reading of the Commerce Clause in light of views such as these, see Richard A. Epstein, "The Proper Scope of the Commerce Power," 73 *Virginia Law Review* 1387 (1987).

As in other areas of constitutional law, one might argue that these liberal and conservative views should be irrelevant to matters of interpretation. But for judges and Justices forced to decide which strand of the "original understanding" to emphasize and how to construe relatively vague constitutional language in light of history and precedent, considerations of which interpretation would lead to the "best" results probably exert a pervasive influence, as the divisions among conservative and liberal Justices in the Violence against Women Act and Affordable Care Act cases would tend to suggest.

Doctrinal and Conceptual History

Supreme Court decisions interpreting the Commerce Clause have followed a twisting path. Roughly speaking, the Supreme Court of John Marshall's era, in the early years of the republic, took an expansive view. Back then, however, Congress did not enact much national regulatory legislation. The Court thus had no occasion to measure the precise scope of congressional authority.

When cases testing the bounds of that authority finally began to arise in the late nineteenth and early twentieth centuries, the Court employed two evaluative frameworks. One was "formalist," or concerned with the form of federal regulation. It focused on whether Congress had directly and specifically regulated the movement of goods in commercial enterprise across state lines. By the narrowest of margins, the Court followed a formalist approach in *Champion v. Ames*[7] (1903), which upheld Congress's power to forbid the interstate transportation of lottery tickets. According to the Court, the statute was valid because it regulated commerce – the shipment of an item of sale from one state to another – in the literal or formal sense. A dissenting opinion protested that the purpose of the statute was to protect the public morals from the evil of gambling and that the regulation of morality was a state function, not

7 188 U.S. 321 (1903).

delegated to Congress by the Commerce Clause.[8] The *Champion* majority brushed this objection aside.

The alternative approach that the Court sometimes employed to analyze congressional power under the Commerce Clause could be described as "realist." This approach focused not on the form of legislation but on its real consequences for the shipment of goods in interstate commerce or, alternatively, on its actual purposes. The Court adopted a realist framework in *The Shreveport Case*[9] (1914). At issue was whether Congress could authorize the Interstate Commerce Commission (ICC) to set rates for the intrastate shipment of rail freight between two cities in Texas. No one disputed that the ICC could regulate the rates a railroad charged for shipments from Texas to Louisiana. But when a railroad began to charge lower rates for shipments along longer routes within the state of Texas, those lower rates skewed incentives to engage in interstate trade: because it was cheaper to ship and sell goods in Texas than to transport them out of state, interstate commerce diminished. In light of this real effect on what was ultimately shipped in interstate commerce, the Court upheld the ICC's regulation of rates on what were formally intrastate rail routes.

Taken by themselves, both the formalist and the realist approaches appeared to make sense. For the Supreme Court, and ultimately for the country, the problem involved fitting both into a coherent overall framework. Just as either a formalist or a realist test could be used to uphold congressional power, as in *Champion v. Ames* and *The Shreveport Case*, either could also be used to restrict congressional power. By the early twentieth century, there were Supreme Court decisions citing realist grounds for invalidating legislation that would have passed a formalist test. For example, in *Hammer v. Dagenhart*[10] (1918) the Court struck down a federal statute forbidding the shipment in interstate commerce

---

8 See ibid. at 364–65 (Fuller, C. J., joined by Brewer, Shiras, and Peckham, J. J., dissenting).

9 *Houston, East & West Texas Railway Co. v. United States*, 234 U.S. 342 (1914).

10 247 U.S. 251 (1918).

of items that had been produced by child labor. Although the statute dealt formally with shipment in interstate commerce, and thus would have passed a formalist test, it was invalid, the Court said, because Congress's real purpose and intended effect involved the regulation of manufacturing that occurred wholly within individual states. Other decisions found that legislation regulating activities with real effects on interstate commerce could not be justified because it formally involved the regulation of manufacturing. To explain when regulation could be justified under a realist theory, the Court distinguished between activities with "direct effects" on interstate commerce, which Congress could regulate, and activities with only "indirect" effects, which it could not. But the line between direct and indirect effects proved elusive, and the Court's judgments were difficult to predict. The doctrine subsisted for decades in this confused state.[11]

Crisis and Revision

The confusion reached a crisis point during the Great Depression of the 1930s. As businesses failed and unemployment mounted, an increasingly desperate public looked to the national government for solutions. In the eyes of commanding political majorities, the experimental policies of President Franklin Roosevelt's New Deal offered the nation's best hope for putting people back to work. The New Deal programs were eclectic, but many rested on the idea that the way to renewed prosperity lay in national economic regulatory legislation, adopted under the Commerce Clause and justified on the "realist" theory that otherwise intrastate activities pervasively influence and ultimately determine what is bought and sold in interstate commerce.

Despite the emergency, and despite plausible doctrinal arguments for upholding the main elements of the New Deal, five and sometimes

11 The account offered here is a relatively standard one. Barry Cushman, *Rethinking the New Deal Court: The Structure of a Constitutional Revolution* (New York: Oxford University Press, 1998), argues that the Court's decisions reflected greater consistency than other commentators have discerned.

six determinedly conservative Supreme Court Justices struck down one piece of New Deal legislation after another. Having won an overwhelming mandate in 1936 when being reelected with more than 60 percent of the popular vote, Franklin Roosevelt – as recounted in the Introduction – proposed his notorious Court-packing plan. With public opinion firmly behind Roosevelt and the New Deal (if not necessarily behind the Court-packing plan, about which the public appeared split), and with Court-packing seriously threatening the Court's independence, two of the Justices did an apparent about-face. Within a few years, the Court had reshaped Commerce Clause doctrine to permit federal legislation whenever it satisfied either a formalist or a realist test. Under what has been termed "the New Deal settlement,"[12] legislation passed constitutional muster if it regulated or forbade shipments in interstate commerce, even if the plain purpose was to regulate manufacturing (for example, by forbidding the shipment in interstate commerce of any goods produced by firms that failed to pay their employees a minimum wage).[13] And intrastate regulatory legislation could equally be defended on the ground that the activity being regulated had substantial effects on interstate commerce[14] – a test that the Court interpreted very loosely. In one celebrated case, the Court unanimously upheld a prohibition against a farmer's exceeding a federal quota for the production of wheat by growing an extra 239 bushels for home consumption.[15] If every farmer did the same, the Court reasoned, the cumulative effect on the purchase and sale of wheat in interstate commerce would be substantial. Congress therefore enjoyed regulatory authority under the Commerce Clause.

The Supreme Court confirmed the breadth of Congress's commerce power in the 1960s. Relying on the Commerce Clause, the Court upheld

---

12 See Larry D. Kramer, "We the Court," 115 *Harvard Law Review* 4, 122 (2001).

13 See, for example, *United States v. Darby*, 312 U.S. 100, 115 (1941) (holding that "the prohibition of the shipment interstate of goods produced under … forbidden substandard labor conditions is within the constitutional authority of Congress").

14 See ibid. at 119 (upholding congressional power to regulate "intrastate activities which have a substantial effect" on interstate commerce).

15 See *Wickard v. Filburn*, 317 U.S. 111 (1942).

central provisions of the 1964 Civil Rights Act, which prohibits race discrimination by restaurants and places of public accommodation, as well
as by public and private employers. In *Katzenbach v. McClung*[16] (1964),
the Court applied the act against a restaurant whose customers admittedly included few or no travelers in interstate commerce. The Court reasoned that much of the food bought and served by the restaurant traveled
across state lines and that restaurant patronage by excluded minorities
would increase, and that purchases connected to interstate commerce
would therefore increase as well, if discrimination by all restaurants were
forbidden. These linkages to interstate commerce sufficed to justify regulation under the Commerce Clause.

A Course Correction of Uncertain Scope

Under precedents such as these, for a period of more than a half century, Congress's regulatory power under the Commerce Clause was
nearly unbounded – despite the original understanding and the Constitution's plain structural aim to endow Congress with only limited powers. Had the Court simply abdicated its responsibilities in the face of
political pressures? At least three powerful arguments supported the
Court's approach. First, if the Commerce Clause was originally understood to empower Congress to deal with all genuinely national problems, prevailing understandings of what constituted genuinely national
problems had changed between 1787 and 1937. By 1937, the national
economy was pervasively interconnected. Nearly all economic matters
affected commerce among the states, at least indirectly. Second, in its
pre-1937 efforts to draw lines restricting Congress's power, the Court
had failed dismally. It had not developed a doctrinal framework capable of yielding sensible and predictable results. Surely, the Constitution
does not require a jurisprudence of confusion. Third, by shifting course
in 1937, the Court acceded to the urgent, palpably manifest wishes of

16 379 U.S. 294 (1964).

large majorities of Congress and the American people. On debatable points not involving individual rights, many people believe that the Court should adopt a deferential stance and possibly even alter its position in response to repeated enactments of legislation.[17] Under the circumstances, the so-called New Deal settlement – permitting Congress broad, if not unbounded, authority to enact regulatory legislation under either formalist or realist tests – was a reasonable judicial response to considerations of constitutional magnitude.

To cite the reasonableness of the New Deal settlement is not, however, to deny the availability of plausible grounds for objection to the resolution of a disputable constitutional issue on such distinctly "liberal" terms. When the Court began its embrace of the New Deal settlement in 1937, the nation was beginning a thirty-six-year period, from 1933 to 1969, in which Democratic Presidents occupied the White House for all but eight years and Congress was even more reliably Democratic. Over the succeeding forty years, from 1969 to 2009, Republicans controlled the presidency for twenty-eight years. By 1995, Republican Presidents had appointed seven of the nine Justices of the Supreme Court. It should thus not be wholly surprising that the Court, in 1995, took a small step toward unsettling "the New Deal settlement."

In *United States v. Lopez*,[18] the Court held by 5–4 that Congress lacked power under the Commerce Clause to enact a statute that criminalized possession of a gun within a school zone. The government argued that guns near schools diminished school attendance and disrupted education, with adverse long-term effects on economic productivity and thus on the interstate movement of goods. But the Court's conservative

---

17 See Charles L. Black Jr., *The People and the Court* (New York: Macmillan, 1960), 59–63 (suggesting that support for the New Deal manifest during the 1936 election would properly provoke doubtful Justices to reconsider their views). For the bolder suggestion that the effect of the 1936 elections, fought over the wisdom and constitutionality of the New Deal, was to enact an informal or unwritten amendment of the Constitution, see Bruce Ackerman, *We The People: Foundations* (Cambridge, MA: Belknap Press of Harvard University Press, 1991), vol. 1.
18 514 U.S. 549 (1995).

majority said that the chain of reasoning needed to link school violence to commerce was too attenuated and that the likely effects on commerce were not sufficiently "substantial." A few years later, the Court decided *United States v. Morrison*, discussed at the beginning of this chapter, in which it found that Congress lacked the power to enact the Violence against Women Act. The majority opinion in *Morrison* emphasized that Congress had not regulated a principally "economic activity." It suggested that Congress could regulate economic activities (such as manufacture and sales of goods), even if they occurred wholly within a single state, but not noneconomic intrastate activities (such as domestic violence against women), on the basis of their substantial cumulative effects on the flow of goods in interstate commerce.

A majority of the Justices drew another line in *National Federation of Independent Business v. Sebelius* when they held that Congress cannot regulate the "inactivity" of individuals who are not already engaged in economic enterprise and do not wish to enter the commercial market to purchase health insurance. Under the Court's rationale, Congress can require those engaged in interstate commerce to take actions that they would not take otherwise. For example, it can compel businesses to pay minimum wages or to hire minority employees whom they do not wish to hire. But the Commerce Clause does not empower Congress to require individuals to enter the market to purchase health insurance, even if their failure to do so has substantial economic effects (for example, when the uninsured show up in emergency rooms and someone else must foot the bill).

Although the Supreme Court has clearly undertaken a doctrinal reassessment, the lines that it has so far drawn, between (1) economic and noneconomic activities and (2) activity and inactivity, have not so far threatened the heart of the governmental regulatory power that emerged during the New Deal era – the power to regulate economic enterprises based on an assumption that the national economy is pervasively interdependent. In concurring opinions in *Lopez, Morrison*, and the Affordable Care Act case, one of the Justices, Clarence Thomas, said that the

Court should consider more sweeping revisions, aimed at bringing current doctrine more nearly in line with the original understanding of congressional power.[19] So far, however, no other Justice has publicly joined this call. Judicial precedent, which the Court usually but not invariably follows, constitutes one obstacle to the course urged by Justice Thomas. The Court's disastrous experience in resisting the New Deal also raises a flag of caution. In addition, any very stringent limitation on congressional power would threaten the constitutionality of a number of criminal prohibitions that conservatives tend to favor, including laws against trafficking in drugs and pornography.

Finally, a substantial cutback on congressional regulatory power under the Commerce Clause might also raise doubts about the continuing validity of the 1964 Civil Rights Act, banning race-based discrimination throughout the national economy, which the Supreme Court has specifically upheld as a valid exercise of the commerce power. Unlike the president wielding a veto pen, the Supreme Court cannot simply reject legislation that it does not like. To hold any particular law unconstitutional, it must provide a principled explanation that would also apply to other laws in other cases, to be decided by lower federal courts as well as by itself. Today, the 1964 Civil Rights Act stands as an entrenched and cherished symbol of the nation's commitment to racial equality. No national politician could attack the 1964 Civil Rights Act without triggering widespread ridicule and contempt. A Supreme Court inhabiting the prevailing political, moral, and intellectual culture seems unlikely either to mount such an attack directly or to embrace a rationale for decision in another case that would thrust the 1964 Civil Rights Act into doubt.

For the time being, however, any prophecy should be cautious. The doctrine concerning congressional regulatory power under the Commerce Clause is in a state of ferment. Many observers believe that the Court's holding that Congress could not mandate individual purchases

---

19 See *Lopez*, 514 U.S. at 602 (Thomas, J., concurring); *Morrison*, 529 U.S. at 627 (Thomas, J., concurring); National Federation of Independent Business, 132 S. Ct. at 2677 (Thomas, J., concurring).

of health insurance under the Commerce Clause signaled the possibility of dramatic, not-yet-specified cutbacks in coming cases.

The Necessary and Proper Clause

At the end of its list of enumerated congressional powers, Article I of the Constitution includes an additional grant of congressional authority "to make all Laws which shall be necessary and proper for carrying into Execution the foregoing Powers."[20] In *McCulloch v. Maryland*[21] (1819), which was discussed in the Introduction, Chief Justice John Marshall held that the word "necessary" need not mean "absolutely necessary" but imports only that an action be "convenient" or "useful" to the attainment of a valid federal aim. Subsequent interpretations have typically been comparably deferential, largely for practical reasons. As Justice Scalia pointed out in a concurring opinion in *Gonzales v. Raich*,[22] which upheld the application of a federal antidrug law to homegrown medical marijuana that would never cross state lines, regulation of intrastate activity may often be necessary and proper as "part of a larger regulation of economic activity, [such as the production of marijuana for sale in interstate markets,] in which the regulatory scheme could be undercut unless the intrastate activity were regulated."[23]

Nevertheless, five Justices rejected an argument that the individual mandate to purchase health insurance in *National Federation of Independent Business* could be sustained as "necessary and proper" to the attainment of permissible ends of the Affordable Care Act. Among its provisions, the ACA requires health insurance companies to provide coverage to would-be purchasers regardless of preexisting conditions. Because health insurance companies are engaged in interstate commerce, a regulation of their sales practices falls squarely within the commerce power.

20 U.S. Constitution, Article I, Section 8, Clause 18.
21 17 U.S. 316 (1819).
22 545 U.S. 1 (2005).
23 Ibid. at 36 (Scalia, J., concurring in the judgment) (quoting *Lopez*, 514 U.S. at 561).

As a practical matter, however, it would be economically infeasible to require insurance companies to sell health insurance without regard to preexisting conditions if people could forgo buying health insurance until they became seriously sick and began to accrue large medical bills. Insurance works by pooling risks before they are realized, not after. Accordingly, the government argued, the individual mandate to healthy people to buy insurance was necessary and proper to make the dictate to companies to provide insurance regardless of preexisting conditions workable in practice. Five Justices rejected this argument, though on somewhat vague grounds. According to Chief Justice Roberts, "[e]ven if the individual mandate is 'necessary' to the Act's insurance reforms, such an expansion of federal power is not a 'proper' means for making those reforms effective," apparently because the individual mandate is so independently consequential and because, he said, the asserted power to enact it is not "derivate of" Congress's recognized powers to establish other, valid regulations.[24] In short, even if the individual mandate was "necessary," it was not "proper" under the standards of constitutional propriety that the Court did not fully articulate. It will take further litigation of future cases to clarify the full significance of *National Federation of Independent Business* for congressional power under the Necessary and Proper Clause. At the very least, it exhibits a mood of wariness by the conservative Justices about reliance on the Necessary and Proper Clause to support new, expansive claims of federal power.

The Spending Power

As the Commerce Clause stands to modern congressional power to regulate the national economy, so stands Congress's power under Article I, Section 8, to "lay and collect Taxes" and to spend money to "provide for the common Defence and general Welfare" to the contemporary welfare state, centrally including the Social Security system. As with the

---

24 *National Federation of Independent Business*, 132 S. Ct. at 2592.

Commerce Clause, the original understanding of this provision is uncertain. James Madison, who played a particularly influential role in drafting the Constitution, maintained that Congress was empowered to tax and spend only to fund the exercise of other powers specifically conferred by the Constitution (such as raising armies and maintaining post offices).[25] By contrast, Alexander Hamilton, another prominent participant in the Constitutional Convention and, like Madison, a coauthor of *The Federalist Papers*, contended that the taxing and spending power was an independent one, permitting Congress to expend funds in any way that it thought appropriate to promote the general welfare.[26] Since the New Deal era, the Court has adhered to the latter, broader view, which was crucial to its rulings upholding the Social Security system,[27] a massive social welfare bureaucracy that the founding generation could not have imagined. In validating the old-age pension program, Justice Benjamin Cardozo wrote that Congress has broad discretion to identify what the general welfare requires. He added: "Nor is the concept of the general welfare static. Needs that were narrow or parochial a century ago may be interwoven in our day with the well-being of the nation."[28] Today, Social Security and other federal spending programs funded out of tax revenues seem too deeply rooted to be vulnerable to constitutional attack even if, for example, historians were to demonstrate that Madison's view, not Hamilton's, reflected the predominant understanding of the Constitution's framers and ratifiers.

As discussed in the prologue, *National Federation of Independent Business v. Sibelius* continued the pattern of broad interpretation of the Taxing and Spending Clause by upholding the Affordable Care Act's individual mandate either to buy insurance or pay a penalty as a permissible "tax" on those who decline to buy insurance – even though Congress

---

25 See *United States v. Butler*, 297 U.S. 1, 65 (1936) (describing Madison's view).

26 See ibid. at 65–66.

27 See *Charles C. Steward Machine Co. v. Davis*, 301 U.S. 548 (1937); *Helvering v. Davis*, 301 U.S. 619 (1937).

28 *Helvering*, 301 U.S. at 641.

had not described it as a tax. Significantly, even the four conservative dissenters did not deny – although they did not expressly concede, either – that Congress could have established a regime of universal national health care through the federal tax code. Instead, they complained that the individual mandate was indeed a "mandate," enforced by a "penalty," and not a "tax" (such as that used to fund Social Security).

Congressional Regulation of State and Local Governments

Among the reasons the Constitution limits congressional power (besides protecting individual liberty) is to preserve a central role for state and local governments. Congress can threaten the independence and power of state and local governments in several distinct ways. First, as already discussed, it can assume regulatory authority in traditional domains of state and local responsibility, thereby diminishing the states' importance. Second, as I discuss presently, Congress can directly regulate state and local governments' activities. Third, as I note more briefly later, Congress can use its power of the purse to entice or coerce the states to do its bidding.

The history of the Fair Labor Standards Act (FLSA) – a statute mandating that employers pay minimum wages – illustrates the use of federal regulatory power to coerce the states and the constitutional concerns to which federal coercion appropriately gives rise. As originally enacted by Congress in 1938 and upheld by the Supreme Court in 1941, the FLSA regulated private employers engaged in manufacturing, which was once viewed as an exclusively state responsibility, but it did not directly regulate the states themselves. In 1966, Congress amended the law to take the further step of regulating the wages and hours of state and local governmental employees. By doing so, it raised the question of whether the Commerce Clause or principles of constitutional federalism limit Congress's power to regulate the activities of state and local governments, even when the comparable activities of private employers are subject to regulation.

Between 1968 and 1985, the Supreme Court's answers to this question veered back and forth. In 1968, the Court concluded that legislation otherwise valid under the Commerce Clause does not become invalid insofar as it imposes obligations on state and local governments.[29] A scant eight years later, however, the Court reversed itself by the narrow vote of 5–4. In *National League of Cities v. Usery*[30] (1976), the Court ruled that general principles of constitutional federalism, as reflected in the Tenth Amendment, forbade Congress "to directly displace the States' freedom to structure integral operations" – for example, by determining the wages and hours of state employees – "in areas of traditional governmental functions." But the regime of *National League of Cities* lasted less than a decade. The decision to overrule it, again by 5–4, came in *Garcia v. San Antonio Metropolitan Transit Authority*[31] (1985). According to *Garcia*, if Congress enacts general legislation that permissibly regulates an activity, the Constitution does not mandate exemptions for state and local governments.

When the Court decided *Garcia* in 1985, Justice William Rehnquist (who would be elevated to the position of Chief Justice a year later) wrote a four-sentence dissenting opinion, distinctly haughty and vaguely taunting in tone. Although Rehnquist did not say so expressly, the trend in national politics appeared to favor conservatives, so that the appointment of more conservative Justices could be expected over time. In his opinion, Rehnquist confidently predicted that the day would come when the "principle" of the *National League of Cities* case would "again command the support of a majority of this Court"[32] and when, presumably, *Garcia* would be overruled.

In several ways, the emerging picture when the Court decided *Garcia* was not an auspicious one. One of the Court's core responsibilities is developing a coherent, reasonably stable body of constitutional

29 See *Maryland v. Wirtz*, 392 U.S. 183 (1968).
30 426 U.S. 833, 852 (1976).
31 469 U.S. 528 (1985).
32 Ibid. at 580 (Rehnquist, J., dissenting).

law. The Justices must, of course, consider how the Constitution should ideally be interpreted and implemented, a matter about which they might understandably differ by shifting divisions of 5–4, but they also need to weigh competing interests in order and predictability. In the case of Congress's power to regulate state and local governments, Justices on both sides plainly believed that those on the other side had engaged in misguided, if not irresponsible, overreaching in overruling recent decisions by only the narrowest of margins. Nevertheless, judicial tit-for-tat in overturning recent precedents by 5–4 majorities sows confusion, imposes costs on those who must adjust to the successive rulings, and breeds disrespect for the Supreme Court and the authority of its decisions.

In the years following the decision of *Garcia* in 1985, changes in the Court's composition made it more conservative, and more interested in protecting federalism, than it had been since before the New Deal – as witnessed, for example, by its decisions in *United States v. Lopez*, *United States v. Morrison*, and, most recently, *National Federation of Independent Business v. Sebelius*. Significantly, however, the conservative majority has made no move formally to overrule *Garcia*. On the contrary, the Court has continued to uphold federal statutes that impose identical obligations on private companies and governmental bodies.[33]

Although it has avoided a frontal attack on congressional power to impose regulations on state and local governments, the Court has barred a particular subcategory of federal regulations: it has held that implicit constitutional principles prohibit Congress from enacting legislation that singles out state and local governments and requires them to perform functions – such as enacting legislation[34] or enforcing the law – that only governmental bodies and their agents can perform. A leading case articulating this principle, *Printz v. United States*[35] (1997), thus ruled that Congress could not compel local sheriffs to enforce a federal statute

33 See, for example, *Reno v. Condon*, 528 U.S. 141 (2000).
34 See *New York v. United States*, 505 U.S. 144 (1992).
35 521 U.S. 898 (1997).

restricting the sale of guns. Law enforcement is a uniquely governmental function, the Court reasoned, and Congress, under the Commerce Clause, cannot single out state and local governments and require them to exercise their distinctively governmental powers.

It remains to be seen whether the Court will go further in protecting state and local governments from direct federal regulation under the Commerce Clause. When the Court previously tried to do so, the standard laid down in the *National League of Cities* case – forbidding Congress "to directly displace the States' freedom to structure integral operations in areas of traditional governmental functions" – proved frustratingly vague and unpredictable in application. By contrast, the narrower limit on congressional power adopted in more recent cases such as *Printz* – forbidding Congress to single out state and local governments and require them to perform uniquely governmental functions – is relatively clear. Clarity and predictability are important legal virtues, to which some of the Justices who most value federalism are also strongly committed,[36] at least most of the time.

Coercion through Spending

Apart from its regulatory powers, Congress frequently attempts to dictate policy to the states by offering them conditional grants of money. When statutory grant conditions merely insist that states spend federal money to achieve Congress's most general intended purposes in making an appropriation for the "general Welfare," there is typically no ground for complaint. No one could object when the federal government demands that states spend highway funds on roads, not education, or Medicaid funds on providing aid to the poor, not subsidizing the arts. But when states are overwhelmingly dependent on federal grant money, champions of federalism understandably worry about the possibility of

---

36 Foremost in this category is Justice Antonin Scalia, author of "The Rule of Law as a Law of Rules," 56 *University of Chicago Law Review* 1175 (1989).

Congress effectively dictating state policy by attaching strings to grants of money, even in domains that would otherwise lie beyond the reach of federal regulatory power.

South Dakota v. Dole[37] – which for thirty-five years was the Supreme Court's leading case on the subject – epitomizes the problem. In 1984, Congress wanted a uniform national drinking age of twenty-one. But it was doubtful that Congress could have mandated one through a direct exercise of regulatory power, and the Supreme Court assumed (without holding) that it could not have done so. Instead of purporting to set a national drinking age by regulating under the Commerce Clause, Congress sought to achieve the same effect by providing that any state with a drinking age of less than twenty-one would forfeit 5 percent of the federal highway funds that it otherwise would have received. South Dakota complained that Congress's threat to withhold highway funds offended principles of constitutional federalism by diminishing its effective scope of quasi-sovereign autonomy to determine a legal drinking age within its borders, but the Supreme Court disagreed. In an opinion by Chief Justice Rehnquist, the Court said that conditions on federal funds were permissible as long as they required otherwise lawful behavior, were clearly stated in advance so that the states knew what they were getting into, and were germane to the purposes for which Congress had decided to give money to the states in the first place. The statute in *South Dakota v. Dole* satisfied the last condition, the Court reasoned, because a twenty-one-year-old drinking age was relevant to Congress's interest in distributing highway funds in ways aimed at achieving safe highways: roads would be safer if young drivers could not legally drink and thereafter drive. The Court then added a final qualification: "the financial inducement offered by Congress [must not] be so coercive as to pass the point at which 'pressure turns into compulsion.'"[38] On the facts of the case, the Court found no compulsion. The states were free to turn

37 483 U.S. 203 (1987).
38 Ibid. at 211.

down the federal money, which amounted to "a relatively small percent-age of certain federal highway funds."[39] From 1987 until 2012, the Court never found a statute conditioning a state's receipt of federal money on a state's compliance with a federal requirement to be impermissibly coercive.

The Court therefore broke new ground in 2012 when it held in *National Federation of Independent Business v. Sebelius*, by a vote of 7–2, that a provision of the Affordable Care Act that required the states to expand their Medicaid programs (to provide health care to more low-income people) or forfeit all federal Medicaid funds was unduly coercive and therefore violated principles of constitutional federalism. According to Chief Justice Roberts, Congress could have refused to give "new funds to States that will not accept the new conditions" of federally mandated Medicaid eligibility, but it could not "threaten[] to withhold ... existing Medicaid funds" without crossing the line into forbidden coercion.[40] Taken in isolation, the Court's holding on this point makes sense, as evidenced by the willingness of two of the "liberal" Justices – Breyer and Kagan – to go along with the conservatives regarding this aspect of the complex, split decision on the constitutionality of the Affordable Care Act. (The ruling on this point did not affect the validity of the rest of the ACA, including the individual mandate.) Federal Medicaid funds make up as much as 10 percent of some states' total budgets. As Chief Justice Roberts wrote, a threat to withdraw all of that money "is a gun to the head."[41] Like several other elements of the Court's decision, how-ever, the ruling with respect to permissible conditions on the accep-tance of federal funds seems certain to invite more litigation. Predictably, states will now challenge a variety of new eligibility conditions for con-tinuing funding under other federal spending programs. In advance of more lawsuits, it is far from obvious which new requirements the Court will deem permissible and which not.

39 Ibid.
40 132 S. Ct. at 2603.
41 Ibid. at 2604.

Concluding Thoughts

The government of the United States remains one of limited powers. But the limits to which Congress is subject have evolved greatly over the course of American history. As the Supreme Court struggles to accommodate competing considerations of constitutional relevance, including varied strands within the "original understanding" of Congress's powers, its role has often been and, indeed, continues to be controversial. The controversy hit its zenith during the New Deal, after which the Court, in retreat, effectively treated Congress's powers as boundless for more than a half century. More recently, a more conservative Court that cares more about federalism has imposed renewed restraints. It has not, so far, threatened the core elements of the kind of economic regulatory and social welfare programs, including Social Security, that began to become common in the New Deal era and continued to proliferate thereafter, including in the 1964 Civil Rights Act. But it is difficult to say more. The Court's decision in the Affordable Care Act case evinced deep divisions on some points and disquiet on others. The process of evolution that produced the body of existing doctrine continues apace.

8 Executive Power

Energy in the Executive is a leading character in the definition of good government. It is essential to the protection of the community against foreign attacks; it is not less essential to the steady administration of the laws.

– The Federalist No. 70

ODAY, THE PRESIDENT OF THE UNITED STATES IS ROUTINELY described as the most powerful person in the free world. It was not always thus. For one thing, the United States did not initially occupy a large space on the world stage. For another, the significance of the President's position within American government has changed enormously over time.

In 1789, fewer than one thousand people worked for the federal government.[1] The State Department had only nine employees[2]; the War Department began with just two.[3] The government's primary day-to-day

---

1 Formal statistics on total federal employment before 1816 are not available. See Bureau of the Census, *Historical Statistics of the United States: Colonial Times to 1970* (Washington, DC: U.S. Department of Commerce, 1975), 2:1103. One detailed review of available records puts the number of federal employees at 780 in 1792, not including deputy postmasters, who likely numbered several hundred. See Leonard D. White, *The Federalists: A Study in Administrative History* (New York: Macmillan, 1948), 255.

2 James Q. Wilson et al., *American Government* (Boston: Wadsworth and Cengage Learning, 2011), 403–04.

3 White, *The Federalists, supra* note 1, 146.

concerns were collecting taxes and delivering the mail.[4] Without a proper staff, the first President, George Washington, relied on just four men to advise him: the members of his Cabinet.[5] Although that group was notably able, considerable duties often fell on Washington alone. Today, by contrast, the President has a staff of more than 1,800 people and oversees a bureaucracy with roughly 2.7 million employees.

Scrupulous to a fault, George Washington strove to acknowledge the coequal status of the other branches of government, especially Congress. Accordingly, as per the mandate of Article II of the Constitution to seek the Senate's "Advice and Consent"[6] regarding a treaty with the Creek Indians, he appeared personally in the Senate chamber. But his visit went poorly from the start. John Adams, the Vice President, read the treaty aloud, but it was hard to hear him over the street noise that filtered in from outside. When some Senators complained, Adams read the treaty again. The Senate then began debating the merits of the agreement while an increasingly impatient Washington looked on in frustration. Finally, when one Senator asked the President to submit the treaty and various supporting documents to a Senate committee for further study, he exploded in what one witness described as "a Violent fret." Washington soon regained a "sullen dignity" and ultimately returned the following week to listen to a few more hours of debate. As he left the assembly following his second visit, he was heard to mutter that he would "be damned if he ever went there again." And he never did. Although Washington continued to involve the Senate in treaty making through informal consultation, he soon established a new precedent: Presidents do not formally seek the body's "advice," just an up-or-down vote.[7]

4 Wilson et al., *American Government, supra* note 2, 403–04.

5 Thomas Engeman and Raymond Tatalovich, "George Washington: The First Modern President? A Reply to Nichols," in *George Washington and the Origins of the American Presidency*, ed. Mark J. Rozell et al. (New York: Greenwood Press, 2000), 37, 61.

6 U.S. Constitution, Article II, Section 2, Clause 2.

7 For accounts of this incident, see Gordon S. Wood, *Empire of Liberty: A History of the Early Republic, 1789–1815* (Oxford: Oxford University Press, 2009), 89, and Michael P.

This changed way of proceeding appeared to satisfy the Senate as much as it did Washington. Indeed, Congress, starting in its very first session, began delegating broad powers to the President. With regard to domestic spending, the first Congress passed lump-sum appropriations and, within broad limits, left it to the President to determine how the money was spent.[8] Congresses also granted Washington enormous discretion in foreign affairs. For example, Congress "authorized" the President "to permit the exportation of arms, cannon and military stores, the law prohibiting the exportation of the same to the contrary notwithstanding," as long as he acted in "cases connected with the security of the commercial interest of the United States, and for public purposes only."[9] During a period of tensions with France, Congress imposed an embargo on French trade but specified that if France "disavow[ed]" and "refrain[ed]" from various aggressive acts, "it shall be lawful for the President of the United States, being well ascertained of the premises, to remit and discontinue the prohibitions and restraints hereby enacted and declared."[10]

Over the sweep of American history, this pattern has repeated itself in countless domains. As the demands on government have grown, power has flowed steadily, almost inexorably, to the President.[11] Congress is a large, often fractious institution. All members must seek election by themselves. All have constituencies to which and for which they attempt to speak. Sometimes one party will control the House while the other has a majority in the Senate. Under these circumstances, coordination can be infuriatingly difficult to achieve. By contrast, the

Riccards, *A Republic, If You Can Keep It: The Foundation of the American Presidency, 1700–1800* (New York: Greenwood Press, 1987), 116.

8 Early Act of September 29, 1789, ch. 23, 1 Stat. 95. See also Act of March 26, 1790, ch. 4, § 1, 1 Stat. 104; Act of February 11, 1791, ch. 6, 1 Stat. 190 (conferring similar discretion).

9 Act of March 3, 1795, ch. 53, 1 Stat. 444.

10 Act of June 13, 1798, ch. 53, §5, 1 Stat. 565, 566.

11 See generally Theodore J. Lowi, *The Personal President: Power Invested, Promise Unfulfilled* (Ithaca, NY: Cornell University Press, 1985).

Executive Branch is headed by the single President of the United States, who is much more capable of decisive and accountable leadership. As an increasing range of governmental functions – from the administration of a welfare bureaucracy (including Social Security and Medicare) to control of regulatory agencies to oversight of foreign affairs – has required effective, coordinated leadership, the President has accumulated responsibility to provide it, typically with the acquiescence of Congress (as in the case of treaty making) and the courts.

These developments have not occurred in defiance of the Constitution, at least when the Constitution is understood in the way that John Marshall, author of *Marbury v. Madison* (1803), once commended – as "intended to endure for ages to come, and consequently, to be adapted to the various *crises* of human affairs."[12] But when adaptation is the order of the day, no firm guides exist as to which elements of the constitutional text should be read strictly and which loosely. When Congress and the President have concurred that the President needs to exercise a power, the courts have most often deferred to that judgment. Indeed, as is emphasized in Chapter 11, which discusses the Constitution in war and emergency, many of the most important issues involving the constitutional separation of powers have been resolved through informal give-and-take between Congress and the President, with the courts not involved at all. Some issues have come to court, however, and the judiciary has struggled to develop and enforce limiting principles fit for a world that the Constitution's framers and ratifiers could not have anticipated.

The *Youngstown* Case

Constitutional lawyers typically regard *Youngstown Sheet & Tube Co. v. Sawyer*[13] (1952) as the leading Supreme Court decision involving presidential power. Curiously, however, they treat the concurring opinion

---

12 *McCulloch v. Maryland*, 17 U.S. 316, 415 (1819).
13 343 U.S. 579 (1952).

of Justice Robert Jackson as more authoritative than the majority opinion. More generally, they explain the result in terms that disavow nearly everything that the majority opinion says.

Youngstown arose when, with the nation at war in Korea, President Harry Truman ordered federal officials to seize and operate the nation's steel mills to avert a planned strike. Truman maintained that an interruption in steel production would threaten the war effort and the safety of troops in the field. Had he wished to do so, Truman could have invoked a federal statute, the Taft-Hartley Act, and obtained a judicial order forbidding a strike for eighty days, during which time he could have sought emergency legislation from Congress. But Truman was a Democratic President with an important union constituency. The Taft-Hartley Act, which the unions despised, had been passed over his veto. Spurning the course available under the Taft-Hartley Act, Truman claimed power directly under the Constitution to seize the steel mills and to run them, presumably on terms acceptable to the Steelworkers Union, until the dispute was settled. As authority for his action, Truman cited his constitutional power as Commander in Chief of the U.S. Armed Forces[14] and provisions of Article II empowering the President to "take Care that the Laws be faithfully executed"[15] and vesting him with "[t]he executive Power."[16]

By a vote of 6–3, the Supreme Court held that none of these provisions either individually or collectively empowered the President to take over the steel mills. Justice Hugo Black – who always claimed to take the Constitution at its literal word – wrote the majority opinion. According to Black, the steel mills were too remote from any battlefield for the President's Commander-in-Chief power to be relevant. Black further maintained that the "take care" power and the grant of executive power both limited the President to executing laws that Congress had enacted. According to Justice Black, the Constitution carefully and specifically

14 See U.S. Constitution, Article II, Section 2, Clause 1.
15 Article II, Section 3.
16 Article II, Section 1, Clause 1.

assigns lawmaking power to Congress and restricts the President to executing congressionally enacted laws. For the President to order seizure of the steel mills in the absence of authorizing legislation was too much like lawmaking, Black thought, possibly because it interfered with the private property rights of the mills' owners. Although Congress could adjust or limit property rights, or even authorize the taking of private property for "public use" (subject to the payment of "just compensation" under the Takings Clause of the Fifth Amendment), the President could not.

Justice Black's analysis reflects what scholars have termed a "formalist" approach to separation-of-powers issues.[17] He assumed that a bright, categorical divide exists between the lawmaking powers given to Congress and the law-executing powers given to the executive, with the content of both categories fixed by original historical understandings. In this way of thinking about separation-of-powers issues, crisis and changing needs play no central role. If this approach were pressed to its logical extreme, it would probably yield the conclusion (as pointed out by the dissenting opinion) that Abraham Lincoln acted unconstitutionally when he issued the Emancipation Proclamation freeing southern slaves in the midst of the Civil War. In the exercise of his Commander-in-Chief power, Lincoln claimed the right to alter the legal relationship between slaves and their masters, not merely to carry out statutes passed by Congress.

Sharply contrasting with Justice Black's opinion was that of Justice Jackson, a former Attorney General under Franklin Roosevelt and a special prosecutor at the Nuremberg trials of Nazi war criminals. More pragmatic than doctrinaire, Jackson was also one of the best writers ever to serve on the Supreme Court, a gifted stylist who never finished law school but who drew heavily on Shakespeare and the Bible. He was the author of many much-quoted epigrams, including an observation that

17 For discussions of formalism, see, for example, Peter L. Strauss, "The Place of Agencies in Government: Separation of Powers and the Fourth Branch," 84 *Columbia Law Review* 573 (1984); Rebecca L. Brown, "Separated Powers and Ordered Liberty," 139 *University of Pennsylvania Law Review* 1513 (1991).

the Constitution is not "a suicide pact" and that judicial interpretation should not turn it into one. Although Jackson agreed with Black about how the *Youngstown* case should come out, his opinion argued that the President's powers are not rigidly fixed under the Constitution, as Justice Black maintained, but at least partly adjustable.[18] Within Jackson's framework, one crucial variable involves the stance taken by Congress. When Congress authorizes the President to act, the politically accountable branches of the national government accord in their judgment about the practical necessity or desirability of executive authority, and courts should give strong deference to their determination. In direct contrast with cases in which Congress has authorized presidential action, Jackson identified a category of cases in which Congress has acted to curb presidential authority. In such cases, Jackson thought that presidential power sank to its "lowest ebb."[19] Between the poles of congressionally authorized and congressionally forbidden assertions of executive authority, Jackson identified a third category that he dubbed a "zone of twilight."[20] Within this category, he suggested, presidential power might depend on practical considerations, including the gravity of the problem that the President confronted.

Commentators have often pointed to Justice Jackson's opinion as epitomizing a "functionalist" approach to separation-of-powers issues (in contrast with Black's "formalism"). As the term is usually used, "functionalism" recognizes that the lines separating executive from legislative from judicial power are often blurry and variable; that ebbs and flows of power are permissible as long as each branch retains its truly core functions and a capacity to check and balance power grabs by other branches; and that practical considerations matter in determining what the Constitution requires and permits, at least in otherwise doubtful cases.

18 See *Youngstown*, 343 U.S. at 635–38 (Jackson, J., concurring).
19 Ibid. at 637.
20 Ibid.

Under Justice Jackson's framework, a presidential seizure of the steel mills might well have appeared defensible in a true national emergency, if no practical alternative existed. (Indeed, in the months immediately preceding the U.S. entry into World War II, President Roosevelt had averted a crippling strike by seizing a California plant that produced one-fifth of the nation's airplanes, and he had done so with the approval of his Attorney General – one Robert Jackson![21]) In *Youngstown*, however, the President had another, statutorily authorized means to protect the national interest: he could have got an injunction barring a strike for eighty days under the Taft-Hartley Act and, if the union still threatened to walk out at the end of that period, could have sought congressional authorization for a seizure. What is more, by enacting the Taft-Hartley Act, Congress had at least implicitly signaled its intent to deny the President the broader, more drastic power simply to order federal takeovers of important industries.

Given that Justice Black's formalism and Justice Jackson's functionalism both pointed to the same result, the *Youngstown* Court almost surely reached the right decision. But which of these two formidable Justices had the better of the argument? This is a debatable question, on which reasonable minds can differ. As we will see, however, there can be no question that Justice Jackson's framework better explains the overall pattern of the Supreme Court's decisions, both before and after *Youngstown*.

Foreign Affairs

The "functionalist" tradition of flexibility in construing presidential power, especially in light of practical needs and congressional acquiescence, manifests itself perhaps most dramatically in the domains of war,

---

21 For details of this episode and a rich account of the political context for the *Youngstown* decision, see Patricia L. Bellia, "The Story of the *Steel Seizure* Case" in *Presidential Power Stories*, ed. Christopher H. Schroeder and Curtis A. Bradley (New York: Foundation Press, 2009), 233.

which is discussed in Chapter 11, and foreign affairs. The President has repeatedly claimed authority to act unilaterally in matters of foreign affairs, largely on the theory that the United States must be able to speak with a single decisive voice on the world stage. For the most part, both courts and Congress have acceded to this claim.[22] The Constitution provides that the President can negotiate treaties "by and with the Advice and Consent of the Senate ... provided two thirds of the Senators present concur."[23] This prescribed process makes secret negotiations difficult; it also permits as little as one-third of the Senate to block a treaty. At the end of World War I, for example, a relatively small band of Senators succeeded in blocking ratification of the Treaty of Versailles and in keeping the United States out of the League of Nations. As an alternative to the treaty process, Presidents have subsequently claimed an authority to enter into "executive agreements," with the same force of law as treaties, without seeking Senate approval. In important cases decided in the 1930s and 1940s, the Supreme Court held that an executive agreement between the Roosevelt administration and the Soviet Union was legally valid. That agreement, which aimed to resolve a number of legal disputes between the Soviet Union and U.S. nationals, both created judicially enforceable federal rights and overrode competing claims based on state law.[24] By permitting an executive agreement to nullify otherwise applicable state law, the Court upheld a power of unilateral presidential lawmaking, the scope of which remains uncertain.

In the 1980s, the Supreme Court again held that the President could eliminate rights to sue a foreign government in American courts, this time under an executive agreement resolving a crisis over the Iranian government's seizure of American hostages. The Court's opinion in

22 For a celebrated judicial statement of this view, see *United States v. Curtiss-Wright Export Corp.*, 299 U.S. 304, 319–21 (1936).
23 U.S. Constitution, Article II, Section 2, Clause 2.
24 See *United States v. Belmont*, 301 U.S. 324 (1937), and *United States v. Pink*, 315 U.S. 203 (1942).

Dames & Moore v. Regan[25] (1981) sounded the pragmatic themes of Justice Jackson's concurring opinion in the *Youngstown* case. The Court emphasized the need for executive flexibility in matters involving foreign relations. It was vital to get back the American hostages and desirable to get the deal done swiftly on terms acceptable to the Iranians. The Court also found implicit congressional authorization for the President to act unilaterally, even though it acknowledged that no statute conferred the power directly.

A rare setback for the cause of executive power in the international realm came in *Medellín v. Texas*[26] (2008), which held that the President lacked authority to order Texas courts to reopen their consideration of a criminal case involving a Mexican defendant. The President issued his directive to bring the United States into conformity with a ruling by the International Court of Justice (ICJ), which held that Texas officials had breached U.S. obligations under an international treaty when they failed to inform Medellín of his right to have the Mexican consulate notified, before trial, of his arrest and detention. In rejecting the President's claim of authority to dictate action to the Texas courts, the Justices divided 6–3. Ordinarily, "conservative" Justices tend to be highly deferential to claims of presidential power. In this case, however, the five most conservative Justices all ruled against the President. As discussed in Chapter 7, conservatives tend to be protective of states' rights as well as executive authority, and *Medellín* involved a clash between competing claims of presidential and state prerogatives. The majority Justices emphasized that the Senate, in ratifying the treaty under which Medellín claimed his rights, had not agreed to make decisions of the ICJ directly binding on the United States or its officials. The majority appeared to view the President's directive to Texas officials to comply with an ICJ ruling as an attempted end run around the treaty's implied limits and, possibly, as an unwelcome subordination of American law and American courts to international law and the ICJ.

25 453 U.S. 654 (1981).
26 552 U.S. 491 (2008).

Delegated Power in Domestic Affairs

In domestic affairs, perhaps the central historical development involving the separation of powers has concerned the growth of the Executive Branch and the flow to it of delegated lawmaking power. The Constitution's framers and ratifiers could not have anticipated federal benefits agencies on the scale of the Social Security Administration, which serves more than fifty-five million people. Nor could they have foreseen regulatory agencies administering complex workplace safety or environmental protection legislation. In the late nineteenth and early twentieth centuries, however, as the population soared and the economy rapidly industrialized, both federal benefit programs and regulatory regimes seemed increasingly imperative. As the number and scope of federal programs grew, Congress proved unable, and sometimes unwilling, to write statutes at the necessary level of detail to guide their implementation. In the environmental area, for example, Congress can decide that factories may not emit dangerous amounts of toxic waste into the air or water, but it may lack the resources to determine exactly which wastes should be deemed toxic at exactly which concentrations. To bridge the gap between general policies and the details of their application, Congress began to vest executive agencies with rule-making power – the authority to write rules or regulations, with the force of law, specifying how often-vague statutory directives should be applied.

The leading case upholding the delegation of rule-making authority to executive agencies, *Yakus v. United States*[27] (1944), came out of World War II. To combat wartime inflation, Congress established a federal agency charged with limiting wage and price increases to those that would be "fair and equitable." The statute, the Emergency Price Control Act, obviously left enormous discretionary authority in the implementing agency, which needed to develop detailed codes specifying permissible and impermissible price increases for various jobs and commodities throughout the country. In practical effect, the act provided for

27 321 U.S. 414 (1944).

lawmaking to occur within the Executive Branch. Nonetheless, the Supreme Court upheld the delegation.

Its reasoning had two elements. First, the Court suggested that Congress had already done all the required lawmaking in the constitutional sense because it had established a legislative policy – that only fair and equitable price increases should be permitted – and had left the agency with the job of implementing the law, not making it. The Court thus purported to honor the so-called nondelegation doctrine, which holds that Congress may not delegate its core legislative powers. In fact, however, the scope of delegated power was enormous, as the second strand of the Court's reasoning acknowledged. That second strand was avowedly pragmatic: "The Constitution as a continuously operative charter of government does not demand the impossible or the impracticable."[28] Congress and the President had reasonably concluded that the stresses of wartime required the development of anti-inflation rules. To develop those rules in their necessary details – determining, for example, how much could be charged for a used car or a loaf of fresh (or day-old) bread – lay beyond Congress's practical competence. The Court thus approved a significant delegation of rule-making power to the Executive Branch.

Yakus set a precedent much exploited by subsequent Congresses and extending well beyond wartime demands. Today, a host of agencies possess the power to issue legally binding regulations involving such matters as federal benefits entitlements, workplace safety, environmental quality, and forbidden employment practices. In delegating lawmaking authority to the Executive Branch, Congress sometimes acts for sound reasons, involving its own lack of technical expertise. But sometimes, too, Congress may find it politically more expedient to legislate in general terms and transfer to the Executive Branch the responsibility for making some of the hardest, most contentious decisions. In either case,

28 Ibid. at 424.

the Executive Branch grows more powerful, and the stakes of presidential elections increase. When the White House changes hands, executive agencies can revise the rules that previous administrations issued. To cite just one notable example, Republican administrations tend to construe environmental protection laws more loosely than do Democratic administrations.

As the country has grown increasingly more conservative in recent decades, and as the Supreme Court has sought ways to rein in congressional regulatory power under the Commerce Clause, some observers have thought that a more conservative Court might – and possibly should – breathe new life into the dictate of the "nondelegation doctrine" that Congress cannot delegate its core legislative authority. There is no doubt that a stringent nondelegation doctrine would make much modern regulation a practical impossibility. Indeed, at the end of the *Lochner* era discussed in Chapter 3, and just before the "switch in time that saved nine," the Court struck down two prominent pieces of New Deal legislation on the ground that they delegated legislative powers that only Congress could exercise.[29] But the Supreme Court, unlike the President with a veto pen, does not get to make ad hoc choices about which schemes and delegations to approve and which to disapprove. Congress delegates power to the Executive Branch to enact regulations in myriad contexts, some involving national defense, foreign affairs, and distributions of benefits to military veterans and the elderly. The task of drawing principled lines would be an enormously daunting one, possibly beyond the practical competence of the Court after it has long ratified such relatively open-ended grants of rule-making authority as that in *Yakus*. Moreover, there are many areas in which judicial (like political) conservatives are even more prone than liberals to see broad executive power as a functional necessity in the modern world.

---

29 See *Panama Refining Co. v. Ryan*, 293 U.S. 388 (1935); *Schecter Poultry Corp. v. United States*, 295 U.S. 495 (1935).

Legislative Vetoes and Line-Item Vetoes

As Congress delegated increasing rule-making power to the Executive Branch, especially in the period from the 1930s through the 1970s, it predictably looked for new ways to oversee and influence the exercise of executive power. In particular, it began to rely increasingly on statutory provisions authorizing so-called legislative vetoes. In a typical statutory design, Congress would authorize executive rule making but provide that the rules drafted by an executive agency – such as environmental regulations – could not take effect if either the House or Senate enacted a "veto resolution" expressing its disapproval.

The Supreme Court addressed the constitutionality of legislative vetoes in *Immigration and Naturalization Service v. Chadha*[30] (1983). With only one dissent, the Court held the arrangement unconstitutional. In an opinion by Chief Justice Warren Burger, the Court reasoned that legislative vetoes violated the plain language and structural design of the Constitution. Congress is the Legislative Branch, charged with lawmaking. When Congress enacts a veto resolution, it must be presumed to act legislatively, Burger wrote; it could not, for example, exercise executive power. But for Congress to legislate, Article I of the Constitution requires that both Houses of Congress must approve the same bill or resolution, which must then be presented to the President for possible veto. Legislative vetoes were unconstitutional, the Chief Justice reasoned, because they departed from this precise, constitutionally mandated scheme. There might be good policy reasons supporting legislative vetoes, the Court said, but it had no business weighing policy arguments. The Court pronounced itself bound by "[t]he choices ... made in the Constitutional Convention."[31]

Chadha exhibits the enormous challenges facing the Supreme Court in applying the Constitution to the circumstances of the modern world and to governmental structures that have evolved, often with the Court's

30 462 U.S. 919 (1983).
31 Ibid. at 959.

approval, to address modern problems that the founding generation could not have imagined. Defenders advanced forceful functionalist arguments that the legislative veto actually helped to realize the basic premise underlying Article I: that valid enactment of federal law requires the joint concurrence of both Houses of Congress. When Congress delegates rule-making authority to the Executive Branch, the risk arises that the executive will promulgate rules that Congress does not in fact approve. Legislative vetoes, the argument continues, defuse this risk and restore the original constitutional balance by ensuring that Congress actually concurs in, or at least does not reject, agency rules possessing the force of federal law. Against such arguments, Burger's wooden invocation of "choices . . . made in the Constitutional Convention" rings slightly hollow. The modern governmental framework departs from original constitutional understandings in many ways. As demonstrated by the *Yakus* case, which upheld rule making by the Executive Branch, the Court is perfectly capable of viewing constitutional norms as adaptable to modern practical imperatives when it wishes to do so.

When all of the complexities of modern government are taken into account and are judged against the Constitution's most fundamental presuppositions, the decision in *Chadha* may well have been the correct one. The ready availability of legislative vetoes created a subtle incentive for Congress to shirk its constitutional responsibility for making hard policy choices. Members could enact legislation with broad language and then pass the buck to administrative agencies. Doing so was essentially cost-free, as long as each House of Congress retained the chance to veto rules that it especially disliked. Without the legislative veto, the delegation of essentially open-ended rule-making authority looks less attractive. Following the Court's decision in *Chadha*, Congress has a greater incentive to do its job responsibly at the legislative stage.

If this or similar analysis is correct, however, it calls for subtle thinking about how courts can best shape constitutional doctrine to protect underlying values – not mechanical recitations about the Constitution's plain text and original understanding. It is possible, of course, that the Court thought about whether to invalidate legislative vetoes in far more sophisticated ways than its *Chadha* opinion revealed. But the formalist methodology of *Chadha*, which is reminiscent of Justice Black's approach in *Youngstown*, is difficult, if not impossible, to reconcile with the flexible approach taken in *Yakus*.

One attempt at reconciliation would proceed as follows: *Chadha* rightly assumes that the Court should prefer narrow, literalist interpretations of the constitutional text and adhere closely to original understandings unless there is some very good reason, arising from changed contexts or practical exigencies, for it not to do so. A good reason – the imperative of stopping economically ruinous price inflation during World War II – arguably existed in *Yakus* but not in *Chadha*. Strikingly, however, the Court did not explain its invalidation of legislative vetoes in these terms.

Clinton v. City of New York[32] (1998) stands with *Chadha* as another of the relatively few post–New Deal cases to invalidate a congressional effort to delegate power to the Executive Branch. Nearly everyone agrees that Congress regularly includes wasteful spending items in the federal budget. Powerful members demand projects for their states or districts, or favors for preferred constituencies, and spending bills get loaded with excess. To deal with the problem, a bipartisan congressional majority enacted the Line Item Veto Act, which authorized the President – after first signing a bill into law – subsequently to determine particular authorized expenditures to be wasteful and thus to decline to make them. The act labeled the President's notifications to Congress of planned nonexpenditures as line-item vetoes.

The Supreme Court struck down the Line Item Veto Act in *Clinton v. City of New York*. In reasoning similar to that of *Chadha*, the Court pointed out that the Constitution provides very specifically for the process by which bills become law and by which presidential vetoes may occur – before a bill becomes law, not after. If the vetoes exercised by

32 524 U.S. 417 (1998).

the President under the Line Item Veto Act were "vetoes" in the constitutional sense, this reasoning would deserve to carry the day. As two dissenting opinions emphasized, however, the title of the Line Item Veto Act was misleading. In determining to withhold spending on wasteful or exorbitant projects, the President did not need to be seen as "vetoing" legislation; he could be viewed, instead, as simply exercising a statutorily conferred authority to withhold unnecessary spending. If, for example, a bill authorized the President to spend up to but not more than $100 billion to meet the nation's defense needs and he spent only $90 billion, no one would say that he had "vetoed" $10 billion worth of spending. The Line Item Veto Act could easily have been viewed in the same way – as creating a discretion to withhold spending of otherwise authorized funds, not as licensing a "veto" of line items in the federal budget.

Perhaps, as Justice Antonin Scalia wrote in dissent, the title of the Line Item Veto Act "fak[ed] out" the Supreme Court.[33] Because the act purported to confer a veto power, the Court assumed that a veto power must be at stake, even though another description of its effect (as authorizing the discretionary withholding of unnecessary spending) would have been more apt. Perhaps the title troubled the Court for other, partly symbolic reasons. The title may have sent a disturbing signal that Congress meant to evade or even flout the Constitution. Or perhaps the Court thought that the Line Item Veto Act threatened to distort the constitutional scheme of checks and balances by giving the President too much discretionary power. However public spirited the act's goals, the act would have greatly enhanced the President's capacity to reward friends (by permitting spending on their preferred projects, however profligate) and punish enemies (by withholding spending on projects of great importance to them, wasteful or not). Only this much seems clear: the Line Item Veto Act presented complex questions of constitutional judgment, not a simple issue about whether Congress can give the President a "veto" power withheld by the Constitution.

33 Ibid. at 468.

Appointments and Removals

Although Article II begins by saying that "the executive Power shall be vested in a President of the United States," the President cannot discharge the obligations of the Executive Branch alone. He (or she) needs subordinates, whose offices must be established by law. Responsibility to establish agencies and departments lies in Congress. And Congress, in establishing agencies and departments, has sometimes attempted to limit the President's power to appoint and remove those who run them. Intricate constitutional questions have thus arisen about whether, when, and to what extent Congress can limit presidential power to appoint and remove high executive officials.

One prominent view is notable for its elegant simplicity. The "unitary executive theory" holds that the Constitution establishes one President, vested with the whole "executive power," and that he must therefore be able to supervise and control all who work for him.[34] According to the unitary executive theory, presidential control requires that the President possess exclusive power to appoint high federal officials and that the President have unrestricted authority to dismiss officials whose performances displease him. This theory promises to deliver coherent, accountable presidential administration.

On the whole, the Supreme Court has agreed with unitary executive theorists that the President must have the power to appoint all high federal officials charged with executing the law.[35] In doing so, the Court has relied on the plain language of Article II, Section 2, Clause 2, which directs that the President "shall nominate, and by and with the Advice and Consent of the Senate, shall appoint" certain named officials and "all other Officers of the United States, whose Appointments are not herein otherwise provided for." (It appears to be agreed on all sides that lower-level employees of the government – often, virtually all those who

---

34 See, for example, Steven G. Calabresi and Kevin H. Rhodes, "The Structural Constitution: Unitary Executive, Plural Judiciary," 105 *Harvard Law Review* 1153 (1992).

35 The leading modern case is *Buckley v. Valeo*, 424 U.S. 1 (1976).

work for a given agency below the very top echelon of management – are not "Officers" in the constitutional sense and that other provisions for their appointment are therefore permissible. For example, no one thinks that secretaries and janitors require presidential or Cabinet-level appointments.)

Even under the "unitary executive" thesis, the President's appointment power is not, of course, unbounded: the Constitution specifically provides that presidential appointees can take office only upon confirmation by the Senate. In deciding whether to "consent" to the appointment of executive officials, however, the Senate has historically given the President considerable latitude. (The deference given to Executive Branch nominees stands in partial contrast with appointments to the Judicial Branch, a subject briefly discussed in Chapters 9 and 13.) Members of the Executive Branch work for the President. The President is accountable for their performance in office. Nevertheless, over the course of history, the Senate has refused to confirm at least nine nominees for Cabinet positions.[36] Some rejections have rested on concerns about the nominees' ethical conduct. Others have reflected the Senate's simple judgment that a particular nominee was temperamentally or otherwise unfit to hold high federal office.

The scope of the President's inherent constitutional authority to fire high executive officials is the subject of recurring constitutional debate. Following the Civil War, in the midst of a struggle between Congress and President Andrew Johnson over Reconstruction policy, the House of Representatives voted to impeach Johnson for unilaterally dismissing a Cabinet officer in defiance of the short-lived Tenure of Office Act, which purported to limit the President's ability to fire members of his own Cabinet without Senate approval. But the Senate refused by a narrow margin to find Johnson guilty of an impeachable offense, apparently because some Senators agreed with him that the Tenure of Office Act

36 See William G. Ross, "The Senate's Constitutional Role in Confirming Cabinet Nominees and Other Executive Officers," 48 *Syracuse Law Review* 1123, 1127 (1998).

was unconstitutional due to its crippling effect on the President's capacity to administer the Executive Branch.

Since the failed Johnson impeachment, disputes about the President's constitutional authority to remove federal officials have moved from impeachment debates into the courts. Two classic cases exhibit the complexity of the resulting judge-made doctrine. *Myers v. United States*[37] (1926) grew from the President's insistence on removing a postmaster, despite a federal statute protecting postmasters from dismissal except for good cause. In an opinion by Chief Justice William Howard Taft, himself a former President, the Court invalidated the statutory limitation on the President's removal power. The President was responsible for the administration of the entire Executive Branch, Taft reasoned, and he must therefore be able to dismiss any subordinate who did not enjoy his full confidence.

A few years later, the Court confronted *Humphrey's Executor v. United States*[38] (1935), involving a statute that limited the President's power to remove commissioners of the Federal Trade Commission. Taking a distinctly flexible or "functionalist" approach, the Court distinguished *Myers* on the basis of the duties performed by Federal Trade Commissioners. Whereas Myers performed traditional executive functions, Congress had empowered the Federal Trade Commission to issue rules and regulations defining unfair trade practices. In some cases, the Court emphasized, the commission even could adjudicate in the first instance whether violations of federal law had occurred (subject to review in a regular federal court created under Article III of the Constitution). According to the Court, when Congress creates "quasi legislative or quasi judicial agencies,"[39] it can limit the President's removal powers in order to protect the independence of those performing legislative and especially judicial functions. Such agencies, the Court said, are "wholly disconnected from the executive department."[40]

---

37 *Myers v. United States*, 272 U.S. 52 (1926).
38 295 U.S. 602 (1935).
39 Ibid. at 629.
40 Ibid. at 630.

Read literally, *Humphrey's Executor* would be an example of constitutional adaptation run riot. It is one thing to say that Congress can confer rule-making and adjudicative powers on administrative agencies; it is another to suggest that Congress can create agencies wholly outside the Executive Branch and presumably outside the Legislative and Judicial Branches as well. The Constitution provides for just three branches. Three are enough. Although it has become common to refer to agencies such as the Federal Trade Commission as "independent agencies," it is better to think of them as "relatively independent" agencies within the Executive Branch.

The crucial point, however, involves substance, not terminology. In the wake of *Humphrey's Executor*, the Supreme Court must decide which federal officials perform predominantly executive functions, and thus come under the rule of *Myers,* and which have duties that are sufficiently judicial or legislative to warrant restraints on the President's removal authority. These questions lack sharp answers. If Congress chooses to do so, it can assign rule-making and quasi-adjudicative functions to Cabinet departments such as the Departments of State, Agriculture, and Commerce; the Constitution does not mandate the use of quasi-independent officials. Yet it seems unimaginable that Congress could limit the President's power to dismiss a Secretary of State in whom he had lost confidence. If this conclusion is correct, then the labels "quasi-judicial" and "quasi-legislative" may guide the Court's thinking in some cases, but they are not the only relevant factors. The Court must assess when the benefits of presidential control of official decision making, and the political accountability that it brings, are outweighed by competing values. An unrestricted removal power ensures clear presidential accountability for the performance of government – a strong presumptive good. But there may be special reasons to think that a few governmental functions are best insulated, at least in part, from the sphere of presidential politics and political calculation.

As *Humphrey's Executor* suggests, certain quasi-adjudicative functions may occupy the category in which insulation from presidential politics makes both practical and constitutional sense. When the Federal

Trade Commission determines whether the specific trade practices of specific companies violate the law – subject to further review in a court – its thinking should not be influenced by political pressure to reward the President's allies or to punish his opponents. The quasi-independent Federal Reserve Board may furnish another example of a federal agency whose functions should be insulated as far as possible from political pressures, including those that a President would predictably bring to bear if he could fire members at will. Through its control over the money supply and interest rates, the Federal Reserve Board has considerable power to stimulate a lagging economy or, conversely, to dampen inflationary tendencies in an overheated economy. In the latter case, its job is to administer painful medicine; in the former, the optimal dosage may be one that brings a gradual improvement, not an immediate recovery. Congress made a deliberate, considered decision to give the powers of the Federal Reserve to a quasi-independent agency, rather than to the President or to officials immediately subject to the President's direction. An incumbent President will always have a strong political incentive to try to cause the economy to boom in election years. If the consequence of presidential control would predictably be a costly cycle of boom followed by bust, then removing certain decisions from direct political control again makes practical sense.

Admittedly, however, "functional" assessments of this kind require calculations of costs and benefits that are inherently contestable. By upholding congressional power to impose limits on the President's power to remove some officials but not others, the Supreme Court has assumed a responsibility for making judgments in an area where the line between law and policy blurs and sometimes vanishes.[41]

41 For an especially forceful statement of this point, see Justice Scalia's dissenting opinion in *Morrison v. Olson*, 487 U.S. 654 (1988).

9   Judicial Power

[T]he judiciary, from the nature of its functions, will always be the
least dangerous [branch of government]....It may truly be said to
have neither FORCE nor WILL, but merely judgment.

> – The Federalist No. 78

The Imperial Judiciary lives.

> – Justice Antonin Scalia, protesting a Supreme Court decision
> upholding abortion rights[1]

I N 1973, DURING A CONGRESSIONAL INVESTIGATION INTO
abuses of power by the presidential administration of Richard
Nixon and illegal activities by the Nixon reelection campaign,
it came to light that Nixon had secretly recorded a large number of conversations in the Oval Office. The special prosecutor charged with inves-
tigating wrongdoing by administration and campaign officials demanded
access to the tapes. When Nixon refused, the special prosecutor sought a
court order directing Nixon to hand them over.

Whatever his personal motivations, Nixon had a serious constitutional argument that the tapes were protected by "executive privilege" – a prerogative of the President, as head of the Executive Branch,
to protect papers, tapes, and other evidence of what his advisers had said
to him and he to them in the course of making presidential decisions.

---

1 *Planned Parenthood of Southeastern Pennsylvania v. Casey*, 505 U.S. 833, 996 (1992)
(Scalia, J., dissenting).

According to Nixon, it would harm the presidency, and thus the country, if Presidents could not receive advice and probe policy options on an absolutely confidential basis. Nixon, of course, acknowledged that Presidents could disclose any information that they saw fit. But he maintained, in essence, that the management of presidential deliberations was the exclusive responsibility of the President, outside the reach of the courts. Beyond their legal argument, White House officials hinted that if the Supreme Court ordered Nixon to surrender the tapes, he might simply refuse as a matter of constitutional principle.

On July 24, 1974, the Supreme Court issued its ruling in *United States v. Nixon* (more commonly known as *The Nixon Tapes Case*),[2] commanding the President to give the tapes to a federal judge, for the judge, rather than the President, to determine which conversations should and which should not be made available to the special prosecutor. Despite his prior bluster, and despite the plausibility of his constitutional arguments, Nixon meekly complied. He really had no choice. If Nixon had refused to surrender the tapes in response to a Supreme Court order, the public would have been outraged. Congress would almost certainly have treated the defiance as a ground for his impeachment and removal from office.

The Nixon Tapes Case made a rather stunning contrast with the earlier case of *Marbury v. Madison*[3] (1803), discussed in the Introduction. In *Marbury*, if the Supreme Court had issued an order directing Secretary of State James Madison to take an action that President Thomas Jefferson had ordered him not to take, Jefferson and Madison let it be known that they would have defied the Court's command. Yet it was widely believed in 1803 that if the Supreme Court ruled against Madison and the Jefferson administration, thereby provoking defiance, then Congress – which supported the President – would actually have impeached Chief Justice John Marshall and removed *him* from office. In *Marbury*, it was the Chief

2 *United States v. Nixon*, 418 U.S. 683 (1974).
3 5 U.S. 137 (1803).

Justice who needed to make a tactical retreat; in *The Nixon Tapes Case*, it was the President.

If one asks why, differences in the facts of the cases undoubtedly matter, as do differences in the legal arguments. It surely matters too that Jefferson was a very popular President in 1803, whereas by 1974, Nixon was a very unpopular one. Perhaps most important, however, the stature of the Supreme Court had changed immeasurably. In 1803, the Court was a weak and vulnerable institution, with the reach of its authority in doubt. By 1974, the Court had achieved a remarkable potency, which it continues to maintain. Today, nearly everyone subscribes to the theory of "judicial supremacy" in constitutional interpretation, which holds that once the Court has spoken, other officials, including the President, must accept the Court's interpretation unless and until the Court changes its mind. A vivid reminder comes from *Bush v. Gore*[4] (2000), discussed in Chapter 6, in which a Supreme Court decision effectively resolved a charged political controversy about who had won a presidential election.

When seen in conjunction with other modern cases – including, in many Americans' minds, *Roe v. Wade* – *Bush v. Gore* may provoke the question: do we have an "imperial judiciary"? Is there anything the Court cannot do? For all their apparent bite, however, such questions cannot survive even a moment's reflection. Although the Court possesses decisive power with respect to a hugely important set of questions, that set is actually quite limited,[5] as I pointed out in the prologue. In recent decades, the most important issues confronting the United States – by nearly everyone's account – have involved the economy and foreign policy. Should the government raise or lower taxes? Should the United States fight wars in Iraq and Afghanistan or support popular uprisings in Libya and Syria? The Supreme Court has had no role in addressing such vital questions. Indeed, if one can even imagine the Court issuing

4 531 U.S. 98 (2000).

5 See generally Frederick Schauer, "The Supreme Court, 2005 Term – Foreword: The Court's Agenda – and the Nation's," 120 *Harvard Law Review* 4 (2006).

an order directing Congress to raise or lower taxes, or to send or withhold aid to rebels in another country, one can just as easily contemplate a perplexed Congress concluding that the Justices had so overstepped their bounds that their ruling could and should be ignored. To understand judicial power under the Constitution, we thus need to grapple with limitations and constraints as well as with sources of authority.

This chapter unfolds in three main parts. The first deals with the character of the judicial role in American constitutional practice. The second discusses limits on judicial power, some of which stem from surrounding cultural and political forces and some from judicially created constitutional doctrines. The third part of the chapter then explores the debates and anxieties that surround the exercise of judicial power even inside the politically constructed bounds within which the public accepts that the judiciary has the last word. It also discusses competing theories or methodologies of constitutional adjudication, including interpretive "originalism."

The Character of Judicial Power

In 1936, Justice Owen Roberts wrote an opinion in an important case invalidating the centerpiece of the New Deal's farm program. Trying to blunt public criticism, he asserted that the Supreme Court's job was not to exercise any independent judgment about the wisdom or even the possibly urgent necessity of challenged legislation. Its job, he explained, was simply "to lay the article of the Constitution which is invoked beside the statute which is challenged and to decide whether the latter squares with the former."[6] The Constitution's meaning, he implied, was almost invariably plain. In cases of doubt, others have suggested that research into the "original understanding" will ordinarily resolve any uncertainty.

As previous chapters of this book have suggested, Roberts's portrait of the judicial role was more fanciful than realistic. (One wonders whether Roberts himself would have acknowledged as much in less

6 *United States v. Butler*, 297 U.S. 162 (1936).

defensive moments – if not in 1936, then surely a year later, when his "switch in time" ended the constitutional crisis that had provoked Franklin Roosevelt's Court-packing plan.) Often, the Constitution's plain text gives no simple answer to modern constitutional questions: Which utterances lie within "the freedom of speech" and which without? When are churches and religiously motivated individuals entitled to exemptions from otherwise generally applicable laws? Which governmental classifications are consistent with "the equal protection of the laws" and which are inconsistent?

When the text gives no obvious answer, few would deny that the original understanding of constitutional language is relevant, but it is often hard to apply eighteenth- and nineteenth-century understandings to modern problems. I emphasized this point in Chapter 7, involving the Supreme Court's historical struggles to interpret and apply the Commerce Clause, but the problem is the same with many other provisions of the Constitution.

Compounding the difficulty, many strands of judicial precedent seem inconsistent with the original understanding of constitutional language, and once precedents have been established, nearly everyone acknowledges that they, too, need to be reckoned with in constitutional adjudication. A particularly clear example involves the constitutionality of paper currency. The issuance of paper money very arguably exceeds the original understanding of Congress's power, conferred by Article I, Section 8, Clause 5 of the Constitution, to "coin Money."[7] Had the framers wished to empower Congress to issue "greenbacks," they could easily have said so; the authorization to "coin Money" seems to speak more narrowly. But the Supreme Court held otherwise in 1871,[8] and a reversal on this issue would provoke economic chaos.

Another example involves race-based discrimination by the federal government. It seems clear that no provision of the Constitution, even as

---

7 See Henry Paul Monaghan, "Stare Decisis and Constitutional Adjudication," 88 *Columbia Law Review* 723, 744 (1988).
8 See *Legal Tender Cases*, 79 U.S. 457 (1871) (overruling *Hepburn v. Griswold*), 75 U.S. 603 (1870)).

amended, was originally understood to bar discrimination by Congress; the Equal Protection Clause, enacted in the aftermath of the Civil War, only limits action by the states. For roughly seventy years, however, the Supreme Court has treated race-based discriminations by the federal government as "suspect" and has subjected them to "strict" or "searching" judicial scrutiny under the Due Process Clause of the Fifth Amendment, which was ratified in 1791.[9] Regardless of whether the earliest cases were rightly reasoned in terms of constitutional text and original understandings, nearly everyone now considers the matter to be settled by precedent and evolving moral understandings. Indeed, even Supreme Court Justices who maintain in other contexts that constitutional adjudication should reflect "the original understanding" of constitutional language have accepted judicial precedents applying equal protection norms to the federal government (and, more controversially, have cited those precedents as authority for condemning federal affirmative action programs).[10]

Of course, the Supreme Court is not absolutely bound by precedent. Sometimes it chooses to "overrule" itself. But the largely discretionary judgment of when to follow precedent and when to overrule it only adds a further judgmental element to constitutional adjudication in the Supreme Court.

When the various relevant considerations are all put into play, I have suggested repeatedly – largely following Professor Ronald Dworkin on this point[11] – that Supreme Court Justices typically decide how the Constitution is "best" interpreted in light of history, precedent, and considerations of moral desirability and practical workability. All of these factors

---

9 The Court first said that "all legal restrictions which curtail the civil rights of a single racial group are immediately suspect" and "that courts must subject them to the most rigid scrutiny" in *Korematsu v. United States*, 323 U.S. 214, 216 (1944).

10 See *Adarand Constructors, Inc. v. Pena*, 515 U.S. 200 (1997), and especially the concurring opinions of Justices Antonin Scalia, ibid. at 239, and Clarence Thomas, ibid. at 240.

11 See Ronald Dworkin, *Law's Empire* (Cambridge, MA: Belknap Press of Harvard University Press, 1986).

are relevant. No clear rule specifies which will be controlling in a particular case. In this context, political scientists often emphasize that the voting patterns of Supreme Court Justices tend to be relatively (though not perfectly) predictable on the basis of their political ideology.[12] In view of the judgmental character of constitutional adjudication, it would be astonishing if the results were otherwise.

To acknowledge such correlation is not to imply that the decisions of Supreme Court Justices are crudely political. The Justices function in what I described in the Introduction to this book as a constitutional "practice," which subjects them to a number of role-based constraints. They must reason like lawyers and take account of text and history as well as precedent. They work in the medium of constitutional law, not partisan politics, and the medium of law – with its characteristic techniques of reasoning – limits, shapes, and channels the Justices' search for the best interpretation of the Constitution.[13] Among the most significant role-based constraints, the Supreme Court, as I have pointed out previously, cannot invalidate laws just because it happens to dislike them analogously to the way that Presidents can veto bills on any grounds that they wish. Instead, the Court must lay down a rule of decision that will apply to future cases, including those to be decided by lower courts. Unless the Court is prepared to live with the across-the-board implications of a legal principle, it cannot rest on that principle to reach a result that a majority of the Justices would prefer for policy reasons in a particular case. At the same time, however, any fair observer must acknowledge that the nature of constitutional interpretation leaves abundant room for the exercise of legal and sometimes moral imagination.

Indeed, in assessing the scope of judicial power, is it not always helpful or even strictly accurate to think of the Supreme Court as engaged solely in constitutional "interpretation." As suggested already, among

12 See, for example, Jeffrey A. Segal and Harold J. Spaeth, *The Supreme Court and the Attitudinal Model* (Cambridge: Cambridge University Press, 1993).

13 I adopt the metaphor of law as a medium from Duncan Kennedy, *A Critique of Adjudication: Fin de Siècle* (Cambridge, MA: Harvard University Press, 1997).

the Court's characteristic modern functions is to formulate rules and tests for application by lower courts in future cases. This process, of course, begins with an interpretive search for the "meaning" of the Constitution." But before the Court comes to a decision, the Justices frequently need to make a great number of practical judgments, informed by their sense of likely consequences. In my view, many of the Court's rules are better viewed as devices to "implement" constitutional values than as "interpretations" of constitutional language.[14] Among the clearest examples of constitutional "implementation" as a function distinct from pure "interpretation" comes from *Miranda v. Arizona*[15] (1966), which introduced the requirement that the police give so-called *Miranda* warnings. These warnings, which make suspects aware of their Fifth Amendment rights against self-incrimination, have no explicit basis in the text of the Constitution. Though admittedly an extreme case, the *Miranda* decision exemplifies a broader phenomenon. Many of the doctrinal tests canvassed in earlier chapters – including the strict scrutiny formula asking whether a statute is necessary to advance a compelling governmental interest – lack clear roots in either the Constitution's language or its early history. The Supreme Court has devised them to implement constitutional values, but they do not emerge from the Constitution through a process that would naturally be described as one of interpretation alone.

One final detail about the role of the Supreme Court deserves mention in a discussion of judicial power. The Supreme Court today enjoys almost complete discretion about which cases to hear and not to hear. Courts in the United States decide tens of thousands of cases every year. The Supreme Court could not possibly review every decision involving a federal constitutional question. After experimenting with various other schemes, Congress, by statute, has provided that the Supreme Court simply gets to choose which cases decided by lower courts it would like to hear. In a typical year, the Court is asked to review approximately ten

14 See generally Richard H. Fallon Jr., *Implementing the Constitution* (Cambridge, MA: Harvard University Press, 2001).
15 384 U.S. 436 (1966).

thousand cases, out of which it has recently selected about seventy-five to eighty. For the most part, the Court agrees to decide those cases that the Justices think most important. The Supreme Court's power to choose its own cases is a significant one, which permits the Court to establish and pursue any agenda that it may wish to adopt – for example, by expanding constitutional rights or powers in some areas or pruning them in others.

Limits on Judicial Power

Partly because of its potency, the judicial power needs to be reigned in, at least to some extent. And it is. Some restraints arise from interaction between the judiciary and other, more overtly political forces and institutions. Others result from legal doctrines with roots in the Constitution's language and structure.

As the introduction to this chapter pointed out, social, cultural, and political considerations play an enormous role in defining and delimiting the power of the Supreme Court.[16] Although the Constitution contemplates the existence of judicial review, the domain within which the Court possesses recognized and effective authority is – in the vocabulary of political scientists – "politically constructed."[17] The political construction thesis has both an affirmative and a negative aspect. Affirmatively, political forces have determined that some issues should be subject to judicial resolution. Negatively, political forces put some issues beyond the sphere of judicial control.

With respect to the kind of issues on which the Court speaks authoritatively, political scientists emphasize that both the American public and elected political officials generally prefer that the Court have the

16 The argument in this and the following paragraphs draws heavily on Richard H. Fallon Jr., "The Supreme Court, Habeas Corpus, and the War on Terror: An Essay on Law and Political Science," 110 *Columbia Law Review* 352 (2010).

17 See, for example, Keith Whittington, *Political Foundations of Judicial Supremacy: The Presidency, the Supreme Court, and Constitutional Leadership in U.S. History* (Princeton, NJ: Princeton University Press, 2007), 4; Mark A. Graber, "Constructing Judicial Review," 8 *Annual Review of Political Science* 425, 425 (2005).

last word. The public values a judicial safeguard against abusive over-reaching by elected officials. Risk-averse political leaders prefer to forgo some opportunities to exercise authority while they hold office to prevent unbounded power by their political adversaries when elections go against them. In addition, national political leaders need a robust judiciary to enforce national values against occasionally wayward states and local officials.

Given the trust that it has earned over time, the Supreme Court today can authoritatively resolve constitutional issues concerning an impressively broad array of issues. For example, almost no one questions the Court's mandate to determine the constitutionality of affirmative action programs, gun-control legislation, or restrictions on contributions to political campaigns – however much critics may dislike the conclusions that the Court reaches. As I have noted already, however, the Court would clearly step outside the bounds of its authority if it identified constitutional questions entitling it to the last word on what tax rates ought to be, whether the federal government should spend more or less money, whether the United States should commit troops to Afghanistan, or whether it should bomb Iranian nuclear sites. To take other, once-controversial examples, the Court would stray outside the politically acceptable space for judicial review if it were to hold, today, that paper money or Social Security is unconstitutional. In the practically unimaginable event that the Court were to upset settled social, political, and economic expectations in such an egregiously disruptive way, its decision almost surely would not stand as the last word – one way or another.

In claiming that the Supreme Court functions within politically constructed bounds, one should distinguish, as political scientists have not always done, between harder and softer versions of the political construction thesis. The harder version holds that political officials, with the public's approbation, would dismiss some otherwise imaginable Court rulings as so obviously exceeding the Justices' constitutional mandate that they could, and should, simply be ignored. For example, Abraham

Lincoln, with the public's support, concluded that Chief Justice Taney had improperly trenched on the President's powers as Commander in Chief in *Ex parte Merryman*[18] (1861), a case that is discussed at length in Chapter 11. Here, suffice it to say that *Merryman* raised issues of military necessity in wartime and that the public agreed with Lincoln that the matter was one for the President, not the courts, to resolve. Franklin Roosevelt's Court-packing plan is a slightly softer example of the politically constructed limits on judicial power. Without "the switch in time that saved nine" in 1937, Roosevelt might well have succeeded in avoiding invalidation of highly popular New Deal programs by persuading Congress to expand the size of the Supreme Court so that he could appoint friendly Justices. The Court's intransigence had ceased to be politically tolerable to the American public. Finally, a still-softer version of the political construction thesis maintains that Court decisions (or patterns of decisions) that provoke sufficiently broad and enduring public outrage will not survive in the long run even if they do not provoke immediate defiance or Court packing. Over time, the voters will elect Presidents who oppose politically intolerable decisions. Those Presidents will then nominate and the Senate will confirm Justices who will undermine or overrule those decisions. An example comes from the 1968 presidential campaign, in which Richard Nixon successfully portrayed the Warren Court as having rendered too many decisions repugnant to the values of "the silent majority" of Americans.

A corollary of the thesis that the Supreme Court operates within politically constructed bounds is the proposition that at least some Justices decide cases in light of the political limits on their authority. Consciously or subconsciously, the Justices endeavor to preserve the public's trust and respect, on which the Court's immediate authority to decide cases, as well as the capacity of those decisions to survive over time, both depend. But one ought not press this corollary too far. As I have repeatedly emphasized, the Supreme Court is a "they," not an "it." There is no

18 17 F. Cas. 144 (C.C.D. Md. 1861) (No. 9487).

good reason to assume that all Justices will appraise the significance of the public's likely response to their decisions in the same way. For the most part, moreover, Supreme Court Justices probably do not need to think self-consciously about public opinion or risks of defiance to reach conclusions that the public, or most of it, is likely to find at least minimally acceptable. The Justices are creatures of the time in which they live (as are the rest of us). Their views are not likely to stray too far from the political mainstream.

The extent to which the Supreme Court tends to, or must, march in step with popular attitudes should not be overstated. Many of the issues decided by the Court draw little or no political interest. With respect to these, the Court can chart its own course without attracting much notice. In addition, individual Justices not only are expected to vote their consciences but also are personally insulated from political retaliation. (Apart from the remote risk of impeachment, the Constitution mandates that all federal judges "shall hold their Offices during good Behaviour," which in essence means that they enjoy life tenure, and their salaries cannot be reduced during their time in office.[19]) Sharp, even bitter, divisions within the Court are not infrequent. It is by no means impossible for a majority of the Justices to be misaligned with the views of political majorities pending the "lag" before appointments and confirmations restore the balance. Overall, perhaps the most that can be said is that the views of the Supreme Court with respect to constitutional issues of substantial political significance are unlikely to diverge very far from those of aroused political majorities for more than a relatively brief period.[20]

It is unclear how this state of affairs should be judged. Although there is some comfort in knowing that the Supreme Court is unlikely to be too

---

19 U.S. Constitution, Article III, Section 1.

20 See Robert A. Dahl, *A Preface to Democratic Theory* (Chicago: University of Chicago Press, 1956), 110 (reporting that there is not a single instance in American history in which a persistent legislative majority has failed to achieve its wishes despite initial Supreme Court resistance).

far out of touch with the American public, a judiciary that tends to share prevailing cultural norms, and thus to decide cases in light of them, is not likely to be a very robust guarantor of minority rights – at least until a particular minority's claim of rights is one that the mass public is generally prepared to accept.[21] As I observed in Chapter 5, it is surely no accident that the Supreme Court generally accepted race-based segregation as constitutionally permissible throughout the Jim Crow era of the late nineteenth and early twentieth centuries. Nor is it coincidental that the Court's pathbreaking decisions forbidding gender-based discrimination did not come until the 1970s, when the movement for women's rights had already begun to transform traditional attitudes.

To maintain that the Court seldom diverges far from the mainstream is not to claim that the Court's rulings make no difference. Sometimes they make a great deal of difference. The point is simply that the difference the Supreme Court makes, both for better and for worse, almost invariably occurs within a politically and culturally bounded range.

Reinforcing the politically constructed limits on judicial power are several complementary legal doctrines, rooted in the Constitution's text and structure, that formally cabin the Supreme Court's role. Article III of the Constitution says clearly that the "judicial power" extends only to "Cases" or "Controversies," or to what the delegates to the Constitutional Convention described as "cases of a Judiciary nature."[22] Although the Court has developed numerous doctrines defining the necessary elements of a constitutional "case" or "controversy," perhaps the most important involves the requirement of "standing." Mostly, standing doctrine requires that a lawsuit be brought by a proper party. To have standing to press a constitutional claim, the challenger must demonstrate that he or she has suffered a concrete "injury" as a result of an allegedly

---

21 See generally Gerald N. Rosenberg, *The Hollow Hope: Can Courts Bring About Social Change?* (Chicago: University of Chicago Press, 1991).

22 See Max Farrand, ed., *The Records of the Federal Convention of 1787* (New Haven, CT: Yale University Press, 1911), 1: 430 (reproducing James Madison's notes of a discussion and vote of August 27, 1787).

unconstitutional act.[23] Imagine that I, a male citizen of Massachusetts and not a doctor, read in the newspaper that Alabama has imposed a restriction on abortions that I believe to be unconstitutional. I would lack standing to challenge the Alabama law because I have not suffered concrete "injury" as that term is used in the legal sense. The proper parties to challenge the imagined statute would be women in Alabama who want or are likely to want abortions and doctors who are threatened with penalties if they perform abortions.

In another application of the case or controversy requirement, the Supreme Court has held that a few disputes about constitutional issues present "political questions" to be decided by either Congress or the President, not the courts. One thread of this doctrine maintains that some constitutional provisions specifically confer interpretive responsibility on a branch of government other than the judiciary. For example, Article I, Section 3, Clause 6 provides that "[t]he Senate shall have the sole Power to try all Impeachments" – actions to remove certain high federal officials from office on the ground that they have committed "Treason, Bribery, or other high Crimes and Misdemeanors."[24] In *Nixon v. United States*[25] (1993), the Court held that this language barred judicial review of whether the Senate had properly discharged its constitutional responsibilities in removing a federal judge named Walter Nixon. The Constitution authorized the Senate, not the courts, to determine the requisites of a fair impeachment trial.

Another thread of the political question doctrine emphasizes that some legal questions are not well suited for judicial resolution, either because of the absence of "judicially manageable standards" or because a judicial answer might create confusion or national embarrassment, especially in foreign affairs.[26] Invoking this rationale, a number of lower

23 See, for example, *Allen v. Wright*, 468 U.S. 737 (1984).
24 U.S. Constitution, Article II, Section 4.
25 506 U.S. 224 (1993).
26 See *Baker v. Carr*, 369 U.S. 186, 210–17 (1962) (reviewing and categorizing grounds on which the Supreme Court had identified political questions not fit for judicial resolution).

courts refused to rule on challenges to the constitutionality of the Vietnam War. (Opponents argued that the war was unconstitutional because Congress had never formally declared war, as they said it was required to do under Article I, Section 8, Clause 11 of the Constitution.) For obvious reasons, a judicial order to withdraw troops from battle would not only embarrass the government but also sow confusion and possibly even put lives at risk.

Apart from the case or controversy requirement, which governs whether a constitutional claim can be adjudicated at all, the Supreme Court has crafted a number of doctrines that call for judicial "deference" to the judgments of other officials in determining what the Constitution requires.[27] For example, the Court has said repeatedly that courts should nearly always accept the judgments of military authorities in assessing constitutional challenges to military regulations and discipline.[28] As was discussed in Chapter 3, the Court has also said that it will almost always defer to the judgments of Congress and state legislatures in determining whether economic regulatory legislation survives challenge under the Due Process and Equal Protection Clauses. Doctrines of judicial deference obviously reduce the tensions that can result from collisions between the courts and other branches of government.

Anxieties about Judicial Power

Although the Supreme Court functions within politically constructed bounds, its authority within those bounds can be enormous. The magnitude of the Court's power – encompassing the authority to invalidate popular legislation that many people may believe to be practically or morally urgent (as in the case of restrictions on abortion) – naturally gives rise to recurrent debates about how, exactly, the Court should go about interpreting and implementing the Constitution. At root, these debates are about how the Justices should conduct themselves such that

27 For general discussion of such doctrines, see Fallon, *Implementing the Constitution*, 87–97.
28 See, for example, *Goldman v. Weinberger*, 475 U.S. 503, 507–08 (1986).

the American people ought to recognize the legitimacy or justifiability of their rulings.

Although disagreements about interpretive methodology and the judicial role are never ending, they occasionally have arisen with special sharpness, typically when the nation is most divided on constitutional questions – as, for example, during the *Lochner* era, or when Richard Nixon promised to appoint "strict constructionist" Justices who would halt what he saw as the excesses of the Warren Court. In recent decades, conservative critics of the Supreme Court have found a focal point for criticism in the Court's 1973 decision in *Roe v. Wade*,[29] which held that absolute prohibitions against abortion violate the Constitution during the period before a fetus becomes viable or capable of surviving outside the womb. Although restrictions on abortion undoubtedly curtail "liberty," no one believes that the Due Process Clause – the provision on which the Court based its decision – was originally understood or intended to protect abortion rights. The Court based its ruling partly on precedent and partly on a contestable judgment that it is unreasonable to make women bear an unwanted fetus.

In objecting to decisions such as *Roe*, critics often maintain not just that the Court reached the wrong decision but also that it is not fair or "legitimate" for the unelected Justices of the Supreme Court to thwart the judgments of political majorities – at least when legislation is not in flat contravention of the Constitution's originally understood meaning. This challenge, to which Alexander Bickel gave the label of "the counter-majoritarian difficulty,"[30] deserves to be taken seriously. As noted previously, worries about countermajoritarianism can be overblown, but surely they cannot be dismissed entirely. Nor should such worries be regarded as distinctly applicable either to "liberal" or "conservative" Court decisions. Although contemporary conservatives probably charge liberals with "judicial activism" more often than the charge runs in the

29 410 U.S. 113 (1973).
30 The label traces to Alexander M. Bickel, *The Least Dangerous Branch: The Supreme Court at the Bar of Politics* (Indianapolis, IN: Bobbs-Merrill, 1962), 16.

other direction, this has not always been so. Conservative Justices nearly crippled the indisputably liberal New Deal. Today, it is conservatives who have stopped cities and states from regulating firearms as they wish, have invalidated politically popular limits on campaign spending, and have voted to subject federal affirmative action programs to strict judicial scrutiny – even though no provision of the Constitution was originally understood to bar affirmative action (or other forms of race-based discrimination) by the federal government.

Against the background of the countermajoritarian difficulty and related anxieties, judges and Justices openly debate questions of judicial role and interpretive methodology, often in the course of opinions deciding actual cases. This is a very striking feature of our constitutional practice. Legal arguments about how the Supreme Court should decide particular cases frequently are intertwined with more general debates about the Court's proper role.

In recent years, at least two (highly conservative) Justices of the Supreme Court, Antonin Scalia and Clarence Thomas, have occasionally maintained that judges and Justices should renounce interpretive methodologies that require them to decide how the Constitution would "best" or most fairly be applied to modern conditions and should decide cases based solely on the original understanding of constitutional language – what it was understood to mean by those who ratified it.[31] Because virtually no one denies that the original understanding is relevant to constitutional adjudication, it is often hard to gauge the precise scope of the difference between so-called originalists and their opponents. Further complicating efforts to make precise comparisons, a number of divisions have emerged among those in the originalist camp. Among other things, originalists disagree about whether the object of

31 See, for example, Antonin Scalia, *Common Law Courts in a Civil-Law System: The Role of United States Federal Courts in Interpreting the Constitution and Laws*, in *A Matter of Interpretation: Federal Courts and the Law*, ed. Amy Guttman (Princeton, NJ: Princeton University Press, 1997), 3, 38–47; Clarence Thomas, "Judging," 45 *University of Kansas Law Review* 1, 6–7 (1996).

historical study should be the "original intent," the "original understanding," or the "original public meaning" of constitutional language.
(Whereas inquiries into the original understanding seek to ascertain
what people actually thought, believed, or understood in the past, the
concept of the original public meaning shifts attention to what reasonable or well informed people who lived in the past would have thought if
they had confronted questions that they may never actually have asked
or answered.) Originalists also disagree about the circumstances, if any,
under which the original understanding should yield to entrenched judicial precedent (such as that holding paper money to be constitutionally
permissible).

Insofar as originalism is sharply distinctive, however, critics urge two
forceful objections. First, the "original understanding" or "original public meaning" of some constitutional provisions may be far out of touch
with current realities.[32] For example, as discussed in Chapter 7, the
principal basis for claims of federal authority to regulate the economy
is a constitutional provision empowering Congress to regulate "Commerce...among the several States." It is highly questionable whether
Congress's regulatory authority in this vital area should depend entirely
on the understanding that prevailed in what President Franklin Roosevelt, in championing the need for federal power to defeat the Great
Depression, referred to as "horse and buggy" days.[33]

A second problem, to which I have called attention already, is that
a great deal of modern constitutional doctrine that now seems to most
people to be too entrenched to give up may be impossible to justify
by reference to the original understanding. If so, originalists face an
uncomfortable choice – and, as noted earlier, they disagree on the solu-
tion. Some originalist law professors say that they would "bite the bul-
let" and stick to their theory: if Social Security and paper money are

---

32 See, for example, Paul Brest, "The Misconceived Quest for the Original Understanding," 60 *Boston University Law Review* 204 (1980).
33 Frank Freidel, *Franklin D. Roosevelt: A Rendezvous with Destiny* (Boston: Little,
Brown, 1990), 163.

unconstitutional as measured against the understood meaning or prevailing understanding on the Constitution in 1789, then we should live with the consequences. Many other originalists, apparently including Justices Scalia and Thomas, concede that their theory must make an exception for issues settled by entrenched judicial decisions[34] – or at least some of them. For them, issues of consistency pose a problem, for they do not contend that all erroneous precedents should be immune from correction. To take perhaps the best-known example, prominent originalists insist tirelessly that *Roe v. Wade*'s recognition of constitutional abortion rights ought to be overruled. But what distinguishes *Roe* from the precedents that originalists would leave unaltered? In essence, originalists reserve the right to pick which precedents to reject and which to accept, largely on the basis of their own judgments concerning which are important, desirable, and undesirable. Once it is recognized that Justices must make judgments such as these, this kind of originalism fails in its aspiration to exclude the Justices' moral and political views from constitutional adjudication. It is a philosophy available to be trotted out in some cases and ignored in others.

Confronted with objections such as these, originalists commonly insist that it takes a theory to beat a theory. Many originalists believe the best defense of their method is that it is the least bad of an imperfect lot. Originalism's critics believe that alternative approaches to constitutional adjudication are better.

Another prominent theory of constitutional adjudication rests on the premise that the Constitution embodies "moral" rights.[35] According to this view, the Constitution's framers and ratifiers did not invent rights such as those of freedom of speech and religion or to the equal

---

34 See, for example, Antonin Scalia, "Response," in Guttman, *A Matter of Interpretation*, 138–40; Robert H. Bork, *The Tempting of America: The Political Seduction of the Law* (New York: Free Press, 1990), 155–8.

35 The great exemplar of this approach is Ronald Dworkin. See especially Ronald Dworkin, *Freedom's Law: The Moral Reading of the American Constitution* (Cambridge, MA: Harvard University Press, 1996).

protection of the laws. Rather, they recognized that such rights already existed as moral rights, and they incorporated those moral rights into the Constitution. Those holding this view would say, for example, that the Equal Protection Clause extends as far as the moral right to treatment as an equal and thus justifies the result in *Brown v. Board of Education*, even if the framers and ratifiers of the Fourteenth Amendment would have thought otherwise. At its foundation, an approach to constitutional adjudication that asks the courts to supply the best "moral reading" of rights-conferring provisions posits that the institutions of political democracy, if left to themselves, would not be morally trustworthy – perhaps because members of Congress and the state legislatures are too susceptible to political pressure. Critics, of course, maintain that this approach invites judges simply to impose their personal moral views. Judges, they insist, have no monopoly on and, indeed, no special insight into moral truth.

In view of the objections to both originalism and a "moral reading" approach, some observers call for greater "judicial restraint" in invalidating legislation. When members of Congress and state legislators enact statutes, they have presumably considered whether the legislation violates the Constitution and determined that it does not. Accordingly, advocates of judicial restraint have long contended – since the *Lochner* era and even before – that the Supreme Court should accord great "deference" to the constitutional judgments of other branches of government, not just with respect to military affairs or economic rights (as the Court now does) but across all areas of constitutional law. According to one famous formulation of this position, the Court should invalidate statutes only when Congress or a state legislature has made a "clear mistake" about what the Constitution permits.[36] This is by no means a wholly implausible position, but it would call for a dramatically reduced judicial role. It would also cast retrospective doubt on many of the

---

36 See James B. Thayer, "The Origin and Scope of the American Doctrine of Constitutional Law," 7 *Harvard Law Review* 129 (1893).

Supreme Court's most celebrated decisions, including some that have protected the rights of racial minorities, safeguarded political speech, and enforced voting rights.[37]

Believing that the Court should retain a robustly protective role in these areas, the late constitutional scholar John Hart Ely argued for deference to majorities except in cases involving claims of minority rights or rights to participate in the political process.[38] He justified this approach by arguing that the Constitution's predominant commitment is to political democracy and that courts should therefore intervene mostly only to make sure that the processes of political democracy function fairly. Fairness is absent, and the democratic process malfunctions, he maintained, when legislative decision making is corrupted by "prejudice" against discrete and insular minorities such as African Americans and when incumbent legislators attempt to silence the speech of their critics or rig the applicable voting rules. Otherwise, courts should be highly deferential. Among its implications, Ely's theory would stop courts from invalidating affirmative action programs (which disadvantage the white majority, not a racial minority, and thus are highly unlikely to reflect prejudice) and recently enacted statutes that discriminate against women (who are a numerical majority, not a minority, of the population). Ely did not claim that the Supreme Court actually follows his theory, only that it should.

Other participants in the debate over constitutional interpretation defend a more flexible approach, partly based on an analogy to the way that judges decided cases under the so-called common law.[39] Well into the nineteenth century, Congress and the state legislatures still had enacted comparatively few statutes, and the most basic law – called the common law – was developed by judges on the basis of "custom" and "reason." In deciding cases at common law, judges begin with the rules

---

37 See Monaghan, "Stare Decisis and Constitutional Adjudication," 727–39.
38 See John Hart Ely, *Democracy and Distrust: A Theory of Judicial Review* (Cambridge, MA: Harvard University Press, 1980), 135–79.
39 See, for example, David A. Strauss, *The Living Constitution* (New York: Oxford University Press, 2010).

as formulated in prior judicial decisions, but they also enjoy some flex-ibility to adapt those rules as circumstances change or as custom and reason require. Under the approach that common-law constitutionalists advocate, Supreme Court Justices should employ a comparably flexi-ble approach in deciding constitutional issues. They should always begin with the text of the written Constitution, with which any interpretation must at least be reconciled. And they should treat the original under-standing as always relevant and often decisive. But under the common-law approach, judges and especially Justices should also give weight to previous judicial decisions, including those that depart from original constitutional understandings. They also should take express account of what is fair, reasonable, workable, and desirable under modern circum-stances because their doing so will yield substantively better constitu-tional law than we would get if they did not. Critics, notably including originalists, argue that the common-law approach gives too large a role to judges, who are invited to thwart the wishes of democratic majorities based on their personal notions of justice and workability.

As the persistence of debate about interpretive methodology per-haps suggests, it may well be that questions about how the Court should interpret the Constitution admit no general answer – and that there can be no categorically persuasive rejoinder to the countermajoritarian dif-ficulty either. The justification of the Supreme Court's role and inter-pretive methodology, if any, may well depend on the substantive fair-ness and popular acceptability of the particular decisions that it makes across the sweep of time.[40] For now, at least, the people of the United States appear to have accepted a judicial role in adapting the Constitu-tion to changing perceptions of need and fairness. But their acceptance of a flexible judicial role should be regarded as contingent, based on an assumption – grounded in our traditions – that judicial review as histor-ically practiced has tended to produce good results overall: it is a useful

40 See Richard H. Fallon Jr., "Judicial Legitimacy and the Unwritten Constitution: A Comment on *Miranda* and *Dickerson*," 45 *New York Law School Law Review* 119, 133–36 (2001).

device for promoting substantive justice and for reaching results that are broadly acceptable to the American public in ways that are at least tolerably consistent with the constitutional ideal of "a government of laws, and not of men."[41]

Alexander Bickel may have had a thought such as this in mind when he wrote, somewhat enigmatically, that the Court "labors under the obligation to succeed."[42] If the Court must somehow succeed in order to justify its role – and if success depends on reconciling the contestable demands of substantive justice with the sometimes competing imperatives of adhering to settled rules of law and of rendering decisions that the public deems acceptable – it is easy to understand why the practice of judicial review provokes anxiety and debate. It is also easy to see why those anxieties and debate have never been, and probably will never be, wholly resolved.

41 *Marbury v. Madison*, 5 U.S. 137 (1803).
42 Bickel, *Least Dangerous Branch*, 239.

Part III FURTHER ISSUES OF CONSTITUTIONAL STRUCTURE AND INDIVIDUAL RIGHTS

10 Structural Limits on State Power and Resulting Individual Rights

[The] principle that our economic unit is the Nation, which alone has the gamut of powers necessary to control of the economy..., has as its corollary that the states are not separable economic units.... [A] state may not use its admitted powers to protect the health and safety of its people as a basis for suppressing competition.

– Justice Robert H. Jackson[1]

T O RAISE REVENUE AND PERHAPS ALSO TO DISCOURAGE people from leaving its borders, Nevada, back in the 1860s, imposed a tax of one dollar on stagecoach and railway tickets for out-of-state destinations. In *Crandall v. Nevada*[2] (1867), the Supreme Court held that the tax was unconstitutional. In ruling as it did, the Court did not point to the language of any particular constitutional provision. None refers expressly to a right to travel from one state to another, much less to a right to travel without being taxed. Instead, the Court found the right to travel among the states, and a prohibition against state legislation penalizing the exercise of that right, to be implicit in the general structure of the Constitution and in the concepts of nationhood and national citizenship.

---

1 *H. P. Hood & Sons, Inc. v. Du Mond*, 336 U.S. 525, 537–38 (1949).
2 73 U.S. 35 (1867).

From a modern perspective, *Crandall v. Nevada* illustrates two important features of American constitutional law. First, just as the existence of the states imposes implied limits on Congress's regulatory powers – a matter discussed in Chapter 7 – the existence of the federal government and the idea of unitary nationhood impliedly restrict the power of the states. Second, the resulting limits, which might be described as arising from the Constitution's structure, in effect give rise to individual rights against the states (such as the right recognized in *Crandall* not to be taxed or otherwise penalized by the government for traveling from one state to another).

How Federal Power and Federal Law Can Restrict State Power

Limits on the powers of the states flow from a number of constitutional sources besides the express rights-conferring provisions discussed in Chapters 1–6. In assigning power to the federal government, the Constitution sometimes explicitly forbids the states to exercise parallel authority. For example, after authorizing Congress to "coin Money" in Article I, Section 8, the Constitution provides separately in Article I, Section 10, that no state shall coin money. After empowering Congress to declare war,[3] Article I again includes a separate provision that "[n]o State shall, without the Consent of Congress,...engage in War, unless actually invaded, or in such imminent Danger as will not admit of delay."[4] When the Constitution empowers the federal government but does not expressly disempower the states, harder interpretive questions arise. As a matter of common sense, the congressional power to levy taxes does not impliedly stop the states from collecting taxes as well; without tax revenues, states could not function. By contrast, the Supreme Court has held that Congress's power to regulate foreign commerce implicitly imposes significant restraints on state regulatory

3 U.S. Constitution, Article I, Section 8, Clause 11.
4 U.S. Constitution, Article I, Section 10, Clause 3.

authority.[5] It would be unacceptable for state law to interfere with federal management of the foreign relations of the United States.

Federal statutes, as well as federal constitutional provisions, can override, nullify, or, as lawyers say, "preempt" state law. This effect occurs through the Supremacy Clause of Article VI, which provides that "this Constitution and the Laws of the United States which shall be made in Pursuance thereof... shall be the supreme Law of the Land..., any Thing in the Constitution or Laws of any State to the Contrary notwithstanding." There are two kinds of statutory preemption. "Express preemption" occurs when a federal statute explicitly provides that federal regulation is intended to be exclusive. "Implied preemption" happens when, even though a federal statute says nothing about preemption, enforcement of a state law would conflict with a federal law.

An example illustrates how preemption works in practice. In 1965, Congress enacted a law requiring cigarette manufacturers to put specific warning labels on their packages as well as in their advertisements. The federal law did not, however, say anything about when, if ever, smokers might be able to sue tobacco companies for harms caused by their products. Some years later, a former smoker who had developed lung cancer sued a cigarette manufacturer in a New Jersey court, claiming an entitlement to damages under New Jersey law. The plaintiff argued in part that New Jersey law required cigarette manufacturers to give fuller disclosures about the dangers of smoking than the federally prescribed warnings provided. When the case came to the Supreme Court, the question was what Congress had intended in enacting the statute that requires federal warnings: had it meant just to establish the minimum that cigarette manufacturers must do, or had it more comprehensively determined that if cigarette manufacturers gave the federal warning, then they had done enough, and thereby "preempted" laws, such as New Jersey's, that previously required fuller warnings? As a matter of constitutional law, no

5 See, for example, *Board of Trustees of the University of Illinois v. United States*, 289 U.S. 48, 56–57 (1933) (holding that congressional power to regulate foreign commerce "may not be limited, qualified, or impeded to any extent by state action").

one doubted Congress's power, under the Commerce Clause, to preempt New Jersey law if it wished to do so. The question was solely one of congressional intent, involving whether Congress meant to displace state law or whether state law was incompatible with the aims of the federal statute. On the facts of the case, *Cipollone v. Liggett Group, Inc.*[6] (1992), a divided Court held that the federal statute preempted state law that would have allowed suit and recovery based on a failure to provide further warnings about the dangers of smoking but that it did not preempt state law permitting suit for affirmative misrepresentations by cigarette manufacturers about the safety of their product.

The Privileges and Immunities Clause

In the early 1970s, Alaska faced an unemployment problem. Although the state's oil industry was thriving, many of the best jobs went to workers newly arrived from out of state, some of whom had no interest in making Alaska their permanent home. In an effort to improve the lot of Alaskans, the state legislature enacted a statute, dubbed "Alaska Hire," requiring that Alaska residents be given a hiring preference over visiting out-of-staters for all jobs "resulting from" oil and gas leases or pipeline projects to which the state was a party. The Supreme Court invalidated Alaska Hire by a unanimous vote.

The Court's ruling, in the case of *Hicklin v. Orbeck*[7] (1978), rested on Article IV's Privileges and Immunities Clause, which provides that "[t]he Citizens of each State shall be entitled to all Privileges and Immunities of Citizens in the several States." Although its language is slightly archaic, the Privileges *and* Immunities Clause – not to be confused with the Privileges *or* Immunities Clause of the Fourteenth Amendment, which was discussed in Chapter 3 and has little, if any, modern significance – establishes an antidiscrimination rule: whatever privileges and immunities a

6 505 U.S. 504 (1992).
7 437 U.S. 518 (1978).

state chooses to grant to its own citizens, it must at least presumptively grant to visiting out-of-staters. As an express constitutional provision, the Privileges and Immunities Clause has distinctive language and a distinctive history, both of which have informed its application. But the Privileges and Immunities Clause also reflects values or suppositions that are implicit in the Constitution's structure and that extend both further and deeper than its specific language. In *Hicklin v. Orbeck*, the Court held in substance that the state's interest in mandating preferences for its own citizens must yield to the national interest in maintaining equal employment opportunities in an open national economy. Under the national Constitution, state interests had to take second place to national interests.

Obviously, however, there is another side of the coin, as was acutely visible to the Alaska legislature. Although the United States exists as a single nation, states persist as political entities separate from the nation as a whole, and they have a special relationship with their citizens that they do not have with citizens of other states. Surely, Alaska can enact welfare programs under which it makes payments only to Alaskans. Surely, the state can give residents preferences in admissions to the state university, and it can charge lower tuition to in-staters than to out-of-staters. Surely, in other words, there must be some balance of state interests and national interests. The Constitution must forbid some kinds of state actions and discriminations against out-of-staters because they would be incompatible with nationhood and national citizenship, but it must permit others because without them statehood and state citizenship would be meaningless. *Hicklin v. Orbeck* put Alaska Hire on the forbidden side of a constitutional line. But where exactly is that line? Although the Supreme Court has not responded as clearly as one might wish to that fundamental constitutional question, at least the outlines of an answer emerge from the Court's decisions.

In applying Article IV's Privileges and Immunities Clause in cases such as *Hicklin v. Orbeck*, the Supreme Court has prescribed two sorts of inquiries. The first aims to distinguish the "privileges and immunities of citizens" from other opportunities or benefits. To make this distinction, the Court has adopted a largely historical test, equating "the privileges and immunities of citizens" with those rights that were historically deemed "fundamental" or understood to "belong...to the citizens of all free governments."[8] This historically based test for fundamental rights under the Privileges and Immunities Clause can easily create confusion because it is different from the not-always-historical tests used to identify "fundamental rights" under the Due Process and Equal Protection Clauses (as discussed in Chapter 6). As a result, a right may be deemed fundamental for purposes of the Privileges and Immunities Clause but not for the Due Process or Equal Protection Clause, or vice versa. But under the historical test used to identify fundamental and nonfundamental rights under the Privileges and Immunities Clause, states can prefer their own citizens when distributing nonfundamental rights. In the leading case of *Baldwin v. Fish and Game Commission*[9] (1978), the Court thus held that a state could charge out-of-staters more than in-staters for elk-hunting licenses because the opportunity to hunt elk was not a historically fundamental right.

Although the "right" to hunt elk may seem trivial, other nonfundamental rights are more important from a practical perspective. Under a historical test, it appears that rights to welfare and education – which I previously suggested states must be able to provide to their own citizens on a preferential basis – would fall into the nonfundamental category. However important they might be today, they would not have been regarded as fundamental in the eighteenth or early nineteenth century.

The second judicial inquiry under the Privileges and Immunities Clause occurs when states attempt to prefer their own citizens in matters involving the recognized "privileges and immunities of citizenship," prominent among which, for historical reasons, is the right (involved in *Hicklin v. Orbeck*) to pursue a lawful trade. Significantly, the Supreme

---

8 *Corfield v. Coryell*, No. 6 F. Cas. 546, 3230, 551 (C.C.E.D. Pa. 1823).
9 436 U.S. 371 (1978).

Court has not held that the Privileges and Immunities Clause forbids all discrimination between citizens and noncitizens even when they involve historically fundamental rights. The Court has said only that such discriminations are presumptively unconstitutional and can be upheld only if the state demonstrates a valid, legitimate, or substantial justification for treating out-of-staters less favorably than in-staters.

In applying this aspect of its test, the Supreme Court has consistently invalidated state laws that flatly forbid out-of-staters from working or seeking jobs in the private sector or that subject them to discriminatory taxes or regulations, as in *Hicklin v. Orbeck*. The Court has distinguished, however, between state laws that impose discriminatory taxes and prohibitions, which it virtually never permits, and those that authorize the distribution of jobs either as government employees or on projects paid for by the government out of tax revenues. With respect to the latter, the Court has suggested that a city or state might have "substantial," and thus constitutionally adequate, reasons to prefer its own citizens to out-of-staters.[10]

The justification for this distinction presumably lies in the need to create sensible incentives for state and local governments, which, as I have said, have special relationships and sometimes special responsibilities to their own citizens. By permitting states to grant hiring preferences to their own citizens when they are spending public funds, the Supreme Court provides an incentive for states to make expenditures that they might not make otherwise. If such preferences were not permitted, then states would be much less likely to fund a variety of beneficial programs – a sad if not disastrous consequence from the perspective of both public policy and constitutional law.

Within the Supreme Court's framework for analyzing claims under the Privileges and Immunities Clause, the hiring preferences mandated by Alaska Hire went too far. The state could have preferred Alaskans in

---

10 See *United Building & Construction Trades Council v. Mayor and Council of Camden*, 465 U.S. 208 (1984).

hiring state employees, but it could not force private employers to prefer Alaskans for all jobs "resulting from" leases and projects to which the state was a party.

The "Dormant" Commerce Clause

Apart from the Privileges and Immunities Clause, which guarantees rights of citizenship, it has long been assumed that the Constitution's Commerce Clause – though framed as a grant of power to Congress to regulate interstate commerce – implicitly restricts the states' ability to impose taxes and regulations that interfere with interstate commerce. This is an important assumption. It is often tempting for states to try to promote the welfare of their own citizens by discriminating against out-of-state businesses (corporations cannot claim the protection of the Privileges and Immunities Clause) or against goods produced out of state. A historically familiar example involves the dairy industry. For decades, the number of dairy farms has been shrinking, especially in the northeastern states, as large milk producers, many from the Midwest, have been able to undersell their competition. Rather than watch the collapse of their domestic dairy industries, a number of states have enacted "protectionist" measures designed to shield in-state farmers from economic competition with out-of-staters. Sometimes the protective efforts have taken the form of discriminatory taxes on milk imported from out of state. In other instances, states have imposed minimum price requirements on the sale of milk by farmers to wholesale distributors – forbidding the sale of milk at cheap prices, regardless of where it is produced – to protect in-state farmers by making it impossible for their out-of-state competitors to undersell them. (Even if out-of-state farmers can produce milk more cheaply than in-state farmers can, minimum price laws stop them from selling it at cheaper prices, and their competitive advantage is thereby destroyed.)

If Congress wished to do so, its Article I commerce power would permit it to displace or preempt state legislation that makes it harder for out-of-staters to sell their goods. But it would be difficult to craft such legislation in general terms. For example, Congress could not sensibly bar all state legislation that tends to diminish the flow of goods in interstate commerce. State laws as sensible as those forbidding the sale and use of dangerous products – firecrackers, for example – diminish interstate commerce in the regulated products. In theory, Congress could also monitor the enactment of state legislation affecting commerce and displace only those specific laws of which it disapproved. As a practical matter, however, the sheer volume of state lawmaking would make it difficult, if not impossible, for Congress to do so effectively.

Believing that Congress could not realistically be expected to oversee all state regulations of commerce and specifically preempt all of those that it found objectionable, the Supreme Court has stepped into the perceived breach by holding that the Commerce Clause impliedly creates presumptive, judicially enforceable limits on state legislation. The resulting body of doctrine is often called "dormant Commerce Clause doctrine" to signify that Congress's regulatory power is dormant, or unexercised. Under this doctrine, the courts determine which state enactments should be deemed invalid because of their effects on interstate commerce. If, however, Congress disagrees with a judicial judgment, it retains its authority to regulate commerce by specifically authorizing a state regulation that the courts have found objectionable.[11]

Under dormant Commerce Clause doctrine, state tax and regulatory statutes that expressly discriminate against goods from other states – for example, by subjecting them to taxes or other regulations to which goods produced within the state are not subjected – are nearly always invalid. The Supreme Court repeatedly has pronounced that the Commerce

---

11 This situation is highly unusual. Under *Marbury v. Madison*, 5 U.S. 137 (1803), Supreme Court rulings of constitutional invalidity normally bind the other branches of government. To be reconciled with *Marbury*, judicial interpretations of the dormant Commerce Clause should probably be thought of as constitutionally mandated "default" rules, to be applied unless Congress legislates to the contrary. See Laurence H. Tribe, *Constitutional Choices* (Cambridge, MA: Harvard University Press, 1985), 29–44.

Clause forbids "economic protectionism – that is, regulatory measures designed to benefit in-state economic interests by burdening out-of-state competitors."[12] As the Court said in *Baldwin v. G. A. F. Seelig, Inc.*[13] (1935), a case involving efforts by the state of New York to prop up its dairy industry, if one state, "in order to promote the economic welfare of her farmers, may guard them against competition with the cheaper prices of [farmers in other states], the door has been opened to rivalries and reprisals that were meant to be averted by subjecting commerce between the states to the power of the nation." For a tax or regulatory statute that discriminates against interstate commerce to be upheld, a state must demonstrate that the discrimination is made necessary by a valid and compelling consideration unrelated to economic "protectionism" – for example, by showing that goods shipped in interstate commerce risk spreading a contagion that cannot be effectively contained except by exclusion.[14] A state engages in forbidden "protectionism," as the Supreme Court uses that term, when it tries to protect its citizens or industries from fair economic competition, but not when it tries to protect against hazards such as disease that are unrelated to fair competition.

When a state law does not expressly discriminate against goods or firms from other states but has an "incidental" effect on the flow of interstate commerce – for example, by forbidding the sale of firecrackers that can be lawfully manufactured and sold in other states – the Supreme Court regularly says that it will determine on a case-by-case basis whether the local benefits are great enough to justify the negative impact on interstate commerce.[15] Virtually never, however, has the Court

---

12 *Wyoming v. Oklahoma*, 502 U.S. 437, 454–55 (1992) (quoting *New Energy Co. of Indiana v. Limbach*, 486 U.S. 269, 273–74 (1988)).

13 294 U.S. 511, 522 (1935).

14 See *Maine v. Taylor*, 477 U.S. 131 (1986) (upholding a state prohibition against the importation of baitfish likely to contaminate Maine baitfish stocks).

15 See, for example, *Pike v. Bruce Church, Inc.*, 397 U.S. 137, 142 (1970): "Where [a state] statute regulates even-handedly to effectuate a legitimate local public interest, and its effects on interstate commerce are only incidental, it will be upheld unless the burden

invalidated a state regulatory statute under the Commerce Clause unless that statute has had the effect of advantaging in-state economic interests over their out-of-state competitors. Thus, if a state were to ban the sale of all firecrackers, the statute would almost surely be upheld against a challenge under the Commerce Clause, even though fewer firecrackers would be sold in interstate commerce as a result. By contrast, if a state were to ban the sale of some firecrackers but not others, and if it happened that the permitted firecrackers were predominantly manufactured in the state and that the prohibited firecrackers were predominantly manufactured out of state, judicial review would be much more searching. The Court's goal would be to "smoke out" a hidden attempt to advantage the in-state manufacturer in economic competition with out-of-state competitors.

Surveying the obvious pattern of the Supreme Court's cases, which tend to invalidate statutes under the dormant Commerce Clause only when they help in-state economic interests in competition with out-of-staters, Professor Donald Regan has surmised that "protectionism" is all that the Court really cares about[16]: although it says it balances competing state and national interests, it actually invalidates state legislation only when it strongly suspects that a state is really trying to protect its residents from fair economic competition. To explain the Court's repeated assertions that it "balances" in-state benefits against harms to the flow of interstate commerce, Regan speculates that the Court is hesitant to accuse state legislatures of constitutionally forbidden discrimination against out-of-staters. The Court may also prefer to preserve its options lest a case come along in which a state law, though not intentionally protectionist, has hugely adverse effects on interstate commerce

imposed on such commerce is clearly excessive in relation to the putative local benefits. If a legitimate local purpose is found, then the question [whether the regulation should be invalidated] becomes one of degree. And the extent of the burden that will be tolerated will ... depend on the nature of the local interest involved, and on whether it could be promoted as well with a lesser impact on interstate activities."

16 See Donald H. Regan, "The Supreme Court and State Protectionism: Making Sense of the Dormant Commerce Clause," 84 *Michigan Law Review* 1091 (1986).

and achieves virtually no local benefit. In any event, if a state regulatory statute does not advantage state residents at the expense of out-of-state economic competitors, it is almost certain to survive judicial challenge under the dormant Commerce Clause.

The States as "Market Participants"

Like the Privileges and Immunities Clause, dormant Commerce Clause doctrine that forbids states from preferring or protecting their own citizens raises a fundamental question about the states' role under the Constitution and about the meaning of state citizenship: once again, aren't states supposed to try to advance the interests of their citizens, sometimes in preference to those of outsiders? In response to that question, the doctrinal structure under the dormant Commerce Clause, like that under the Privileges and Immunities Clause, generally prohibits the states from trying to aid their citizens by subjecting out-of-staters to discriminatory regulations and taxes, but it permits the states to favor their own citizens when buying or selling goods or services. Under the "market participant exception" to dormant Commerce Clause doctrine, a state that engages in economic activity can hire its citizens on a preferential basis, and it can similarly grant preferences to its own citizens as purchasers of goods sold by the state.

In *Reeves, Inc. v. Stake*[17] (1980), which involved a challenge to a state-owned cement plant's practice of selling cement to in-state customers on a preferential basis, the Court attempted to rationalize its practice of subjecting the states to different rules when they act as market participants than when they act as market regulators. *Reeves* intimated that when a state enters the market, it does not act in a sovereign or governmental capacity and that norms applicable to the state-as-sovereign therefore do not apply. This suggestion will not withstand analysis. A state remains a state, and thus subject to constitutional limits, as much in the market as

17 447 U.S. 429 (1980).

STRUCTURAL LIMITS ON STATE POWER

in any other context. No one contends that a state should be able to discriminate on the basis of race or religion when buying or selling goods. On the contrary, it is because the state remains a state that it should be able to prefer its residents when buying goods and services and when selling or dispensing other goods. As noted earlier, it is the function of states, as political communities, to attempt to benefit their citizens, sometimes in preference to noncitizens. For a variety of sound reasons involving national union and national citizenship, states cannot attempt to protect their residents by imposing discriminatory taxes that would be likely to cause resentment and trigger retaliation by other states. But states can and should be encouraged to create goods – such as educational opportunities, public housing, and welfare benefits – that would not otherwise exist. For states to have an incentive to do so, they are reasonably permitted to prefer their own residents when they buy, sell, or distribute such goods and opportunities. (Once again, the situation is different when a state, without having used taxpayer-generated funds to created opportunities, tries to thrust onto the citizens of another state the burden of making its own residents better off by, for example, subjecting out-of-staters to discriminatory taxes or regulations.)

Traditionally, states have also been permitted to provide economic subsidies to domestic industries.[18] The line between a discriminatory tax against out-of-staters (which would be clearly impermissible) and a subsidy for domestic industries can often be a fine one – a point that has troubled the Court in some cases and might possibly trigger a rethinking of the doctrine at some time in the future.[19] By tradition, however,

---

18 See *New Energy Co. of Indiana v. Limbach*, 486 U.S. 269, 278 (1988) (observing that the dormant Commerce Clause "does not prohibit all state action designed to give its residents an advantage in the marketplace" and that "[d]irect subsidization of domestic industry does not ordinarily run afoul of [the constitutional] prohibition").

19 See *West Lynn Creamery, Inc. v. Healy*, 512 U.S. 186 (1994) (invalidating a state subsidy scheme that, in effect though not in form, called for the rebate of special taxes imposed to fund the scheme to in-staters but not out-of-staters); *DaimlerChrysler Corp. v. Cuno*, 547 U.S. 332 (2006) (reviewing a package of city and state tax incentives designed to keep a manufacturing plant in Toledo, Ohio, and upholding the incentives

314 THE DYNAMIC CONSTITUTION

a state that has permissibly accumulated revenues through taxes on its own citizens is permitted to prefer its own citizens when making voluntary expenditures.

Conclusion

As I noted at the outset of this chapter, if the concept of unitary nationhood makes it impermissible for the states to favor their own residents by enacting laws that discriminate against out-of-staters, it effectively creates rights in out-of-staters to be free from discrimination. But not all state discriminations against out-of-staters are forbidden. If they were, the states could not fulfill some of their most basic functions. The doctrine distinguishing permissible from impermissible discriminations is sometimes murky, but its basic aim is crystal clear. Constitutional law must permit an accommodation between the ideal of unitary nationhood and national citizenship, on the one hand, and the concept of meaningful statehood and state citizenship, on the other.

offered by the city but finding that the plaintiffs lacked standing to challenge the state tax breaks). Academic literature reconsidering the traditional line between permitted subsidies and forbidden discriminatory taxes includes Dan T. Coenen, "Business Subsidies and the Dormant Commerce Clause," 107 *Yale Law Journal* 965 (1998), and Peter D. Enrich, "Saving the States from Themselves: Commerce Clause Constraints on State Tax Incentives for Business," 110 *Harvard Law Review* 377 (1996).

11 The Constitution in War and Emergency

[While] the Constitution protects against invasions of individual rights, it is not a suicide pact.

– Kennedy v. Mendoza-Martinez (1963)[1]

War is hell.

– General William Tecumseh Sherman

ON APRIL 12, 1861, CONFEDERATE MILITARY FORCES FIRED on Fort Sumter, in the harbor of Charleston, South Carolina, and within a few days forced the surrender of Union soldiers stationed there. Confronted with the gravest crisis in American history, President Abraham Lincoln knew that he must convene the Congress of the United States – which was then out of session and absent from Washington, not due to return until the fall. But Congress was large, even then, and opinionated and divided. Lincoln therefore thought that he could manage the crisis better alone. So he called Congress into a special session but postponed the meeting date until July 4.[2]

In the period between April 12 and July 4, Lincoln ordered a blockade of Southern ports – a step almost universally regarded as an act of

1 372 U.S. 144, 160 (1963).

2 The relevant developments are succinctly summarized in Daniel Farber, *Lincoln's Constitution* (Chicago: University of Chicago Press, 2003), ch. 6.

war. Article I of the Constitution assigns the power "[t]o declare War" to Congress, which had not yet convened.[3] Also before July 4, Lincoln called for volunteers for the army and ordered fifteen ships added to the navy, even though the Constitution specifically gives Congress, not the President, the powers to "raise and support Armies" and to "provide and maintain a Navy."[4] Doubting the loyalty of officials in the Treasury and War Departments, many of whom were Southerners, Lincoln directed the Secretary of the Treasury to transfer $2 million in federal funds to three private citizens charged by him to make requisitions "for the defence and support of the government"[5] – notwithstanding the constitutional provision that "[n]o Money shall be drawn from the Treasury, but in Consequence of Appropriations made by Law."[6]

In a further response to secessionist activity, Lincoln, in the language of the Constitution, either suspended or authorized suspension of "the Privilege of the Writ of Habeas Corpus" in selected regions of the country. Technically, this step barred courts from examining the legality of the detention of civilians by military officials. As a practical matter, it permitted military leaders to lay down rules binding on civilians as well as on military personnel and to imprison those believed to be engaged in disloyal activities without needing to prove in civilian courts that the detainees had committed any actual crimes. Although the Constitution specifically provides for suspension of the writ of habeas corpus "when in Cases of Rebellion or Invasion the public Safety may require it," it does so in Article I, which lists the powers of Congress, not in Article II, which deals with the powers of the President.[7]

---

3 U.S. Constitution, Article I, Section 8, Clause 11.

4 U.S. Constitution, Article I, Section 8, Clauses 12 and 13.

5 Message of Abraham Lincoln to the Senate and House of Representatives, May 26, 1862, reprinted in Abraham Lincoln, *Selected Speeches and Writings 1859–1865* (New York: Library of America, 1989), 325–26.

6 U.S. Constitution, Article I, Section 9, Clause 7.

7 U.S. Constitution, Article I, Section 9, Clause 2.

Did Lincoln violate the Constitution? Should we care?[8] Did his ends – preservation of the Union and ultimately the eradication of slavery – justify his chosen means? Does the Constitution confer expanded or even unlimited powers on the government and its officials in times of war and possibly other emergency?

Historians, lawyers, and concerned citizens continue to debate these questions.[9] For his own part, Lincoln, who was a lawyer, took pains to offer constitutional defenses for nearly every step that he took. In addition, when Congress finally convened, he sought and Congress voted for legislation declaring his actions "respecting the army and navy of the United States" to be "hereby approved and in all respects legalized and made valid."[10] A few years later, the Supreme Court held that Lincoln also had constitutional authority to order a blockade of Southern ports.[11] For all practical purposes, the Court said, the nation was at war, even if no war had formally been declared, and in wartime the decision to order a blockade comes within the President's Article II power as Commander in Chief of the armed forces.

Only with respect to the suspension of habeas corpus and resulting assaults on individual liberties did either Congress or the judiciary show much resistance. After Lincoln had authorized a suspension, Union military officials arrested a suspected Confederate collaborator named John Merryman. Merryman's lawyer went to the Chief Justice of the United States, Roger Taney, and sought "the Writ of Habeas Corpus" to which the Constitution refers – an order directing Merryman's jailer to come

8 I adapt this line of questions from Sanford Levinson, "Was The Emancipation Proclamation Constitutional? Do We/Should We Care What the Answer Is?," 2001 *University of Illinois Law Review* 1135.

9 An excellent recent discussion is Farber, *Lincoln's Constitution*, ch. 6. See also James G. Randall, *Constitutional Problems under Lincoln*, rev. ed. (Urbana: University of Illinois Press, 1951; originally published in 1926).

10 "An Act to Increase the Pay of the Privates in the Regular Army and of the Volunteers in the Service of the United States, and for Other Purposes," Ch. 63, Section 3, 12 Stat. 326, 326 (1861).

11 See *The Prize Cases*, 67 U.S. 635 (1863).

to court, bringing Merryman with him, and either to justify the imprisonment as a matter of law or to release the prisoner. Taney issued the writ.
Merryman had not been convicted of or even charged with any crime
in a civilian court. Military officials believed him guilty of treason as a
result of his having taken up arms against the United States, but the writ
of habeas corpus was designed to ensure that government officials could
not lock up whomever they chose on mere suspicion that the person had
committed, or might in the future commit, a crime – unless, of course,
"the privilege of the writ of habeas corpus" had been validly suspended.
Taney ruled that it had not. Although President Lincoln had tried to
suspend the privilege of the writ, Taney held that he had no power to
do so: the Constitution gave the power to suspend the writ of habeas
corpus to Congress (which was not in session at the time), not to the
President.[12]

Lincoln refused to yield. He ordered his military officers to ignore
Taney's ruling, and the officers obeyed the President, not the Chief Justice. Merryman thus remained under military arrest. Meanwhile, Lincoln
prepared and published a constitutional defense of his actions. The Constitution did not say in so many words that only Congress, not the President, could suspend the writ of habeas corpus. In wartime, with Congress
not in session, Lincoln argued that the President could lawfully exercise
the power in his capacity as Commander in Chief.[13] In his view, the Constitution should be read as giving the President the power to do what
needed to be done to preserve the nation and the Constitution itself –
at least if there was any way in which it could plausibly be so read. To
invoke a later-coined phrase, the Constitution is not a suicide pact, and
those interpreting it should not turn it into one.

Lincoln's argument provides an important perspective on the complex interconnection between constitutional argument and more broadly
political, prudential, or pragmatic argument. Sometimes "political"

12 See *Ex parte Merryman*, 17 F. Cas. 144 (C.C.D.Md. 1861).
13 See Abraham Lincoln, "Message to Congress in Special Session of July 4, 1861,"
   reprinted in Lincoln, *Speeches and Writings 1859–65*, at 252–53.

concerns and prudential values influence the courts. In the *Merryman* case, one might have expected Chief Justice Taney, as much as Lincoln, to hold that with Congress out of session, the power to suspend the privilege of the writ of habeas corpus – which was by all accounts an emergency power – could be exercised by the one official capable of swift and decisive action to meet an emergency. But in extraordinary cases, in which the stakes are high enough, law and politics can also come together in a different way. The American people care about the Constitution. It would not have gone down well, even in wartime, for Lincoln to claim an entitlement to flout the Constitution. Rather, the tenability of his position in suspending the writ of habeas corpus and then ignoring an order from the Chief Justice depended, as a matter of politics, on his ability to make a constitutional argument that would prove persuasive, under the circumstances, to Congress and the American people. To put the point a bit differently, in cases of true emergency, such as that which Lincoln confronted at the outset of the Civil War, the ultimate court under the Constitution of the United States may be the court of public opinion. When the President and the courts differ in their interpretations of the Constitution, the American people ordinarily think the President should accept the courts' judgment. In wartime, the situation may sometimes be different. Lincoln's political stature did not suffer much from his defiance of a judicial order in *Ex parte Merryman*, nor has his historical reputation diminished. (He is nearly always rated as American's greatest President, trailed by George Washington and Franklin Roosevelt.)

Although distinctive in some ways, in others Lincoln's argument that the Constitution is a flexible instrument sounded very much in the tradition of John Marshall, the great Chief Justice, who had emphasized that the Constitution was designed to be adaptable to "crises of human affairs" and should be construed accordingly.[14] This has been the dominant tradition of American constitutional interpretation. I have emphasized that tradition and lauded it throughout this book. Flexibility, I have

14 *McCulloch v. Maryland*, 17 U.S. 316, 407 (1819).

suggested, is a great virtue, and our Constitution has served so well precisely because it is and has been interpreted to be so flexible.

But if flexibility is a virtue, it is sometimes a risky one because a constitution that is completely flexible is also a constitution that imposes no hard, intractable restraints on governmental power and thus no absolute guarantees of individual rights. Especially in time of war and emergency, the Constitution frequently does more to provide a framework for arguments than it does to resolve them. Nor, again, are wartime arguments about constitutional law always addressed exclusively, or even principally, to the courts.

In the remainder of this chapter, I briefly summarize constitutional doctrines and history involving the scope of presidential and congressional power in war and related emergencies. I then consider individual rights in war and emergency before discussing, without pretending to resolve, a few issues arising from the ongoing "war on terror" that began following the Al Qaeda attacks of September 11, 2001.

The Power to Initiate War

Throughout American history, Presidents have claimed authority to send troops into battle or otherwise engage in warlike acts without awaiting a congressional declaration of war. Thomas Jefferson deployed ships into the Mediterranean to battle the Barbary Pirates. Lincoln took it upon himself to blockade Southern ports and otherwise begin fighting the Civil War. By one count, "[f]rom 1798 to 2000, there were over 200 cases where the President transferred arms or other war material abroad or actually sent troops [into hostile environments], all without Congressional involvement."[15]

Some of the arguments supporting unilateral presidential power to enter military hostilities are pragmatic: American lives and interests

---

15 John E. Nowak and Ronald D. Rotunda, *Constitutional Law* (St. Paul, MN: West Group, 2000), 255.

would be compromised if the President could not take swift, unhesitating action to protect the national interest against foreign threats. Other arguments now appeal to historical practice. Still others claim that those who wrote and ratified the Constitution intended to permit the President to initiate war making. Although scholars are divided, some maintain that Congress's power to declare war is a narrow one, which merely triggers the international laws of war,[16] and need not be exercised in order to authorize military action by the United States. On this view, the President can launch military operations unilaterally, subject only to constraints arising from Congress's power to deny funding.

Although the Supreme Court has never specified the scope of unilateral presidential authority to commit troops to battle, Congress reviewed the pattern of executive war making during the early 1970s, when a Democratic Congress sought to impose modest strictures on the President, then a Republican. Enacted in 1973, the War Powers Resolution[17] provides that whenever the President initiates military hostilities he (or she) should notify House and Senate leaders within forty-eight hours and that presidentially directed military actions should cease after not more than sixty days (with a provision for extension to ninety days in cases of "unavoidable military necessity") unless authorized by Congress. By nearly everyone's account, the War Powers Resolution has proved a failure. Presidents have occasionally ignored or defied it. Some have argued insistently that the War Powers Resolution is unconstitutional.

16 See, for example, John C. Yoo, "The Continuation of Politics by Other Means: The Original Understanding of War Powers," 84 *California Law Review* 167, 242 (1996). The contrary view is that although the President has inherent constitutional authority to repel sudden attacks and to protect lives imminently at risk, Congress possesses exclusive constitutional power to commit the country to war, whether declared or undeclared. See, for example, John Hart Ely, *War and Responsibility: Constitutional Lessons of Vietnam and Its Aftermath* (Princeton, NJ: Princeton University Press, 1993), 3–10; Harold Hongju Koh, *The National Security Constitution: Sharing Power after the Iran-Contra Affair* (New Haven, CT: Yale University Press, 1990), 74–77.

17 87 Stat. 555, Public Law No. 93–148, 93d Cong. (H. J. Res. 542, adopted over presidential veto on Nov. 7, 1973).

Although the War Powers Resolution has not worked as intended, it has not been wholly without influence either, partly because its sixty-day limit on the President's unilateral power to commit troops to hostilities accords with a widely shared judgment about how the Constitution does and ought to operate in practice. When American lives and vital interests are at stake, the President needs to be able to respond quickly, with military force if necessary, without waiting for approval from cumbersome (and sometimes partisan) congressional processes. But there is a practical and constitutional difference between relatively minor military interventions of short duration and major wars that would require large, long-term commitments of forces and commensurate risks of losses of life. To speak much too crudely, large-scale and drawn-out military operations should require congressional authorization, even if smaller fights of shorter duration do not.

Events surrounding the 1991 Persian Gulf War and the 2003 war in Iraq illustrate how the division of war-making powers between Congress and the President has tended to work. In both cases the President's representatives initially maintained that he could conduct large-scale military operations without needing congressional approval. Had the President insisted on this position, it is at least highly doubtful that a court would have tried to stop him. The "political question" doctrine (discussed in Chapter 9) arguably applies;[18] troops in the field should not have to await judicial pronouncement on the lawfulness of military orders.

It bears repeated emphasis, however, that the Constitution is not just a document for the courts, especially in matters of war and peace. As I have said, even when the Judicial Branch sits on the sidelines, the Constitution matters to Congress and the President, not least because it matters to the American people. In the case of both the Gulf War and the Iraq War, the President ultimately found it politically indefensible to begin a

---

18 For discussion of whether the existence of "war" is a political question, see the concurring opinions in *Campbell v. Clinton*, 203 F. 3d 19 (D.C. Cir. 2000).

war without first obtaining congressional authorization. When the President sought such authorization, Congress followed determined presidential leadership and went along.

The congressional resolutions authorizing these recent conflicts were not labeled as "declarations of war," but the terminology should not matter. The crucial practical point, as resolved in the court of public opinion, was that the country should not launch a major, long-term military action unless the President and both Houses of Congress were solemnly and publicly committed to it.

Federal Powers during Wartime

Once war or its practical equivalent is under way, the courts have usually responded sympathetically to claims that the government possesses all reasonably necessary powers to make the venture succeed. Because the federal government is one of limited powers, courts must ask first whether some provision of the Constitution authorizes Congress or the President to act at all. Only if that question yields an affirmative answer must courts face the further question of whether a presumptively valid governmental action under Article I or II of the Constitution nevertheless violates another provision, such as those of the Bill of Rights, that creates an overriding constitutional "right." As I discuss shortly, questions of governmental powers and individual rights are not always as sharply separate as this sequential mapping might imply. For now, however, it suffices to recall Justice Robert Jackson's famous observation in the *Youngstown* case,[19] discussed in Chapter 8, that when Congress and the President concur that governmental action is necessary, the powers of the national government are at their zenith. Never is this truer than in war and emergency.

When the President asserts a wartime power to take steps not approved by Congress, matters are potentially more difficult, especially

19 *Youngstown Sheet & Tube Co. v. Sawyer*, 343 U.S. 579 (1952).

if the presidential action occurs at home, rather than abroad. But when wartime Presidents have claimed power, Congress has usually acquiesced – as, for example, when Congress retroactively approved Lincoln's actions regarding the army and navy during the Civil War. To be sure, there are exceptions to this pattern. In the *Youngstown* case, the Court found that the President lacked the power to take over the nation's steel mills. Overall, the President's authority had probably not diminished from Lincoln's time, but the Court in *Youngstown* concluded that Congress had meant to deny the President the power that he claimed. It did not say so, but it probably also believed (as discussed in Chapter 8) that the emergency was not great enough to justify an otherwise impermissible presidential action.

War and Individual Rights

As governmental powers expand in wartime, protection for individual rights notoriously suffers. First, a few rights may wholly disappear. The Third Amendment provides that "[n]o Soldier shall, in time of peace be quartered in any house, without the consent of the Owner," but it makes an exception for wartime. To take another plain example, the right to "the Privilege of the Writ of Habeas Corpus" to test the legality of arrests and detentions can be suspended "when in Cases of Rebellion or Invasion the public Safety may require it."[20]

Second, some rights are expressly defined by reference to what is reasonable. For example, the Fourth Amendment does not ban all searches and seizures but only "unreasonable" ones. Some searches and seizures that would be unreasonable in peace may be reasonable in war and emergency.

Third, in probably the most typical case, even rights ordinarily regarded as "fundamental" may yield when "necessary to promote a compelling governmental interest." This is a telling formulation. It suggests

20 U.S. Constitution, Article I, Section 9, Clause 2.

that courts must do something like "balancing" the interests of those claiming constitutional rights against the government's interests or those of the public as a whole.[21] In war and emergency, risks to the public interest may be greater than in other times, and they may appear even greater than they are.

Among America's wars, the Civil War was probably the worst for individual rights.[22] First without and later with congressional authorization, Lincoln oversaw the suspension of habeas corpus throughout much of the nation and empowered Union generals to impose martial law – effectively to rule by military decree – insofar as they judged it necessary. Over the course of the war, the Union Army arrested and detained thousands of people without civilian trials, at least some of them for exercising what would today be regarded as basic speech rights (for example, by expressing sympathy for the Confederacy).

World War I brought enactment of the Espionage Act and its enforcement by the Supreme Court in the famous cases under the "clear and present danger" test, discussed in Chapter 1. In the first of those cases, *Schenck v. United States*[23] (1919), Justice Holmes, himself a Civil War veteran, asserted pointedly that "[w]hen a nation is at war many things that might be said in time of peace are such a hindrance to its effort that their utterance will not be endured [or deemed protected under the Constitution] so long as men fight."

During World War II, speech rights generally fared better, but the government pursued its infamous policy of excluding all persons of Japanese descent, citizens as well as noncitizens, from the West Coast of the United States. Writing nearly twenty years later and attempting to draw lessons from the Supreme Court's decision to uphold the exclusion, Chief Justice Earl Warren (who had himself played a role in executing

---

21 See generally Richard H. Fallon Jr., "Individual Rights and the Powers of Government," 27 *Georgia Law Review* 343 (1993).

22 See generally Mark E. Neely Jr., *The Fate of Liberty: Abraham Lincoln and Civil Liberties* (New York: Oxford University Press, 1991).

23 249 U.S. 47, 52 (1919).

the policy while Attorney General of California) wrote that "there are some circumstances in which the Court will, in effect, conclude that it is simply not in a position to reject descriptions by the Executive of the degree of military necessity."[24]

The Supreme Court's decision in *Korematsu v. United States*[25] (1944) may be explainable on that basis, but the potential of wartime fears and emotion to distort judgment should not be denied. The history of Earl Warren – who, for better and occasionally for worse, was probably the most conspicuously humane Chief Justice in U.S. history – is again revealing. As David Halberstam wrote: "The one serious blot on [Warren's] record was [his role as California's Attorney General in the Japanese relocation]. He was playing to the growing fear of sabotage and the country's anger against the Japanese, particularly in California. Later he expressed considerable regret for his actions...: In 1972, when he was interviewed on the subject, he broke down in tears as he spoke of the little children being taken from their homes and schools."[26]

Looking backward at the history of civil liberties in wartime, commentators have reached differing assessments and, perhaps even more strikingly, have drawn sharply different conclusions about how courts ought to behave in the future. Perhaps the most common view maintains that past wars have produced not merely violations but also egregious violations, of constitutional liberties. Those who hold this view tend to argue that current and future courts should scrutinize claims that rights must yield to wartime imperatives with great, great skepticism.[27]

Judge Richard Posner – a brilliant former law professor who has continued to comment provocatively on public issues while serving as a federal appeals court judge – has advanced a challengingly contrary

---

24 Earl Warren, "The Bill of Rights and the Military," 37 *New York University Law Review* 181, 192–93 (1962).

25 323 U.S. 214 (1944).

26 David Halberstam, *The Fifties* (New York: Villard Books, 1993), 417–18.

27 See, for example, David Cole, "The New McCarthyism: Repeating History in the War on Terrorism," 38 *Harvard Civil Rights-Civil Liberties Law Review* 1 (2003).

view. "[T]he lesson of history," he argues, is not that governmental officials "habitually exaggerate dangers to the nation's security" but "the
opposite": "It is because officials have repeatedly and disastrously under-
estimated these dangers that our history is as violent as it is," including
such events as the terrorist attacks of September 11, 2001.[28] Although
there are plain mistakes that have become obvious in hindsight, Posner
appears to believe that America's wartime record with civil liberties is
actually quite good. He sees no reason to ratchet up the level of judicial scrutiny in cases requiring a balance of individual liberties against
national security interests. To the contrary, he appears to believe that it
could be a grave, potentially disastrous mistake to do so.

A third group of commentators, prominently including William
Rehnquist, who wrote a book on civil liberties in wartime[29] while he
was serving as Chief Justice but before the 9/11 attacks, emphasize what
they take to be an encouraging historical trend: although wartime has
been bad for constitutional liberties, there have tended to be fewer, or
less serious, abuses in each war than in those that preceded it. As a
factual matter, this claim is hard to judge. There is no adequate metric
with which to compare the World War I deprivations of speech rights,
for example, with the Japanese relocation during World War II. Nevertheless, it is surely true that the American people and their elected
leaders have learned from experience. In the aftermath of the Civil
War, no branch of government seriously considered broadly suspending "the privilege of the writ of habeas corpus" in either World War I
or World War II.[30] With the Holmes-Brandeis view about freedom of
speech having won increasing acceptance in the years following World
War I, Congress did not reenact an Espionage Act in World War II,

---

28 Richard A. Posner, "The Truth about Our Liberties," 13 *Responsive Community* 4, 5
(2002).
29 William H. Rehnquist, *All The Laws But One: Civil Liberties in Wartime* (New York:
Knopf, 1998).
30 The Supreme Court invalidated a declaration of martial law in Hawaii, which was then
a territory rather than a state, in *Duncan v. Kahanamoku*, 327 U.S. 304 (1946).

though it did later pass laws under which communists were punished for speech and association during the Cold War.

With respect to the role of the courts, Rehnquist maintained that they, too, have drawn lessons from wars past. One example comes from *Brandenburg v. Ohio* (1969), which was discussed in Chapter 1. Reflecting the Court's conclusion that wartime courts were too quick to suppress speech under the clear and present danger test, *Brandenburg* gives more nearly categorical protection to even loosely political speech; it recognizes no wartime exception. Rehnquist concluded his book with cautious prophecy and with equally cautious judgments about the role of courts in wartime:

> [Although there] is no reason to think... that future Justices of the Supreme Court will decide questions differently from their predecessors[,]... there is every reason to think that the historic trend against the least justified of the curtailments of civil liberty in wartime will continue in the future. It is neither desirable nor is it remotely likely that civil liberty will occupy as favored a position in wartime as it does in peacetime. But it is both desirable and likely that more careful attention will be paid by the courts to the basis for the government's claims of necessity as a basis for curtailing civil liberty.[31]

The Constitution and the "War on Terror"

Following the terrorist attacks of September 11, 2001, the United States embarked on what the Bush administration, in particular, often described as a "war on terror." Military operations in Iraq and Afghanistan have involved war under nearly anyone's definition. By contrast, other actions to combat terrorist groups – which are not nation states and do not typically fight as traditional armies on battlefields – have framed the question of whether terrorists are better analogized to enemy soldiers or to ordinary criminals. As a general rule, criminals must be arrested, not summarily killed or subjected to drone attacks, and then

31 Rehnquist, *All The Laws But One*, 224–25.

must be given speedy trials before juries in ordinary criminal courts. To date, no full answer has emerged to the question of which actions in the war on terror fall under the heading of military operations, which largely lie outside the jurisdiction of the courts, and which come under the heading of criminal law enforcement, in which suspects enjoy a broad panoply of rights. Although much remains unsettled, four generalizations will explain much – though not all – of how the government and the courts have applied the Constitution to the war on terror.

First, the civil liberties of U.S. citizens within the United States have fared rather well, even though there have been some, probably predictable, compromises, especially immediately following 9/11, when fear ran highest. Most notably, the month after the attacks, Congress passed and President Bush signed into law the Patriot Act.[32] Among its many provisions, the act gave the government new authority to conduct searches and surveillance. The act allows the government to obtain secret court orders for access to personal records held by third parties, which critics charge could include information such as lists of books read by library patrons.[33] The government also has authority under the act to issue, without judicial oversight, "national security letters" ordering Internet service providers to produce detailed customer records.[34]

The government has also conducted an initially secret program of national security wiretaps, administered by the National Security Agency. In the early period of its operation, the program bypassed restrictions imposed by the Foreign Intelligence Surveillance Act, a law Congress adopted in 1978 following revelations about previous government wiretapping abuses. After the *New York Times* revealed

---

32 Uniting and Strengthening America by Providing Appropriate Tools Required to Intercept and Obstruct Terrorism (USA PATRIOT) Act of 2001, Pub. L. No. 107–56, 115 Stat. 272 (codified in scattered sections of the U.S.C.). For an overview of the act's key provisions, see Charles Doyle, "The USA PATRIOT Act: A Legal Analysis," *CRS Report for Congress*, April 15, 2002.

33 See Patriot Act § 215, 115 Stat. at 287–88 (codified as amended at 50 U.S.C. §1861 (2006)).

34 See ibid. § 505, 115 Stat. at 365–66 (codified as amended at 18 U.S.C. § 2709(b) (2006)).

the existence of the secret program in 2005, Congress amended these restrictions to permit various elements of the National Security Agency's program.

In *Hamdi v. Rumsfeld*[35] (2004), a fractured Supreme Court held that an American citizen captured fighting for the Taliban and against American allies on a battlefield in Afghanistan could be detained indefinitely as an enemy combatant – essentially a prisoner of war – without the government needing to prove him guilty of any crime beyond a reasonable doubt. Language in the Justices' opinions in that and another case suggested that the result would have been different if the citizen had been apprehended in the United States, not Afghanistan.

Second, the various actions grouped together under the heading of the "war on terror" have served as a reminder that the Constitution confers few if any rights on noncitizens outside of U.S. territory.[36] When American armies engage in bombing or shelling in military operations abroad, or when the United States mounts drone attacks on suspected terrorists in other countries, no victim, no matter how innocent, can claim a violation of constitutional rights.

Seeking to exploit this limitation on the reach of constitutional rights, the Bush administration opened a large detention facility at Guantánamo Bay, Cuba, which the United States controls under a permanent lease but does not technically own. In *Boumediene v. Bush*[37] (2008), the Supreme Court, by a 5–4 vote, ruled that foreigners held as enemy combatants at Guantánamo have at least some constitutional rights, including a right to fair hearings to determine whether they really are enemy combatants and thus subject to indefinite detention. But the Court did not make clear whether its ruling had any application to noncitizens held in any foreign locale other than Guantánamo Bay, which is for all functional purposes within the territorial jurisdiction

35 542 U.S. 507 (2004).
36 See, for example, *United States v. Verdugo-Urquidez*, 494 U.S. 259 (1990); *Johnson v. Eisentrager*, 339 U.S. 763 (1950).
37 553 U.S. 723 (2008).

of the United States. Crucially, even if the *Boumediene* ruling were subsequently extended to ensure rights to fair hearings to detainees in Afghanistan, for example, the decision in no way signals the recognition of constitutional rights of noncitizens not to be subjected to bomb or drone attacks abroad. Nor does the decision point directly to the conclusion that noncitizens have constitutional rights not to be tortured – no matter how morally heinous torture may be – when they are not in the United States or at Guantánamo. (It would be possible to argue that at least some constitutional rights, including a right not to be tortured, attach at the point when United States officials take someone into custody, but the Supreme Court has so far had no occasion to decide.)

Third, even within the United States, noncitizens do not always have the same rights as American citizens.[38] To take the most obvious case, noncitizens, or "aliens," cannot vote. In addition, the Supreme Court has ruled that federal policies discriminating against aliens (in ways other than denying them constitutional guarantees of fair procedures in criminal trials) are presumptively permissible, not "suspect," under applicable equal protection doctrine: only rational basis review applies.[39]

The starting point for the Court's reasoning is the commonsense notion that Congress must be able to exclude noncitizens from coming to live in the United States. From Congress's power to exclude aliens entirely, the Court has inferred that the government has sweeping powers to enforce the immigration laws and, what is more, that these powers imply either the limitation or the nonexistence of constitutional rights in the context of investigations of suspected immigration violations. In the immediate aftermath of 9/11, governmental officials rounded up more than 750 foreign citizens living in the United States. Almost all were of Arab descent. Many were held for relatively long periods without access to courts or lawyers. In defense of its actions, the government cited its

38 For a survey of the rights of aliens, see Gerald L. Neuman, *Strangers to the Constitution: Immigrants, Borders, and Fundamental Law* (Princeton, NJ: Princeton University Press, 1996).
39 See, for example, *Mathews v. Diaz*, 426 U.S. 67 (1976).

special prerogatives in enforcing the immigration laws – or, what comes to the same thing, the very limited rights that noncitizens can assert against enforcement of the immigration laws.

Fourth, for at least some purposes, as was noted at the outset, the Constitution recognizes a distinction between ordinary criminal laws, the enforcement of which triggers ordinary constitutional guarantees, and the laws of war – a body of international and American law that governs the rights and duties of combatants during wartime. When and where the laws of war apply, they constitute exceptions to ordinarily applicable constitutional guarantees in at least two respects. First, the laws of war permit captured combatants for the other side to be detained until the cessation of hostilities without proof of criminal wrongdoing. The parties to a conflict can hold prisoners of war who are not war criminals, as most prisoners of war are not. Second, if the government chooses to charge a violation of the laws of war, it can try the alleged offenses before a military commission, consisting of military officers, rather than a civil jury. Trials before military commissions afford far fewer procedural guarantees than a civil court would provide.

Questions about the outer boundaries of the law of war and about the exceptions to ordinary constitutional guarantees permissible in "war crimes" cases seem virtually certain to arise at some point in the future, but the Supreme Court has not confronted them yet in a case involving modern terrorism. *Ex parte Quirin*[40] (1942), a World War II case involving would-be Nazi saboteurs who entered the United States after exiting German submarines, suggests that any case alleging a violation of the laws of war can be tried before a military commission, even if the accused is an American citizen (as one of the captured German soldiers was) apprehended far from any traditional battlefield. But *Quirin* is difficult, if not impossible, to reconcile with an earlier Civil War precedent holding that a U.S. citizen (other than a member of the military) who is apprehended within the United States has a right to trial in a civilian

40 317 U.S. 1 (1942).

court as long as the courts are open and functioning.[41] It is not obvious
which of these two decisions the modern Court would find controlling in
the case of a suspected terrorist who was captured in the United States.
Perhaps it would matter whether the terrorist was a citizen or a noncit-
izen. Although the Court attached no significance to that distinction in
Quirin, the facts of that case were peculiar. The Justices issued their decision after President Roosevelt had informally made it known to them
that he would defy any Court ruling that purported to bar him from
summarily trying the captured Nazis before a military commission and
promptly executing them. In 1942, the public would undoubtedly have
rallied behind Roosevelt and in opposition to the Court in any showdown about the procedural niceties owed to Nazis who did not deny their
membership in the German army, even if one of them was an American
citizen. If nothing else, the 1942 decision in *Ex parte Quirin* may illustrate the vagaries surrounding the enforcement of constitutional rights
in wartime.

Conclusion

It is sometimes said that *inter arma leges silent* – in times of war, the laws
are silent.[42] This old Latin maxim claims too much. During every war in
the history of the United States, the Constitution has remained in force.
Elections have occurred on schedule. Public servants have continued to
perform their constitutional duties. Most citizens have retained most of
their ordinary constitutional rights.

But if the Constitution does not go silent in wartime, it undoubtedly
speaks to some issues in more muted, equivocal tones than it does in
time of peace.[43] During the Civil War, after ordering the suspension of
the writ of habeas corpus and defying an order by the Chief Justice to
release a prisoner, Abraham Lincoln at least tacitly acknowledged that

---

41 See *Ex parte Milligan*, 71 U.S. 2 (1866).
42 For discussion, see Rehnquist, *All The Laws But One*.
43 See ibid.

his position could be squared with the Constitution only with difficulty (even though he insisted that it could indeed be squared). In defending his stance, Lincoln emphasized that the constitutional provision that he was alleged to have violated – preserving rights to the writ of habeas corpus – was only one among many and that he, in taking his oath of office, had pledged to preserve, protect, and defend the entire Constitution of the United States. The entire Constitution was in jeopardy, he maintained, unless he could take necessary steps, which he thought included the suspension of habeas corpus, to win the war. Assuming this to be the case, was he obliged to honor the letter of the provision dealing with the writ of habeas corpus? If he preserved and protected what he described as "all the laws, *but one*,"[44] was that not better, constitutionally speaking, than to put the entire constitutional order at risk?

War and emergency sometimes require the compromise of ideals, if not deals with the devil. Unfortunately, not every wartime leader asserting claims to extraordinary power or demanding the sacrifice of constitutional liberties will share the equable spirit of Abraham Lincoln. The challenges of war and emergency require practical wisdom. The Constitution creates a framework within which such wisdom can be exercised but does not, alas, ensure that it will always be furnished. No constitution could.

---

44 Abraham Lincoln, "Message to Congress in Special Session of July 4, 1861," reprinted in Lincoln, *Speeches and Writings, 1859–65*, at 246.

12 The Reach of the Constitution and Congress's Enforcement Power

[C]ivil rights, such as are guaranteed by the constitution against state aggression, cannot be impaired by the wrongful acts of individuals, unsupported by State authority.

– The Civil Rights Cases (1883)[1]

Congress does not enforce a constitutional right by changing what the right is. It has been given the power "to enforce," not the power to determine what constitutes a constitutional violation.

– City of Boerne v. Flores (1997)[2]

THIS CHAPTER DEALS WITH THREE SEPARATE BUT RELATED issues concerning the nature and reach of constitutional rights. One involves the applicability of the Constitution: against whom does the Constitution create rights? Another has to do with the character of the rights that the Constitution creates. Nearly all are rights to be free from one or another kind of hostile governmental action. Few are rights to affirmative governmental assistance. Why? The final topic involves the scope of Congress's power to "enforce" constitutional guarantees. When making judgments about whether to enact legislation enforcing the Constitution, can Congress interpret the Constitution as creating rights that the Supreme Court would not recognize otherwise?

1 109 U.S. 3, 17 (1883).
2 521 U.S. 507, 519 (1997).

State Action Doctrine

A little more than a decade ago, a major league baseball pitcher named John Rocker gave a magazine interview in which he denounced New York City, the New York City subways, and gays. He mocked foreigners and referred to an African American teammate as "a fat monkey." Rocker's comments disturbed many people, including officials of Major League Baseball, a private, for-profit organization of private, for-profit baseball teams. In response, the baseball commissioner – an employee of Major League Baseball, not associated with the government in any way – ordered Rocker to undergo sensitivity training, fined him, and suspended him from a number of games. Many applauded the commissioner's response to Rocker's outburst. Some complained that the situation called for even harsher discipline.

Others, however, worried about Rocker's constitutional rights. Across the country, sportswriters began to ring the phones of lawyers and constitutional law professors. Hadn't the commissioner and Major League Baseball violated Rocker's First Amendment right to freedom of expression? Didn't Rocker have a constitutional case?

To the evident surprise of many sportswriters and presumably some nonsportswriters as well, the answer to these questions was simply no. Almost without exception, constitutional rights exist only against the government, not against private citizens or private businesses or organizations. Neither Congress nor a state legislature could have made Rocker's remarks a crime. Nor would the First Amendment have let the government fine Rocker for what he said. But the First Amendment creates no rights enforceable against Major League Baseball or its commissioner. In other words, the First Amendment prohibits the government from interfering with freedom of speech, but it does not prevent Major League Baseball from doing so.

The general rule that the Constitution creates rights only against the government, and not against private citizens, has one important exception. The Thirteenth Amendment, which abolished slavery, says that "[n]either slavery nor involuntary servitude...shall exist within the United States." Private attempts at enslavement violate the Thirteenth Amendment.

The rule that only the government can violate the Constitution (other than the Thirteenth Amendment) is usually referred to as "the state action doctrine," but it would be less confusingly called "the governmental action requirement," for the Constitution applies as much to Congress, the President, and other governmental officials as it does to the states. Once this terminological point is understood, the state action doctrine is virtually self-applying in most cases. On the affirmative side, Congress engages in state action whenever it enacts a law, as do state legislatures, city councils, and other governmental bodies. Similarly, governmental officials engage in state action when they enforce the law or otherwise exercise official responsibility. The school officials involved in *Brown v. Board of Education* were state actors, as were the prosecuting attorneys who stood ready to enforce the antiabortion law in *Roe v. Wade*. Police officers interrogating criminal suspects, as in *Miranda v. Arizona*, are state actors as well. All can violate the Constitution.

On the negative side, private citizens are generally not state actors, and thus cannot violate the Constitution, for the obvious reason that they are neither the government nor the government's agents. There are a few exceptions, involving special circumstances that occasionally make it appropriate to treat action by private parties as if it were taken by the government itself. One exceptional category includes otherwise private citizens performing what the Supreme Court has characterized as inherently "public functions." For example, the Court has held that operating a prison is an inherently public function. If a state hires a private, for-profit company to incarcerate and supervise those convicted of crimes, the company and its officials are state actors, and prisoners possess constitutional rights against them.[3] By contrast, the Court has held that operating a school is not an inherently public function. Private

3 See *Richardson v. McKnight*, 521 U.S. 399 (1997).

schools and their employees are therefore not state actors, and they are not subject to constitutional restraints (even though public schools and public school employees are).[4]

The Court has also found that private citizens can be treated as state actors and sued for constitutional violations when state law empowers them to act in the name of the government or control the conduct of governmental officials. For example, in both civil and criminal trials, the law permits parties to exclude a certain number of would-be jurors by exercising "peremptory challenges." Because peremptory challenges direct the court – plainly a governmental actor – to dismiss potential jurors, the Supreme Court has held that the Equal Protection Clause applies to their use. Under the Equal Protection Clause, private parties cannot use their peremptory challenges to exclude jurors on the basis of race.[5]

Again, however, cases such as these are the exception, not the rule. Although the details of the state action doctrine are sometimes tangled, the Supreme Court has generally resisted efforts to characterize private parties as state actors subject to the Constitution – even when they are heavily regulated by the government or enjoy governmentally conferred monopoly power (as do public utility companies). When constitutional rules apply, they operate as constraints. The Court clearly thinks it best to limit the reach of those constraints and thus to preserve a large space for the exercise of private, unconstrained liberty. Major League Baseball should be free to suspend John Rocker if he makes comments that alienate fans. John Rocker (who is no more a state actor than Major League Baseball) should be free to make bigoted decisions, not bound by the Equal Protection Clause.

As is probably obvious, protecting the "liberty" of some often entails costs for others. For example, the liberty of Major League Baseball to impose a fine and suspension on John Rocker arguably diminished his liberty to speak his mind and thus imposed a cost on him. (In an earlier

4 See *Rendell-Baker v. Kohn*, 457 U.S. 830 (1982).
5 See, for example, *Georgia v. McCollum*, 505 U.S. 42 (1992); *Edmonson v. Leesville Concrete Co., Inc.*, 500 U.S. 614 (1991).

era, the liberty of baseball owners to decide for themselves whom to hire and not to hire resulted in the total exclusion of African American players until the Brooklyn Dodgers broke ranks and gave Jackie Robinson a chance in 1947.) In a case closer to the edge of the state action doctrine, to deem a utility company a private rather than a state actor means that it can cut off service to customers – who have no place else to turn for water, or gas, or electricity – without first needing to provide "due process of law" under the Due Process Clause.[6] Without denying that costs to such an approach exist, the Supreme Court reads the Constitution as relying on the political process, rather than on the courts, to balance the competing interests. Democratically accountable legislatures frequently pass laws restricting the liberty of some in order to protect the interests of others. Congress did so, for example, when it passed the 1964 Civil Rights Act, which would bar Major League Baseball from engaging in race discrimination today, even if it wished to do so. Similarly, state and local laws often protect consumers from having their power or water shut off at the whim of utility companies. But the rights of private citizens against other private citizens or organizations come from statutes, not the federal Constitution.

The Paucity of "Positive" Fundamental Rights

The reach of the Constitution is also bounded in another way: as construed by the Supreme Court in the light of both text and history, it confers very few "positive" rights or entitlements to affirmative governmental assistance. Rather, most recognized rights are "negative" ones that operate as shields against hostile government action.[7] Thus, to use obvious examples, the First Amendment protects against governmental interferences with speech, but it does not oblige the government to furnish anyone with a microphone or a printing press. The Fifth and

6 See *Jackson v. Metropolitan Edison Co.*, 419 U.S. 345 (1974).
7 See generally David P. Currie, "Positive and Negative Constitutional Rights," 53 *University of Chicago Law Review* 864 (1986).

Fourteenth Amendments forbid deprivations of property without due process of law, but they do not confer a positive right to be given property, even for those who otherwise have none.

Positive constitutional rights are surely not impossible. The constitutions of some other countries guarantee rights to education, medical care, shelter, and food. Indeed, the Supreme Court has recognized a few positive rights under the American Constitution. People accused of crimes have a right to a government-appointed lawyer if they are too poor to afford one. Inmates in prisons have an affirmative right to health care and a decent diet.[8] In a broader-reaching example, all citizens have a right to have the streets and sidewalks maintained as a "public forum" available for speech and expressive activities. But these and a few more examples complete the list.

From time to time, commentators have argued that the Supreme Court should recognize various positive rights as fundamental rights implicit in or presupposed by the Constitution. Their obvious concern has involved the poor. Someone who is hungry, impoverished, homeless, sick, or uneducated may have no practical opportunity to enjoy or exercise express constitutional rights that others take for granted. According to some commentators, when the Constitution confers rights, it must presuppose that people will be able to exercise or enjoy them, and thus it must implicitly create positive rights to such things as education, health care, food, and shelter.[9] As we have seen, the Supreme Court interprets the Constitution as securing such "unenumerated" rights as the right to vote in state elections, the right to marry, and the right to an abortion. Once some unenumerated rights are recognized, it becomes appropriate to ask whether there might be a good case for adding a few positive rights to the list.

---

8 See *Estelle v. Gamble*, 429 U.S. 97 (1976).

9 See, for example, Charles L. Black Jr., "Further Reflections on the Constitutional Justice of Livelihood," 86 *Columbia Law Review* 1103 (1986); Frank I. Michelman, "On Protecting the Poor through the Fourteenth Amendment," 83 *Harvard Law Review* 7 (1969).

If positive rights such as rights to education, housing, and health care were recognized, they might take one of two forms. First, they might be absolute, in which case the government would have no choice but to honor them. Alternatively, they might be fundamental rights under the Equal Protection Clause. The government need not always confer rights that are fundamental under the Equal Protection Clause on anyone, but if it distributes them at all, then any inequalities trigger strict judicial scrutiny. Voting rights cases, which were discussed in Chapter 6, provide an example. A town need not allow anyone to vote for members of the school board. It could provide for the school board to be appointed by the mayor or town council. But if a town allows anyone to vote for school board members, then restrictions on who can vote will trigger strict judicial scrutiny because of the fundamental status of voting rights (once they are conferred).[10] So it might also be with rights to education, welfare, or housing.

In cases decided during the 1950s and 1960s, the Warren Court took some tentative, isolated steps toward the recognition of positive constitutional rights and also of equal protection rights framed in part to protect the poor. The Warren Court recognized the right of indigent criminal suspects to have a lawyer appointed for them. It required the states to waive fees and expenses that made it impossible for the poor to file criminal appeals. The Warren Court also held that because the right to vote is fundamental, a state may not impose a "poll tax" that made it difficult or impossible for the poor to exercise that right.

It will never be known whether the Warren Court, in time, might have recognized positive constitutional rights to welfare, education, and health care, or might have held that these are fundamental rights such that, once the government furnishes them to anyone, it must provide them equally to others. The Warren Court never reached such questions, and the decisive cases came later, after Earl Warren had retired and after the 1968 presidential campaign, in which Richard Nixon pledged

10 See *Kramer v. Union Free School District No. 15*, 395 U.S. 621 (1969).

to appoint conservative "strict constructionist" Justices. Four Nixon appointees joined the bare 5–4 majority in *San Antonio Independent School District v. Rodriguez*[11] (1973), which held that education is not a fundamental right.

The plaintiffs in *Rodriguez* were the parents of schoolchildren who lived in relatively poor Texas communities. In essence, they challenged the constitutionality of the state's overall scheme for funding public education. That scheme relied heavily on local property taxes. In wealthy communities, it was possible to raise lots of money through the property tax, and the schools were generously funded. In poorer communities, the property tax generated much less revenue, and the average per-pupil expenditure on public education was as much as 60 percent lower. In light of the accepted constitutional assumption that cities and towns are "arms of the state" for which the state is ultimately responsible, the *Rodriguez* plaintiffs argued that Texas should be forced to adopt a different funding scheme that would more nearly equalize per-pupil expenditures across public school districts. Education, they argued, was a fundamental right under the Equal Protection Clause, which the state of Texas (and, by implication, other states too) must therefore distribute on a more equal basis. The challengers also argued that Texas's financing system was unconstitutional because it disadvantaged the poor, who should be deemed a "suspect" class.

Nixon appointee Justice Lewis Powell, a courtly Virginian who had once served as chairman of the Richmond School Board, wrote the Court opinion rejecting the constitutional challenges. Education, he ruled, was not a fundamental right because it was neither explicit nor implicit in the Constitution. Nor, he held, do the poor constitute a suspect class. To support the conclusion that fundamental rights cannot be recognized unless they are "implicitly or explicitly guaranteed by the Constitution"–a formulation that is unexceptionable in itself because it leaves open the question of how the Court should identify implicit rights – Powell's opinion

11 411 U.S. 1 (1973).

cited *Roe v. Wade*,[12] a case decided only months earlier, as having so recognized. Although *Roe* included some language to the effect that the courts cannot enforce any rights that the Constitution does not either implicitly or explicitly guarantee, *Rodriguez*'s invocation of *Roe* as authority for this proposition might seem simply bizarre. Many would say that *Roe* reveals the wide, almost boundless breadth of the Court's authority to identify fundamental rights. What is more, the argument that education is a fundamental right was in many ways stronger than the parallel argument with respect to abortion. *Brown v. Board of Education*[13] (1954) strongly suggested that education had become a fundamental right because of its practical importance in modern life. In addition, because education is practically necessary to the enjoyment of other rights, its claim to fundamental status is structurally similar to the accepted argument for recognizing a constitutional right to freedom of association. Freedom of association is constitutionally protected because it facilitates speech; education can be equally crucial in making speech rights meaningful.

Nevertheless, the contrast between *Roe* and *Rodriguez* is revealing. Whereas the abortion right is a "negative" right to be free from governmental interference, the asserted fundamental right to education was a "positive" right, which would have taken affirmative governmental steps to implement. If the Court had characterized education as a fundamental right, distributed by the state, it could quickly have found itself enmeshed in complex disputes about when Texas (and other states) had achieved the equality that the Constitution requires. To escape those disputes, the Court might have adopted a financial measure: the fundamental right to education is distributed equally when per-pupil expenditures on education are roughly equal in every school district within a state. But a ruling to this effect would have forced Texas and many other states to alter their historic reliance on local property taxes to fund local

12 410 U.S. 113 (1973).
13 347 U.S. 483 (1954).

education. As a practical matter, property taxes will not permit relatively poor communities to achieve equality of funding with wealthier communities. To achieve equalized funding at acceptable levels would therefore have required substantial economic redistribution from the better-off to the less well-off, likely sparking loud protests from politically influential middle- and upper-class communities. (Interestingly, a number of state supreme courts have subsequently held that their state constitutions require the state legislature to take steps either to equalize educational funding within the state or to ensure every child a minimal level of educational quality. In doing so, however, state supreme courts have generally relied on state constitutional provisions that specifically refer to education. The Constitution of the United States includes no such provision.)

Both parties in *Rodriguez* had plausible cases, as reflected in the 5–4 division among the Justices. The question presented was an unusually testing one. Arguably, it is the job of the Supreme Court to mandate economic redistributions – involving such basic goods as education and health care – to guarantee all citizens "the equal protection of the laws." Arguably it is not, in light of historical understandings of the Equal Protection Clause, which no one believes to have been targeted at economic inequality. To be sure, the Court has departed from original constitutional understandings in many other areas. But when it has done so successfully, it has usually reflected or helped crystallize broadly shared judgments of fairness, necessity, or propriety. In 1973, there was scant evidence of an emerging national consensus supporting more equal distributions of educational funding (or of funding for health care or welfare either) to benefit the poor. To the contrary, the victory of Richard Nixon in the 1968 presidential election had marked a turn away from the egalitarian aspirations of Lyndon Johnson's Great Society program.

Today, given the country's further move to the right in the years since 1973, what is perhaps most clear with respect to positive rights is that the Supreme Court will not and, in the long run, probably could not enforce broad-based economic redistributions opposed by governing political majorities. For several generations, *Rodriguez* has epitomized the view of a conservative Court in a generally conservative political era about both positive rights and economic equality. As construed by the Court, the Constitution is overwhelmingly a charter of negative, not positive, liberties, and the Equal Protection Clause, as currently interpreted, imposes very few affirmative governmental obligations to redress economic inequality.

Congressional Power to "Enforce" the Reconstruction Amendments

The Thirteenth Amendment, which abolishes slavery; the Fourteenth Amendment, which includes the Due Process and Equal Protection Clauses; and the Fifteenth Amendment, which bars race discrimination in state and national elections, all include clauses that authorize Congress to "enforce" their substantive provisions "by appropriate legislation." Because Congress cannot legislate at all in the absence of an affirmative grant of authority to do so (as was discussed more generally in Chapter 7), the specific terms of the authority granted by these Reconstruction Amendments assume great importance. What does it mean for Congress to enforce the Constitution? Does Congress possess a power to determine what counts as a constitutional violation? If so, how would that congressional authority fit with the Supreme Court's power, as recognized in *Marbury v. Madison*[14] (1803), to "say what the law is"?

For many years, the leading case addressing these questions was *Katzenbach v. Morgan*[15] (1966). At issue in *Katzenbach* was a provision of the federal Voting Rights Act, which was enacted by Congress to enforce the Equal Protection Clause of the Fourteenth Amendment, prescribing that no one who had completed the sixth grade in a non-English-speaking school in Puerto Rico could be denied the right to vote because of lack of English literacy. New York officials challenged the provision's constitutionality. In an earlier case, *Lassiter v. Northampton*

14 5 U.S. 137, 178 (1803).
15 384 U.S. 641 (1966).

County Board of Electors[16] (1959), the Court had upheld an English-literacy requirement for voters against a constitutional challenge based on the Equal Protection Clause. In light of *Lassiter*, New York election officials argued, legislation barring New York from insisting on English literacy as a voting requirement could not qualify as "appropriate legislation" to "enforce" the Fourteenth Amendment: rather than "enforc[ing]" the Equal Protection Clause, Congress had attempted to go further than the Fourteenth Amendment required, by banning literacy tests that the Court had held permissible, and no provision of the Constitution authorized it to do so.

The Supreme Court disagreed. Justice William Brennan's opinion for the Court offered three theories on which, despite *Lassiter*, Congress's limited prohibition against literacy tests might count as "appropriate legislation" to "enforce" the Fourteenth Amendment. The first theory was simultaneously remedial and preventative. According to Brennan, Congress could rationally have concluded that unconstitutional discrimination against Puerto Ricans occurred in a variety of settings, not limited to voting but also including public schools, welfare administration, and law enforcement. Brennan suggested that Section 5 of the Fourteenth Amendment authorized Congress to provide a remedy for those violations, and a safeguard against their recurrence, by investing Puerto Ricans with an expanded right to vote. The right to vote, he wrote, was "preservative of all rights."[17]

Brennan's second theory postulated that Congress could justify the enactment of legislation to "enforce" the Fourteenth Amendment by invoking its "specially informed" fact-finding abilities. In upholding the particular literacy test that was challenged in *Lassiter*, the Supreme Court had not held that all literacy tests were constitutionally valid. Under well-established principles, literacy tests would be invalid if they were enacted for the discriminatory purpose of excluding as many racial

16 360 U.S. 45 (1959).
17 *Katzenbach v. Morgan*, 384 U.S. at 652 (quoting *Yick Wo v. Hopkins*, 118 U.S. 356, 370 (1886)).

minorities as possible from being able to vote. Based on its own knowledge and the facts presented by the parties in *Lassiter*, the Court was unwilling to presume that most literacy tests were enacted for discriminatory purposes or that they were not a "necessary or appropriate means" of furthering legitimate state ends.[18] But Congress, Brennan suggested in *Katzenbach*, might know better. If Congress concluded that many or most literacy tests were adopted for the discriminatory purpose of disqualifying minority voters or were otherwise unnecessary to further legitimate state interests, the Court should defer to these largely factual judgments by Congress and should uphold the challenged prohibition against literacy tests as "appropriate" to "enforce" the Fourteenth Amendment.

Finally, and most controversially, Brennan hinted that when legislating under Section 5 to enforce constitutional rights, Congress could permissibly define those underlying rights at least slightly more broadly than the Supreme Court would otherwise define them. Under this theory, which commentators dubbed the "ratchet theory,"[19] Brennan maintained that Congress had "no power to restrict, abrogate, or dilute" constitutional guarantees,[20] but he suggested that Congress might indeed have power to ratchet up the level of constitutional protection beyond that afforded by the Court.[21]

If accepted, *Katzenbach v. Morgan*'s ratchet theory would dramatically expand the scope of congressional authority and correspondingly diminish the centrality of the judicial role. In effect, it would call for the

---

18 Ibid. at 654.
19 See, for example, Douglas Laycock, "RFRA, Congress, and the Ratchet," 56 *Montana Law Review* 145, 155 (1995).
20 *Katzenbach v. Morgan*, 384 U.S. at 651, n.10.
21 On the surface, the ratchet theory might appear inconsistent with *Marbury v. Madison*, 5 U.S. 137 (1803), and especially with its celebrated assertion that "[i]t is emphatically the province and duty of the judicial branch to say what the law is." Ibid. at 177. But *Marbury* need not be read to hold more than that courts must determine whether legislative enactments comport with the Constitution. If Section 5 of the Fourteenth Amendment gives Congress a limited power to interpret constitutional guarantees, *Marbury* requires only that the Court assess whether legislation enacted under Section 5 comes within the Section 5 grant of congressional power.

Supreme Court to share its power to interpret the Constitution. Under the ratchet theory, judicial rulings would establish the minimum content of constitutional guarantees but not necessarily the maximum. Perhaps troubled by this implication, the Court pointedly failed to embrace the ratchet theory in a couple of subsequent cases, but without expressly renouncing it either.

Equivocation ended in *City of Boerne v. Flores*[22] (1997). *City of Boerne* decisively rejects the ratchet theory and sharply limits Congress's enforcement powers under the Thirteenth, Fourteenth, and Fifteenth Amendments. Specifically at issue in *Boerne* was the constitutionality of the Religious Freedom Restoration Act (RFRA). Congress enacted the RFRA in response to the Supreme Court's decision in *Employment Division v. Smith*[23] (1990), discussed in Chapter 2, which gave a narrow interpretation of the Free Exercise Clause. Previous free exercise decisions had held that statutes could not be enforced against religious practices (such as the sacramental use of peyote at issue in *Smith*) unless the burden on religion was "necessary to promote a compelling state interest." *Smith* substituted a narrower test, under which the Free Exercise Clause usually affords no right to religious exemptions from generally applicable laws. Congress, invoking its power under Section 5 of the Fourteenth Amendment, passed the RFRA in an attempt to restore the pre-*Smith* regime. The RFRA prohibited federal, state, and local governments from "substantially burdening" a person's exercise of religion, even through the enforcement of neutral laws of general applicability, unless the burden on religious practice was necessary to further a compelling governmental interest.

With no Justice dissenting on this point, the Supreme Court held that Congress has no power "to enact legislation that expands the rights contained in Section 1 of the Fourteenth Amendment" (including those, such as free exercise rights, that the Fourteenth Amendment

22 521 U.S. 507 (1997).
23 494 U.S. 872 (1990).

"incorporates" under the so-called incorporation doctrine discussed in Chapter 4).[24] Congress's power is to enforce constitutional rights as defined by the Court, not to define constitutional rights for itself, the Justices ruled.

Having dismissed the ratchet theory, the Court acknowledged that Congress could provide remedies for constitutional rights violations and, under some circumstances, could legislate to prevent them – provided that what counted as a constitutional rights violation was defined by the courts, not Congress. But the Court insisted that preventive and remedial legislation must be "congruen[t] and proportional[]"[25] to an underlying pattern of identified constitutional violations. The Court suggested that the legislation involved in *Katzenbach v. Morgan* met this test: "The provisions restricting and banning literacy tests ... attacked a particular type of voting qualification ... with a long history as a 'notorious means to deny and abridge voting rights on racial grounds.'"[26] Even if not every literacy test had this invidious purpose, many of them did, and the statutory prohibition was thus congruent and proportional to the problem that it addressed. By contrast, the Court said, the RFRA was wholly "out of proportion to a supposed remedial or preventive object":[27] Congress was trying to redefine the rights guaranteed by the Free Exercise Clause, not to remedy or prevent violations of the narrow right that the Court had identified in *Employment Division v. Smith*.

Cases subsequent to *City of Boerne* are not entirely consistent in interpreting its requirement that congressional legislation to enforce the Fourteenth Amendment must be "congruen[t] and proportional[]" to a pattern of judicially cognizable constitutional violations. At a minimum, the cases make clear that Congress must demonstrate more than a "rational basis" for thinking legislation appropriate, a stance that, as in *Boerne* itself, presents a puzzle: why do the Justices think that Congress should

24 *City of Boerne v. Flores*, 521 U.S. at 527–28.
25 Ibid. at 508.
26 Ibid. at 533.
27 Ibid. at 532.

attract unusually searching judicial review when it exercises a specifically delegated constitutional power to enforce constitutional rights? I would conjecture that at least three factors have influenced the Justices' interpretation of the Constitution's text and history.

First, *Boerne*'s restrictive interpretation of Congress's power to enforce the Constitution reflects the Court's commitment – also manifest in a number of roughly contemporaneous cases discussed in Chapter 7 – to reinvigorate constitutional federalism. Legislation enacted under Section 5 typically imposes obligations directly on state and local governments. (Because the Constitution generally creates rights only against the government and its officials, legislation to enforce the Reconstruction Amendments will almost invariably apply only to state and local governments and their employees. The RFRA, for example, would have forced state and local governments to exempt persons engaged in religiously motivated conduct from otherwise applicable laws.) *Boerne* promotes federalism by constraining Congress's power to regulate state and local governments and thus expanding state and local governments' freedom of action.

Second, *Boerne* manifests the modern Supreme Court's sense of its own vital role and special capacities. As reflected not only in *Boerne* but also in *Bush v. Gore*[28] (2000) and myriad other cases discussed in earlier chapters, the Justices appear to believe that they possess a disinterested wisdom not shared by other institutions of government, especially those that operate in the messy domain of electoral politics. The Court wants to protect its own turf, not simply because it enjoys the exercise of undiluted power, but also because it believes that a dominant role for the Supreme Court in constitutional matters serves the nation's best interests. By giving a narrow interpretation of Congress's power to enforce the Reconstruction Amendments, *Boerne* helped preserve that dominant judicial role.

28 531 U.S. 98 (2000).

A third consideration is more subtle and, in suggesting that it may have influenced the *Boerne* decision, I necessarily become more speculative. This consideration involves the Supreme Court's apparent perception of the nature of constitutional interpretation and the Justices' stake in maintaining that perception. In *Boerne*, the Court formulated the issue before it as whether Section 5 of the Fourteenth Amendment authorizes Congress to "expand" constitutional rights. To this question, the answer is surely no. But in framing the question as it did, and then answering it, the Court did not pause, as it might have, to consider exactly what constitutional rights are and, in particular, to consider what it does in adjudicating constitutional claims. Without being self-conscious that it was doing so, the *Boerne* Court assumed what might be called a Truth Model of constitutional adjudication and constitutional rights. Under that model, there is one truth about what the Free Exercise Clause, for example, protects and does not protect, and the Court's job is to find that single, determinate, nondiscretionary truth. After the Court had performed that job in *Employment Division v. Smith*, for Congress to adopt a broader view of the right to free exercise of religion when it enacted the Religious Freedom Restoration Act necessarily amounted to an attempted expansion of constitutional rights.

Although the Truth Model is alluring in many ways, its central premises are deeply contestable. An alternative model, which might be called the Reasoned Judgment Model, contemplates that sometimes there may be no single, ultimate truth about constitutional meaning; the reach of a constitutional guarantee can be vague and indeterminate, at least to some extent. Along a spectrum, it may be clear that some formulations would afford too much protection to religious liberty, for example, whereas other formulations would afford too little. In the middle of the spectrum, however, the Reasoned Judgment Model postulates that the Supreme Court does not attempt so much to identify a timeless truth about constitutional meaning as to exercise reasoned judgment about how best to implement a constitutional provision – such as the Free

Exercise Clause, the Due Process Clause, or the Equal Protection Clause – at any particular time. Within the Reasoned Judgment Model, legislation such as the RFRA would not necessarily need to be seen as "expanding" the rights conferred by the Constitution. Insofar as a right is vague or indeterminate, there would be some room, within a range, for Congress to substitute its reasoned judgment for that of the Court about how that right would best be implemented. If the Reasoned Judgment Model were adopted, the Court's job in Section 5 cases would be to assess whether Congress moved beyond the vague or indeterminate range and thereby expanded or contracted a constitutional guarantee. Within that range, Congress could substitute its reasoned judgment for that of the Supreme Court.

In many ways, the Reasoned Judgment Model explains better than the Truth Model the nature of the most difficult and important decisions that the Supreme Court has to make. In at least some of the cases that they decide, the Justices do not seek constitutional truth so much as make practical judgments about how to implement vague constitutional values. History matters to constitutional adjudication, but original understandings do not always bind the Court. The Justices adjudicate in light of moral and political ideals, but sometimes they temper their judgments to accommodate prevailing public sentiments and considerations of prudence and practicality.

In *City of Boerne v. Flores*, however, the Justices implicitly disavowed the Reasoned Judgment Model and embraced the Truth Model. It is easy to see why they would want to do so. The Reasoned Judgment Model may reflect the reality of Supreme Court decision making, but it also diverges in sharp, even shocking ways from familiar, comforting views that the Court should simply find the law and apply it, without the Justices allowing their own views to come into play. What is more, the Reasoned Judgment Model acknowledges an enormous personal responsibility of the Justices for decisions that they make in the name of the Constitution. The Justices may hesitate to admit even to themselves the burdens of judgment that they bear in implementing the Constitution.

13 Conclusion

[The] constitution [was] intended to endure for ages to come, and consequently, to be adapted to the various crises of human affairs.
– Chief Justice John Marshall[1]

I have a dream.
– Dr. Martin Luther King Jr.

N THE INTRODUCTION, I EMPHASIZED THAT THIS WOULD BE a book about American constitutional practice – not just about the Constitution as a written text but also about the social, cultural, and political processes through which constitutional law emerges. To a large and possibly excessive extent, the Supreme Court has tended to dominate the book because the Court stands center stage in the production of constitutional doctrine. But the Court is not the only actor in the drama. In this concluding chapter, I therefore want to step back from the details of constitutional doctrine and offer a few summary theses about the role of the written Constitution and the Supreme Court in our constitutional practice.

Our Constitution is an adaptable document, which draws its meaning partly from evolving thinking and the pressure of events. In the course of

---

1 *McCulloch v. Maryland*, 17 U.S. 316, 415 (1819).

this book, I have offered many illustrations of this claim, such as the historical flow of power to the Executive Branch, the expansion – and more recently the partial contraction – of congressional power under the Commerce Clause, the recognition of increasingly broad rights to freedom of speech and association, and the evolving interpretation of the Equal Protection Clause. To reiterate just one vivid example, the Constitution as originally written imposed no obligation on the federal government to accord all citizens "the equal protection of the laws," and no subsequent amendment has added such a requirement. Nevertheless, the Supreme Court has held consistently for roughly seventy years that the Due Process Clause of the Fifth Amendment, which was written and ratified at a time when the Constitution tolerated slavery, subjects the federal government to the same equal protection norms as the states. It has thus invalidated federal legislation that discriminates on the basis of race and gender.

In theory, many of the changes in our constitutional practice might have occurred through constitutional amendments. Generally, they have not.[2] The Constitution is difficult to amend. Also, many Americans regard it worshipfully and hesitate to change it or even to think it needful of change. For better or for worse, American constitutional practice thus relies more on flexible, pragmatic practices of constitutional interpretation than on frequent formal amendment.

Despite the dynamism of American constitutional practice, the Constitution anchors decision making and debate. Americans revere their Constitution. Both in the courts and outside, constitutional argument is a reasoned process, in which justifications for governmental action must ultimately trace back to the written Constitution.[3] For example, we tend not to say, "It is an emergency, and therefore the Constitution does not

---

2 See generally David A. Strauss, "The Irrelevance of Constitutional Amendments," 114 *Harvard Law Review* 1457 (2001).

3 For emphasis of this point, and argument that it is crucial to perceived constitutional and judicial legitimacy, see Jack M. Balkin, *Living Originalism* (Cambridge, MA: Harvard University Press, 2011).

apply," or "The Constitution does not control because the situation is one that the framers and ratifiers could never have foreseen." Rather, for better or worse, we tend to echo the famous words of Chief Justice John Marshall, quoted at the beginning of this chapter, that the Constitution was "intended to endure for ages to come, and consequently, to be *adapted* to the various crises in human affairs."[4] In some circumstances, we defend interpretations restricting constitutional guarantees by recalling Justice Robert Jackson's equally famous observation that the Constitution should not be interpreted as "a suicide pact."[5] Always, however, interpretations of the Constitution are required.

Despite the Constitution's flexibility on some points, it is inflexible on others. Although the President's "war powers" are flexible, and various rights may be limited when necessary to promote a compelling government interest, elections for Congress are reliably held every two years and for President every four years. Americans can be confident, largely because of the Constitution, that the head of government next year will be the elected President of the United States, not some other official who may command greater support from the Joint Chiefs of Staff. They can also be confident that no one will be detained or punished simply for criticizing the government or taxed to support an establishment of religion.

It is important to understand, however, that claims such as these depend as much on constitutional practice as do other claims about constitutional law. It takes knowledge of constitutional history and American political culture, not just the constitutional text, to know which elements of the Constitution are likely to be regarded as most flexible and which as most unyielding. If President Abraham Lincoln and the Congress had jointly decided to postpone the 1864 elections on grounds of military necessity, and if their doing so had won approval in the court of public opinion, it would be harder to say with confidence today that whatever else may be subject to compromise, the Constitution flatly

4 *McCulloch v. Maryland*, 17 U.S. 316, 415 (1819) (emphasis added).
5 *Terminiello v. Chicago*, 337 U.S. 1, 37 (1949) (Jackson, J., dissenting).

demands regular elections. In American constitutional practice, precedent and historically grounded expectations matter greatly.

*Actors besides the courts influence the development of constitutional
law.* As I have emphasized, constitutional questions involving the scope
of presidential power in war and foreign affairs have mostly been
resolved in informal political struggles between Congress and the President. The courts have generally stood on the sidelines, either because the
issues present "political questions" in the formal sense (as discussed in
Chapter 9) or because judges and Justices have recognized that management of issues of war and peace lies beyond their practical competence.

Presidents, in particular, have influenced the course of constitutional law. Franklin Roosevelt persuaded the American public, eventu-
ally including bench and bar, to adopt a constitutional philosophy that
shaped American constitutional law for more than a generation. Other
presidents, too, have appointed Justices with transformative visions to
the Supreme Court. Richard Nixon began the dismantling of the Warren
Court. Ronald Reagan pushed the project of conservative reconstruction
even further.

The Supreme Court operates within politically constructed bounds. As
Alexander Hamilton wrote in *The Federalist* No. 78, the Judicial Branch
has the power neither of the sword nor of the purse.[6] It possesses its
authority because and only insofar as the great mass of elected officials
and the American people trust it to have the last word about the Constitution's meaning. Today, that trust is great. Over time, the Court has
earned it. But the trust it has earned and the authority it exercises depend
on the Court's decisions being politically tolerable.

The bounds of politically tolerable judicial authority are probably
impossible to define with precision. Because the Justices have so thor-
oughly internalized the lesson that their power depends on their retaining the trust of the American people, there have been few cases testing

---

6 Alexander Hamilton, "No. 78: The Judiciary Department," in *The Federalist Papers*,
  ed. Clinton Rossiter (New York: Mentor, 1999), 464.

the outer boundaries of tolerable judicial authority in recent decades. In the past, however, Presidents have occasionally defied or credibly threatened to defy judicial rulings purporting to limit their authority, especially – as discussed in Chapter 11 – in times or war or emergency. When the President and the Court stand at loggerheads, the ultimate arbiters are Congress, which possesses the power of impeachment, and the American people.

During the Great Depression, when the Supreme Court threatened to scuttle New Deal programs that an aroused political majority thought vital to stabilize the national economy, President Franklin Roosevelt proposed Court-packing legislation. If the Court had not backed down, Congress might well have adopted his proposal.

In a softer illustration of the thesis that the Supreme Court operates within politically constructed bounds, presidential candidates have sometimes made Court decisions a campaign issue and pledged to appoint Justices with specifically different judicial philosophies. Although Roosevelt's Court-packing plan foundered after the Court reversed course, the eight Justices whom he got to appoint to the Court during the remainder of his more than three terms in office swept away the discredited jurisprudence of the *Lochner* era. In 1968, Richard Nixon criticized the Warren Court for tying the hands of the police in fighting crime and promised to appoint "strict constructionist" Justices who would not overstep the proper limits of judicial authority. Whatever else might be said about the Warren Court, some of its decisions tested the bounds of political tolerability, which shifted to the right as the country's politics became more conservative. When conservative Presidents beginning with Nixon appointed more conservative Justices, a number of Warren Court precedents were either flatly overruled or more subtly undermined.

The Supreme Court seldom diverges too far from the central values of popular political majorities. This possibly obvious yet important point – which could be viewed as an entailment of the proposition that the Court operates within politically constructed bounds – was first stated with respectable precision and documentation by the distinguished political scientist Robert Dahl.[7] (It had been anticipated roughly a half century earlier by political cartoonist Finley Peter Dunne, whose "Mr. Dooley" offered the pungent observation that "th' supreme coort follows th' iliction returns."[8]) Indeed, only twice in American history does the Court appear to have veered seriously out of line with generally prevailing views: an aged and conservative court notoriously outraged the public by threatening to stop the New Deal in one era, and the Warren Court prompted a political demand for "law and order" and "strict constructionist" judges in another. The appointments process, of course, contributes importantly to this result, but it is not the only factor. In cases that do not provoke sharp ideological divisions, judges and Justices are likely both to share and to apply the prevalent values of their time.

Although the courts have an important role in protecting minority rights, the protection that has historically been afforded to minorities should not be exaggerated. As people of their times, judges and Justices of the Supreme Court have seldom been at the forefront of movements to protect minorities, whether African Americans before *Brown v. Board of Education*,[9] or women before the 1970s, or gays and lesbians before recent years. In addition, judges and Justices are as prone to fear in fearful times as is nearly everyone else. It is therefore no surprise that civil liberties have tended to fare badly in periods of war and emergency.

Once a view about basic fairness has achieved broad acceptance, however, courts can be expected to insist that the shared ideal should be enforced consistently throughout the nation. To take an obvious example, once the ideal of racial equality became widely accepted, the Supreme Court moved determinedly to stamp out pockets of resistance. More recently, the Court invalidated a statute barring homosexual

7 See Robert A. Dahl, *A Preface to Democratic Theory* (Chicago: University of Chicago Press, 1956), 109–12.

8 Finley Peter Dunne, *Mr. Dooley's Opinions* (New York: Harper & Brothers, 1906), 26.

9 347 U.S. 483 (1954).

sodomy[10] after, but only after, such statutes had become rare, apparently because of an emerging consensus that the government has no business regulating private sexual conduct among consenting adults.

Political movements help shape constitutional law. The altered norms of fairness that lead to the recognition of previously unrecognized rights, including minority rights, do not crystallize spontaneously and often reflect the success of political mobilization. The civil rights movement undoubtedly had a profound effect on the Justices of the Supreme Court as well as on public opinion. Many of the Court's decisions of the 1960s and 1970s enforcing civil rights are the legacy of that movement. The Court's steps to protect rights of gender equality, beginning in the 1970s, again show the tendency of politics, in its various manifestations, to influence constitutional law.

Conservative political activism has also made its mark. The National Rifle Association helped promote a revised understanding of the Second Amendment right to "keep and bear arms," which the Supreme Court long treated as subject to restriction by laws defining the needs, if any, of a "well regulated Militia." More generally, the political movements that pushed the nation's politics to the right after Lyndon Johnson's Great Society also altered the direction of constitutional law.

The Supreme Court is a "they," not an "it." Although it is often irresistible to speak of "the Court" as if it were a monolithic institution with a single collective mind, it in fact comprises nine Justices, who sometimes disagree sharply with one another. The Justices have varied judicial philosophies. They respond differently to legal arguments, shifting public opinion, and practical exigencies. To take one example, I have spoken of "the Court" as having changed course in 1937, after Franklin Roosevelt advanced his Court-packing proposal. Even then, however, four Justices held firm in their anti–New Deal stances. Only one Justice, Owen Roberts, exhibited conspicuously changed views. (Chief Justice Hughes appeared to move to a lesser extent.) To take another

10 See *Lawrence v. Texas*, 539 U.S. 558 (2003).

example, commentators tend to refer to the Court as having a "swing" Justice whose vote is likely to tip the balance one way or another on hotly contested issues. In trying to persuade "the Court," good lawyers often pitch their arguments to appeal most directly to the swing Justice. On a number of issues, Sandra Day O'Connor was the swing Justice for much of her tenure on the Court. When she retired, the role fell to Justice Anthony Kennedy. Among the consequences was that the Court, by 5–4, very swiftly overruled one of the most important decisions written by Justice O'Connor and invalidated restrictions on spending by corporations in political campaigns.

Judicial decision making is inevitably "political" in one sense of that term. Interpreting the Constitution is an inherently practical affair, not a merely intellectual one. As I emphasized at an early point, in trying to draw guidance from the Constitution's text and history and from judicial precedents, judges and Justices must often ask which interpretation would be "best." This is a practical judgment, sometimes with a moral dimension, about what will give us the best law that our Constitution permits. Judgments of this kind will often be controversial, with liberals and conservatives disagreeing in ways that ultimately trace back to their political views.[11]

Nevertheless, judicial decisions are not characteristically political in the same way that decisions by Congress or the President are political. Judicial decisions are both made and expressed in the medium of law, not electoral politics, and the medium of law demands considered attention to the Constitution's text, history, and structure, as well as to judicial precedent. In addition, judges and Justices vote not just for outcomes but also for rules that will be applied in future cases. They do, or should, care about the integrity of constitutional doctrine – about having sensible and consistent rules governing freedom of speech, for example, and not just about deciding whether a particular speaker gets to utter a particular

---

11 See generally Ronald Dworkin, *Law's Empire* (Cambridge, MA: Belknap Press of Harvard University Press, 1986).

statement. Finally, judicial decisions rarely are (and never should be) partisan in the sense of being designed to favor one or another political party.

The role of politics appropriately triggers concern. In discussing the role of politics in judicial decision making, I have repeatedly made both a descriptive and a normative claim. The descriptive claim is that moral and political values influence constitutional decision making. The normative claim is that when there is a choice between one otherwise plausible interpretation that would be morally or practically better and another that would be morally or practically worse, judges and Justices are right to take the moral or practical implications into account. For them not to do so would seem to me wrongheaded.

I should emphasize, however, that my normative claim is a limited one, which does not rule out the possibility that Supreme Court Justices may give too much weight to their views of moral or practical desirability and thereby make constitutional decision making too political. If the Justices attach excessive significance to their normative preferences, in disregard of other factors that also ought to matter in constitutional adjudication (including text, history, precedent, and interests in consistency and predictability), we lose at least some of the benefits of what John Marshall called "a government of laws, and not of men."[12] In addition, the Justices acquire an unjustified amount of political power, including power to frustrate democratic self-government.

Precisely how much weight should Supreme Court Justices give to their views of what would be morally or practically best? Do the current Justices tend to give too much weight to their own substantive values? Do they owe more "deference" to Congress and the President than many of them give at the present time? These are complex questions, with no short or easy answers. Indeed, the question whether the Justices generally let their moral and practical judgments have too much influence in their decision making may well be misleading. It seems unlikely that

12 *Marbury v. Madison*, 5 U.S. 137, 163 (1803).

there is one "right" formula about the role that moral and practical considerations ought to play in all cases, equally applicable to run-of-the-mill disputes under the Due Process and Equal Protection Clauses (currently governed by a "rational basis" test) and, for example, to *Brown v. Board of Education*.[13] Moreover, as the example of *Brown* may also suggest, we should not let concern with the degree to which the Justices are influenced by moral and practical considerations distract attention from substantive questions involving which moral values and practical factors should guide the Justices. Perhaps the most infamous cases in Supreme Court history – including *Dred Scott v. Sandford*,[14] *Lochner v. New York*,[15] and *Korematsu v. United States*[16] – are those in which the Court arrayed itself on the wrong side of an issue with an irreducibly moral aspect.

There are fewer simple truths about constitutional law than most Americans would probably expect. The life of the law, as Oliver Wendell Holmes once wrote, has not been logic but experience. In the past, constitutional law has taken many turns that would not have been easy to predict. The Constitution's future remains to be shaped. The principal aim of this book has been to assist those who want to understand our constitutional practice in all of its daunting, sometimes maddening, and occasionally inspiring complexity.

13 387 U.S. 483 (1954).
14 60 U.S. 393 (1857).
15 198 U.S. 45 (1905).
16 323 U.S. 214 (1944).

Appendix: The Constitution of the United States

Preamble

We the People of the United States, in Order to form a more perfect Union, establish Justice, insure domestic Tranquility, provide for the common defence, promote the general Welfare, and secure the Blessings of Liberty to ourselves and our Posterity, do ordain and establish this Constitution for the United States of America.

Article I

Section 1. All legislative Powers herein granted shall be vested in a Congress of the United States, which shall consist of a Senate and House of Representatives.

Section 2. [1] The House of Representatives shall be composed of Members chosen every second Year by the People of the several States, and the Electors in each State shall have the Qualifications requisite for Electors of the most numerous Branch of the State Legislature.

[2] No Person shall be a Representative who shall not have attained to the Age of twenty five Years, and been seven Years a Citizen of the United States, and who shall not, when elected, be an Inhabitant of that State in which he shall be chosen.

[3] Representatives and direct Taxes shall be apportioned among the several States which may be included within this Union, according to their respective Numbers, which shall be determined by adding to

the whole Number of free Persons, including those bound to Service for a Term of Years, and excluding Indians not taxed, three fifths of all other Persons. The actual Enumeration shall be made within three Years after the first Meeting of the Congress of the United States, and within every subsequent Term of ten Years, in such Manner as they shall by Law direct. The Number of Representatives shall not exceed one for every thirty Thousand, but each State shall have at Least one Representative; and until such enumeration shall be made, the State of New Hampshire shall be entitled to chuse three, Massachusetts eight, Rhode Island and Providence Plantations one, Connecticut five, New York six, New Jersey four, Pennsylvania eight, Delaware one, Maryland six, Virginia ten, North Carolina five, South Carolina five, and Georgia three.

[4] When vacancies happen in the Representation from any State, the Executive Authority thereof shall issue Writs of Election to fill such Vacancies.

[5] The House of Representatives shall chuse their Speaker and other Officers; and shall have the sole Power of Impeachment.

Section 3. [1] The Senate of the United States shall be composed of two Senators from each State, chosen by the Legislature thereof, for six Years; and each Senator shall have one Vote.

[2] Immediately after they shall be assembled in Consequence of the first Election, they shall be divided as equally as may be into three Classes. The Seats of the Senators of the first Class shall be vacated at the Expiration of the Second Year, of the second Class at the Expiration of the fourth Year, and of the third Class at the Expiration of the sixth Year, so that one third may be chosen every second Year; and if Vacancies happen by Resignation, or otherwise, during the Recess of the Legislature of any State, the Executive thereof may make temporary Appointments until the next Meeting of the Legislature, which shall then fill such Vacancies.

[3] No Person shall be a Senator who shall not have attained to the Age of thirty Years, and been nine Years a Citizen of the United States,

and who shall not, when elected, by an Inhabitant of that State for which he shall be chosen.

[4] The Vice President of the United States shall be President of the Senate, but shall have no Vote, unless they be equally divided.

[5] The Senate shall chuse their other Officers, and also a President pro tempore, in the Absence of the Vice President, or when he shall exercise the Office of President of the United States.

[6] The Senate shall have the sole Power to try all Impeachments. When sitting for that Purpose, they shall be on Oath or Affirmation. When the President of the United States is tried, the Chief Justice shall preside: And no Person shall be convicted without the Concurrence of two thirds of the Members present.

[7] Judgment in Cases of Impeachment shall not extend further than to removal from Office, and disqualification to hold and enjoy any Office of honor, Trust, or Profit under the United States: but the Party convicted shall nevertheless be liable and subject to Indictment, Trial, Judgment, and Punishment, according to Law.

Section 4. [1] The Times, Places and Manner of holding Elections for Senators and Representatives, shall be prescribed in each State by the Legislature thereof; but the Congress may at any time by Law make or alter such Regulations, except as to the Places of chusing Senators.

[2] The Congress shall assemble at least once in every Year, and such Meeting shall be on the first Monday in December, unless they shall by Law appoint a different Day.

Section 5. [1] Each House shall be the Judge of the Elections, Returns, and Qualifications of its own Members, and a Majority of each shall constitute a Quorum to do Business; but a smaller Number may adjourn from day to day, and may be authorized to compel the Attendance of absent Members, in such Manner, and under such Penalties as each House may provide.

[2] Each House may determine the Rules of its Proceedings, punish its Members for disorderly Behavior, and, with the Concurrence of two thirds, expel a Member.

[3] Each House shall keep a Journal of its Proceedings, and from time to time publish the same, excepting such Parts as may in their Judgment require Secrecy; and the Yeas and Nays of the Members of either House on any question shall, at the Desire of one fifth of those Present, be entered on the Journal.

[4] Neither House, during the Session of Congress, shall without the Consent of the other, adjourn for more than three days, nor to any other Place than that in which the two Houses shall be sitting.

Section 6. [1] The Senators and Representatives shall receive a Compensation for their Services, to be ascertained by Law, and paid out of the Treasury of the United States. They shall in all Cases, except Treason, Felony and Breach of the Peace, be privileged from Arrest during their Attendance at the Session of their respective Houses, and in going to and returning from the same; and for any Speech or Debate in either House, they shall not be questioned in any other Place.

[2] No Senator or Representative shall, during the Time for which he was elected, be appointed to any civil Office under the Authority of the United States, which shall have been created, or the Emoluments whereof shall have been increased during such time; and no Person holding any Office under the United States, shall be a Member of either House during his Continuance in Office.

Section 7. [1] All Bills for raising Revenue shall originate in the House of Representatives; but the Senate may propose or concur with Amendments as on other Bills.

[2] Every Bill which shall have passed the House of Representatives and the Senate, shall, before it become a Law, be presented to the President of the United States; If he approve he shall sign it, but if not he shall return it, with his Objections to the House in which it shall have originated, who shall enter the Objections at large on their Journal, and proceed to reconsider it. If after such Reconsideration two thirds of that House shall agree to pass the Bill, it shall be sent together with the Objections, to the other House, by which it shall likewise be reconsidered, and if approved by two thirds of that House, it shall become a Law. But in all

such Cases the Votes of both Houses shall be determined by Yeas and Nays, and the Names of the Persons voting for and against the Bill shall be entered on the Journal of each House respectively. If any Bill shall not be returned by the President within ten Days (Sundays excepted) after it shall have been presented to him, the Same shall be a Law, in like Manner as if he had signed it, unless the Congress by their Adjournment prevent its Return in which Case it shall not be a Law.

[3] Every Order, Resolution, or Vote, to Which the Concurrence of the Senate and House of Representatives may be necessary (except on a question of Adjournment) shall be presented to the President of the United States; and before the Same shall take Effect, shall be approved by him, or being disapproved by him, shall be repassed by two thirds of the Senate and House of Representatives, according to the Rules and Limitations prescribed in the Case of a Bill.

Section 8. [1] The Congress shall have Power To lay and collect Taxes, Duties, Imposts and Excises, to pay the Debts and provide for the common Defence and general Welfare of the United States; but all Duties, Imposts and Excises shall be uniform throughout the United States;

[2] To borrow money on the credit of the United States;

[3] To regulate Commerce with foreign Nations, and among the several States, and with the Indian Tribes;

[4] To establish an uniform Rule of Naturalization, and uniform Laws on the subject of Bankruptcies throughout the United States;

[5] To coin Money, regulate the Value thereof, and of foreign Coin, and fix the Standard of Weights and Measures;

[6] To provide for the Punishment of counterfeiting the Securities and current Coin of the United States;

[7] To Establish Post Offices and Post Roads;

[8] To promote the Progress of Science and useful Arts, by securing for limited Times to Authors and Inventors the exclusive Right to their respective Writings and Discoveries;

[9] To constitute Tribunals inferior to the supreme Court;

[10] To define and punish Piracies and Felonies committed on the high Seas, and Offenses against the Law of Nations;

[11] To declare War, grant Letters of Marque and Reprisal, and make Rules concerning Captures on Land and Water;

[12] To raise and support Armies, but no Appropriation of Money to that Use shall be for a longer Term than two Years;

[13] To provide and maintain a Navy;

[14] To make Rules for the Government and Regulation of the land and naval Forces;

[15] To provide for calling forth the Militia to execute the Laws of the Union, suppress Insurrections and repel Invasions;

[16] To provide for organizing, arming, and disciplining the Militia, and for governing such Part of them as may be employed in the Service of the United States, reserving to the States respectively, the Appointment of the Officers, and the Authority of training the Militia according to the discipline prescribed by Congress;

[17] To exercise exclusive Legislation in all Cases whatsoever, over such District (not exceeding ten Miles square) as may, by Cession of particular States, and the Acceptance of Congress, become the Seat of the Government of the United States, and to exercise like Authority over all Places purchased by the Consent of the Legislature of the State in which the Same shall be, for the Erection of Forts, Magazines, Arsenals, dock-Yards, and other needful Buildings; – And

[18] To make all Laws which shall be necessary and proper for carrying into Execution the foregoing Powers, and all other Powers vested by this Constitution in the Government of the United States, or in any Department or Officer thereof.

Section 9. [1] The Migration or Importation of Such Persons as any of the States now existing shall think proper to admit, shall not be prohibited by the Congress prior to the Year one thousand eight hundred and eight, but a Tax or duty may be imposed on such Importation, not exceeding ten dollars for each Person.

[2] The privilege of the Writ of Habeas Corpus shall not be suspended, unless when in Cases of Rebellion or Invasion the public Safety may require it.

[3] No Bill of Attainder or ex post facto Law shall be passed.

[4] No Capitation, or other direct, Tax shall be laid, unless in Proportion to the Census or Enumeration herein before directed to be taken.

[5] No Tax or Duty shall be laid on Articles exported from any State.

[6] No Preference shall be given by any Regulation of Commerce or Revenue to the Ports of one State over those of another: nor shall Vessels bound to, or from, one State be obliged to enter, clear, or pay Duties in another.

[7] No money shall be drawn from the Treasury, but in Consequence of Appropriations made by Law; and a regular Statement and Account of the Receipts and Expenditures of all public Money shall be published from time to time.

[8] No Title of Nobility shall be granted by the United States: And no Person holding any Office of Profit or Trust under them, shall, without the Consent of the Congress, accept of any present, Emolument, Office, or Title, of any kind whatever, from any King, Prince, or foreign State.

Section 10. [1] No State shall enter into any Treaty, Alliance, or Confederation; grant Letters of Marque and Reprisal; coin Money; emit Bills of Credit; make any Thing but gold and silver Coin a Tender in Payment of Debts; pass any Bill of Attainder, ex post facto Law, or Law impairing the Obligation of Contracts, or grant any Title of Nobility.

[2] No State shall, without the Consent of the Congress, lay any Imposts or Duties on Imports or Exports, except what may be absolutely necessary for executing its inspection Laws: and the net Produce of all Duties and Imposts, laid by any State on Imports or Exports, shall be for the Use of the Treasury of the United States; and all such Laws shall be subject to the Revision and Controul of the Congress.

[3] No State shall, without the Consent of Congress, lay any Duty of Tonnage, keep Troops, or Ships of War in time of Peace, enter into any

Agreement or Compact with another State, or with a foreign Power, or engage in War, unless actually invaded, or in such imminent Danger as will not admit of delay.

Article II

Section 1. [1] The executive Power shall be vested in a President of the United States of America. He shall hold his Office during the Term of four Years, and, together with the Vice President, chosen for the same Term, be elected, as follows:

[2] Each State shall appoint, in such Manner as the Legislature thereof may direct, a Number of Electors, equal to the whole Number of Senators and Representatives to which the State may be entitled in the Congress; but no Senator or Representative, or Person holding an Office of Trust or Profit under the United States, shall be appointed an Elector.

[3] The Electors shall meet in their respective States, and vote by Ballot for two Persons, of whom one at least shall not be an Inhabitant of the same State with themselves. And they shall make a List of all the Persons voted for, and of the Number of Votes for each; which List they shall sign and certify, and transmit sealed to the Seat of the Government of the United States, directed to the President of the Senate. The President of the Senate shall, in the Presence of the Senate and House of Representatives, open all the Certificates, and the Votes shall then be counted. The Person having the greatest Number of Votes shall be the President, if such Number be a Majority of the whole Number of Electors appointed; and if there be more than one who have such Majority, and have an equal Number of Votes, then the House of Representatives shall immediately chuse by Ballot one of them for President; and if no Person have a Majority, then from the five highest on the List the said House shall in like Manner chuse the President. But in chusing the President, the Votes shall be taken by States the Representation from each State having one Vote; A quorum for this Purpose shall consist of a

Member or Members from two thirds of the States, and a Majority of all the States shall be necessary to a Choice. In every Case, after the Choice of the President, the Person having the greater Number of Votes of the Electors shall be the Vice President. But if there should remain two or more who have equal Votes, the Senate shall chuse from them by Ballot the Vice President.

[4] The Congress may determine the Time of chusing the Electors, and the Day on which they shall give their Votes; which Day shall be the same throughout the United States.

[5] No person except a natural born Citizen, or a Citizen of the United States, at the time of the Adoption of this Constitution, shall be eligible to the Office of President; neither shall any Person be eligible to that Office who shall not have attained to the Age of thirty five Years, and been fourteen Years a Resident within the United States.

[6] In case of the removal of the President from Office, or of his Death, Resignation or Inability to discharge the Powers and Duties of the said Office, the Same shall devolve on the Vice President, and the Congress may by Law provide for the Case of Removal, Death, Resignation or Inability, both of the President and Vice President, declaring what Officer shall then act as President, and such Officer shall act accordingly, until the Disability be removed, or a President shall be elected.

[7] The President shall, at stated Times, receive for his Services, a Compensation, which shall neither be increased nor diminished during the Period for which he shall have been elected, and he shall not receive within that Period any other Emolument from the United States, or any of them.

[8] Before he enter on the Execution of his Office, he shall take the following Oath or Affirmation: "I do solemnly swear (or affirm) that I will faithfully execute the Office of President of the United States, and will to the best of my Ability, preserve, protect and defend the Constitution of the United States."

Section 2. [1] The President shall be Commander in Chief of the Army and Navy of the United States, and of the militia of the several

States, when called into the actual Service of the United States; he may require the Opinion, in writing, of the principal Officer in each of the Executive Departments, upon any Subject relating to the Duties of their respective Offices, and he shall have Power to grant Reprieves and Pardons for Offenses against the United States, except in Cases of Impeachment.

[2] He shall have Power, by and with the Advice and Consent of the Senate to make Treaties, provided two thirds of the Senators present concur; and he shall nominate, and by and with the Advice and Consent of the Senate, shall appoint Ambassadors, other public Ministers and Consuls, Judges of the supreme Court, and all other Officers of the United States, whose Appointments are not herein otherwise provided for, and which shall be established by Law; but the Congress may by Law vest the Appointment of such inferior Officers, as they think proper, in the President alone, in the Courts of Law, or in the Heads of Departments.

[3] The President shall have Power to fill up all Vacancies that may happen during the Recess of the Senate, by granting Commissions which shall expire at the End of their next Session.

Section 3. He shall from time to time give to the Congress Information of the State of the Union, and recommend to their Consideration such Measures as he shall judge necessary and expedient; he may, on extraordinary Occasions, convene both Houses, or either of them, and in Case of Disagreement between them, with Respect to the Time of Adjournment, he may adjourn them to such Time as he shall think proper; he shall receive Ambassadors and other public Ministers; he shall take Care that the Laws be faithfully executed, and shall Commission all the Officers of the United States.

Section 4. The President, Vice President and all civil Officers of the United States, shall be removed from Office on Impeachment for, and Conviction of, Treason, Bribery, or other high Crimes and Misdemeanors.

Article III

Section 1. The judicial Power of the United States, shall be vested in one supreme Court, and in such inferior Courts as the Congress may from time to time ordain and establish. The Judges, both of the supreme and inferior Courts, shall hold their Offices during good Behaviour, and shall, at stated Times, receive for their Services a Compensation, which shall not be diminished during their Continuance in Office.

Section 2. [1] The judicial Power shall extend to all Cases, in Law and Equity, arising under this Constitution, the Laws of the United States, and Treaties made, or which shall be made, under their Authority; – to all Cases affecting Ambassadors, other public Ministers and Consuls; – to all Cases of admiralty and maritime Jurisdiction; – to Controversies to which the United States shall be a Party; – to Controversies between two or more States; – between a State and Citizens of another State; – between Citizens of different States; – between Citizens of the same State claiming Lands under the Grants of different States, and between a State, or the Citizens thereof, and foreign States, Citizens or Subjects.

[2] In all Cases affecting Ambassadors, other public Ministers and Consuls, and those in which a State shall be a Party, the supreme Court shall have original Jurisdiction. In all the other Cases before mentioned, the supreme Court shall have appellate Jurisdiction, both as to Law and Fact, with such Exceptions, and under such Regulations as the Congress shall make.

[3] The trial of all Crimes, except in Cases of Impeachment, shall be by Jury; and such Trial shall be held in the State where the said Crimes shall have been committed; but when not committed within any State, the Trial shall be at such Place or Places as the Congress may by Law have directed.

Section 3. [1] Treason against the United States, shall consist only in levying War against them, or, in adhering to their Enemies, giving them Aid and Comfort. No Person shall be convicted of Treason unless on the

Testimony of two Witnesses to the same overt Act, or on Confession in open Court.

[2] The Congress shall have Power to declare the Punishment of Treason, but no Attainder of Treason shall work Corruption of Blood, or Forfeiture except during the Life of the Person attainted.

Article IV

Section 1. Full Faith and Credit shall be given in each State to the public Acts, Records, and judicial Proceedings of every other State. And the Congress may by general Laws prescribe the Manner in which such Acts, Records and Proceedings shall be proved, and the Effect thereof.

Section 2. [1] The Citizens of each State shall be entitled to all Privileges and Immunities of Citizens in the several States.

[2] A Person charged in any State with Treason, Felony, or other Crime, who shall flee from Justice, and be found in another State, shall on demand of the executive Authority of the State from which he fled, be delivered up, to be removed to the State having Jurisdiction of the Crime.

[3] No Person held to Service or Labour in one State, under the Laws thereof, escaping into another, shall, in Consequence of any Law or Regulation therein, be discharged from such Service or Labour, but shall be delivered up on Claim of the Party to whom such Service or Labour may be due.

Section 3. [1] New States may be admitted by the Congress into this Union; but no new State shall be formed or erected within the Jurisdiction of any other State; nor any State be formed by the Junction of two or more States, or Parts of States, without the Consent of the Legislatures of the States concerned as well as of the Congress.

[2] The Congress shall have Power to dispose of and make all needful Rules and Regulations respecting the Territory or other Property belonging to the United States; and nothing in this Constitution shall be

so construed as to Prejudice any Claims of the United States, or of any particular State.

Section 4. The United States shall guarantee to every State in this Union a Republican Form of Government, and shall protect each of them against Invasion; and on Application of the Legislature, or of the Executive (when the Legislature cannot be convened) against domestic Violence.

Article V

The Congress, whenever two thirds of both Houses shall deem it necessary, shall propose Amendments to this Constitution, or, on the Application of the Legislatures of two thirds of the several States, shall call a Convention for proposing Amendments, which, in either Case, shall be valid to all Intents and Purposes, as part of this Constitution, when ratified by the Legislatures of three fourths of the several States, or by Conventions in three fourths thereof, as the one or the other Mode of Ratification may be proposed by the Congress; Provided that no Amendment which may be made prior to the Year One thousand eight hundred and eight shall in any Manner affect the first and fourth Clauses in the Ninth Section of the first Article; and that no State, without its Consent, shall be deprived of its equal Suffrage in the Senate.

Article VI

All Debts contracted and Engagements entered into, before the Adoption of this Constitution shall be as valid against the United States under this Constitution, as under the Confederation.

This Constitution, and the Laws of the United States which shall be made in Pursuance thereof; and all Treaties made, or which shall be made, under the Authority of the United States, shall be the supreme

Law of the Land; and the Judges in every State shall be bound thereby, any Thing in the Constitution or Laws of any State to the Contrary notwithstanding.

The Senators and Representatives before mentioned, and the Members of the several State Legislatures, and all executive and judicial Officers, both of the United States and of the several States, shall be bound by Oath or Affirmation, to support this Constitution; but no religious Test shall ever be required as a Qualification to any Office or public Trust under the United States.

Article VII

The Ratification of the Conventions of nine States shall be sufficient for the Establishment of this Constitution between the States so ratifying the Same.

Amendments of the Constitution of the United States

of America, Proposed by Congress and Ratified by

the Legislatures of the Several States Pursuant to

the Fifth Article of the Original Constitution

Amendment I [1791]

Congress shall make no law respecting an establishment of religion, or prohibiting the free exercise thereof; or abridging the freedom of speech, or of the press; or the right of the people peaceably to assemble, and to petition the Government for a redress of grievances.

Amendment II [1791]

A well regulated Militia, being necessary to the security of a free State, the right of the people to keep and bear Arms, shall not be infringed.

Amendment III [1791]

No Soldier shall, in time of peace be quartered in any house, without the consent of the Owner, nor in time of war, but in a manner to be prescribed by law.

Amendment IV [1791]

The right of the people to be secure in their persons, houses, papers, and effects, against unreasonable searches and seizures, shall not be violated, and no Warrants shall issue, but upon probable cause, supported by Oath or affirmation and particularly describing the place to be searched, and the persons or things to be seized.

Amendment V [1791]

No person shall be held to answer for a capital, or otherwise infamous crime, unless on a presentment or indictment of a Grand Jury, except in cases arising in the land or naval forces, or in the Militia, when in actual service in time of War or public danger; nor shall any person be subject for the same offence to be twice put in jeopardy of life or limb; nor shall be compelled in any criminal case to be a witness against himself, nor be deprived of life, liberty, or property, without due process of law; nor shall private property be taken for public use, without just compensation.

Amendment VI [1791]

In all criminal prosecutions, the accused shall enjoy the right to a speedy and public trial, by an impartial jury of the State and district wherein the crime shall have been committed, which district shall have been previously ascertained by law, and to be informed of the nature and cause of the accusation; to be confronted with the witnesses against him; to have compulsory process for obtaining witnesses in his favor, and to have the Assistance of Counsel for his defence.

Amendment VII [1791]

In Suits at common law, where the value in controversy shall exceed twenty dollars, the right of trial by jury shall be preserved, and no fact tried by jury, shall be otherwise re-examined in any Court of the United States, than according to the rules of the common law.

Amendment VIII [1791]

Excessive bail shall not be required, nor excessive fines imposed, nor cruel and unusual punishments inflicted.

Amendment IX [1791]

The enumeration in the Constitution, of certain rights, shall not be construed to deny or disparage others retained by the people.

Amendment X [1791]

The powers not delegated to the United States by the Constitution, nor prohibited by it to the States, are reserved to the States respectively, or to the people.

Amendment XI [1798]

The Judicial power of the United States shall not be construed to extend to any suit in law or equity, commenced or prosecuted against one of the United States by Citizens of another State, or by Citizens or Subjects of any Foreign State.

Amendment XII [1804]

The Electors shall meet in their respective states and vote by ballot for President and Vice-President, one of whom, at least, shall not be an inhabitant of the same state with themselves; they shall name in their ballots the person voted for as President, and in distinct ballots the person voted for as Vice-President, and they shall make distinct lists of all persons voted for as President, and of all persons voted for as Vice-President, and of the number of votes for each, which lists they shall sign and certify, and transmit sealed to the seat of the government of the United States, directed to the President of the Senate; – The President of the Senate shall, in the presence of the Senate and House of Representatives, open all the certificates and the votes shall then be counted; – The person having the greatest number of votes for President, shall be the President, if such number be a majority of the whole number of Electors appointed; and if no person have such majority, then from the persons having the highest numbers not exceeding three on the list of those voted for as President, the House of Representatives shall choose immediately, by ballot, the President. But in choosing the President, the votes shall be taken by states, the representation from each state having one vote; a quorum for this purpose shall consist of a member or members from two-thirds of the states, and a majority of all the states shall be necessary to a choice. And if the House of Representatives shall not choose a President whenever the right of choice shall devolve upon them before the fourth day of March next following, then the Vice-President shall act as President, as in the case of the death or other constitutional disability of the President. – The person having the greatest number of votes as Vice-President, shall be the Vice-President, if such number be a majority of the whole number of Electors appointed, and if no person have a majority, then from the two highest numbers on the list, the Senate shall choose the Vice-President; a quorum for the purpose shall consist of two-thirds of the whole number of Senators, and a majority of the whole number shall be necessary to a choice. But no person constitutionally ineligible to the office of President shall be eligible to that of Vice-President of the United States.

Amendment XIII [1865]

Section 1. Neither slavery nor involuntary servitude, except as a punishment for crime whereof the party shall have been duly convicted, shall exist within the United States, or any place subject to their jurisdiction.

Section 2. Congress shall have power to enforce this article by appropriate legislation.

Amendment XIV [1868]

Section 1. All persons born or naturalized in the United States, and subject to the jurisdiction thereof, are citizens of the United States and of the State wherein they reside. No State shall make or enforce any law which shall abridge the privileges or immunities of citizens of the United States; nor shall any State deprive any person of life, liberty, or property, without due process of law; nor deny to any person within its jurisdiction the equal protection of the laws.

Section 2. Representatives shall be apportioned among the several States according to their respective numbers, counting the whole number of persons in each State, excluding Indians not taxed. But when the right to vote at any election for the choice of electors for President and Vice President of the United States, Representatives in Congress, the Executive and Judicial officers of a State, or the members of the Legislature thereof, is denied to any of the male inhabitants of such State, being twenty-one years of age, and citizens of the United States, or in any way abridged, except for participation in rebellion, or other crime, the basis of representation therein shall be reduced in the proportion which the number of such male citizens shall bear to the whole number of male citizens twenty-one years of age in such State.

Section 3. No person shall be a Senator or Representative in Congress, or elector of President and Vice President, or hold any office, civil or military, under the United States, or under any State, who having previously taken an oath, as a member of Congress, or as an officer of the United States, or as a member of any State legislature, or as an executive or judicial officer of any State, to support the Constitution of the United States, shall have engaged in insurrection or rebellion against the same, or given aid or comfort to the enemies thereof. But Congress may by a vote of two-thirds of each House, remove such disability.

Section 4. The validity of the public debt of the United States, authorized by law, including debts incurred for payment of pensions and bounties for services in suppressing insurrection or rebellion, shall not be questioned. But neither the United States nor any State shall assume or pay any debt or obligation incurred in aid of insurrection or rebellion against the United States, or any claim for the loss or emancipation of any slave; but all such debts, obligations and claims shall be held illegal and void.

Section 5. The Congress shall have power to enforce, by appropriate legislation, the provisions of this article.

Amendment XV [1870]

Section 1. The right of citizens of the United States to vote shall not be denied or abridged by the United States or by any State on account of race, color, or previous condition of servitude.

Section 2. The Congress shall have power to enforce this article by appropriate legislation.

Amendment XVI [1913]

The Congress shall have power to lay and collect taxes on incomes, from whatever source derived, without apportionment among the several States, and without regard to any census or enumeration.

Amendment XVII [1913]

[1] The Senate of the United States shall be composed of two Senators from each State, elected by the people thereof, for six years; and each Senator shall have one vote. The electors in each State shall have the qualifications requisite for electors of the most numerous branch of the State legislatures.

[2] When vacancies happen in the representation of any State in the Senate, the executive authority of such State shall issue writs of election

to fill such vacancies: *Provided*, That the legislature of any State may empower the executive thereof to make temporary appointments until the people fill the vacancies by election as the legislature may direct.

[3] This amendment shall not be so construed as to affect the election or term of any Senator chosen before it becomes valid as part of the Constitution.

Amendment XVIII [1919]

Section 1. After one year from the ratification of this article the manufacture, sale, or transportation of intoxicating liquors within, the importation thereof into, or the exportation thereof from the United States and all territory subject to the jurisdiction thereof for beverage purposes is hereby prohibited.

Section 2. The Congress and the several States shall have concurrent power to enforce this article by appropriate legislation.

Section 3. This article shall be inoperative unless it shall have been ratified as an amendment to the Constitution by the legislatures of the several States, as provided in the Constitution, within seven years from the date of the submission hereof to the States by the Congress.

Amendment XIX [1920]

[1] The right of citizens of the United States to vote shall not be denied or abridged by the United States or by any State on account of sex.

[2] Congress shall have power to enforce this article by appropriate legislation.

Amendment XX [1933]

Section 1. The terms of the President and Vice President shall end at noon on the 20th day of January, and the terms of Senators and Representatives at noon on the 3d day of January, of the years in which such terms would have ended if this article had not been ratified; and the terms of their successors shall then begin.

Section 2. The Congress shall assemble at least once in every year, and such meeting shall begin at noon on the 3d day of January, unless they shall by law appoint a different day.

Section 3. If, at the time fixed for the beginning of the term of the President, the President elect shall have died, the Vice President elect shall become President. If the President shall not have been chosen before the time fixed for the beginning of his term, or if the President elect shall have failed to qualify, then the Vice President elect shall act as President until a President shall have qualified; and the Congress may by law provide for the case wherein neither a President elect nor a Vice President elect shall have qualified, declaring who shall then act as President, or the manner in which one who is to act shall be selected, and such person shall act accordingly until a President or Vice President shall have qualified.

Section 4. The Congress may by law provide for the case of the death of any of the persons from whom the House of Representatives may choose a President whenever the right of choice shall have devolved upon them, and for the case of the death of any of the persons from whom the Senate may choose a Vice President whenever the right of choice shall have devolved upon them.

Section 5. Sections 1 and 2 shall take effect on the 15th day of October following the ratification of this article.

Section 6. This article shall be inoperative unless it shall have been ratified as an amendment to the Constitution by the legislatures of three-fourths of the several States within seven years from the date of its submission.

Amendment XXI [1933]

Section 1. The eighteenth article of amendment to the Constitution of the United States is hereby repealed.

Section 2. The transportation or importation into any State, Territory, or possession of the United States for delivery or use therein of intoxicating liquors, in violation of the laws thereof, is hereby prohibited.

Section 3. This article shall be inoperative unless it shall have been ratified as an amendment to the Constitution by conventions in the several States, as provided in the Constitution, within seven years from the date of the submission hereof to the States by the Congress.

Amendment XXII [1951]

Section 1. No person shall be elected to the office of the President more than twice, and no person who has held the office of President, or acted as President, for more than two years of a term to which some other person was elected President shall be elected to the office of President more than once. But this Article shall not apply to any person holding the office of President when this Article was proposed by the Congress, and shall not prevent any person who may be holding the office of President, or acting as President, during the term within which this Article becomes operative from holding the office of President or acting as President during the remainder of such term.

Section 2. This article shall be inoperative unless it shall have been ratified as an amendment to the Constitution by the legislatures of three-fourths of the several States within seven years from the date of its submission to the States by the Congress.

Amendment XXIII [1961]

Section 1. The District constituting the seat of Government of the United States shall appoint in such manner as the Congress may direct:

A number of electors of President and Vice President equal to the whole number of Senators and Representatives in Congress to which the

District would be entitled if it were a State, but in no event more than the least populous state; they shall be in addition to those appointed by the states, but they shall be considered, for the purposes of the election of President and Vice President, to be electors appointed by a state; and they shall meet in the District and perform such duties as provided by the twelfth article of amendment.

Section 2. The Congress shall have power to enforce this article by appropriate legislation.

Amendment XXIV [1964]

Section 1. The right of citizens of the United States to vote in any primary or other election for President or Vice President, for electors for President or Vice President, or for Senator or Representative in Congress, shall not be denied or abridged by the United States or any State by reason of failure to pay any poll tax or other tax.

Section 2. The Congress shall have power to enforce this article by appropriate legislation.

Amendment XXV [1967]

Section 1. In case of the removal of the President from office or of his death or resignation, the Vice President shall become President.

Section 2. Whenever there is a vacancy in the office of the Vice President, the President shall nominate a Vice President who shall take office upon confirmation by a majority vote of both Houses of Congress.

Section 3. Whenever the President transmits to the President pro tempore of the Senate and the Speaker of the House of Representatives his written declaration that he is unable to discharge the powers and duties of his office, and until he transmits to them a written declaration to the contrary, such powers and duties shall be discharged by the Vice President as Acting President.

Section 4. Whenever the Vice President and a majority of either the principal officers of the executive departments or of such other body as Congress may by law provide, transmit to the President pro tempore of the Senate and the Speaker of the House of Representatives their written declaration that the President is unable to discharge the powers and duties of his office, the Vice President shall immediately assume the powers and duties of the office as Acting President.

Thereafter, when the President transmits to the President pro tempore of the Senate and the Speaker of the House of Representatives his written declaration that no inability exists, he shall resume the powers and duties of his office unless the Vice President and a majority of either the principal officers of the executive department or of such other body as Congress may by law provide, transmit within four days to the President pro tempore of the Senate and the Speaker of the House of Representatives their written declaration that the President is unable to discharge the powers and duties of his office. Thereupon Congress shall decide the issue, assembling within forty-eight hours for that purpose if not in session. If the Congress, within twenty-one days after receipt of the latter written declaration, or, if Congress is not in session, within twenty-one days after Congress is required to assemble, determines by two-thirds vote of both Houses that the President is unable to discharge the powers and duties of his office, the Vice President shall continue to discharge the same as Acting President; otherwise, the President shall resume the powers and duties of his office.

Amendment XXVI [1971]

Section 1. The right of citizens of the United States, who are eighteen years of age or older, to vote shall not be denied or abridged by the United States or by any State on account of age.

Section 2. The Congress shall have power to enforce this article by appropriate legislation.

*Amendment XXVII [1992]**

No law, varying compensation for the services of Senators and Representatives, shall take effect, until an election of Representatives shall have intervened.

---

* On May 7, 1992, more than two hundred years after it was first proposed by James Madison, the Twenty-Seventh Amendment was ratified by a thirty-eighth state (Michigan). Although Congress set no time limit for ratification of this amendment, ten of the other amendments proposed at the same time (1789) – now known as the Bill of Rights – were ratified in a little more than two years.

Index

Abington School District v. Schempp
 (1963), 82n12
abortion, 32, 126, 194, 209, 290. *See also*
 specific decisions
 partial-birth abortion, 213
Abrams v. United States (1919), 48
Adams, John, 12, 254
Adamson v. California (1947), 128n8
Adarand Constructors, Inc. v. Pena (1997),
 280n10
advertising, 63–65
affirmative action, 149, 171, 173–175, 176,
 177, 178, 189, 295. *See also* equal
 protection; *specific groups*
Affordable Care Act. *See* Patient
 Protection and Affordable Care Act
Affordable Care Act case. *See National
 Federation of Independent Business v.
 Sebelius*
after-the-fact punishments, 42
Ali, Muhammad, 77
aliens, 331. *See also* citizenship,
Alito, Samuel, xi, 35, 69, 91, 177, 213
Allegheny, County of v. ACLU (1989),
 80n6, 90n32, 91n33
Allen v. Wright (1984), 302n4
Allied Structural Steel Co. v. Spannaus
 (1978), 119n39
American Supreme Court, The
 (McCloskey), xv
anti-canon, 117, 163

Aronson, Michael, xviii
Articles of Confederation, 3
assisted suicide. *See* death, right to
association, freedom of, 73, 194
Atkins v. Virginia (2002), 142n46

Baker v. Carr (1962), 288n26
Baldwin v. Fish and Game Commission
 (1978), 306
Baldwin v. G. A. F. Seelig, Inc. (1935),
 310
Bank of the United States, 21, 23
bankruptcy laws, 106
Barron v. Baltimore (1833), 127
Barron, David, xviii
Beard, Charles, 101
Berghuis v. Thompkins (2010), 136n23
Berra, Yogi, 186
Betts v. Brady (1942), 130n10
Bickel, Alexander, 290, 297
 countermajoritarian difficulty. *See*
 countermajoritarianism
Bill of Rights, 8, 126. *See also specific
 amendments*
bin Laden, Osama, xxv
Bipartisan Campaign Reform Act, 68, 69
Black, Charles, 161
Black, Hugo, 60, 116, 128n8, 162, 257
Blackmun, Harry, 216
*Board of Trustees of the University of
 Illinois v. United States* (1933), 303n5

Boerne, City of, v. Flores (1997), 335, 348, 352
Bolling v. Sharpe (1954), 153n3
Boumediene v. Bush (2008), 330
Bowers v. Hardwick (1986), 215–216, 219
Boy Scouts of America v. Dale (2000), 75, 76
Bradwell v. Illinois (1872), 180n56
Brandeis, Louis, 49, 50, 53
Brandenburg v. Ohio (1969), 51–54, 328
Braunfeld v. Brown (1961), 92n38
Brennan, William, 131, 346
Breyer, Stephen, 36, 145, 205, 250
broadcast media, 71, 72
Brown v. Board of Education (1954), xxii, 31, 126, 152, 163–165, 166, 167, 168, 171, 173, 174, 179, 188, 198, 294, 343, 358, 362
Brzonkala case. *See United States v. Morrison*
Buckley v. Valeo (1976), 67–68
Burger, Warren, 32, 134, 215, 266
Bush v. Gore (2000), 19, 203–206, 277
Bush, George H. W., 87, 211
Bush, George W., 33, 87, 204, 329
busing, 172

cable television, 72–73
Calder v. Bull (1798), 106, 113
Callins v. Collins (1994), 141n41
Cantwell v. Connecticut (1940), 77
capital punishment. *See* death penalty
Cardozo, Benjamin, 244
Carlin, George, 71
case or controversy requirement, 287
Catholics, 86
censorship, 49, 57
Central Hudson Gas & Electric Corp. v. Public Service Commission (1981), 64
Champion v. Ames (1903), 234
Chaplinsky v. New Hampshire (1942), 59
Chase, Samuel, 106
Chemerinsky, Erwin, xviii
child pornography, 62, 232

children, 62, 65, 72, 73, 166, 194, 221
child labor, 236
Choper, Jesse, xviii
churches. *See* religion
Cipollone v. Liggett Group, Inc. (1992), 304
Citizens United v. Federal Election Commission (2010), 69–70
citizenship, 108, 109, 196, 331
civil rights, 51, 74, 165, 169, 359. *See also specific decisions*
Civil Rights Act of 1964, 165, 169, 171, 238, 241, 339
Civil Rights Cases (1883), 335
Civil War, 9, 26, 109, 152, 258, 315–318, 320, 325
Clay, aka Ali, v. United States (1971), 78, 97
clear and present danger, 46–47, 48, 49, 50, 54, 325
Cleburne, City of, v. Cleburne Living Center (1985), 189n75
Clinton v. City of New York (1998), 268
Clinton, Bill, 183, 185
Coase, Ronald, 64
Cohen v. California (1971), 58
Coker v. Georgia (1977), 142n43
Cold War, 50
Colegrove v. Green (1946), 197n11
commerce clause, xxvii, 229, 234, 236, 238–239, 248, 292, 309
original understanding, 231, 241
commercial speech, 63, 64
common law, 295
communism, 50
Communist Party. *See* communism
compelling interest, 93, 176
conditional grants, 248–250
Congress, U.S., xxv
Article I and, 6
commerce power. *See* commerce clause
enforcement power, 335, 345
House of Representatives, 5
powers of, xxvii, 6, 22, 227, 335

Senate, 5

spending power. *See* taxing and spending clause

state governments and, 350

war powers, 316

Connolly v. Pension Benefit Guaranty Corp. (1986), 122n46

conservatism, xxi, 27, 32, 86, 122, 144, 146, 185, 187, 195, 211, 233, 262, 265, 345, 359

Constitution, U.S.

amendments to, 7, 376. *See also* Bill of Rights; *specific amendments*

Article I, 6, 21, 26, 102, 114, 228, 243, 279, 302, 363

Article II, 7, 254, 270, 317, 370

Article III, 7, 13, 373

Article IV, 7, 108, 374

Article V, 7, 375

Article VI, 8, 12, 303, 375

Article VII, 8, 376

Articles of Confederation and, 4

as higher law, 10

Bill of Rights. *See* Bill of Rights

Constitutional Convention, 4, 12

due process. *See* due process

equal protection. *See* equal protection

historical practice and, 90

interpretation of, 1, 2, 11, 18, 20, 132, 234, 280

judicial review. *See* judicial review

noncitizens and, 330, 331

politics and, 22, 90

Preamble, 6, 363

race and. *See* race

ratification of, 8

reach of, 335

rhetoric and, 6

slavery and. *See* slavery

Supreme Court and. *See* Supreme Court

women and. *See* women

Continental Congress, 3

contraceptives, 207, 209. *See also Griswold v. Connecticut; Eisenstadt v. Baird*

contracts, 27, 30, 101, 105–107, 112, 115, 118, 126

Corfield v. Coryell (1823), 108, 306n8

Corporation of Presiding Bishop of Church of Jesus Christ of Latter-Day Saints v. Amos (1987), 97n51

counsel, right to, 131, 340. *See also* Sixth Amendment

countermajoritarianism, 290

Craig v. Boren (1976), 181–183

Crandall v. Nevada (1867), 301

criminal procedure, 32, 130, 134

DaimlerChrysler Corp. v. Cuno (2006), 313n19

Dames & Moore v. Regan (1981), 262

Davis v. Bandemer (1986), 199–200

death penalty, 138–143

death, right to, 219–221

Debs v. United States (1919), 47, 52

Debs, Eugene, 47

Declaration of Independence, 152

Democrats, 163, 197, 199, 203, 204, 239, 265

Dennis v. United States (1951), 50, 52

Department of Agriculture v. Moreno (1973), 158–159

Dickerson v. United States (2000), 135

discrimination, xxiii, xxvi, 9, 31, 35, 96, 151, 153, 155, 156, 159, 160, 162, 165, 167, 168, 170, 174, 176, 177, 179, 183, 185, 186, 238, 241, 279, 287. *See also* equal protection; *specific decisions, topics*

discriminatory purposes, 170

dissent, freedom of, 47

District of Columbia v. Heller (2008), 144–146

domestic affairs, 263

dormant commerce clause, 308, 309

market participant exception, 312

Dothard v. Rawlinson (1977), 183n62

Douglas, William, 60, 193, 207

draft cards, 55. *See also United States v. O'Brien*

Dred Scott v. Sandford (1857), 25, 109, 163, 214, 362
drugs, prescription, 63
drunk driving, 182
due process, 27, 102, 111, 128, 186, 188, 207, 217, 219, 280, 289, 339
    economic legislation, 114, 116, 117
    equal protection and, 153
    fundamental rights and, 194
    incorporation doctrine. *See* Fourteenth Amendment
    privileges or immunities clause and, 111
    substantive due process, 111, 114, 117, 126, 130, 192
Duncan v. Louisiana (1968), 130n10
Dunne, Finley Peter, 358
Dworkin, Ronald, 280
dying, rights of, 219

Eastern Enterprises v. Apfel (1998), 117n33
economic legislation, 30, 64, 101, 114, 115, 116, 124, 240
Edmonson v. Leesville Concrete Co., Inc. (1991), 338n5
education, 82, 86, 154, 157, 163, 171, 176, 306, 338, 342
    discrimination and, 163, 164, 166, 168, 178
Eighteenth Amendment, 382
Eighth Amendment, xxiv, 9, 138, 192, 378
Eisenhower, Dwight, 164
Eisenstadt v. Baird (1972), 208, 210
elections
    campaign finance, 33, 36, 66, 67, 68, 69
    districting, 197, 199
    speech and, 66, 68, 69–70
    voting and, 194, 195, 196, 341, 345
Eleventh Amendment, 378
Elk Grove Unified School District v. Newdow (2004), 90n32
Ely, John Hart, 51, 295
Emancipation Proclamation, 258
emergencies, 118, 236, 260, 315, 319

Emergency Price Control Act, 263
eminent domain. *See* takings clause
Employment Division v. Smith (1990), 94, 96, 98, 348
Engel v. Vitale (1962), 82n11
Enmund v. Florida (1982), 142n43
environmental legislation, 232
Epperson v. Arkansas (1968), 83
equal protection, xxii, 9, 31, 126, 153, 156, 166, 176, 183, 186, 192, 205, 289, 338
    affirmative action. *See* affirmative action
    antisubordinationism, 174–175
    classifications and, 151, 156, 159, 172, 175, 189
    disparate impact, 169
    districting and, 197, 198, 200
    due process and, 157, 162
    fundamental rights and, 194, 211, 341
    gender classifications, 180, 189
    integrationism, 179
    positive rights and, 344
    race. *See* race
    sexual orientation, 184, 187, 188, 216
    voting and, 195, 197
Espionage Act, 325
establishment clause, xxvi, 77, 78, 79
    accommodationism, 80, 81, 91
    ceremonial deism, 90, 90n32
    free exercise clause and, 97, 98
    Lemon test, 83, 91
    neutrality rationale, 87
    original understanding, 79
    public schools and, 83, 84
    separationism, 80, 81, 83, 85
Estelle v. Gamble (1976), 340n8
Everson v. Board of Education (1947), 80n8
Ex parte Merryman (1861), 285, 317–318
Ex parte Milligan (1866), 333n41
Ex parte Quirin (1942), 332
exclusionary rule, 134, 136
Executive, 253. *See also specific presidents, decisions*

appointments and, 270
Article II and, 7
Cabinet and, 271, 272, 273
delegated powers, 263
executive privilege, 275
impeachment, 271
powers of, 253
removals and, 270
term limits, 10
unitary executive theory, 270
veto power, 7
war powers, 7, 317, 321, 324. *See also*
    war
executive agreements, 261
express preemption, 303
expressive organizations, 74–76

Fair Labor Standards Act, 245
fair procedures, right to. *See* procedural
    rights
fairness doctrine, 71
family, rights and, 221–222
farmers, 237
FCC v. Beach Communications, Inc.
    (1993), 157n8
FCC v. Pacifica Foundation (1978), 71–72
Federal Communications Commission,
    71
Federal Corrupt Practices Act, 66
Federal Election Campaign Act, 67
Federal Reserve Board, 274
Federal Trade Commission, 272
federalism, 9, 245, 249, 251, 350
Federalist Papers, 12, 244
Feingold, Russell, 68
Ferguson v. Skrupa (1963), 117n31
Fifteenth Amendment, 9, 128, 345, 381
Fifth Amendment, 9, 102, 119, 132, 153,
    282, 339, 377
    due process clause. *See* due process
    takings clause. *See* takings clause
First Amendment, xxvi, 9, 41, 54, 55, 56, 60,
    63, 64, 68, 127, 194, 336, 339, 376
    absolutists, 60

Espionage Act, 45, 47
establishment clause. *See* establishment
    clause
free exercise clause. *See* free exercise
    clause
freedom of association. *See* association,
    freedom of
freedom of speech. *See* speech, freedom
    of
literalists, 60
original understanding, 42, 60
flag-burning, 56
Fletcher v. Peck (1810), 105
food stamps, 158
Ford v. Wainwright (1986), 142n45
foreign affairs, 260
foreign commerce, 303
Foreign Intelligence Surveillance Act,
    329
formalism, 234, 258, 268
Fourteenth Amendment, 9, 31, 102, 108,
    128, 149, 153, 294, 340, 345, 380
    due process clause. *See* due process
    equal protection clause. *See* equal
        protection
    incorporation doctrine, 10, 127, 129, 130,
        130n10, 147, 192
    original understanding, 108, 152,
        154–155, 174, 344
    privileges or immunities clause. *See*
        privileges or immunities clause
    ratification of, 108
    section 5 of, 346, 348
Fourth Amendment, 9, 131, 133, 137, 324,
    377
Frankfurter, Felix, 164, 166, 197, 201
free exercise clause, xxvi, 77, 78, 92, 348
    establishment clause and, 94, 98
    exemptions and, 92–96
    ministerial exception, 96
    original understanding, 95
    Smith and, 95, 96
free speech. *See* speech, freedom of
Frontiero v. Richardson (1973), 180

functionalism, 259, 272
fundamental rights, 109, 125, 129, 147, 154,
    160, 186, 193, 219, 306, 324, 340
  unenumerated rights, 126, 209
Furman v. Georgia (1972), 139

gambling, 235
Garcia v. San Antonio Metropolitan Transit
    Authority (1985), 246
gay rights, 76, 185, 214
  don't ask, don't tell, 185
  gay marriage, 185, 188, 218
gender issues, 75, 151, 179, 181, 287
George III, King, 143
Georgia v. McCollum (1992), 338n5
Gerken, Heather, xviii
gerrymandering, 36, 199–201
Gideon v. Wainwright (1963), 132, 134
Ginsburg, Ruth Bader, 35, 180, 183, 205,
    213
Goesaert v. Cleary (1948), 180n57
Goldman v. Weinberger (1986), 289n28
Gonzales v. Carhart (2007), 213
Gonzales v. Raich (2005), 242
Good News Club v. Milford Central School
    (2001), 84n19
Gore, Al, 204
Gratz v. Bollinger (2003), 150–152, 176
Great Depression, 27, 118, 236, 357
Great Society, 344, 359
Green v. County School Board (1968),
    172n46
Gregg v. Georgia (1976), 140–141
Griswold v. Connecticut (1965), 207–208,
    215
Grutter v. Bollinger (2003), 177, 178
Guantánamo Bay, 330. *See also*
    Boumediene v. Bush
guns, 143, 144, 239, 248. *See also* Second
    Amendment

H. P. Hood & Sons, Inc. v. Du Mond
    (1949), 301n1
habeas corpus, 316, 318, 324

Halberstam, David, 326
Hamdi v. Rumsfeld (2004), 330
Hamilton, Alexander, 12, 23, 244
Hammer v. Dagenhart (1918), 235
Harlan, John Marshall, 161
Harlan, John Marshall, II, 191
Harper v. Virginia Board of Elections
    (1966), 195
healthcare case. *See National Federation of*
    Independent Business v. Sebelius
heath insurance, 240
Heller v. Doe (1993), 189n75
Helvering v. Davis (1937), 244n27
Hicklin v. Orbeck (1978), 304
Holmes, Oliver Wendell, 1, 41, 46, 101, 113,
    206, 362. *See also specific decisions*
  free speech and, 45, 47, 48, 54, 325
  great dissenter, 48
  legal mind of, 50
  Lochner and, 113
  marketplace of ideas and, 48–49
  regulatory powers and, 121
  Yankee from Olympus, 50
Home Building Loan Association v.
    Blaisdell (1934), 118
homosexuality, 151, 215, 218. *See also* gay
    rights; equal protection
Hosanna-Tabor Evangelical Lutheran
    Church and School v. Equal
    Employment Opportunity
    Commission (2012), xxvi, 96, 98
Houston, East & West Texas Railway Co. v.
    United States (1914), 235n9
Hughes, Charles Evans, 359
Humphrey's Executor v. United States
    (1935), 272

Immigration and Naturalization Service v.
    Chadha (1983), 266
immigration laws, 266, 331
impeachment, 288
implied preemption, 303
incorporation doctrine. *See* Fourteenth
    Amendment

independent agencies, 272, 273
individual rights, 30, 306, 324
intermediate scrutiny, 182
International Court of Justice, 262
Internet, 73
Interstate Commerce Commission, 235
Iraq War, 322
Islamic faith, 77

Jackson v. Metropolitan Edison Co. (1974), 339n6
Jackson, Robert, 257, 258, 301, 323, 355
Jacobson v. Massachusetts (1905), 221n69
Japanese internment. *See Korematsu v. United States*
Jefferson, Thomas, 12, 23, 276, 320
Johnson v. Eisentrager (1950), 330n36
Johnson, Andrew, 271
Johnson, Lyndon, 344, 359
judicial review, 12, 125, 297
    Article III and, 7, 11
    constitutionality of, 11
    deference, 239, 289
    foundations of, 11
    history of, 12, 24
    judicial restraint, 294
    Marbury and, 15, 19
    Marshall and, 17, 18, 24–25
    politics and, 17–19
    state judges, 12
judicial supremacy, 277

Kagan, Elena, xii, 36, 250
Katzenbach v. McClung (1964), 238
Katzenbach v. Morgan (1966), 345–347
Kelo v. City of New London (2005), 102–104, 119, 122
Kennedy v. Louisiana (2008), xxiv, 142n43
Kennedy v. Mendoza-Martinez (1963), 315
Kennedy, Anthony, xxiv, 35, 91, 177, 179, 187, 201, 212, 213, 217, 360
Kersch, Ken, xviii
King, Martin Luther, Jr., 353

Korean War, 257
Korematsu v. United States (1944), 162–163, 169, 326, 362
Kramer v. Union Free School District No. 15 (1969), 341n10
Ku Klux Klan, 51, 74

labor, 257
Lafler v. Cooper (2012), 135n21
laissez-faire, 123
Lassiter v. Northampton County Board of Electors (1959), 346
Lawrence v. Texas (2003), 185, 188, 216–218
League of Nations, 261
Lee v. Weisman (1992), 84
Legal Tender Cases (1871), 279n8
legislative veto, 266
Lemon v. Kurtzman (1971), 83n13
Levinson, Sandy, xviii
libel, 59
liberalism, 30, 130, 146, 195, 233
liberty interests, 218
Lincoln, Abraham, 26, 214, 258, 285, 315–318, 320, 325, 333
line-item veto, 268
literacy, 345, 347
Lochner v. New York (1905), 27n33, 105, 112–114, 126, 163, 164, 194, 208, 362, 387
    aftermath of, 30, 114
    Holmes and. *See* Holmes, Oliver Wendell
    Lochner era, 27, 105, 128, 134, 192, 265, 290
    repudiation of, 115–116, 125
    Warren Court and, 31
Lorillard Tobacco Co. v. Reilly (2001), 65, 69
lotteries, 234
Loving v. Virginia (1967), 166
Lucas v. South Carolina Coastal Council (1992), 121n44
Lynch v. Donnelly (1984), 90n32, 91n33

Madison, James, 244, 276
magazines, 71
Maine v. Taylor (1986), 310n14
majority-minority districts, 203
Mapp v. Ohio (1961), 133
Marbury v. Madison (1803), xix, 2, 14, 25, 28, 256, 276, 345
markets, regulation of. *See* economic legislation
marriage, 194, 208, 218, 222
Marsh v. Chambers (1983), 85n22
Marshall, John, 13, 22, 24, 234, 319, 353, 355, 361
   contract rights and, 105, 107
   judicial review and. *See Marbury v. Madison*
   state laws and, 107
Maryland v. Wirtz (1968), 246n29
Mathews v. Diaz (1976), 331n39
McCain, John, 68
McCarthy, Joseph, 51
McCleskey v. Kemp (1987), 139n33, 142
McCloskey, Robert, xv
McConnell v. Federal Election Commission (2003), 68, 69, 70
McCreary County v. ACLU (2005), 91n33
McCulloch v. Maryland (1819), 20–23, 118, 242
McDonald v. City of Chicago (2010), 147
Medellín v. Texas (2008), 262
Medicaid, 250
Medicare, 256
Meltzer, Daniel, xviii
military commissions, 332
military service, 163, 186
militias, 143, 145
Miller v. California (1973), 61, 62, 71
minimum wage, 115, 240
minorities, 30, 53, 58, 168, 173, 358. *See also* equal protection; *specific groups*
Minow, Martha, xviii
Miranda v. Arizona (1966), 132, 135, 136, 282

Missouri v. Frye (2012), 135n21
Mitchell v. Helms (2000), 87, 89
money, 279, 302
moral reading, 293
Mormon Church, 92
Morrison v. Olson (1988), 274n41
Myers v. United States (1926), 272

NAACP v. Alabama (1958), 73
Naim v. Naim (1955), 166
National Association for the Advancement of Colored People, 74, 140, 163
National Federation of Independent Business v. Sebelius (2012), xx, xxvii, 23, 228, 230, 240, 242, 244, 247, 250
National League of Cities v. Usery (1976), 246
National Rifle Association, 359
National Security Agency, 329
Native American Church, 94, 95
natural rights, 106, 114, 123, 155
necessary and proper clause, 7, 242–243
New Deal, 27, 115, 236, 240, 251, 265, 278, 357
   New Deal settlement, 237, 239
New Energy Co. of Indiana v. Limbach (1988), 310n12
New York v. Ferber (1982), 62
New York v. United States (1992), 247n34
newspapers, 71
Nguyen v. Immigration and Naturalization Service (2001), 184n66
Nineteenth Amendment, 10, 382
Ninth Amendment, 9, 378
Nixon tapes case. *See United States v. Nixon*
Nixon v. United States (1993), 288
Nixon, Richard, 31, 61, 67, 134, 275, 285, 290, 341, 357
Nixon, Walter, 288
nondelegation doctrine, 264, 265
Northern Securities Co. v. United States (1904), 206n27

O'Connor, Sandra Day, xi, 35, 69, 91, 104, 177, 212, 217, 221, 360
Obama, Barack, xix, xxii, xxv
obscenity, 60–62
Ogden v. Saunders (1827), 106–107, 118
originalism, xvi, 23, 34, 144, 291–293

pain, rights and, 220
Palko v. Connecticut (1937), 130n10
Palmore v. Sidoti (1984), 166
Panama Refining Co. v. Ryan (1935), 265n29
paper currency, 279, 284
Parents Involved in Community Schools v. Seattle School District No. 1 (2007), xxii, 178–179
parents, children and, 221–222
parliamentary sovereignty, 11
parochial schools, 86, 87
Parsons, Ed, xviii
Patient Protection and Affordable Care Act, xix, xxvi, 228, 230, 242, 245, 250
Patriot Act, 329
Pearl Harbor, 162
Pennsylvania Coal Co. v. Mahon (1922), 120, 121
peremptory challenges, 338
Persian Gulf War, 322
peyote, 94
Pike v. Bruce Church, Inc. (1970), 310n15
piracy, 320
Planned Parenthood of Southeastern Pennsylvania v. Casey (1992), 211
plea bargaining, 135
Plessy v. Ferguson (1896), 159–161, 163, 168, 169
Poe v. Ullman (1961), 191n1
police power, 231
police practices, 133, 135, 136–138
political parties, 6, 12
political question doctrine, 198, 199, 201, 288, 322
polygamy, 92
pornography, 62

positive rights, 339
Posner, Richard, 326
poverty, 114, 131, 136, 340
Powell, Lewis, 125, 139, 175, 177, 342
precedent, 96, 135, 178, 241, 280, 292
predominant factor test, 202
preemption, statutory, 303–304
President. *See* Executive
Printz v. United States (1997), 247
prior restraint, 42
prisons, 183, 337, 340
privacy, 207, 215, 218
privileges and immunities clause, 7, 108, 304
    citizenship and, 109
    individual rights and, 306
privileges or immunities clause, 108, 128, 128n8, 155
    citizenship and, 110
    privileges and immunities clause and, 108
    states and, 110
Prize Cases (1863), 317n11
procedural rights, 130, 134
Proffitt v. Florida (1976), 141n39
Progressive Era, 112
Prohibition, 95
property rights, 101, 104, 119, 122, 123
property taxes, 342
protectionism, 308, 310, 311
Protestants, 87
protestors, 55
public schools. *See* education

Quick Bear v. Leupp (1908), 80n7

race, xxii, 151, 162, 163, 174–175, 179, 238, 241, 279
    affirmative action. *See* affirmative action
    death penalty and, 139, 142
    discrimination and. *See* discrimination
    education and, xxii
    equal protection and. *See* equal protection

race (*cont.*)
  gender and, 181
  interracial marriage, 166
  minority groups, 168, 169, 170
  quota systems, 176, 177
  racism, 53, 153, 161, 163, 167
  voting and, 201
radio, 71, 72
railroads, 235
ratchet theory, 347. *See also Katzenbach v.
  Morgan*
rational basis test, 116, 155, 156–158, 187,
  189, 192
  heightened rationality review, 158
Reagan, Ronald, 32, 87, 211
realism, 178, 235
reasoned judgment model, 351
Reconstruction period, 128, 152, 165, 271
Red Lion Broadcasting Co. v. FCC (1969),
  71, 72
Reed v. Reed (1971), 180n58
Reeves, Inc. v. Stake (1980), 312
Regan, Donald, 311
*Regents of the University of California v.
  Bakke* (1978), 175–176
regulatory taking, 120, 122. *See also* takings
  clause
Rehnquist, William, xi, 32, 63, 217, 219,
  246, 249, 327
religion, 77, 78
  Amish groups, 93, 94
  conservative coalition, 87
  establishment clause. *See* establishment
    clause
  exemptions and, 92–96, 97
  free exercise clause. *See* free exercise
    clause
  governmental aid to, 85
  minorities and, 95, 99
  public schools and, 82
  symbolic support of, 89
Religious Freedom Restoration Act,
  348
Rendell-Baker v. Kohn (1982), 338n4

Reno v. American Civil Liberties Union
  (1997), 73
Reno v. Condon (2000), 247n33
Republicans, 12, 197, 199, 203, 204, 211,
  239, 265
Revolutionary War (U.S.), 3
Reynolds v. Sims (1964), 196–198
Reynolds v. United States (1878), 92, 93
Richardson v. McKnight (1997), 337n3
Roberts v. Louisiana (1976), 141n40
Roberts v. U.S. Jaycees (1984), 74
Roberts, John, xi, xx, xxi, xxvi, xxviii, 33,
  91, 178, 250
Roberts, Owen, 27, 278, 359
Rocker, John, 336
Roe v. Wade (1973), xxi, 32, 126, 130,
  209–211, 215, 223, 277, 290, 293, 343
  Lochner and, 117
Romer v. Evans (1996), 186–188
Roosevelt, Franklin, xvi, 27, 29, 116, 130,
  166, 236, 260, 292, 319, 333, 357
  court-packing, 27, 115, 237, 279, 285, 357
Roper v. Simmons (2005), 142n44
Rostker v. Goldberg (1981), 183n63
Roth v. United States (1957), 60

Sabbatarianism, 93
Saenz v. Roe (1999), 111n23
*San Antonio Independent School District v.
  Rodriguez* (1973), 342, 344
*Santa Fe Independent School District v.
  Doe* (2000), 84n21
Scalia, Antonin, 34, 91, 144, 177, 217, 218,
  269, 275, 291
Schauer, Fred, xviii
Schecter Poultry Corp. v. United States
  (1935), 265n29
Schenck v. United States (1919), 45–46, 52,
  325
Schlanger, Margo, xviii
schools. *See* education
Second Amendment, 9, 143, 359, 376
  original understanding, 145, 146
seditious libel, 42

separate but equal. *See Plessy v. Ferguson*

separation of powers, 8, 258, 259

September 11 attacks, 327, 328, 331

Seventeenth Amendment, 381

Seventh Amendment, 9, 129, 378

sexual revolution, 209

Shaw v. Reno (1993), 202

Sherbert v. Verner (1963), 93

Sherman, William Tecumseh, 315

Shreveport Case (1914), 235

Sixteenth Amendment, 10, 381

Sixth Amendment, 9, 129, 131, 377

Skinner v. Oklahoma (1942), 191, 193, 207, 210

Slaughter-House Cases (1872), 109–111, 112, 128, 155, 193

slavery, 5, 9, 25, 152, 337

Social Security, xxix, 34, 116, 230, 244, 256, 263, 284

Sotomayor, Sonia, xii, 36

Souter, David, xii, 205, 212

South Dakota v. Dole (1987), 249

speech, freedom of, 41, 54, 336

  Black and, 60

  Brandeis and, 49

  broadcast media. *See* broadcast media

  commercial speech. *See* commercial speech

  corporate speech, 68, 70

  crowded theater argument, 44

  expressive conduct, 54, 56

  Holmes and, 44, 45, 47, 48

  incidental restrictions on, 57

  libel. *See* libel

  marketplace of ideas, 44, 48, 70

  modern doctrine, 44

  obscenity. *See* obscenity

  offensive speech, 58

  persuasion principle, 69

  public forum, 340

  terrorism and, 42, 52

  unprotected categories, 59

  war and, 46, 325

standing, 287

state action doctrine, 10, 336, 337

  public function exception, 337

states

  admission of, 7

  appeals from, 12

  citizenship and, 110

  constitutions of, 8, 344

  criminal procedure and, 131

  individual rights and, 302

  interstate commerce and, 308, 310

  limits on, 302

  out-of-state competitors, 308, 310

  powers of, 228

  privileges and immunities, 304

  regulation of, 245

  rights of, 262

  role of, 9

  sovereignty of, 232

  subsidies and, 313

Steel Seizure case. *See Youngstown Sheet & Tube Co. v. Sawyer*

Stenberg v. Carhart (2000), 213n41

Stevens, John Paul, xii, xxiv, 103, 146, 179, 202, 205

Steward Machine Co. v. Davis (1937), 244n27

Stewart, Potter, 60, 92, 140, 222

Stone v. Graham (1980), 83

Stone, Harlan Fiske, 192

strict scrutiny, 93, 155, 166, 167, 193, 282

Stuart v. Laird (1803), 14, 28

Sturges v. Crowninshield (1819), 105

suicide. *See* death, right to

supremacy clause, 8, 12, 303

Supreme Court

  antiregulatory stance, 27

  appointments to, 29, 87, 134, 211, 239, 285, 357

  Article III and, 7

  case selection, 282

  conservatism. *See* conservatism

  judicial deference and, xxix

  judicial power, 283, 289

  judicial review. *See* judicial review

Supreme Court (*cont.*)
  jurisdiction of, 15
  legitimacy of, xxx, 191, 212, 215, 285, 290, 356
  liberalism and. *See* liberalism
  mandamus and, 15
  nominations, xxi
  politics and, xii, xvii, xxiv, 28, 134, 165, 197, 241, 281, 283, 356
  role of, xvi, 11, 350
suspension clause. *See* habeas corpus
Swann v. Charlotte-Mecklenburg Board of Education (1971), xxiii, 172

Taft, William Howard, 272
Taft-Hartley Act, 257, 260
takings clause, 102, 103, 105, 119, 122, 258
  original understanding, 121
Taney, Roger, 26, 285, 318
taxation, xxviii, 10, 156
taxing and spending clause, xxviii, 230, 243
  original understanding, 243
television, 71, 72
Tenth Amendment, 9, 228, 246, 378
Tenure of Office Act, 271
Terminiello v. Chicago (1949), 355n5
Texas Monthly, Inc. v. Bullock (1989), 97n51
Texas v. Johnson (1989), 56
Thanksgiving, 80
Third Amendment, 9, 324, 377
Thirteenth Amendment, 9, 128, 152, 336, 345, 379
Thomas, Clarence, 34, 91, 177, 217, 240, 291
Thornburg v. Gingles (1986), 199n14
Tillman Act, 66
tobacco products, 65, 303
torture, 331
travel, right to, 195, 301
treaties, 254, 261. *See also* executive agreements
Treaty of Versailles, 261
trial by jury, 129
Trop v. Dulles (1958), 138n29

Troxel v. Granville (2000), 221
Truman, Harry, 163, 257
truth model, 351
Twelfth Amendment, 378
Twentieth Amendment, 382
Twenty-Fifth Amendment, 385
Twenty-First Amendment, 383
Twenty-Fourth Amendment, 385
Twenty-Second Amendment, 10, 384
Twenty-Seventh Amendment, 387
Twenty-Sixth Amendment, 386
Twenty-Third Amendment, 384

United Building & Construction Trades Council v. Mayor and Council of Camden (1984), 307n10
United States v. Belmont (1937), 261n24
United States v. Butler (1936), 244n25, 278n6
United States v. Carolene Products Co. (1938), 125, 131, 173, 188
  footnote four, 125, 129, 131, 168
United States v. Causby (1946), 120
United States v. Curtiss-Wright Export Corp. (1936), 261n22
United States v. Darby (1941), 237n13
United States v. Debs (1919), 57, 70
United States v. Eichman (1990), 56
United States v. Lee (1982), 94n42
United States v. Lopez (1995), 239, 240, 247
United States v. Miller (1939), 143
United States v. Morrison (2000), 228, 240, 247
United States v. Nixon (1974), 276
United States v. O'Brien (1968), 55–56
United States v. Pink (1942), 261n24
United States v. Seeger (1965), 79n4
United States v. Verdugo-Urquidez (1990), 330n36
United States v. Virginia (1996), 183

Vacco v. Quill (1997), 219
Van Orden v. Perry (2005), 91n33
Vieth v. Jubelirer (2004), 201

Vietnam War, 55, 58, 77, 289
Vinson, Fred, 164
Violence against Women Act, 228, 229, 240
Virginia Military Institute, 184
Virginia State Board of Pharmacy v. Virginia Citizens Consumer Council Inc. (1976), 63, 64
Voting Rights Act, 201, 345
voucher programs, 88

Wallace v. Jaffree (1985), 80n5, 83
Walz v. Tax Commission (1970), 85
war, 289, 315
    free speech and, 325
    individual rights and, 26, 324, 358
    laws of, 332
    terrorism and. *See* War on Terror
    war criminals, 332
    war powers, 323
War on Terror, 328
War Powers Resolution, 321
Warren, Earl, 30, 31, 61, 130, 134, 164, 325, 341
Washington v. Davis (1976), 170–171
Washington v. Glucksberg (1997), 219

Washington, Bushrod, 109
Washington, George, 12, 23, 80, 254, 319
Weinreb, Lloyd, xviii
welfare, 306
Welsh v. United States (1970), 79n4
West Coast Hotel Co. v. Parrish (1937), 115
West Lynn Creamery, Inc. v. Healy (1994), 313n19
White, Byron, 191, 200, 215
Whitney v. California (1927), 49, 53
Wickard v. Filburn (1942), 237n15
Wills, Garry, 143
Wisconsin v. Yoder (1972), 93
women, 6, 10, 35, 62, 179, 211, 214
Woodson v. North Carolina (1976), 141n40
World War I, 45, 325
World War II, 263, 325
Wyoming v. Oklahoma (1992), 310n12

Yakus v. United States (1944), 263
Youngstown Sheet & Tube Co. v. Sawyer (1952), 256–260, 323

Zablocki v. Redhail (1978), 221n68
Zelman v. Simmons-Harris (2002), 88, 89
zoning, 120